EX LIBRIS
MAY BLESSINGS BE UPON THE HEAD OF CADMUS, THE PHOENICIANS
OR WHOEVER IT WAS THAT INVENTED BOOKS
CARLYLE
Helen Ray Bremer
Dale Thompson Mendelsohn

Presidents' Sons

PRESIDENTS' SONS

The Prestige of Name in a Democracy

by

J. J. PERLING

The Odyssey Press · · New York

PRINTED IN THE UNITED STATES
FIRST EDITION

AMERICAN BOOK–STRATFORD PRESS, INC., NEW YORK

To My Wife

Esther Ruth Perling

Whose Unwavering Faith

Made This Work Possible

Foreword

Sociologists have traced the progeny of the Jukes and the Mathers, seeking to appraise the influence of heredity; historians have chronicled the careers of princes and nobles, noting successes due to inherited title and wealth; when men have risen to high estate, genealogists have charted the achievements of their ancestors. But neither sociologist nor historian has inquired to what degree those Americans who achieve the highest office in the land have affected their offspring.

The cynic may say that fortuitous circumstances have combined to make men Presidents of the United States; that Death, or self-interest of political manipulators, or emotional public outbursts have raised some men to the Presidential chair. Nevertheless, those men must have possessed resourcefulness and political astuteness even if all did not have dominating personalities or achieve conspicuous greatness. Did their sons inherit traits of shrewdness and ability? Or, in the absence of such qualifications, to what degree did their fathers' high place contribute to the advancement of the sons?

Biographers of our Chief Executives have usually passed over with indifference the activities of Presidents' sons. True, in many instances, they were young when their fathers came to the White House. But, with rare exceptions, even adult sons have failed to receive any notice from those who have chronicled the activities of their fathers. In fact, they have been *purposely* excluded.[1]

Thus, few relevant data were at hand regarding the lives of Presidential sons. So-called "gossip" books on the occupants of the White House seldom afford salient facts other than those about the sons' childhood. The researcher must, therefore, combine patience and perseverance with good fortune to discover authentic information. And yet the theme is worthy of the effort: in a Democracy where every boy is said to have an equal opportunity it is interesting to test that thesis on the basis of the facts regarding the sons of Presidents.

[1] Numbers in the Foreword and succeeding chapters refer to notes in "References and Explanatory Notes," pages 377 to 451.

Nineteen Presidents had sons when they entered the White House; another, Grover Cleveland, became a father of sons after his Presidential terms.[2] The careers of all these Presidents' sons are reviewed in this book; in addition, there are included the adopted son of Andrew Jackson and the legendary "adopted son" of George Washington.

In the "References and Explanatory Notes" will be found the primary sources from which facts have been gleaned: unpublished letters of Presidents and their sons, diaries of Presidential advisors and family friends, Army reports, official documents, Congressional debates, newspapers, college annuals, memoirs of political personalities. These records have been appraised with full consideration of the motives which prompted the authors, and of the epochs in which they lived. While this is a chronicle of Presidents' sons, brief résumés of the fathers' careers are an essential part of it. They afford an opportunity to compare the successes of parent and offspring; and in "References and Explanatory Notes" there are further historical sidelights on events which influenced the careers of sons and fathers.

The record ends with the sons of Franklin D. Roosevelt. The only child of his successor, Harry Truman, is a daughter. But, outside the White House, the sons of six former Presidents have continued active in business enterprises, in public office, in the professions. Some are directors of prominent corporations; they draw enviable salaries and share in substantial dividends. Some are attorneys, with wealthy clients and lucrative fees. Others are high in party councils; their political influence brings them the friendships of the rich and the great. It is not unlikely that, with the passing months, the names of some will again make headlines.[3] It was always thus. Astute politicians may seek to capitalize the renown of their sires; promoters, to beguile investors, may recall their paternal integrity; advocates of social and economic theories may persuade them to add their signatures to public appeals. Or, of their own accord, they may seek to realize political ambitions or to amass fortunes. They are Presidents' sons; and—even in a democracy—there is prestige of name.

J. J. P.

Chevy Chase, Md.
September, 1947

Contents

Illustrations

1

Sons of John Adams

From Amsterdam, Holland, in December, 1781, an impatient father wrote to his son in St. Petersburg, Russia, upbraiding him for not improving his handwriting and censuring him for his failure to describe in detail all the characteristics of the Russian mode of living and the appearance of the Russian capital. Complained the father:

> You have not informed me whether the houses are brick, stone, or wood; whether they are seven stories high, or only one; how they are glazed; whether they have chimneys as in Spain; what public buildings, what maisons de ville or state houses; what churches, what palaces; what statuary; what paintings, music, spectacles, etc. You have said nothing about the religion of the country; whether it is Catholic or Protestant; what is the national church; whether there are many sectaries; whether there is a toleration of various religions, etc.[1]

To this paternal reprimand and demand for an elaborate report on Russia and its customs, the son respectfully pleaded: "Honored sir, you make me a great number of questions at a time, but I will answer them as well as I can." And his replying letter describes with minuteness the architecture, worship, royal residences, educational system and peasant customs in Russia. The father who expected such erudition was John Adams, then in Europe seeking aid for the American colonies fighting the Revolutionary War and, fifteen years later, the second President of the newly created United States of America. The son was John Quincy Adams, then fourteen years of age. John Quincy was the eldest of three sons—the other two being named Charles and Thomas Boylston. But it was not alone to the father that these sons owed their fervent patriotism,

[1] Figures refer to correspondingly numbered notes for each individual chapter in "References and Explanatory Notes" in Appendix.

their knowledge of languages and their taste for classical literature. For much of their childhood was under the tutelage of their illustrious mother, Abigail Smith Adams.

The family of Abigail Smith did not favor her marriage, in 1764, to John Adams. He was a farmer's son, with an uncertain future in the profession of law for which he had studied at Harvard. She was the descendant of a long line of prominent men who had played important roles in the settlement and progress of the Massachusetts colony. Her mother was the daughter of colorful John Quincy, who served many years as a member of the provisional legislature, and for a long period was Speaker of the House of Representatives, and also a member of the Council of the colony; [2] her father was the Reverend William Smith, the minister of a fashionable church in Weymouth. For a hundred years writers have repeated the legend that, at the ceremony uniting his daughter in marriage with John Adams, the Reverend Smith took as his text, "For John came neither eating bread nor drinking wine." [3]

Whether or not the father-in-law made such a reference to the lack of material prosperity of his daughter's husband there is no historical proof; but we do have evidence from John Adams himself that, for ten years after his marriage, he was still unable to achieve monetary success. It was then customary for lawyers to go to surrounding towns, attending sessions of the courts which convened as the presiding judges went around their circuits; and John Adams sojourned first in one town and then in another in search of clients. His wife remained at Braintree and we find him writing to her from Boston, during the first week of May, 1774, "There is no prospect of any business in my way in this town this whole summer. I don't receive a shilling a week." Two months later he is equally unsuccessful in Falmouth, and his letter bespeaks his despair: "I shall bring home as much as I brought from home, I hope, and not more, I fear. I go mourning in my heart all the day long, though I say nothing. I am melancholy for the public and anxious for my family. As for myself, a frock and trousers, a hoe and a spade would do for my remaining days. For God's sake make your children hardy, active and industrious; for strength, activity and industry will be their only resource and dependence." [4]

Abigail Adams, separated year after year from the father of her children, read her husband's pleas with understanding and determination, and inculcated in her sons high ideals, a passionate love of freedom, and a taste for literature. No woman in American history, through her own talents and inherent greatness, has been more distinguished in her own time, has contributed so much to the lives of men who rose to high place in the councils of the nation, or has left to posterity such a rich heritage of letters as these which record the epochal events at the birth of the Republic. And what is more remarkable is that this daughter of a minister had no formal schooling. In her day, colleges on this side of the Atlantic did not open their doors to "females," and the elementary schools restricted themselves to the three R's: reading, 'riting and 'rithmetic. Those of the upper social circles added to these music and, in those sections of the country where strict religious tenets did not forbid such frivolities, dancing. But Abigail's health prevented her from attending school, and the surprising store of her knowledge was acquired from her father and her grandfather, from self-study, and from listening to the educated men who came to the minister's study. Yet, with equal familiarity her letters discuss the philosophy of the ancients, incisively analyze military and political problems of the Revolution, and quote with easy grace from the classics and the literature of her own age.

But not only in beauty of diction and in erudition did Abigail Adams stand distinguished; she was great also in all those qualities which constitute nobility in woman. Those who knew her best—even staid and exacting Puritans—paid her homage. The austere moralist, the Reverend T. Sharp, included her among his "heavenly sisters," adding to his *Lives of Thirty Eminently Pious Females* a "memoir of Mrs. Adams, wife of the late President Adams"; [5] and other patriots who created the Republic listened to her brilliant conversation and spoke of her with respect and admiration.[6] During the Revolutionary War, while John Adams was absent in the Congress or on other missions, his wife was in the midst of the conflict between the British and American armies. She watched the Massachusetts farmers battling the English soldiers as the conflict shifted from Bunker Hill to Breed's Hill; she nursed the wounded "rebels," and sheltered under her roof the dominant personalities of the Revolution—General George Washington among them. And, during that period when battles, disease, hunger and fire endangered her and her family, Abigail Adams reared her children and taught them morals, literature, and courage. To her husband went forth messages of encouragement and comprehension which lightened the difficult tasks assigned him. From the despairing days when John Adams was a struggling lawyer to the happier and prosperous period when he acquired fame as a diplomat and President, the incisive understanding and sage counsel of Abigail Adams played a vital part in the lives and careers of her husband and her sons.

Slowly, John Adams increased his law practice and improved his financial condition. In the biography of his father, John Quincy Adams summarizes the attributes which contributed to the ultimate success of our second President, telling us that "for the profession of law, John Adams had been preeminently gifted with the endowments of nature: a sound constitution of body, a clear and sonorous voice, a quick conception, a discriminating judgment, and a ready eloquence. His natural temper was as quick as his conception. His confidence in his own judgment founded on the consciousness of his powers, gave it a cast of stubbornness and inflexibility, perhaps necessary for the successful exercise of the duties of a lawyer, nor sometimes less necessary, though requiring more frequently the countercheck of self-control, in the halls of legislation and at the courts of kings." [7] But it was not ability alone which accounted for John Adams' progress in the legal profession; his alliance with Abigail Smith contributed much to pave the way. For this we have the admission of John Quincy Adams, who wrote of his father, "By this marriage, Mr. Adams became allied with a numerous connection of families, among the most respectable for their weight and influence in the province, and it was immediately perceptible in the considerable increase in his professional practice." [8]

It was not in law, however, that John Adams achieved honor and position in his time and a lasting place in the history of the United States. Within a decade after his marriage the thirteen colonies resolved to sever their bond with the mother country, Britain, and to establish in the New World an independent English-speaking Republic. In the events which led to that decision and the resulting war to make freedom a reality, John Adams played an important part. He was a member of the Continental Congress in Philadelphia which appointed him, with Thomas Jefferson and three others, as a committee to draft the Declaration of Independence. Absent from home, he considered what his children might say in after years about this consecration of his time and efforts to the cause of freedom instead of to the amassing of worldly goods for their security and comfort. These thoughts he confided to Abigail, writing her from Philadelphia in April, 1776, again entreating his wife to model the characters of their sons:

I believe my children will think I might as well have thought and labored a little, night and day, for their benefit. But I will not bear the reproaches of my children. I will tell them that I studied and labored to procure a free constitution of government for them to solace themselves under, and if they do not prefer this to ample fortune, to ease and elegance, they are not my children, and I care not what becomes of them. They shall live upon thin diet, wear mean clothes, and work hard with cheerful hearts and free spirits, or they may be the children of the earth, or of no one, for me.

John has genius and so has Charles. Take care that they don't go astray. Cultivate their minds, inspire their little hearts, raise their wishes. Fix their attention upon great and glorious objects. Root out every little thing. Weed out every meanness. Make them great and manly. Teach them to scorn injustice, ingratitude, cowardice and falsehood. Let them revere nothing but religion, morality and liberty.

Abby and Tommy are not forgotten by me although I did not mention them before. The first, by reason of her sex, requires a different education from the two I have mentioned. Of this, you are the only judge.[9]

The replies which came to John Adams from his wife, and the letters which the oldest son wrote him, filled the absent father with assurance and pride. The mother had already instilled in her little brood a passionate love of country. John Quincy was eight, Charles six, and Thomas Boylston three. John Adams tells Abigail, "John writes like a hero, glowing with ardor for his country, and burning with indignation against her enemies."[10] Three months after the Declaration of Independence was signed, little John Quincy Adams assumed the role of dispatch carrier between the villages surrounding his town, and John Adams acknowledges information about this from Abigail, writing her, "I am glad master John has an office so useful to his mamma and papa as that of post-rider."[11] Still far from home, the father reflects, "If I live much longer in banishment, I shall scarcely know my own children. Tell my little ones that, if they will be very good, Papa will come home."[12] In the beginning of 1778 John Adams returned to his home, but his stay was brief. He was starting upon a mission to France, and his eldest son, John Quincy, now eleven years old, accompanied him across the Atlantic. Before he embarked upon a ship for the European voyage, John Adams wrote to his wife that "Johnny sends his duty to his mamma and his love to his sister and brothers. He behaves like a man." [13] Abigail Adams wrote to her son, upon his arrival in Europe, a touching letter with admonition to "adhere to those religious sentiments which were early instilled in your mind, and remember that you are accountable to your maker for all your words and actions. . . . Dear as you are to me, I would much rather you should have found a grave in the ocean you have crossed, than see you an immoral, profligate or graceless child." And to her husband she wrote: "To my dear son remember me in the most affectionate terms. Enjoin it upon him never to disgrace his mother, and to behave worthily of his father." [14]

Thus the child John Quincy Adams began a long career in public service. The boy became his father's secretary, copying official letters and state documents, or writing what his father dictated. Remaining in Europe for several years, he traveled in France, Holland and Russia. In St. Petersburg, while his father went to Holland, John Quincy Adams was made an attaché of the American Mission as copyist. It was from that Russian city, as we have seen, that he wrote to his father the description which John Adams deemed lacking in completeness and detail.

During the several years abroad John Adams continued to write to Abigail letters imbued with affection for her and for the children; but these missives often embodied also long discourses on the rearing of the little sons he had left in America.[15] In letters from Passy, L'Orient, Paris, and Amsterdam, John Adams alternates between expression of pleasure that the eldest son, John Quincy, is with him and regret that the expense of maintaining the boy in Europe is high. "My son has had a great opportunity to see this country; but this has unavoidably retarded his education in other ways," he writes to the mother. "He has enjoyed perfect health, from first to last, and is respected wherever he goes, for his vigor and veracity both of mind and body, for his constant good humor, and for his rapid progress in French as well as his general knowledge which, for one of his age, is uncommon." [16]

In Europe, John Quincy's education is intermixed with his "official duties," and he shifts from school to school. He attends school in France, in Holland, in England; he studies under private tutors in Russia. He reads Greek and Latin classics, becomes familiar with French and German authors. He writes long letters to each of his parents, and meticulously records in his diary all that he sees, all that he thinks. Twice he recrosses the Atlantic, remains a short while at the parental home, then again accompanies his father to the other continent.

Upon his return to the United States from his last youthful sojourn abroad, John Quincy entered Harvard; in eighteen months he completed the entire classical course. This youth had seen in many foreign lands far more than could be taught him by textbooks; as a spectator and as a participant he learned much of current history, of government, of world personalities. He himself, long after he had achieved the highest office in his native land, described his early education:

> I was graduated at Harvard University in 1787. I had already traversed the Atlantic Ocean four times, three of them in the midst of the American revolutionary War, had travelled over a great part of Europe, and had served the public in the not altogether irresponsible capacity of Secretary and interpreter to the mission of the United States to the Empress Catherine of Russia, and afterwards at the Negotiation of the Treaty of Peace and Independence at Paris in 1783, at the Treaty with Prussia at the Hague in 1784, and under the Commission of my father, Dr. Franklin and Mr. Jefferson at Paris in 1785. I had served my father as his private Secretary. I had thus served a practical apprenticeship of seven years, to the trade and mystery of American Politics before I entered the walls of Harvard as a student. My public life began, as it were, with the Declaration of Independence.[17]

After his graduation from Harvard, he prepared himself for the legal profession by studying law, as was then the custom, in the office of an attorney already practicing in the courts; going to Newburyport, he chose as his preceptor the lawyer Theophilus Parsons, who, fifteen years later, became the Chief Justice of the Massachusetts Supreme Court. That the profession which he chose for his career was not held in high esteem by the people of Massachusetts after the Revolution, John Quincy Adams learned soon after beginning his legal studies, and he wrote to Abigail Adams that "the popular odium which has been excited against the practitioners in this Commonwealth prevails to so great a degree that the most innocent and irreproachable life cannot guard a lawyer against the hatred of his fellow citizens."[18] But he assured his mother of his determination not to be deterred from completing his preparation for the bar.

John Quincy read legal treatises assiduously, studied carefully the arguments of opposing counsel, analyzed court decisions, and meticulously performed all the tasks allotted to him by the barrister Theophilus Parsons. But, while diligently applying himself to the profound discourses of Blackstone and Coke, and the beauties of Virgil, Homer, and the French classics, like other gentlemen in their twenties John Quincy enjoyed lighter moments in Newburyport and in the surrounding villages. His diary, not included in the *Memoirs* edited by his son, contains numerous accounts of dances, card playing, drinking parties, and excursions in coach and sleigh with flattering girls. He partakes of frivolities, and his Puritan soul pens contrite phrases on the following day moralizing on his stupidity or lamenting the waste of time. On New Year's Day in 1787, he recalls the pastime of the preceding evening: "It was playing pawns; a number of pledges were given all around, and kissing was the only condition upon which they were redeem'd." There is no hint that he protested nor that he was aloof from redeeming a pawn; but, after the game, John Quincy Adams reflects that it was "stupid" and pronounces his disapproval: "Ah! What kissing! 'tis a profanation of one of the most endearing demonstrations of love. A kiss unless warm'd by sentiment and enlivened by affection may just as well be given to the air as to the most beautiful or the most accomplished object in the Universe."[19]

The diary of this law student and classical scholar is replete with keen analyses of involved legal dicta and incisive commentaries on poets and dramatists; but there are also many lengthy appraisals of female attractiveness. Although he was glad to change to another partner because he enjoyed conversation, and Miss Frazier "could talk only in monosyllables," he noted while dancing with her that "she is not tall, but has what is called a genteel shape";[20] Miss Sally Jenkins was "of middling female size and has a fine form, the features of her face are regular, and were not her nose too much aquiline, would be very handsome";[21] Nancy Jenkins "holds her head too stiff for elegance and has read too many novels"; [22] Miss Cazneau "has nothing in her person to recommend her but a very good shape . . . a capricious, passionate, imprudent character"; [23] Miss Deblois "puckers her mouth a little, and contracts her eyelids a little, to look very pretty—is not wholly unsuccessful." [24] Nor does he forget that "Mrs. Jones is young, uncommonly handsome, educated in Europe, . . . exhibited an arm, the beautiful contour and snowy whiteness of which might fire the imagination of a sensual voluptuary, but which I unfortunately did not think of admiring till it was too late." [25]

One wonders, in noting the date of this last-quoted diary entry, to what degree youthful John Quincy was affected by the letter which John Adams, then in London, had written to him five weeks earlier. Admonishes the father, "My dear John: Morals, my boy, morals should be, as they are eternal in their nature, the everlasting object of your pursuits." [26] Morals! The Puritanic code of the seventeenth century was handed down by the Adamses from father to son, and John Quincy clung to its harsh credo throughout his life. At fourteen, near Paris, he saw a lovely little girl of his own age, and he treasured her image in his memory for forty years. He never spoke to her, though his heart yearned to know her. She was with a troupe of child players and, as John Quincy Adams explained at fifty-five, "She was the first woman I ever loved . . . but with respect to morals, I made it a rule to make no acquaintances with actresses . . . to which I have since invariably adhered." [27]

At the end of three years, being then twenty-three, John Quincy Adams completed the required apprenticeship in the law office, was admitted to the bar, and opened an office in Boston. The year was 1790. Seven years earlier, after the Americans had won the Revolutionary War, the thirteen states had been formally acknowledged by Britain as a sovereign nation. When the Constitution had been approved by eleven states, even though Rhode Island and North Carolina had not yet ratified and were still outside the Union, George Washington was inaugurated President on April 30, 1789. There was little call for the untested legal knowledge of young attorneys such as John Quincy Adams, and his clients were few. Writing to his brother Thomas after several years of practice, he appeared reconciled to his slow progress: "I argued one more cause, and was successful. I gain my causes, but I get no business; that is as low an ebb as ever, but I am tolerably habituated to the lot."[28]

However, he was no novice in knowledge of world history or in acquaintance with the countries of Europe, their governmental and economic systems, and their political leaders. He possessed, too, a gifted pen. Here was a field more promising for him than the profession of law. The transition from the status of a British colony to that of an independent nation brought many perplexing political and economic problems to the infant Republic, and John Quincy Adams began writing articles on them for newspapers and magazines. His incisive analyses of domestic and international questions were widely discussed and praised by those who were guiding the destinies of the Nation during those crucial years.

There was one subject which was of particularly vital concern to President George Washington and his Administration: our relations with France. That nation overthrew and executed its king, and established a Republic. Unquestionably, its revolutionary leaders drew inspiration from the American revolt against the tyranny of the British monarch; the French people recalled that their Lafayette, their Rochambeau, their ships and their loans had aided the thirteen colonies in achieving independence. In 1793 France declared war against England, and looked to the sister Republic across the Atlantic not only to supply ships and munitions but also to enter the conflict as an ally of the French. They sent an emissary to the United States—Citizen Genêt. The sympathies of the American people were largely for the French cause, and everywhere Genêt was greeted with enthusiasm. The capital of the United States was then in Philadelphia, and Genêt—assured of popular support—went there in an effort to obtain for his nation the active aid of the American President, George Washington, and his Administration—in which the Vice-President was John Adams, father of John Quincy Adams. Washington, however, considered it unwise for the United States, organized just four years under the Constitution, to engage in another war. He declared neutrality in the struggle between France and England. In support of this policy John Quincy Adams wrote compelling arguments under the pseudonym "Publicola." Years later, in a confidential letter, John Adams asserted that "John Quincy's writing turned the tide against Genêt";[29] it was gratitude for this effective writing, John Adams insisted, that prompted George Washington to appoint the younger Adams to a foreign post.

Monday 20th Feb. 1797.

Dear Sir

I thank you for giving me the perusal of the enclosed. – The sentimts do honor to the head & heart of the writer – and if my wishes would be of any avail they should go to you in a strong hope that you will not withhold merited promotion from Mr John Adams because he is your son. – For without intending to compliment the father or the mother, or to censure any others, I give it as my decided opinion that Mr Adams is the most valuable public character we have abroad – and that he will prove himself to be the ablest of all our Diplomatic Corps.

If he was now to be brought into that line, or into any other public walk, I could not, upon the principle which has regulated my own conduct, disapprove the caution which is hinted at in the letter. – But he is already entered; – the public more & more, as he is known, are appreciating his talents and

and worth; — and his country would
sustain a loss if these are checked
by over delicacy on your part —
With sincere esteem & affectionate regard
I am ever Yours
G^o Washington

To
The Vice-President
20th Feby 1797

GEORGE WASHINGTON ADVISES ABOUT A PRESIDENT'S SON

John Adams, elected President to succeed Washington, was perplexed about his son, John Quincy Adams, whom Washington had appointed Minister to Holland. Should the father reappoint him to a foreign post? Adams asked the advice of Washington; in this letter the Father of his Country replied. (*Papers of George Washington,* Library of Congress)

Whatever the controlling reason for choosing John Quincy Adams, President George Washington had no need to inquire about the antecedents of this young writer: he remembered that this was the eldest son of John Adams and Abigail Adams at whose home he had found refuge when the Revolutionary War broke out around Boston; he had heard that this John Quincy Adams had been of great help to his father on several missions in Europe. At that moment the father of this brilliant commentator on public affairs was the Vice-President of the United States—the colleague of George Washington in guiding the young Nation. Thus, in 1794, the first President appointed John Quincy Adams Minister to Holland, then one of the prominent nations in the Old World. The appointee was just twenty-seven.

In March, 1797, John Adams succeeded Washington as President of the United States.[30] But, a month before he assumed the highest office the father of John Quincy Adams was troubled about his son: what would be said if, as President, he reappointed John Quincy to some foreign mission? John Adams turned to the Father of his Country for counsel; he wrote to George Washington and indicated his reluctance to continue his own son in public service. Washington replied to the perplexed President-elect; his letter of February 20, 1797, tells us what the first Chief Executive considered ethical and in the public interest when a President's son was involved:

> If my wishes would be of any avail they should go to you in a strong hope that you will not withhold merited promotion from Mr. John Adams because he is your son. For without intending to compliment the father or the mother or to censure any others, I give it as my decided opinion that Mr. Adams is the most valuable public character we have abroad—and that he will prove himself to be the ablest of all our Diplomatic Corps. If he was now to be brought into that line, or into any other public walk, I could not, upon the principle which has regulated my own conduct, disapprove the caution which is hinted at in the letter. But he is already entered;—the public more & more, as he is known, are appreciating his talents and worth;—and his country would sustain a loss if these are checked by over-delicacy on your part.[31]

Thereupon, the second President appointed his son Minister to Prussia. The Senate did not immediately confirm the appointment, but the objection was mainly to the continuance of a legation in Berlin and not especially because of disapproval of John Quincy. When, finally, Senatorial consent was given, the President's son, then in Holland, visited London before taking up his post in the German capital. He had become engaged to Louisa Catherine Johnson, the daughter of the American Minister to England; the marriage took place in the closing week of July, 1797. The record of the license, filed in the Faculty Office of the Archbishop of Canterbury, made no mention that the groom was the son of the President of the United States, a nation which only twenty-one years previously had renounced its allegiance to the mother country, Britain; neither did it make reference to the fact that it was the father of the groom, John Adams, who aided in drafting the Declaration of Independence declaring the thirteen British colonies free and independent. The official notation read: "John Quincy Adams esq. of Boston, in North America, bachelor, above 21, and Louisa Catherine Johnson, of All Hallows Barking, London, spinster, above 21—at All Hallows Barking aforesaid. 24 July, 1797." [32] The wedding ceremony was indeed a quiet affair; there are few entries in the diary of John Quincy Adams less impressive than this:

> July 26—At nine this morning I went, accompanied by my brother, to Mr. Johnson's, and thence to the Church of the parish of All Hallows Barking, where I was married to Louisa Catherine Johnson, the second daughter of Joshua and Catherine Johnson, by Mr. Hewlett. Mr. Johnson's family, Mr. Brooks, my brother, and Mr. J. Hill were present. We were married before eleven in the morning, and immediately after went out to see Tilney House, one of the splendid country seats for which this county is distinguished.[33]

A quarter of a century after the wedding Louisa Johnson Adams still was not aware of her husband's innermost thoughts or his deep-rooted tastes.[34]

John Quincy Adams continued as America's Minister to Prussia until the spring of 1801. In the preceding autumn his father had been defeated for a second term; and, before yielding the Presidency to his successful rival, Thomas Jefferson, John Adams considered it his "duty" to recall his son. He believed, too, that John Quincy was entitled to a more distinguished post in London or Paris.[35]

Returning to his Massachusetts home, the ex-President's son obtained, from a friendly Federal judge, an appointment as commissioner in bankruptcy. He felt that, after so long an absence abroad, this connection would afford him the opportunity to resume his law practice and to become known in the courts. However, after the inauguration of Thomas Jefferson, the politicians of the incoming Administration managed to displace John Quincy with a commissioner of their own party. Abigail Adams, believing that Jefferson had deliberately ousted her son, became embittered against the author of the Declaration of Independence. Three years elapsed before Jefferson learned the cause of her resentment; he then assured her that it had not been with his consent or knowledge that John Quincy had been deprived of the post, that he himself would have preferred the son of John and Abigail Adams to any other aspirant in Massachusetts, regardless of political affiliation.[36]

John Quincy was elected to the State Senate, and was chosen by that body, in 1802, to be United States Senator. Here, as throughout his political career, he refused to adhere blindly to the principles of the party which had selected him. Failing to be re-elected, he resigned his Senatorial post before the term ended. Harvard had just established a professorship of rhetoric and oratory and, in June, 1806, John Quincy Adams was installed as the first professor.[37] His duties were not arduous, being limited to giving a course of public lectures to the resident graduates and the two senior classes, and presiding at the declamations of those classes. It was an era of deep interest in public speaking, and many newspapers devoted many columns to lectures on reading and declaiming before audiences. John Quincy Adams was peculiarly fitted as an instructor: he was steeped in the eloquence of Greece and Rome; he was equally familiar with the great orators of Britain and France; his own writings and addresses were models of convincing polemics and literary elegance. His lectures were extremely popular and, at the request of the students attending them, were published. For four years he devoted himself to the literary work which always afforded him deep pleasure. Then he resigned to undertake again a diplomatic mission abroad. James Madison, succeeding Jefferson as President in 1809, recalled John Quincy Adams to foreign service—appointing him Minister to Russia. Even political enemies acknowledged that the son of the second President was the outstanding diplomat, recalling that the great George Washington himself had first chosen him as an American Minister.

On Christmas Eve, 1814, he was one of the commissioners signing the Treaty of Ghent intended to end our second war with England although, after it was signed, General Andrew Jackson on this side of the Atlantic, not aware that the treaty-makers had agreed on the end of hostilities, fought a battle and defeated the British army at New Orleans. From 1815 to 1817 John Quincy Adams was our Minister in London; in the latter year he became Secretary of State in the Cabinet of President James Monroe. Thus, up to 1825, under every President except Jefferson, John Quincy Adams served either as a Minister abroad or directed our foreign affairs.

James Monroe held office for two terms; and, in 1824, an election was held to choose a succeeding President to take office on March 4, 1825. The story of the nomination, the rancor of the campaign, the test of Constitutional procedure and popular sentiment, the eclipse of eminent statesmen and the rise of new personalities—all these comprise one of the most absorbing chapters in the history of the Republic.[38] Here it need only be noted that the principal candidates for the Presidency were John Quincy Adams and Andrew Jackson, that in the eighteen states in which the people cast ballots (in the eight remaining states, the legislatures made the choice) Jackson was given the larger popular vote. In electoral votes, too, Jackson won a larger number than his rival—the former receiving 99 and Adams 84; however, as 74 electoral votes were cast for two other candidates, Henry Clay and William Crawford, no candidate had obtained a majority of the total electoral votes; thus, as provided in the Constitution,[39] it devolved upon the House of Representatives to make a choice from the three candidates receiving the highest number of votes. The House did make the choice: thirteen states cast their ballots for Adams, seven for Jackson, four for Crawford. John Quincy Adams was duly declared elected President of the United States, and was inaugurated March 4, 1825, the only President's son ever himself to hold that high office.[40]

It was to be expected that after an election so bitter in its contest and so unique in its final determination there would continue to be animosity toward the victor. Ill feeling was aggravated by the personality of the new President: John Quincy Adams lacked the tact and the inclination to pacify political antagonists. He had many enemies when he began his term and the number increased during his four years in office. An antagonistic Congress and a violently partisan press belittled all that he did or attempted to do.[41] With equal ardor, his followers claimed that future generations would acclaim him a great President. "The events of the past administration already belong to history, and when the passions, prejudices and excitement connected with them have passed away, we have no doubt history will do them justice," was the verdict of a prominent Boston paper after he ended his term.[42] "The time is approaching when justice will be done to the administration of John Quincy Adams," prophesied the Boston *Journal* two decades after he had ended his Presidential term, "the passions of that day are already fast subsiding . . . and the clear verdict of posterity may almost be heard, even now, in the formal acknowledgment of its merits to the people of the country." [43]

The prediction has not been realized. The four years of Adams' Administration were not distinguished either in achievements or in epochal events, even though there was neither lack of great men nor of a great problem. That astute British statesman and scholar, James Bryce, pronounced the reasons for the absence of lustre: "The generation to which John Quincy Adams, Jackson, Webster, Clay, Calhoun belonged is less impressive, perhaps because they failed to solve a question which may have been too hard for any one to solve." [44] Bryce had in mind the slavery question, the solution of which was made in blood on the battlefields of the Civil War three decades later. The statesmen in the eighteen-twenties were aware that, sooner or later, both economic factors and an awakened conscience would make Negro bondage a paramount political issue; but they were too close to the generation which evolved the Constitution to forget that in it slavery had legal sanction. To John Quincy Adams that document was incompatible with the loftier principles of human freedom expounded in the Declaration of Independence, and he was foremost among the public men of his time who crusaded for the ending of slavery.

On the day he left the White House, with the realization that the people had refused to elect him for another term, John Quincy Adams wrote in his diary:

March 4, 1829—This day Andrew Jackson of Tennessee was inaugurated President of the United States. I can yet scarcely realize my situation. Hitherto I have prayed for direction from above in concerns of my country and of mankind. I need it not less, and pray for it with equal fervor, now, for those of myself, my family, and of all whose dependence is upon me. From indolence and despondency and indiscretion may I specially be preserved.[45]

He returned to the family home in Quincy, and devoted himself to the writing which he loved and for which he was so well equipped. The respite was not very long.

Three years after relinquishing the Presidency, John Quincy Adams was elected a member of the Congress of the United States. "My return to public life is with disastrous forebodings," he wrote in his diary on the closing day of 1831;[46] but he probably welcomed the prospect of so prominent a forum in which to voice publicly his views. To him it mattered little whether he held exalted place or less distinguished office as long as there was opportunity to serve his country and to battle for the causes he championed. This unusual consecration to public service impressed even foreign historians, and Bryce exclaims in admiration, "Although several Presidents have survived their departure from office by many years, only one, John Quincy Adams, played a part in politics after quitting the White House. . . . Adams was elected to the House of Representatives within three years from his presidency, and there became for seventeen years the fearless and formidable advocate of what may be called the national theory of the Constitution against the slaveholders."[47]

Nearing his sixty-fifth year when he took his seat in the House of Representatives, this ex-President in his first few terms rivaled the fervor and alertness of members half his age, and became the acknowledged spokesman for those who dedicated their lives to the eradication of slavery. There was another principle for which John Quincy Adams fought with uncompromising zeal—the right to present petitions to the Congress of the United States. He shunned the credo of expediency, the belief of some leaders that political controversy should be avoided; in fact, he deliberately set in motion events which aroused against him the most violent criticism and censure. Then he would stand up against his accusers and denounce their actions or their principles. It was then the custom in the House of Representatives to set aside certain days when petitions from citizens and groups might be presented; usually the procedure was a mere formality, the petitions being referred perfunctorily to some committee or "laid on the table"—a parliamentary consignment to oblivion. We have a glimpse of John Quincy Adams as he appeared to observers in the galleries; Julia Gardiner, later the wife of President John Tyler, tells us how she looked down upon the members: "I remember the appearance of Mr. Adams as he sat day after day watching his opportunity to present his mammoth petition on the subject of slavery. Mr. Adams was excessively bald, and as he sat in the middle of the House, with his immense petition rolled around a kind of windlass to sustain it, his excitement was manifest in the flaming redness of his bald head, which acted as a chronometer to his audience." [48]

Though most of the petitions which Adams presented were in condemnation of slavery, his devotion to the principle that it was an inherent right to address Congress prompted him to present also petitions which were at variance with the causes he espoused and even antagonistic to himself personally. Let the historian McMaster relate a typical example: "When petition day came around again and Massachusetts was called, Adams presented a memorial from the citizens of Georgia who considered it a grievance that he had been placed at the head of the Committee on Foreign Relations. His talents, patriotism, and statesmanship the petitioners freely admitted, but complained that he was 'possessed of a species of monomania on some subjects' . . . and was, therefore, unfit to be intrusted with our relations with Mexico. Objection was made to its receipt, but Adams claimed the right to be heard in his defense and four days were wasted in a profitless and unseemly debate." And, when the call for petitions was resumed, Adams again presented a petition from citizens of his own state, arousing a furious and bitter debate, with members attempting to pass a resolution of censure against Adams for presenting the petition; arguments in the House on the subject continued for two weeks amid confusion, and the public press entered the fray with censure, ridicule, and anger.[49]

It did not matter to John Quincy Adams that he had aroused an avalanche of criticism; it was not the first instance, and was not to be the last. At every opportunity he spoke out against slavery, or attempted to present petitions from anti-slavery organizations. The House attempted to end this agitation, voting a refusal even to accept the petitions. Against this "gag rule" Adams fought with impassioned eloquence; finally he won his fight, the gag rule was repealed. But he was realizing a growing need to entrust to younger men the banner of human freedom, and to them he repeatedly wrote counsel and encouragement. In July, 1838, at seventy-one, we find him writing to youthful Edmund Quincy, who had invited him to a celebration of the Massachusetts Anti-Slavery Society on the anniversary of the day upon which slavery was abolished in the colonial possessions of

Great Britain; every phrase breathes the consuming hatred which the venerable ex-President felt toward slavery:

> I rejoice that the defence of human freedom is falling into younger and more vigorous hands. That in three score years from the day of the Declaration of Independence, its self-evident truths should be yet struggling for existence against the degeneracy of an age pampered with prosperity and languishing into servitude, is a melancholy truth from which I should in vain attempt to shut my eyes. But the summons has gone forth. The youthful champions of the rights of human nature have buckled and are buckling on their armor; and the scourging overseer, and the lunching lawyer, and the servile sophist, and the faultless scribe, and the priestly parasite, will vanish before them like Satan touched with the spear of Ithuriel. I live in the faith and hope of the progressive advancement of Christian liberty, and expect to abide by the same in death. You have a glorious and arduous career before you, and it is among the consolations of my last days, that I am able to cheer you in the pursuit and exhort you to be steadfast and unmovable in it.[50]

Despite the animosities he had aroused, John Quincy Adams was regarded with admiration and reverence by the members of the House of Representatives to which he was re-elected every two years from 1831 on. When, in the spring of 1847, he fell ill, friends and antagonists alike watched his vacant seat with regret; when he returned, in the closing days of February, the entire membership rose in respect and tribute; the newspapers were filled with encomiums in prose and verse.[51]

The final events in his career were now approaching; his spirit and mind reflected the vigor of youth, but his body was frail with advancing years. At noon, on February 21, 1848, when the House of Representatives convened, he was in his chair, carefully arranging papers on the desk before him. Voting had begun on a pending resolution, and he expressed "No" in an unusually loud tone. He rose to address the Speaker, and suddenly reeled, falling at the side of his chair.[52] He was taken to the Speaker's room, and was heard to mutter, "This is the last of earth, I am content." The Washington correspondent of a New York newspaper, who had witnessed the tragic event, wrote in his report, "His own wishes are gratified, for it was the wish of John Quincy Adams that he die in harness." Physicians were summoned and attempts were made to "cup" him—a deliberate bleeding process customary in that period; at an earlier period a similar process hastened the end of George Washington.[53] Removed to his Washington residence, he lingered for two days, dying on February 23. Throughout the land friends and former political enemies alike paid him tribute. When the body of the ex-President journeyed from the Nation's Capitol to its Massachusetts tomb, saddened crowds stood in reverence in the towns through which the funeral train passed. In New York City, where it was necessary to transfer the casket from one railway station to another at the opposite side of the city, the hearse, drawn by "eight white horses, with eight grooms in Turkish costume," [54] was preceded by mounted troops, and followed by a long procession of high dignitaries and groups of men representing numerous professions and trades. In Philadelphia, the coffin rested in the State House, in the room where his father—John Adams—had signed the Declaration of Independence.[55] When the casket reached Boston, all business was suspended, all flags were at half-mast. At last, the body came to Quincy and John Quincy Adams was entombed near the grave of his father. Upon the casket, the silver plate bore the inscription written by Daniel Webster:

JOHN QUINCY ADAMS
BORN
AN INHABITANT OF MASSACHUSETTS
JULY 11, 1767
DIED FEBRUARY 23, 1848
A CITIZEN OF THE UNITED STATES
IN THE CAPITOL AT WASHINGTON
HAVING SERVED HIS COUNTRY FOR HALF A CENTURY,
AND ENJOYED ITS HIGHEST HONORS [56]

Perhaps the most succinct tribute to this President's son was the announcement which George Bancroft, then our Minister to England, sent to the London newspapers. The official news of the death of John Quincy Adams did not reach the American Legation until March 27; and on the following day the London *Times* published Bancroft's eulogy: "So full of years that he numbered more of them than our Republic—the companion of the fathers of our Constitution—he was a patriot firm in the faith in man's capacity for self-government, and always loving his country above all lands of the earth." [57]

Such was the career of the most famous of Presidents' sons—the oldest of the second President. In comparison, the lives of his younger brothers—Charles and Thomas Boylston—were unimportant and unspectacular; no biographers have accorded them more than a sentence or two, and few newspapers noted their passing in more than a single phrase.[58] They played no roles in political controversy, their names were not acclaimed by devoted partisans or besmirched by political slanderers. Yet they matched the brilliant scholarship of their elder brother John Quincy; and, in the legal profession for which all three sons of John Adams were educated, at least one brother achieved greater success.

Charles Adams, two years younger than John Quincy, was nine when his father took him to Europe after the older brother had already made four crossings of the Atlantic. With motherly anxiety Abigail Adams awaited news from her husband. "My delicate Charles, how has he endured the fatigue of his voyage?" she inquired. "John is a hardy sailor, seasoned before. I do not feel so much for him." [59] A letter from John Adams calmed her fears: "Charles has sustained the voyage and behaved as well as his brother ever did." [60] It had been the plan of the father to put both young sons in the Leyden University in Holland; John Quincy was enrolled, but admission was denied to Charles because he was under twelve. Instead, this youngster was sent to school in Paris.[61] But in two years his health was impaired and his longing for his American home prompted John Adams to put him aboard ship in charge of a friend. "What have I not suffered since I heard my dear Charles was on board and no intelligence to be procured of the vessel for four months," wrote the anguished mother.[62] Her apprehensions did not end until he was again in her arms.

Later, Charles attended Harvard, graduating at nineteen. There were turbulent events at the college while he was a sophomore; both he and his younger brother Thomas Boylston, in the lower class, were suspected of being participants. John Quincy, then studying law in nearby Newburyport, records in his diary that he "had with Mr. Shaw some conversations upon the subject of the disorders which happened at the College in the course of the last quarter. His fears for my brothers are greater than mine. I am persuaded that Charles did not deserve the suspicions which were raised against him; and I have great hope that his future conduct will convince the governor of the University that he was innocent." [63] Rebellions among Harvard students were not infrequent; usually, these were protests against the inferior and unpalatable food served in the college dining halls.[64] But

I was graduated at Harvard University in July 1787. I had already traversed the Atlantic Ocean, four times, three of them in the midst of the American revolutionary War—had travelled over a great part of Europe, and had served the public, in the not altogether irresponsible capacity of Secretary and interpreter to the mission of the United States to the Empress Catharine of Russia and afterwards at the Negotiation of the Treaty of Peace and Independence at Paris in 1783—at that of the Treaty with Prussia, at the Hague in 1784—and under the Commission of my father, Dr Franklin, and Mr Jefferson at Paris in 1785 I had served my father as his private Secretary—I had thus served a practical apprenticeship of seven years, to the trade and mystery of American Politics before I entered the walls of Harvard as a Student—My public life began, as it were with the Declaration of Independence—

When I took my first degree at Cambridge, the federal Convention which formed the present Constitution of the United States, were in Session at Philadelphia—In September of that year, the Constitution was presented to the People, for their acceptance. My father was then in England—I was reading Law, in the office of Theophilus Parsons at Newbury-Port. In March 1789—the Government of the Union was organized under the new Constitution—My father was the first Vice-President of the United States.—In July 1790 I was admitted to the Bar at the Courts of Common Pleas, in the Counties of Essex and Suffolk, and opened an Attorneys office in Boston

J. Q. Adams

A PRESIDENT'S SON RECALLS HIS PRECOCIOUS YOUTH

At seventy, John Quincy Adams, son of the second President, recounted his youthful education—within college classrooms and among the statesmen of Europe. (New York Public Library) the riots during the student days of Charles Adams were due to another reason: more stringent oral examinations were instituted, and the innovation aroused the ire of the students.[65] Assuredly, no sons of John and Abigail Adams had need to fear additional tests of scholarship, however comprehensive. Even John Quincy, steeped in classical lore and accomplished in ancient and modern tongues, admired the linguistic and debating talents of his younger brother; in his diary he noted, "Charles had a dialogue with Emerson. The circumstance gave me more pleasure than any allotment that I ever had myself." [66]

After completing his classical courses, Charles served the required period in a law office and was admitted to the bar. He took up residence in New York City, and gradually gained clients. In 1795, at twenty-five, he married, and fathered two children. Thenceforth, his career is shrouded in mystery; the published diaries and letters of his father and brothers make no reference to his activities.[67] On the last day of November, 1800, he died. The researcher seeks in vain for some documentary evidence that either parent came from the Capital to attend the funeral of their son.[68]

The cryptic phrases in the letters of John Adams lead to the conclusion that the untimely death of Charles was hastened by dissipation. Writing to a friend, a month after the death of Charles, the Presidential father both mourned his loss and found solace in belief that his surviving sons would not fail in the Adams credo of righteousness. Said John Adams:

> The affliction in my family from the melancholy death of a once beloved son has been very great, and has required the consolation of religion as well as philosophy to enable us to support it. The prospects of that unfortunate youth were very pleasing and promising, but have been cut off. . . . I have two sons left, whose conduct is worthy of their education and connection. I pray that their lives be spared and their characters respected.[69]

The same implication that Charles had been delinquent to the parental ideals finds expression again in a letter to another close friend: "I thank the Supreme that I have yet two sons, who will give me some consolation by a perseverance in those habits of virtue and industry which they have hitherto preserved." [70] And still more indicative that Charles Adams, dying at thirty, had saddened his sire not only by his death but by the manner of his dying is the anguished outburst of the father when he mentions to Thomas Jefferson "the funeral of a son, who was once the delight of my eyes, and a darling of my heart, cut off in the flower of his days, amidst very flattering prospects, by causes which have been the greatest grief of my heart, and the deepest affliction of my life." [71]

Far happier and longer than the life of Charles—though far less conspicuous or distinguished than that of John Quincy—was the career of Thomas Boylston Adams, the third and youngest son of the second President. Not yet four when his father aided Jefferson in drafting the Declaration of Independence, little Tommy toddled along by his mother's side while Abigail Adams was in the midst of the dramatic events which began the Revolutionary War in the Massachusetts towns. Abigail taught her youngest as she did her two older boys, and he became imbued with her intense liking for history, philosophy, and literature. For his mother he retained a deep affection throughout her life, and with this love a reverence for her scholarship and wisdom; but Abigail Adams did not want respectful deference to chill his filial affection and she wrote him, when he had reached manhood, "My dear son Thomas, when you address me again let it be by the endearing epithet of Mother instead of the formal one—Madam." [72]

Thomas graduated from Harvard, at eighteen, in 1790. Two years later he became Treasurer of Quincy. He studied law, and was admitted to the Massachusetts bar in 1795. But he did not begin immediately to practice the legal profession; instead he went to Europe where, as we have seen, his brother John Quincy was already an experienced diplomat. For nine months Thomas acted as chargé d'affaires of the American Legation at The Hague, in Holland; shortly thereafter he became secretary of the Berlin Legation where John Quincy was accredited Minister to Prussia. The official duties were not difficult, and Thomas Boylston Adams spent his leisure visiting ancient castles, and struggling with Adams inhibitions. He was then twenty-four. In his meditative moments he jotted down in a diary his opinions and his impressions; these observations were later published in book form.[73] These notations, as do his letters in later years, reflect more than a philosophical interest in women. Near Wittenberg he enjoyed "a very good breakfast served by a tidy and pretty waiting maid"; [74] he went to the theater where "the actors were very tolerable . . . but one beautiful girl in the number"; he visited the Prince's palace and other castles at Wörlitz, but while he noted that "my deliberate opinion is that they neither pay the time, expense, nor trouble of going out of one's way to see them," he was intrigued with a large painting "of a bathing scene of females, in which they are surprised by a male intruder . . . rather well than otherwise, for anybody to have done . . . extremely so for a lady and a princess." Other entries make it clear that Thomas was susceptible to feminine youth and beauty; at Dessau he "took a walk in the park & ogled a couple of young girls, who returned it with interest, but though I thought myself invited, I dared not speak to them, for one reason only, namely lest they should not understand me." But when he finds "a female old and uninviting" traveling alone he declines to share the chaise with her and engages his own conveyance.

When he returned to the United States his father was President and the Capital was at Philadelphia. Thomas remained with his father and John Adams found his company interesting; when the son planned to visit his mother at their Massachusetts home, the President wrote to his wife, "Thomas is my delight and I know not how to resign him; but as I know you will not be quite well till you see him, I shall consent to his going next week." [75] Later the seat of Government was moved to "Washington City on the banks of the Potomac" and there John Adams was the first Chief Executive to occupy the "Presidential Palace"—later called the Executive Mansion, and finally the White House. Thomas himself went to the new Capital and balls were given in his honor. He realized that the eagerness to entertain him was because he was a President's son; and he wrote to a friend, "What a fine thing it is to have a father when his merits are thus visited upon his child." [76]

Thomas had decided to settle in Philadelphia, and practice law. Like his father and brother before him, his beginning was difficult. He found his means too limited to indulge in the style of young gentlemen. He was obliged to forego the purchase of a horse to "rather buy a few law tools to decorate the bare walls & empty tables of my Office, & trust to my heels for exercise." [77] Soon thereafter, alarmed by an epidemic of yellow fever, he went to nearby Germantown until the courts reopened in the fall. Around Philadelphia he found few who shared his interest in literature, and he preferred the company of his books. "Since I came out here, I have been infinitely more amused, instructed, & gratified with the company I have kept than that I was obliged to frequent in the City," he wrote to his friend, William Shaw. "I converse with Cicero, Tacitus, Ovid, Horace, in addition to professional writers." Nevertheless, he was aware that he needed more than the classics to survive in a materialistic world, and he wrote: "But these will not give me bread, no! we must dwell with bricks & stones, filth & heat & all the disagreeables of life, because there dwells man, sordid, money-making animals." [78] With this realization that the practice of law and not indulgence in literary tastes would increase his monetary income, Thomas gave more attention to the promotion of his legal abilities. He wrote: "Since my return I have been more occupied with my profession than I had been, for a long time before. My ambition does not aspire to anything out of the pale of Bar promotion, but it is by no means an easy task to obtain eminence in this sphere. The number of competitors added to the difficult and laborious duties in the exercise of our profession, make it a perfect lottery as to success & profit. Every opportunity I get, of holding forth, at the Bar, invigorates zeal, but I have not yet vanquished the terrors of palpitation incident to inexperienced speakers." [79]

Political events intrigued him, too; and he wrote with finality his verdict on the prominent personalities of that period, and with equal definiteness he voiced his opinions about books, orations, judicial decisions, and Governmental activities. In the consciousness of his superiority, he lavished praise and heaped ridicule; he even censured the letters of his correspondent, five years his junior: "Dear William, you write a very slovenly hand and you spell shockingly ill. Truth is sometimes disagreeable, but ought not to be disguised. She is, you know, the only female that wants no fig leaf to cover her nakedness."

Despite his enchantment with the Greek and Latin poets, Thomas was not immune to the charms of young ladies. We find him confiding to his cousin William that he was not unaffected by their presence in a conveyance from the Capital to Philadelphia. The President's son was then twenty-eight; he writes: "I had a remarkably pleasant journey from Washington—rendered more delightful by the society of two fine, accomplished, & tolerably handsome females. You know what charming creatures they are. And though neither your experience nor mine extends beyond their enlivening powers in the journey of a stage coach—some faint notion, I apprehend, may be gathered of their happy influence upon the journey through life." [80] He had progressed in his law practice, "though not full of business—a small portion falls to my share, and I look to time & perseverance for a moderate increase." The court appointed him to defend a man accused of highway robbery, and he obtained the acquittal despite the judge's charge to the jury suggesting a verdict of guilty. With the passing months, however, his progress did not satisfy him. "It matters little whether there be few or many lawyers in the same place, for business will always be done by a few. . . . I cannot help feeling gloomy at times, under the conviction that my business will not be sufficient to support me for two or three years to come. Will this be enough to satisfy me? Do I not wish for something beyond this? Perhaps I do —what then? Why wait two or three years more, until the best part of your Life is spent, and there is a chance that you may gain a livelihood by your profession. Very consolatory." [81]

Several years later Thomas married and returned to his native State of Massachusetts. Settling in Quincy, he continued in the legal profession, but his love of literature was still strong. Around Boston, in the environs of Harvard, he found the intellectual and cultural atmosphere he missed in Philadelphia.

In August, 1806, Thomas Boylston was chosen to deliver the oration at the annual meeting of Phi Beta Kappa, the fraternity in which membership even then was regarded as a badge of scholarship. His theme was "Philosophy," and a Boston paper reported that "Mr. Adams manifested diligent and laborious research . . . and instructed the assembly by a very learned and deep research into the opinions of the different sects of ancient philosophers"; and, aware that the lecturer was the son of the ex-President, the editor continued, "He honorably maintained the reputation of the family from which he is descended; which family is rendered noble, not by office and power in the State, but by a taste and capacity for acquiring ancient and modern literature." [82] We have another version of the occasion in the notes of a fellow member. The meeting opened with prayer, then "brother Thomas B. Adams delivered an oration on philosophy. Although there was such a numerous concourse of brethren, but thirty of us dined at Porter's." The "numerous concourse" included some fifty members, but nearly half of those who listened to the lecture must have felt it sufficient for an evening's entertainment and did not attend the repast and music which followed it—leaving uneaten twenty dinners for which advance payment had been made in expectation of their attendance.[83]

Thus Thomas gratified his literary interests while progressing in his law practice, with an occasional appointment by the Governor to investigating commissions. Finally, his knowledge of legal procedures and his judicial temperament, coupled with his prestige as the son of John Adams, led to his selection as judge of a State Court.[84]

Although this youngest son of the second President resided in Massachusetts most of his sixty years, the press of that State took little notice of his activities. Even in death, in 1832, some newspapers made no mention whatsoever of him; the few which noted his passing merely included his name in the customary list: "Died, at Quincy, Hon. Thomas B. Adams, age 60." [85]

Thus lived and died the three sons of John Adams. At least two of them could have said with their sire: "The great Anxiety of my Life has been to do my Duty and avoid just Reproach; and I know very well, that my Life has been passed at such a remote Distance from every bad Principle and foul Course, that no Authority will be credited which may be so abandoned as to ascribe to me any Thing very vicious or very vile." [86]

2

Sons of John Quincy Adams

The three Presidents who, from 1801 to 1825, followed John Adams—Jefferson, Madison, and Monroe—had no sons. The sixth President, as we have seen, was John Quincy Adams, whose career as a Presidential son we have already traced; now, our task is to view him as a Presidential father.

John Quincy Adams had three sons. The eldest was born on July 4, 1801, and was christened George Washington Adams. But, despite the fact that his birthday was on the most consecrated day of the Republic and that he was named after the Father of his Country, and even though his grandfather and his father were both presidents, George Washington Adams could never have been an occupant of the Presidential chair: the Constitution of the United States restricted that office to native born citizens, and George Washington Adams had been born in Germany. His early education also was in Europe, but he completed his studies at Harvard and acquired his knowledge of law in the office of the able and eloquent Daniel Webster. John Quincy Adams was much attached to this eldest son; and, during the intervals on this side of the Atlantic, the father would take little George for evening strolls around Braintree and Boston, explaining to him the localities where so many epochal events of the Revolution had taken place.[1] George was the only son who inherited his parents' love of literature; the father tells us in his diary that when on a Christmas day he gathered his family about him and read aloud Pope's "Messiah" to "make an experiment on the tastes of the children, . . . not one of them excepting George appeared to take the slightest interest." [2]

But, even though he was barred from any possibility of being President, George nevertheless followed in the footsteps of his distinguished forebears in pursuing a career of law and public life.[3] At the beginning of his father's Presidential term, George was a confidential aide at the White House; but later he returned to Massachusetts. Living in Boston or in its suburbs, he was elected to the State Legislature, and also became a captain in a State regiment. It was George who was at the bedside of his grandfather John Adams on that 4th of July, 1826, when that venerable patriot passed away. John Quincy Adams, journeying from Washington by steamer, tells us how he alighted at Boston on July 12, and heard from George that John Adams had died at the family home at Quincy, Massachusetts, eight days previously: "My son George came in shortly after, and was with me till near one in the morning. He informed me of the circumstances of my father's last moments, and of those attending the funeral. George himself was on the 4th in Boston expecting to attend with his company at the celebration of the day. An express was sent for him, and he came out about noon. My father recognized him, looked upon him, and made an effort to speak, but without success. George was with him at the moment when he expired, a few moments before six in the evening." [4]

George occasionally visited his parents in Washington, and there was gossip that he had fallen in love with a cousin who preferred his younger brother John, whom she later married. Whether it was this disappointment in romance or the friendships which he formed which led him into dissipation, we do not know. Neither do we know whether it was with deliberation or by accident that he fell overboard from a steamboat [5] en route to New York. The reports of what contemporary newspapers called "a melancholy circumstance" were based entirely on hearsay, influenced by affection or dislike of the Presidential father. No one witnessed the tragedy.

George, then twenty-eight, embarked at a Rhode Island port—either Providence or Newport—on the *Benjamin Franklin.* When, on the morning of April 30, 1829, the boat was nearing New York it was discovered that George Washington Adams was not aboard. His hat was found on the upper deck; his cloak in the wheelhouse. The ship's captain, obliged by law to report the missing passenger, made an affidavit in which he "presumed," "inferred," and "believed" that "it was more than likely that he fell accidentally from the upper deck." [6] "The public mind was a good deal excited yesterday in consequence of a circumstance which occurred on board the steam packet *Benjamin Franklin,*" said the New York *Journal of Commerce,* repeating the assertion by the captain that passengers had later recalled incidents which indicated that "Mr. Adams was laboring under mental derangement." Other papers recounted the episodes on the preceding night: George had been in a sociable mood during the evening, had conversed lengthily with an Indian missionary and her two red-skinned converts. Later he complained of a violent headache. After retiring he rose suddenly, dressed, and awakened other passengers, demanding whether they were circulating a rumor that he intended to jump overboard.[7] "It is strange," exclaimed the New York *Commercial*, "that under these circumstances the unfortunate young gentleman was not watched and the catastrophe prevented." [8] Several of the journals spoke of the ex-President's son as "an attorney of talents," "a lawyer of prominence and a young man of considerable acquirements," and "a most amiable man and excellent citizen in every relation of life." [9]

Where or when George sank into the waters was not known, and it was assumed that it would be his fate to remain forever in his ocean grave. However, six weeks later, his body was washed ashore and the villagers of the then existing Eastchester, on the north shore of Long Island Sound, accorded the remains entombment with reverent religious ceremonies.[10] The father mourned the loss of his first-born, and his diary often reflected his heartache and his sad memories of George; Puritan resignation vied with grief in his thoughts on the last day of the year in which the eldest son died: "At the close of the year the only sentiment that I feel to be proper is of humble gratitude to God for the blessings with which it [the year] has been favored. Its chastisements have been more afflictive, but I have experienced mercy with judgment. The loss of power and of popular favor I could have endured with fortitude, and relief from the slavery of public office was more than a compensation for all the privations incident to the loss of place. Its vanities I despised, and its flatteries never gave me a moment of enjoyment. But my beloved son! Mysterious Heaven! Let me bow in submission to thy will. Let me no longer yield to a desponding or distressful spirit. Grant me fortitude, patience, perseverance and active energy, and let thy will be done." [11]

The second son, John, like his brother, was born on July 4th—in the year 1803. Named after his grandfather, the John Adams who was the second President of the United States, this second John became the favorite grandson and it was to him that the aging John Adams gave the medal which was engraved at his direction in 1783 to commemorate the treaty by which England formally recognized the independence of the United States.[12] Like George, this second son of John Quincy Adams graduated from Harvard and studied law. When his father became President, John became the White House secretary. In this position, he met many men of prominence and distinction. It was he whom the President sent out to meet General Lafayette, and he also accompanied his father and that distinguished Frenchman on the visits which they made to ex-President Monroe and to other statesmen who no longer occupied official posts in Washington.[13] John performed his secretarial duties not only with efficiency but also with aggressiveness; and his resentment of any adverse opinions regarding his father often brought him into difficulties with antagonistic politicians or their partisans in Washington. One of these assumed considerable notoriety, and led to Congressional discussion. On April 15, 1828, John took to the Capitol a document listing nominations made by his father; the events which followed are described in the diary of John Quincy Adams:

> In carrying these messages, my son John, after having delivered them to the House, was passing through the rotunda with that to the Senate, when he was personally assaulted and struck in the face by Russell Jarvis, one of the printers of the Senate. He returned the blow, and an affray between them was arrested by the interference of persons who were accidentally there. The origin of this outrage was, that Jarvis came to the last drawing room, and my son, indignant at seeing here a man who lives by the detail of daily slander upon me, said to Mr. Stetson that if Jarvis had the feelings of a gentleman he would not show himself here. This was on the 2d of the month. On the 8th, Jarvis wrote a note to John, stating that he had learned that while he was here on the Wednesday before he had spoken of him disrespectfully. He sent this note by a man named McLean who, he said, would receive any explanation. John repeated to McLean what he had said, declined giving any written answer, and said he would hold no correspondence with Jarvis. That day Jarvis followed him out from the House of Representatives, came up to him from behind, accosted him by name, asked him if he had given him the final answer and, upon John's answering that he had, struck him on the face and retreated back, so that John could only strike at him in return before they were separated.[14]

Political opponents of John Quincy Adams gleefully made use of this incident which involved his son, and partisan newspapers opened their columns to stories which depicted the affray as the inevitable result of young John's lack of manners and disregard of others' sensibilities. Colonel Jarvis himself, in addition to being the printer of Senatorial documents, was the editor of a Washington newspaper which had assailed the Adams Administration in the vituperative phraseology characteristic of that period.[15] Other journals throughout the land, in keeping with their political affiliations, denounced or defended the principals in the fray. The Boston *Statesman,* with a keen dislike of the President, printed another version of the affair which it styled "The Fracas at Washington," saying that the altercation originated in "the wanton insult offered by young Adams to a most accomplished and amiable lady, in the presence of her parents and the public"—the amiable lady being the wife of Colonel Jarvis. The newspaper published a letter from a Washington correspondent, "a gentleman whose correctness cannot be doubted," and this anonymous writer asserted that when, at a levee at the White House, someone asked John the identity of Mrs. Jarvis, the President's son replied, "in a tone sufficiently loud for the colonel and his lady to hear him, that it was 'the wife of one Jarvis who, if he had any sense of decency or good breeding would not show his head here'—or something to that amount." [16] The New York *Enquirer,* pretending to be an impartial judge of the episode, left no doubt that it considered the President's son the aggressor, arguing, "Colonel Jarvis, one of the editors of the *Telegraph,* had assaulted and beaten Mr. John Adams, Jr., the President's private secretary. We always have deprecated acts of personal violence; but it is but right to hear the provocation. Colonel Jarvis has been caricatured and ridiculed by the Adams men, and if the private secretary had a hand in it, he cannot expect to escape attack himself." [17]

With equal heat the Administration journals heaped torrents of invective upon the Washington editor. Typical of these defenders of young Adams was a Vermont paper which called the attack on John "a dastardly outrage," asserting that "an affair took place in the rotunda of the Capitol . . . at the recital of which every true American bosom ought to thrill with honest indignation. The notorious Russell Jarvis, co-editor of the 'Tell-lie-graph' . . . as a parade of mischief and falsehood, made an assault upon John Adams (son and private secretary to the President). . . . Jarvis met him in the rotunda, attacked him unaware, threw him down and attempted to wring his nose. The cause of this affray seems to have been that this Jarvis had the audacity and effrontery at the last Presidential levee to intrude his tainted carcase into the President's house—to exhale the poison of his breath where 'Peace and Honor and Virtue Dwells,' polluting as it were the very air and soiling with his infamy the very carpet on which he trod. Young Adams expressed surprise." [18] Other papers excoriated Jarvis for taking advantage of a weaker man, which led the anti-Adams Boston *Statesman* to protest that "the hired writers from Washington to the coalition papers are attempting to excite sympathy for young Mr. Adams because, as they say, there is a disparity of strength between Col. Jarvis and Mr. A. This is not so." [19]

Then began a series of conferences between the President and his political advisors. They all knew that the majority in Congress were unfriendly to John Quincy Adams and that their hatred of him kindled antagonism toward his son. Some of his intimate friends counseled that the matter be dropped, and the diary to which Adams confided his thoughts reflects doubts in his own mind about how to proceed. However, since Congress took no action on its own initiative, the President finally decided to call the incident to the attention of the legislators; on April 17 he sent a brief message to the Senate and the House of Representatives describing the incident in the rotunda of the Capitol and asking that the Congress consider "whether any further laws or regulations are necessary to ensure security in the official intercourse between the President and Congress, and to prevent disorders in the Capitol itself." John Quincy Adams disclaimed any personal motive in bringing the affair to the attention of the legislators, saying that "in the deliberations of Congress on this subject it is neither expected nor desired by me that any consequence should be attached to the private relation in which my secretary stands to me."

The official communication from the Chief Executive made it necessary for Congress to take some action. A special committee was appointed by the House of Representatives, and hearings were held.[20] Colonel Jarvis, John Adams, and a score of witnesses testified regarding the attack and also about the remarks made by the President's son at the White House reception. Russell Jarvis readily admitted that he had twitched Adams' nose, claiming that John's offensive expression was sufficient provocation. He protested that he intended no disrespect to the dignity of the House, even though his onslaught occurred in the halls of the Capitol; and he argued that his offense was answerable only to the civil authorities. John and his friends asserted that he did not use the objectionable language "with a view of injuring the feelings of the ladies who accompanied Mr. Jarvis, nor with a knowledge that it was overheard by them." [21] The Committee made its report on May 17; its members were divided in their opinions as to whether Jarvis had infringed upon the "privileges" and dignity of the House. A bare majority expressed the view that "the conduct of Mr. Jarvis was obnoxious [and subject] to the censure of the House, yet they can hardly suppose he was conscious, at the time of committing the assault, that he was offering a contempt to its authority," and a resolution was recommended which would say that "the assault . . . was a violation of privilege which merits the censure of the House, [but] it is not expedient to have any further proceedings in this case." The minority was not content merely to save Colonel Jarvis from punishment; to "decide a great question of Constitutional law"—whether the House, even if it felt so inclined, could punish Jarvis—the minority report traced the history of "privileges" in the British Parliament and the Congress of the United States, cited in detail examples of transgressions and disciplinary action, and formally resolved that "it is not competent for the House to punish Russell Jarvis for the assault upon the private secretary of the President." [22] Thus the majority considered action "not *expedient*," the minority "not *competent*"; all agreed to let the matter drop; and both reports were "ordered to lie upon the table"—the euphonious parliamentary phrase for ending all discussion. For several weeks there were reported to the President repeated threats of physical violence against John; ultimately the excitement subsided.

John remained in Washington for some months after the expiration of his father's Presidential term. They were in the Capital when news reached them of George's drowning. Then John accompanied the ex-President on the long journey home.[23] John survived his brother six years, but his name disappeared from the newspaper columns. He died in 1834.

The best known of the three sons of John Quincy Adams was the youngest, Charles Francis, born in Boston in 1807. When he was two years old, his father was appointed Minister to Russia, and young Charles Francis spent his childhood at St. Petersburg. Here he began to acquire a knowledge of all the languages then spoken in the leading countries of Europe. The admiring father recounts in his diary how, strolling with little Charles, they met the Emperor of Russia, "who asked me what language Charles spoke. I told him a little English, a little French, a little German, and even a little Russian. 'Ah!' said he, 'the young gentleman is very clever.' But which language did he speak best? I answered that I believed it was the German." [24] In the winter of 1815 he started on a journey to France; when he had children of his own he told them how, with his mother, he had traveled in a carriage from the Russian capital to Paris where John Quincy Adams was negotiating the treaty which ended our second war with England.[25] Charles Francis was then eight; all around him he heard stories of Waterloo and the other events which led to the fall of Napoleon Bonaparte, whom he saw in France. Later the youngster went to London, and there he received some schooling, but textbooks must have been dull for this boy whose eyes had observed so much. Upon his return to America, he again heard of great events from one who was a principal actor in the drama which created the United States—for Charles Francis spent his winter vacation with his grandfather, John Adams.[26] John Quincy Adams has left his appraisal of this youngster, recording that "Charles has a great fondness for books, and a meditative mind, but neither disposition for public speaking nor correct reading. Charles must teach himself all that he learns. He will learn nothing from others." [27]

Like his grandfather and father, Charles Francis Adams had studied at Harvard and prepared for the practice of law, but he never became active in that profession. His father, John Quincy Adams, had yearned for a career in literature, and had confided to his diary that "literature has been the charm of my life and, could I have carved out my own fortune, to literature would my whole life have been devoted. I have been a lawyer for bread, and a statesman at the call of my country." [28] What his father could not achieve, was realized by the son; Charles Francis Adams had the financial means to "carve out his own fortunes." At twenty-two he married the daughter of Peter Brooks of Boston who, dying twenty years later, left to Charles Francis Adams and his wife a fortune of over $300,000. Charles was freed from financial problems long before this inheritance was received; he had engaged in literary work two decades earlier. The memory which his own son had of him was that "in Quincy he seemed to me to correct proof sheets endlessly." [29] The proof sheets were the diaries and other writings of his famous grandfather and father; to these he devoted much of his time and energies. It was he, too, who edited and published the engrossing letters of his grandmother, Abigail Adams.

Occasionally, this youngest son of John Quincy Adams turned to economic problems. In 1837 he wrote *Reflections upon the Present State of the Currency,* and its phraseology, more than that of his later writings, reflects the caustic comments which characterized the utterances of John Quincy Adams. In fact, he speaks of those hold-

George W Childs Esq Philadelphia. Penn.

Quincy 8 June 1852

Dear Sir

I return to you the biography of Mrs Adams which I wrote originally, corrected, and with the additions which you requested. My time has been so much absorbed of late that I have been unable as yet to complete the other - but I will do so in a few days, if in time for your purpose

I am, very truly

Yr obedt Servt

Charles Francis Adams.

AN EX-PRESIDENT'S SON TURNS BIOGRAPHER OF HIS FAMOUS GRANDMOTHER

Charles Francis Adams, youngest son of the sixth President, wrote the biography of his illustrious grandmother Abigail Adams, and edited her remarkable letters.

ing opposite views with deliberate sarcasm; his reference to Daniel Webster is typical: "Mr. Webster, a gentleman from whom as well on account of position as of exalted reputation, a thorough examination of the truth might have been expected, has as it seems to me, not merely failed in this regard but has contributed a good deal to lead the Nation into error." [30] That the object of his criticism was the Daniel Webster in whose office he studied law did not deter his censure.

His Presidential grandfather, John Adams, had remarked that even in a democracy it was not merit but family prestige that paved the way for political advancement.[31] Probably both these factors prompted political leaders in Boston to offer Charles a nomination to the State Legislature in 1839. He declined it, feeling that the family had become unpopular; but his father induced him to accept the nomination in the following year and he was elected.[32] Thereafter, John Quincy Adams told his son not to expect consideration from his opponents; said the father to Charles, the newly elected legislator: "Your father and grandfather have fought their way through the world against hosts of adversaries, open and close, disguised and masked; with many lukewarm and more than one or two perfidious friends. The world is and will continue to be prolific of such characters. Live in peace with them. But—'don't give up the ship!' Fortify your mind against disappointments—keep up your courage and go ahead!" [33]

It was to be expected that, as the son of the ex-President John Quincy Adams who had fought so zealously and so uncompromisingly against slavery, Charles Francis Adams would be drawn into the councils of those who were seeking either to destroy the institution or to restrict the spread of Negro bondage. In 1848 he was a delegate to the convention which met at Buffalo, and he was chosen to preside over that body. It was a gathering of individuals previously affiliated with all the existing political parties, but now united by a single impulse—their hatred of slavery. They assumed the name "Free Soil Party," and proclaimed that "we will inscribe on our banner 'Free Soil, Free Speech, Free Labor, Free Men'; and under it we shall fight on, and fight ever, until a triumphant victory shall reward our exertions." [34] Ex-President Martin Van Buren was selected to head the national ticket, and Charles Francis Adams was selected as the nominee for Vice-President. Leaders of the established parties belittled this attempt to establish a new party with expectation of winning the Presidency; their derision was reflected in the comment made by James K. Polk, then President, in his diary: "I learn that the Buffalo convention of Whigs, Abolitionists, and Barnburners have nominated Charles F. Adams, the son of the late John Quincy Adams, for the Vice-Presidency on Mr. Van Buren's ticket, the latter having been nominated for the Presidency. Mr. Van Buren is the most fallen man I have ever known." [35] The Free Soil Party did not win in the subsequent election; twelve years were to elapse before these moving spirits mustered sufficient strength to create and popularize the Republican Party and to elect a candidate, Abraham Lincoln, in 1860.

Despite the defeat in 1848, the crusade for "free soil, free speech, and free men" went on, and Charles Francis Adams was among the foremost adherents of this anti-slavery movement. Though usually preaching the creed of compromise, he occasionally gave utterance to more pronounced comment.

In 1851, he was invited to preside over the Freedom Convention, held at Ravenna, Ohio, but he was ill at his home in Quincy and instead of attending wrote a long letter which was given prominence in the leading newspapers of the North. This communication breathes the spirit of independence and crusading zeal for human liberty which characterized his father; there were some political leaders who counseled that the slavery question be kept in the background because they believed that agitation by anti-slavery advocates would endanger party success. Against this doctrine of silence Charles Francis Adams spoke out: "Now we are to be denied even this poor privilege of complaint on the plea that the Union cannot be maintained unless we are dumb! Out upon such timid, crawing servility, I say. As long as God gives me life and health, I will retain and exercise the privilege of denouncing the wretched doctrines which would place the liberty of the human race at the feet of every tyrant whose caprice happens to be attended with power to do mischief. . . . My interest in public affairs always has been, and is now, confined to a single purpose, the redemption of one great principle, Human Liberty." [36]

But even though this ringing challenge by Charles Francis Adams was reminiscent of his father's denunciation of "gag rule," later utterances of Charles Francis Adams lack the impassioned hatred of slavery which marked the writings and speeches of John Quincy Adams. In 1855, Charles Francis was invited to discuss the slavery question before audiences in New York City and Syracuse. The policy he counseled was the restriction of slavery to the slaveholding states; and he held that time might lead to voluntary emancipation there. Said he:

Am I asked what I desire to see done? The answer is plain. I would have the people do no injury to the slave-holder, rob him of none of his rest, nor harm a hair of his head, nor any of those dear to him. But I would have them do all that is possible to deprive him of the power of harm to the country or to them. To this end, it seems indispensable that he be dislodged from the strongholds in the federal government. Neither he, nor anyone that he will select, should be made President of the United States, or be placed in any other situation of responsibility in which he could avail aught to prevent an entire reversal of the policy which has, for a long time back, been prompted to promote his peculiar interests. Instead of perpetuating and extending slavery, every effort should be directed to the great object of releasing the general government from all responsibility for it or connection with it. The *word* should not be seen in a statute-book. The *thing* should not be known where the national flag waves over natural territory.[37]

In 1858, Charles Francis Adams was elected to Congress. Still he voiced no fervent denunciations of slavery; he did not match the eloquence of zealous abolitionists or the defiant pronouncements of pro-slavery statesmen. When secession was threatened, he delivered a speech in which premise follows premise to objective conclusions. It was a speech which recognized the legality of slavery, but argued that it was irreconcilable with the underlying principles of the Constitution which gave it lawful status; it admitted the possibility of secession, but contended that the secessionists themselves would discover that they could not survive apart from the other states.[38]

Charles Francis Adams' service in the Congress of the United States did not impress the American people. Said *Harper's Weekly*, "He has not been a prominent member of the House; but the first proposition for a compromise came from him." But the periodical believed that his argument against secession "possibly was the most finished speech delivered in Congress on the crisis.[39]

At the end of his term in Congress, Adams was appointed Minister to Great Britain. He was then fifty-three. Charles Francis Adams came to London neither unknown nor unknowing. Official England, as well as those dominant in industry, finance and society, recalled that his grandfather and father had not only been Ministers to the Court of St. James but also Presidents of the United States. "His reputation had come before him," said the London *News* in reviewing his career, "the grandson of the second President of the United States, the son of the sixth President . . . he was justly regarded as representing the best culture and the highest tradition of the American public." [40] Other emissaries from America were greeted with critical appraisal and some were accorded scant recognition beyond the bare requirements of diplomatic courtesy, but this scion of the Adams clan was "to the manner born"; his family prestige and the wealth of his wife paved the way into the inner circles of British society; Adams treated the aristocracy with casual calm. "It is a common belief that our ministers and ambassadors to Great Britain succumb to the charm of English society," commented the historian Rhodes, "that dinners of the duchesses in London and country visits to persons of quality, distinction and influence are apt to weaken the American fibre. That was not the case with Adams. He went much into society in London and was frequently invited by persons of influence to visit them in their houses in the country. But with him the dinners, receptions and country visits were all in the line of his work, which was to do his part toward saving the republic." [41]

Apart from the recognition accorded him in high circles, Adams possessed another advantage: he knew the English people, their institutions, and their national characteristics. As a boy he had traveled over the British Isles, he had been tutored by English teachers, had begun friendships which developed with the passing years. There are some historians who assert that Charles Francis Adams lacked the graciousness and tact essential in diplomacy; certain it is that, at times, his notes to the British Foreign Office were couched in terse phrases such as are usually avoided in international communications, but the occasions demanded firmness and directness. If, as Hoar concluded in his autobiography, "Adams rarely betrayed any deep emotion on any public occasion, however momentous," [42] he certainly gave vent to his feelings in private conferences with Britain's great. An English journal asserted that "Mr. Adams adopted no apologetic tone. He firmly and energetically submitted the cause of the North at a Court which was passionately opposed to it." [43]

Charles Francis Adams became our diplomatic representative in Britain at a time when the British-American relations were strained —when there was talk of war between the two nations. The war then raging in the United States, between the Union and the slave-owning States, was endangering the economic stability of large sections of England, because the mills of Lancashire could not operate without the cotton of the American Southland, and the Union Navy was blockading the ports of the Confederacy. Though the British detested slavery, their own material prosperity depended in large degree on the unhampered flow of cotton to England; not only the cloth manufacturers but also many other industries and trades were vitally affected. The "cotton question" was of paramount importance, therefore; meetings were called to discuss the events in America and their effect on the British Isles. When the Prime Minister of Nova Scotia and important officials of Canada came to England the halls where they spoke were "crowded to excess, the audience consisting chiefly of the working class"; [44] the London *Post* quoted the chairman of the meeting as expressing the opinion that "no question could more vitally concern the working class." "Let the mills of Lancashire stand idle for one week," prophesied another speaker, "and no statesman in this country could hold his position for an hour who did not meet that exigency, and provide for it by the highest exercise of national prerogative." [45]

The difficulties and economic distress which Englishmen were enduring because of the war across the Atlantic, between the states which had comprised the United States, were further aggravated by an incident which wounded British pride and "national honor." The Confederate Government was sending to England two emissaries, Mason and Slidell. They had managed to reach Havana and there boarded a Royal Mail steamer, the *Trent,* en route to the British West Indies. A Union warship, the *San Jacinto,* commanded by Captain Wilkes, stopped the English vessel, and removed the Confederate commissioners.[46] That action was entirely in accord with the international law to which Great Britain had clung, even though the United States had long endeavored to obtain strict inviolability of neutral ships. The incident occurred in November, 1861. When the news reached England, in the closing days of that month, there was a storm of denunciation against the Washington Government. "Wherever two or three men met together yesterday," reported the London *Times,* "the single topic of conversation was the recent outrage that has been offered by the Federal Government of America to the British flag." [47] And it commented editorially, "It requires a strong effort of self-restraint to discuss with coolness the intelligence we published today." [48] Accounts of the removal of Mason and Slidell —and two other men—were embellished with reports of brutal conduct on the part of the American officers who boarded the *Trent;* the purser of the English vessel wrote to the newspapers that sailors from the warship were about to bayonet the daughter of Slidell when she barred the way to his cabin.[49] The first outburst of anger, however, gave way to more restrained resentment. The following day the London *Globe* told its readers that "reports from all quarters of the country show that the first feeling of the country on the receipt of the intelligence that a British mail steamer had been boarded and her passengers seized, was one of strong indignation;

but that on reflection the feeling cooled down, because there was an universal confidence that the government of Lord Palmerston would be certain to do the right thing, and uphold the national honor." [50]

Mason and Slidell were released, but other events brought friction between the Government at Washington and the British statesmen who were not averse to aiding the Southern States. In English shipyards there was much activity in the building and equipping of war vessels intended for the Confederacy. Under the subterfuge that the ownership of the completed ships was to vest in citizens of other countries, the British authorities permitted a violation of the international law which prohibited the fitting out of ships of war in neutral harbors. Charles Francis Adams protested vigorously.[51] If he could not prevent the sailing of several vessels which preyed on Union shipping, he had the satisfaction a decade later to win from the British Government the payment of damages. Above all, he kept England from giving to the seceding states recognition as an independent nation. His countrymen in the North recognized the difficulties of his task, and had confidence that he was doing all in his power to protect the rights of his country. The press eulogized his ability and his efforts.[52] But the praise was not unanimous. Some Northern papers found fault with his accomplishments as Minister; a few indulged in acrimonious censure, maintaining that he was not only beguiled by the British, but was also a pawn of the Confederates! The chief critic was the fiery Samuel Medary, editor of *The Crisis,* a four-page journal published in Columbus, Ohio, but circulated widely throughout the Union states. Medary gave rein to his partisan hate; said *The Crisis:* "By the late arrivals from England, it appears that the Matamoras cotton speculators have not only got permits from Jeff Davis, but have our minister Adams sucked in, either as a partner or judy, and he has been granting permits to secure these vessels against the dangers of our blockaders." [53] Of course, there was no truth in the insinuation; but editor Medary raised doubts in the minds of his credulous readers. Objective historians, however, regard the service of this President's son as Minister to England as "a career of singular distinction and usefulness." [54] He remained in London until December, 1867, and then resigned.

Apart from his service as our Minister in Great Britain, the greatest achievement of Charles Francis Adams was his work in settling the *Alabama* claims. The *Alabama* was the most destructive of the dozen ships built for the Confederates in English yards; during the Civil War it sent to the ocean's bottom fifty-eight Union vessels. The United States maintained that the British Government, permitting the construction of these ships in violation of international law, was responsible for the losses brought about by the Confederate raiders. We demanded damages; and, after long negotiations, it was agreed that a High Commission of British and American members should sit at Geneva, Switzerland, to judge the claims of the United States and assess the damages. The Commission convened in 1871. Ulysses S. Grant was then President, and it devolved upon him to select the American representatives. General Badeau, who had been his aide and confidant for several decades, tells us that Grant had a strong dislike for the entire Adams family;[55] and there was at that time a movement to make Charles Francis Adams a Presidential candidate in opposition to Grant, who was seeking a second term. Nevertheless, Grant appointed this Adams. The tribunal awarded to the United States an indemnity of fifteen million dollars; Adams had not been able to stop the building and equipping of the ships, but he played an important part in obtaining monetary compensation. The Boston *Transcript,* much later, justly appraised his work: "Mr. Adams' successful conduct of the case of the United States at Geneva, while a member of the council of arbitration, challenged the admiration of diplomats everywhere, as well as of his own countrymen."[56] Even those English newspapers which opposed his efforts as our Minister to prevent the building of the ships paid tribute to his staunch defense of American rights; said the biased London *Mail:* "To say that he comported himself throughout the arbitration in a manner friendly to this country would be inaccurate . . . but, at all events, he did not err from lack of patriotism."[57]

In 1872, a number of influential Republicans, discontented with the Grant Administration, laid plans to prevent Grant's re-election for a second term. The corruption and scandals which beset the Government agencies in Washington prompted many citizens to desire another President, and astute leaders of the anti-Grant factions gave impetus to the movement for an independent Republican party. The "Liberal Republicans" was organized, and gained extensive following in important states. The new party arranged to hold a nominating convention in Cincinnati; a candidate for the Presidency was needed. Horace Greeley, the famed editor, was receptive, but not popular with the German press; the leaders turned to Charles Francis Adams. He had the support of important newspapers not only in his own state, but also in other sections of the country; among these journals was the influential New York *World,* which declared that "if Mr. Adams should be nominated, we have not the slightest doubt that the Democratic national convention will also indorse him." [58] But there were other papers, equally potent in molding public opinion, which did not share the opinion that Charles Francis Adams would prove a popular candidate; the Brooklyn *Eagle* asserted that "for Mr. Adams we have, as the whole country has, profound respect as a scholar and a diplomat. . . . We do not believe he has the running qualities for the race." [59] Editors who understood the mass psychology predicted that he could not sway the electorate, that he was generally viewed as regarding himself superior to his fellows. Though it argued that "such a conception is but a travesty . . . upon Charles Francis Adams," his leading champion, the Springfield *Republican,* accurately described public opinion: "The popular idea of him is that he was the most prominent living representative of a blue-blooded family, cold and reserved in manner, and undemocratic, if not haughty in spirit—holding himself aloof from the world as of a superior mold." [60]

However, if Charles Francis Adams lacked "personal magnetism" he did have the prestige of family name and the support of large segments of voters: the considerable German population, the anti-Grant bloc, and probably Democratic voters discontented with their own nominee.

Those who launched the new Liberal Republican Party weighed all these factors, and it appeared that most of them preferred Adams to Greeley. The initiative was taken by the party committee in Missouri, which instructed its delegates to vote in the national convention for Charles Francis Adams as the candidate for President. It was decided to obtain from Adams a written expression that he would accept the nomination; and a letter was sent asking a clear definition of his attitude.

Charles Francis Adams wrote his reply, and immediately sailed for Europe. He answered:

> I do not want the nomination, and could only be induced to consider it by circumstances under which it might possibly be made. If the call on me were an unequivocal one, based on confidence in my character

earned in public life, and a belief that I would carry out in practice the principles which I professed then, indeed, would come a test of my courage in an emergency. But if I am to be negotiated for, and have assurance given that I am honest, you will be so kind as to draw me out of that crowd. . . . I never had a moment's belief that when it came to the point anyone so entirely isolated as I am from all political associations of any kind could be made acceptable as a candidate for public office. But I am so unlucky as to value that independence more highly than elevation which is brought by a sacrifice of it. This is not inconsistent with a sense of grateful recognition of the very flattering estimate made of my services in many and high quarters. But I can not consent to peddle them for power.[61]

An outburst of criticism followed the publication of the letter. Most of the newspapers regarded it as proof of a cold and haughty personality. "The letter is high-toned, manly and honorable in itself and in relation to Mr. Adams," exclaimed the Brooklyn *Eagle*, "but it justifies and encourages no special enthusiasm in his behalf as a Presidential candidate."[62] Other editors, eager to sow discord in the new party, singled out the phrase "draw me out of *that crowd*." That some of the delegates did consider "that crowd" a derogatory reference to them is probable; possibly, the letter did alienate votes.

The convention of the Liberal Republicans met in May. On the dais of the Cincinnati auditorium where the delegates assembled there was a constant reminder that Charles Francis Adams was a scion of the Adams who helped to create the Republic: there had been brought to the convention hall, as the seat for the presiding officer, the identical chair in which John Adams had sat when he signed the Declaration of Independence.[63] It is not unlikely that, had there been nominating speeches, supporters of Charles Francis Adams would have reminded the delegates that he was a President's son; but the voting began without formal nominations.[64] The leading candidates were Adams and Greeley, but there were three others for whom votes were cast. For the first five ballots the son of John Quincy Adams received the largest vote, reaching 309 against Greeley's 251. "When Adams' highest vote was announced, at the close of the fifth ballot, there broke out a storm of applause such as human ears have seldom heard," reported a Cincinnati paper.[65] "With such a backing, and lacking only forty-nine votes of a nomination, Adams' success seemed certain." But Charles Francis Adams did not acquire the remaining votes he lacked. The votes scattered among the three trailing aspirants were to be the deciding ballots: the Greeley managers obtained these, and Charles Francis Adams emerged the loser.

But his political career had not yet ended: four years later the political leaders who dictated nominations in Massachusetts still considered that the prestige of his name would again attract voters, and they named him the candidate for Governor of their State. They had miscalculated the public interest in this President's son: his opponent was elected by a plurality of thirty thousand votes. After this defeat no further attempts were made to elect him to public office. Charles Francis Adams thenceforth devoted himself to literary tasks. He became active in the Historical Society and was made its vice-president.[66]

When this son of John Quincy Adams died in 1886 nearly sixty years had passed since his father had been President of the United States, and a decade had elapsed since Charles Francis Adams himself had taken any part in political affairs; several generations had dimmed the events in which father and son had played their roles. "The American public of today cannot by any means recall the period of the last public appearance of Charles Francis Adams, and still less can it recall the period of his greatest service to his country," observed the Massachusetts journal which had once championed him as a Presidential candidate.[67] It was true: some editors had even forgotten that the sixth President had two other sons, the prominent Boston *Transcript* saying that "Charles Francis Adams was the only child of John Adams . . . *second* President of the United States"! [68] But most of the American newspapers had prolific files and there were still writers who remembered the exciting period of the elections in the seventies; some recalled that he was a President's son. The dominant opinion was expressed by the Boston *Post,* that "Mr. Adams united in his own person perhaps more of ancestral inheritance and achievement than any other person." [69] In England, too, the press noted his passing with lengthy editorials, observing that "an eminent man himself, he was the son of one famous citizen and the grandson of another." [70] The London *Times,* remarking that the sixth American President was John Quincy Adams, argued that "Charles Francis Adams was his child, and his career offers interesting proof that even in a Republic hereditary talent will make itself felt."[71]

The Boston papers which had recorded the births, careers and deaths of the Adams family for more than a century described the last rites: he was laid to rest among those whose names were linked with the crucial events of the Republic from its very beginning. "The funeral service was held in the church, beneath which are entombed the bodies of Presidents John Adams and John Quincy Adams, grandfather and father of Charles Francis Adams. Tablets to their memory grace the walls of the solid stone edifice, and the statue to John Quincy Adams, erected by his son, looked down upon the ivy-crowned casket containing all that was mortal of that distinguished descendant." And, added the Boston *Transcript*, "Judging the deceased by what he accomplished, . . . he was as great in public office as any of his illustrious ancestry."[72]

3

Sons of the Little Magician

Martin Van Buren, President of the United States from 1837 to 1841, acquired the sobriquet "Little Magician" because he conjured up events which advanced his career and transformed seeming political defeats into victories. He was one of the most astute and resourceful men in all the history of American politics.[1] He inspired ardent attachments and aroused violent hatreds. He intrigued his adherents and infuriated his enemies with his reticence; like the awakening of a slumbering volcano his attacks on his opponents burst forth after periods of unbearable tranquility. His antagonists ascribed to his silence the brewing of sinister plans; a typical doggerel of the period gave vent to their resentment:

> Good Lord! what is VAN!—for though simple he looks
> 'Tis a task to unravel his looks from his crooks;
> With his depths and his shallows, his good and his evil,
> All in all, he's a *Riddle* must puzzle the devil.[2]

Whatever Van Buren did was interpreted as having an ulterior motive; even his courtesy, viewed as a mark of refinement in other men, was regarded as a suspicious omen in him. Thus, John Quincy Adams, who had just relinquished the Presidential office to Andrew Jackson in whose cabinet Van Buren became Secretary of State, joins praise with distrust when he records in his diary a call by Van Buren. "Mr. Van Buren, the new Secretary of State," he wrote, "paid me a morning visit. Of the new Administration he is the only person who has shown me this mark of civility. Van Buren, by far the ablest man of them all, but wasting most of his ability upon mere personal intrigue, retains the favor of civility, and pursues enmity as if he thought it might be one day his interest to seek friendship. His principles are all subordinate to his ambition."[3]

His personal characteristics have been described thus: "rather under medium height with high forehead, a quick eye and pleasing features. He wore short sideburns and was slightly bald. In dress he was immaculate, almost dainty. He made a fetish of good manners and deportment. It is said that when he left the Senate and his household goods were sold, 'the carpet before a long mirror in an upstairs room was worn threadbare from his standing there so much to practice grace and gesture.'"[4] His enemies portrayed him with less kindness. In a period when scurrility was a political weapon and ridicule of personal traits a favorite pastime, Martin Van Buren was a target for both. Even when he already occupied the Presidential chair his opponents not only denounced his political career but also derided his physical appearance; an example of these partisan outbursts was *Childe Martin: An Epic Poem,* which was published anonymously in 1840:

Now see his picture. Body stout and short,
Ears lengthened, high cheek-bones, a chin to sort;
Nose rounding, and withal a handy snout
Where things obnoxious must be rooted out;
And for hair that lacked upon his skull
Were placed large sandy whiskers on the gull:

A pair of legs he had, so short, 'tis true,
They might be thought his body split in two;
An eye he had that noted all things down,
Though never resting long on any one;
He gained by smiling all his private ends,
For he could smile on foes as well as friends.[5]

Born six years after the American colonies proclaimed their Declaration of Independence, he could later boast that he was the first President of the United States who had not been born a subject of the British king. The son of a tavern keeper in the little village of Kinderhook, New York, he studied law and coupled with his legal practice the profession of politics. His rise in public popularity was rapid: he was elected to the State Senate, became Attorney General of New York, United States Senator, Governor, Secretary of State in the Cabinet of President Jackson.[6]

But, with all his political acumen, it is doubtful whether Martin Van Buren would ever have reached the White House had it not been for the determination of Andrew Jackson to have him as his successor, not merely because of Van Buren's great ability, not because he was the most popular political figure at that time: there were others more brilliant, far better known throughout the land. President Andrew Jackson felt grateful that Van Buren did not desert him when he championed Peggy O'Neal.

Peggy O'Neal, as has been recounted often, was the pretty, vivacious daughter of William O'Neal who owned the tavern where General Andrew Jackson, before his election to the Presidency, had rooms, and where other prominent politicians frequented the dining hall or bar room.[7] The shapely girl, aiding her father in serving drink and food, knew them all; her beauty and lively spirit intrigued many of the lonely statesmen far from home. She married a Navy purser, named Timberlake, and there were insinuations that she had been neither virginal when she became a wife nor virtuous after.[8] Later, while at sea, Timberlake committed suicide. Peggy took as her second husband Major John Eaton, later Secretary of War in Jackson's Cabinet.[9] Eaton had expected for his attractive bride the companionship and cordiality of the wives of his Cabinet colleagues, but they refused to associate with her. When the President gave receptions where Peggy would also be a guest, the other invited Cabinet wives pleaded sudden illness to avoid attendance and contact with her. Others prominent in Washington society likewise ignored her; the Eatons were not invited to a party given by the Dutch Minister's wife, and they were similarly overlooked when invitations were sent out for large evening parties given by the Secretary of the Treasury, the Attorney General, or the Secretary of the Navy.[10] Mrs. John C. Calhoun, wife of the Vice-President, particularly refused to have any social relations with Peggy Eaton; when the Secretary of War and Peggy unexpectedly called at the Calhoun home she was received with cold decorum, and the Vice-President's wife asserted definitely after the unwanted visit that she would never return the call. Calhoun himself had been absent when his Cabinet associate came with Peggy, but he announced publicly that he was in entire accord with his wife's attitude. He realized the difficulties facing him, but he "viewed the question involved as paramount to all political considerations, and was prepared to meet the consequences . . . be they what they may." [11] "Happily for our country," wrote Calhoun in the closing pages of his *Reports and Public Let-*

ters, "this censorship is too high and too pure to be influenced by any official considerations whatever. It is equally beyond the scope of power or influence to exclude the virtuous and unsuspected female from society, as experience has found it is to raise the suspected to that elevation . . . the great victory has been achieved, in favor of the morals of the country, by the high-minded independence and virtue of the ladies of Washington." [12]

John C. Calhoun was mistaken: the "ladies of Washington" had not triumphed over Peggy O'Neal Eaton without a heavy price. Peggy had as her champion the President of the United States! "Questions of female virtue," observes one historian, "have broken more than one cabinet in some parts of the world, but Mrs. Eaton stands much alone among us." [13] Andrew Jackson believed Peggy virtuous. "I have been and ever will remain steadfast in the opinion of her innocence," he wrote to General Call, who claimed to have definite proof of Peggy's loose morals and her affair with Eaton while Timberlake was still her husband.[14] Jackson remembered with intense bitterness that when he had married his beloved Rachel without knowledge that her divorce from a first husband had not been formally recorded there were slanders and whispered innuendoes which shortened her life.[15] His political enemies on the stump and in print proclaimed that Andrew Jackson had lived for months with another man's wife. He now regarded Peggy as a victim of equally unjust scandal. "In this unholy wicked and unjust conspiracy against female character, by which I was to be reached, and the memory of my D'r wife is indirectly or directly assailed," he wrote to the niece of his deceased wife; [16] and he denounced the Cabinet wives as "those wicked ones who live and thrive upon slander, and are base enough to assail female character." The Eatons became the favored guests at White House receptions, and about Peggy there gathered crowds prompted either by a desire to please the President, to taunt the absent Vice-President Calhoun and his wife, or merely to satisfy curiosity. President Andrew Jackson could not sway the women of his official family, but he could oust them from their high positions in Washington society; he proclaimed an ultimatum to members of his Cabinet: their wives either would accept the wife of Secretary Eaton or the husbands would be deprived of their Cabinet posts. He could not deprive Calhoun of his elected post as Vice-President, but the other members resigned. All but Martin Van Buren, Secretary of

State. He was a widower, and had no recalcitrant wife to snub Peggy O'Neal Eaton. Probably, too, he remembered that his own father had been an innkeeper. Martin Van Buren accorded Peggy every courtesy, until Eaton, eager to escape the unhappy social tempest, resigned his Cabinet post and went on an official mission to Spain, taking Peggy with him.[17]

Andrew Jackson did not forget that Martin Van Buren was the sole member of his Cabinet who accorded Eaton and his ostracized wife the friendship which Jackson himself demanded for them. He did not forget that the Vice-President had scorned to let his wife associate with the glamorous Peggy and had publicly inferred that President Andrew Jackson was championing a Jezebel.[18] With one stroke the enraged Jackson was determined to reward Van Buren and to punish Calhoun. Calhoun's Vice-Presidential term was nearing its end; certain of his own nomination and election as President for another four years, Jackson planned to displace Calhoun as his running mate, and make Martin Van Buren the candidate for Vice-President. Van Buren was in Europe when Jackson sent word of his intentions, and the Little Magician realized what the friendship and support of President Andrew Jackson meant. From London he wrote to Jackson, "Of one thing be forever certain, that whatever course this matter or any other question in relation to myself may take, it is not in the power of circumstances to disturb the settled conviction of my mind—that I have not in the world a more faithful and sincere friend than yourself. With this conviction I left you, and in this faith I mean to die." [19] Jackson and Van Buren were victorious in the election of 1832; in March, 1833, Martin Van Buren became Vice-President of the United States. Four years later he was himself elected Chief Executive. On March 4, 1837, the Little Magician moved into the White House. With him were four President's sons.

Martin Van Buren had married Hannah Hoes, the daughter of a wealthy Dutch farmer who had settled in an upper county of New York, close to the place where Martin's father was operating a tavern.[20] Her brother married one of Martin's sisters, thus forming double bonds between the two families. The future President and his wife were a devoted couple; after her death he remained a widower for twenty-eight years, despite the many designing women who became interested in him when he rose to high rank both in the United States and as its representative in foreign lands. The union brought him four sons: Abraham, John, Martin, Jr., and Smith Thompson. From their early childhood the boys were his constant concern, their mother having died when the eldest son was twelve years old. The father, though submerged in political strife, watched over them, directed them, and reproved their lapses from the principles he considered essential for their progress.

In Washington, on official missions abroad, on pleasure sojourns in France and Italy, one of the sons was always with him. They acted as his secretaries, they fought his political battles and neglected their own opportunities so that their father might achieve still greater prominence, they hurried to his bedside during his last illness and received his dying blessing. Of all Presidents' sons none were more attached to their sire. And none intentionally made less use of their father's prestige to advance their own interests.

For his eldest son the future President had planned a military career. At sixteen Abraham entered West Point, graduating as a second lieutenant in 1827. He was assigned to an infantry regiment, and served two years on the Western frontier. His record as an officer reflects no spectacular strides; he was not catapulted into high rank as were other Presidents' sons in subsequent generations. It required five years for Abraham Van Buren to become a first lieutenant.[21] Nine years elapsed after he left the Military Academy before he was promoted to captain to fill a vacancy caused by the resignation of an officer of that rank.[22] For seven years he was aide to General Alexander Macomb, but there is not the slightest evidence that the political advancement of the father influenced the appointment. With this son, as with the other sons of Martin Van Buren, it was the father's welfare to which the personal interests of the younger men were subordinated. Abraham Van Buren interrupted his progress in the Army whenever the elder Van Buren required his presence as an aide, and he either obtained military leaves or resigned during the periods when his father wanted him as his secretary. He was his father's companion and confidant when the latter was Secretary of State; but, although he had much to lose in leaving Washington, he encouraged the elder Van Buren to resign when moving from the Capital would benefit the father. This filial devotion Martin Van Buren recorded in his autobiography, noting that "the only inmate of my household at that time, besides the servants, was my son Colonel Van Buren,[23] to whom alone I confided my intention [of resigning] and who after hearing my reasons, unhesitatingly concurred in them, notwithstanding the professional and social advantage which he derived from my official position and residence and which surrounded him with strong inducements to regret the step I was about to take."[24]

In 1837, when Martin Van Buren became Chief Executive, Abraham resigned his Army commission to become the Presidential secretary. Van Buren's foremost biographer asserts that Abraham aided in the writing of the Inaugural Address;[25] at a later period this eldest son did develop literary ability, but at this time he must have been limited in his knowledge of national affairs and without experience in the writing of important State papers.

Despite his arduous secretarial duties, which involved writing by hand his father's correspondence, Abraham found time for love-making. The object of his affections was Angelica Singleton, the daughter of a wealthy plantation owner in South Carolina. Angelica, as was the custom of many Southern belles, had been a student for several years at a fashionable girls' seminary in Philadelphia; and, en route home, she spent several months in the Capital. There, it is said, her cousin Dolly Madison assumed the role of match-maker, and Angelica became engaged to the President's son. The wedding took place in her father's mansion in November, 1838, and the honeymoon was spent in Europe, most of it in London where Angelica's cousin was the American Minister to Great Britain. Upon their return to the United States, Abraham and his bride made their home at the White House, where the young wife acted as official hostess until the end of Martin Van Buren's term in March, 1841.

In 1846 war broke out with Mexico and, as indicated in the Army records, Abraham was commissioned major in June of that year. We read of him in every battle of the campaign, across Mexico from Vera Cruz to the Mexican capital. He was promoted to the rank of lieutenant colonel, in recognition of "gallant and meritorious conduct at Contreras and Churubusco."[26] Abraham remained in the Army until 1854—resigning twenty-seven years after the date of his first commission.

The eldest son of Martin Van Buren survived his Presidential father nearly eleven years. During that decade he lived part of the time on the Kinderhook estate and spent the winters in New York, devoting himself to the editing and publication of his father's works.

In the sixty-sixth year of his life he died. His passing did not receive the editorial comments or even the review of his life which, as will be seen later, were accorded to his brother John. A single New York paper printed a paid notice of six lines noting his death and that "relatives and friends of the family are invited to attend the funeral, from Grace Church, corner Broadway and Tenth Street, on Tuesday without further notice." [27]

The most colorful personality among the sons of Martin Van Buren was John—three years younger than Abraham—known as "Prince John." From early boyhood to death this President's son lived gaily, aggressively, challengingly. Extravagant, talented, bold, his career was marked with escapades and accomplishments which kept him in public view, won him legions of devoted followers and hosts of bitter enemies. While it is undeniable that his status as a President's son made easier his progress both as a lawyer and as a politician, it is equally certain that his successes would have been noticeable had his father never been Chief Executive. Even after the elder Van Buren was in the White House, John relied on his own talents and his own efforts; possibly, had he marshalled his ability to the utmost for his personal advancement, he would have become a more prominent figure in national affairs, but he subordinated his own opportunities to the ambitions of his sire.[28]

Born in 1810, he grew to manhood at that period of the eighteen-thirties when it was fashionable for "young gentlemen" to exhibit prowess in drinking, gambling, and love-making. John was proficient in liquor and betting, but there is no evidence of "affairs with women." In his father's letters are recurrent admonitions to restrain his liking for drink and to abandon his habit of wagering; but John Van Buren did not give up these vices. At Yale he divided his time between classrooms and taverns—with a marked partiality for the latter.[29] He became involved in debt, in card playing and horse racing; but, despite these diversions, his brilliant mind kept pace with the required studies. Upon his graduation from Yale, he studied law in the office of a prominent Albany attorney. At twenty he was admitted to the New York bar, but he did not begin immediately the practice of his profession.

His father, whom President Andrew Jackson selected as Minister to England, sailed for London without waiting for confirmation of his appointment by the Senate, and John accompanied him to serve as secretary of the American Legation. Here we have the beginning of friendships with influential foreigners which always awed and intrigued the father: in his autobiography Martin Van Buren recalled, "I sailed from New York on the execution of my English mission on the 16th day of August, 1831 . . . accompanied by my son, Mr. John Van Buren. . . . There were only three other passengers, among them an apparently amiable and certainly modest and retiring young gentleman who was the son of the celebrated Duke of Otrante."[30] It was this reverence for aristocracy, and the eagerness for his sons to cultivate the friendship of those possessing privileged status or power, that subjected Martin Van Buren, in the White House and out of it, to the censure of his political enemies, who asserted that he was defiling the democratic ideals of the Republic.[31] Returning to the United States after two years in London, John Van Buren opened an office in Albany and began a very lucrative legal practice. Such success is usually the result when a lawyer combines knowledge of the law with activity in the political field. Self-confident, an able speaker, he matched his knowledge, his eloquence, and his wits with eminent lawyers twice his age and riper in learning and experience.[32]

Martin Van Buren, in Washington, heard of the growing reputation of his son, but his pride was mixed with apprehension when he learned that John was still drinking heavily. Even though the father considered some of the rumors to be without foundation, he was well aware of John's weakness and in his alarm he wrote a warning to his son:

> What you may regard as an innocent & harmless indulgence will take you years to overcome in the public estimation. . . . The light & vain feeling of desiring to be regarded as a dashing fellow is surely gratified at too great an expense in this way. *Washington is full of reports at your expense.* It was no longer than last evening that I was informed by a friend—well-meaning but fond of gossip—that Major Fane should have said here that you had been twice carried drunk from the race course. *I knew of course that this was untrue.*[33]

In the spring of 1838, John Van Buren made plans for a trip to Europe. His shrewd father, anticipating that the sojourn abroad would prove more pleasant and profitable if his son "met the right kind of people," wrote to Andrew Jackson, then in Tennessee, for a note of introduction to the Duke of Wellington, the conqueror of

Napoleon and the most prominent man then in England. The name and fame of General Andrew Jackson aroused in England a mixture of hatred, awe, and admiration; he had fought the British, had defeated them. But the Duke of Wellington, a soldier, had respect for this American warrior; and though Van Buren was the President, he knew that, across the Atlantic, Andrew Jackson's name carried more prestige. "My son John is called to England on professional business," Martin Van Buren told Jackson, "he proposes to sail the middle of May & I should be proud to have him bear a letter of introduction from you to the Duke of Wellington. If you find no objection to giving him one it may be sent after him if it should not comport with your convenience to send it in season before his departure." Andrew Jackson did find it convenient to send the requested letter promptly; upon the envelope which brought Van Buren's request Jackson noted in ink, "Martin Van Buren, rc'd 10th. answered same day enclosing letter of introduction for his son John to Duke of Wellington A. J."[34]

With the Duke of Wellington as his sponsor, the President's son was cordially received among the royalty and nobility of the British Isles. A few months after John Van Buren reached London, Queen Victoria gave a State ball and John was among the invited guests. The British press detailed the magnificence of the entertainment, the profusion of rich foods and costly wines, the splendor of costumes and jewels. The newspapers published also the Court Circular, giving the names of those attending the brilliant function, listing the guests in order of rank. And there, between the names of princes appeared the name of "John Van Buren, son of the President of the United States."[35]

The political press in the United States did not overlook its opportunity; it heralded far and wide that the son of the Chief Magistrate, who should be democratic, was hobnobbing with royalty abroad. A congressman from Pennsylvania consumed several hours on the floor of the House of Representatives to denounce this flagrant departure from the ideals of equality for which the Founding Fathers fought against England. "There was a time in this land when Kings, and aristocrats, and noblemen were not countenanced as they are now," exclaimed Charles Ogle, "there was a time when there were not such strong affinities between us and the monarchs on the other side of the Atlantic; there was a time when you would not find the son of a President of the United States invited and set down to the royal table in England before the highest noblemen in that land. Just look at it! Do you not see how we are growing in favor with the potentates of Europe? When Scott went to England, was he taken by the hand in this way? No, he had whipped the British at Lundy's Lane and at Bridgewater too much. No! But when the son of President Van Buren goes there, he is put down by the side of Prince Esterhazy, and takes precedence even of the Duke of Wellington. I tell you we are growing in favor with crowned heads." [36]

Newspapers unfriendly to President Martin Van Buren delighted in printing reports sent across the Atlantic by their correspondents in London, depicting how the son of the President of the democratic United States became the favorite of the British monarch, and Ogle sarcastically quotes from a description of the Queen's banquet—a "graphic sketch" from an American reporter in London, and how John Van Buren was favored by the Queen:

On each side of the Queen, when she is at table, is a chair generally vacant. When she wants to talk to any of her guests, she sends her page to the person with a request to drink wine with her majesty. The person thus honored immediately gets up and walks up to one of the vacant chairs, drinks with her majesty, and enters into conversation. When John had the invitation, he entered into quite an interesting tête-à-tête with the pretty little Queen. He talked of the United States—of our big rivers, big mountains, and big prairies. The Queen was delighted with young John, indications of which crossed her fair cheeks in the form of sweet smiles.

Henceforth, this second son of Martin Van Buren was known as "Prince John"; foe and friend alike seldom referred to him by any other name.[37] Having mingled with Old World royalty and nobility, John Van Buren became a much-sought guest at social affairs in democratic America. He had the *savoir faire* which assured his popularity—and the prestige of being a President's son.

Although, like his father, John Van Buren was adept in all the social graces and the courtesies which were requisite in official circles, he occasionally wounded the pride of those whose friendship he did not at the moment regard as important to his political progress. While men hid their resentment of his hauteur, women were less forgiving. James K. Polk, President of the United States, con-

COURT CIRCULAR.

Her Majesty gave a state dinner last evening to the Royal Family, the Foreign Princes, the Foreign Ambassadors and Ministers, and a party of the nobility.

The company arrived at seven o'clock, and were ushered into the green drawing-room. The Royal Family were received in the grand hall, and conducted by the Hon. Col. Cavendish, Clerk Marshal, and Col. Buckley, the Equerry in Waiting, to the Throne-room. At half-past seven dinner was served in the picture gallery. The tables extended the whole length of the gallery, which was brilliantly illuminated and ornamented with splendid candelabra, vases, and candlesticks of silver gilt, with circular baskets of silver gilt, filled with artificial flowers interspersed. In the middle, opposite to her Majesty, was the magnificent Prince of Wales's candelabrum, and at each extremity of the table were some fine Egyptian candelabra. The gallery was also illuminated with several chandeliers. At the south end of the gallery was a large sideboard of gold plate, occupying the whole of the space between the Corinthian columns, which separate the gallery from the alcove. It was covered with rich crimson cloth, finished at the top with a cornice of white and gold. Some of the finest shields, salvers, vases, tankards, and cups in the royal collection were here tastefully displayed amongst a variety of gold branches and candelabra. In the middle compartment were Flaxman's shield of Achilles, the urn captured on board the Admiral's vessel commanding the Spanish Armada; a beautiful cup, the body of which is ivory exquisitely sculptured with a subject from ancient history; the cover is of gold, surmounted by figures in gold of young Bacchuses, squeezing the grape into a cup held by a nymph; the handle on the one side is a satyr, and on the other a beautiful bacchante, wrought in the same precious metal, as also the supporters, and a magnificent candelabrum in two divisions, the lower supported by seahorses, and the upper by dolphins, surmounted by a statue of Neptune. Among the pieces was a small basso-relievo, recently added to the royal collection, elegantly mounted; the subject, "Rebecca at the well." In front of the column which formed the entrance to the alcove were placed the two recumbent female figures in marble by Canova.

In an adjoining room the band of the Coldstream Regiment of Foot Guards was in attendance, and performed during dinner several favourite pieces.

All the company appeared in full court dress; the members of the orders of knighthood wore their respective insignias.

The Yeomen of the Guard were on duty in the Grand Hall.

There were present their Royal Highnesses the Duchess of Kent, the Duchess of Gloucester, the Duke of Sussex, the Duke and Duchess of Cambridge, Prince George and the Princess Augusta of Cambridge; their Serene Highnesses the Princess Hohenlohe, the Hereditary Prince of Nassau, Prince Maurice of Nassau, Prince Furstenberg, Prince Esterhazy, the Austrian Ambassador; Count Pozzo di Borgo, the Russian Ambassador, the French Ambassador and Countess Sebastiani, the Neapolitan Ambassador and Countess Ludolf, Prince de Ligne, the Belgian Ambassador; the Russian Ambassador Extraordinary and Countess Strogonoff, the Austrian Ambassador Extraordinary and Princess Schwartzenburg, the Netherlands Ambassador and Baroness Van der Capellen, the Marquis de Miraflores, Spanish Ambassador Extraordinary; the Prince de Putbus, Prussian Ambassador Extraordinary; General Count Alten, Hanoverian Ambassador Extraordinary; the Sardinian Ambassador and the Marchioness de Brignolles; Count de Lowenhielm, Swedish Ambassador Extraordinary; the Portuguese Ambassador Extraordinary and the Duchess de Palmella; Marshal Soult, French Ambassador Extraordinary; Baron Bulow, the Prussian Minister; Count Mandelslohe, the Wurtemberg Minister; M. Van de Weyer, the Belgian Minister; the Danish Minister and Baroness Blome; the Bavarian Minister and Baroness de Cetto; M. Dedel, the Netherlands Minister; the United States Minister and Mrs. Stevenson; Chevalier de Aguilar, the Spanish Minister; Count Pollen, the Sardinian Minister; the Grecian Minister and Princess Soutzo; Baron Munchausen, the Hanoverian Minister; Baron Gersdorff, the Saxon Minister; Prince Nicholas Esterhazy, Prince Windisch Gratz; John Van Buren, son of the President of the United States; the Lord Chancellor and Lady Cottenham, the Dukes of Norfolk, Cleveland, Wellington, Sutherland, Argyll, and Devonshire; the Duchess of Sutherland, the Marquis and Marchioness of Lansdowne, the Marquis Conyngham, the Marquis of Headfort, the Earls of Minto, Grey, and Albemarle, the Countess Charlemont, Viscount and Viscountess Howick, Viscount Melbourne, Viscount Palmerston, Lord and Lady John Russell, Lords Hill, Glenelg, Holland, and Plunkett, Lady Flora Hastings, the Chancellor of the Exchequer and Lady Theodosia Spring Rice, Sir John Hobhouse, Sir Henry Wheatley, Sir Hussey Vivian, the Right Hon. C. Poulett Thomson, the Count and Countess Zavadowsky, Count Alexis Strogonoff, the Marquis of Dalmatia, the Marquis de Mornay, the Hon. Miss Cocks, the Hon. Miss Cavendish, Lady Caroline Barrington, the Baroness Lehzen, the Hon. C. A. Murray, the Hon. Colonel Cavendish, the Hon. William Cowper, and Colonel Buckley.

The Duchess of Cambridge visited her Majesty yesterday.

The Duke of Devonshire and Viscount Melbourne had audiences yesterday of the Queen.

A PRESIDENT'S SON AMONG PRINCES

John Van Buren, son of the eighth President, attended a State dinner given by the British Queen to royalty and nobility. In the "Court Circular" his name was listed among those of princes. Thereafter he was called "Prince John." (London *Chronicle*, July 26, 1838)

sidered it tactful to invite to White House receptions this son of a former President, but Mrs. Polk refused because John Van Buren had never extended to her the recognition due a President's wife by making a formal call. Polk recorded in his diary that "upon two or three occasions I had decided that he should be invited to dinner, and in each case Mrs. Polk had countermanded the order. This she did upon the ground that if he so far neglected the courtesies of life as not to call and pay his respects to her that he should not be honored with an invitation to dinner by the President. Upon one of these occasions I was amused when she told me she had burned John Van Buren's dinner ticket, which I had requested my Private Secretary to send to him." [38] Finally, John Van Buren made the required call, on "the regular weekly evening for receiving company," nonchalantly mingling among the company, even though, during the preceding months he had traveled about the country making violent political speeches against the Polk administration.

It was true, as was said by the famed editor, Bigelow of the New York *Evening Post,* that "John Van Buren was the son of a President; from his youth therefore a pet of society." [39] But social triumph was not the goal John Van Buren had set for himself. The yearning for political combat was in his blood. It was not merely parental favoritism which prompted Martin Van Buren to admit this second son at twenty-four to the inner councils of New York party leaders; John Van Buren had demonstrated political acumen, incisive appraisal of popular opinion, oratorical eloquence which swayed voters. Upon his return from England he was elected to Congress.

John Van Buren took his seat in the House of Representatives on the last day of May, 1841.[40] He was in distinguished company; about him were an ex-President of the United States, John Quincy Adams, and a President-to-be, Millard Fillmore; there was also James Roosevelt, a forebear of future Presidents, and other members destined to play important roles in the unfolding drama of the Civil War—Henry Wise, to be Governor of Virginia, and David Levy Yulee who was to have so dominant a part in creating Florida as a state. He found around him, too, members who had attacked his father, Martin Van Buren, who, just a few months previously, had ended his four years as President of the United States. John Van Buren was not awed. In his first speech he voiced his challenge and defiance to the detractors of his sire: "I will tell the gentleman that, after he and those who act with him shall have passed into that contempt which is their doom, the integrity of Martin Van Buren, and the wisdom of the measures for which he contended, will be fully established." [41] John Van Buren's speeches discussed pending legislation with clarity and logic; they analyzed the divergent views expressed by proponents and antagonists of a measure; they were calm expositions of the subject under consideration.

But there was one topic which always aroused an impassioned outburst of eloquence—unfavorable references to the personality or policies of his father. Six weeks after becoming a member of Congress, he debated a loan bill. Suddenly, he recalled that previous speakers had criticized his father's Administration; John Van Buren hurled his reply: "In behalf of the Democracy of the State of New York, who venerate Martin Van Buren as one of her noblest sons, as one of the proudest pillars of the Democratic cause, permit me to cast back all such insinuations with scorn, and to say to his puny assailants, that even before the short period shall have elapsed which shall consign them and those apostates who, in the hour of difficulty, abandoned their political faith and turned recreant to the Democratic cause, into merited insignificance, a just and discerning public will become not only fully satisfied of the purity and unbending integrity of character of the late President, but also of the wisdom of the measures which he recommended." [42] Generally, John Van Buren espoused the principles of his party. He opposed high tariff rates, pleaded for currency in which businessmen could have confidence, introduced resolutions for the payment of pensions to some of his constituents.[43] In short, he proposed no startling legislation; and his Congressional colleagues did not hail him as an outstanding leader.[44]

Political enemies who had attacked John because he was the son of Martin Van Buren now hurled invective with John himself as the target. That was an era of political pamphlets; biographies of public men were written not only by their friends but also by their enemies.[45] The "Life" of a candidate was part of every campaign—it was printed in books, in the newspapers,[46] or as a leaflet for distribution at political rallies. The procedure did not stop there; these "lives" were promptly answered in similar form by the partisans of rival candidates—usually, anonymously. Thus, when an admirer of Martin Van Buren wrote a praising "Life," an antagonist calling himself "Corrector" immediately issued another *Life of Martin Van Buren* allegedly "correcting" paragraph by paragraph statements in the first volume.[47] It was a contest of scribes, a marathon between eulogy and scurrility. Name-calling, the revelation of unknown scandals or the revival of forgotten ones, the fabrication of libelous stories—these constituted the accepted political weapons of the early eighteen-hundreds. As regards John Van Buren, his adversaries made political capital of his personal shortcomings—real and imagined.

The bitterest attacks on John Van Buren came long after his father had ended his Presidential term. There were many such tracts, reeking with rancor and villification; a volume which concentrated all the spleen of those who hated ex-President Martin Van Buren and his sons was that written by one William L. MacKenzie, titled *Life and Times of Martin Van Buren.* The author, who detested the father and was lavish also in his hate of John, had obtained letters written by and to the Van Burens and publicized them. Several of these missives related to John's wagers—on horses and elections; others embodied words objectionable to the ears of pious voters—such as "damn" and "hell." MacKenzie denounced John Van Buren for his vices of betting and cursing, accused the ex-President's son of every chicanery and lack of personal integrity. "John Van Buren is a rowdy, the associate of rowdies," fumed MacKenzie; and he concluded with a verse typical of the low level to which political slander had fallen in the middle of the nineteenth century; John Van Buren, because he used in his letters words not sanctioned in polite society, was

matched in mouth with
Mastiff, blood-hound, mongrel grim,
Cur and spaniel, hack and lym,
Bob-tail-tyke and trundle-tail.[48]

The revelation and denunciation of John's "vices" probably won for him more followers than inimical voters; in an imperfect world human frailties often arouse sympathetic understanding in fellow men. At any rate, his popularity increased with each passing year; John Van Buren was a political power in the State of New York and stood high in party councils in other parts of the country. It is the opinion of very incisive students that he could have gone far in national politics had he not sacrificed his own opportunities to advance the interests of his father; there is much evidence to warrant the conclusion of the New York State historian that, in 1850, "John, who took the stump for his father, spoiled his own chances for the Presidency at Democratic hands." [49] What John Van Buren did or said was considered important news, and prominent newspapers reported his public addresses. His long, involved legal arguments were given place and printed in full on the first page of the *Evening Post,* at that time the most influential newspaper in New York. When opponents of the fugitive-slave law met in Boston in 1851, a letter was received from John Van Buren, "the reading of which was deferred in consequence of its length," but the *Evening Post* published it in its entirety—in three columns on its first page—with the comment that the letter was "marked with its author's characteristic clearness of statement, orderliness of logic, and felicity of language. It presents, withal, a compact and irresistible array of constitutional objections to the law to which it relates." [50]

Political adversaries in his own day, and history writers in succeeding generations, have asserted that John Van Buren changed his principles for the sake of political expediency. An objective review of factual data does not corroborate this viewpoint. It is never easy to appraise the inner motives which prompt the actions of men in public life; our greatest statesmen have alternated unselfish devotion to great causes with deeds which even their most ardent partisans viewed as activated only by personal interest. Gold is usually combined with baser metals. Often, however, leaders of great movements, wholly dedicated to an ideal, are beset with sincere doubts regarding the means to attain it, while more reckless or less foresighted followers have no hesitancy. Often, leaders compromise and yield part of a declared credo to save and to achieve the more important elements of their objective.

John Van Buren lived in an epoch of momentous problems—political, economic, and social. Chief among the questions which agitated Americans was Negro slavery. This traffic in humans had aroused the conscience of every generation since the founding of the Republic. The movement to abolish slavery had grown in the North, and there were many in the South who also fervently wished that the nation were free of the scourge. But how to bring about the freedom of the black man, how to end the system which was clearly recognized by the Constitution of the United States, was the unsolvable difficulty. John Van Buren hated slavery, and he was outspoken in his condemnation of it. An example of his repeated utterances is in the speech he delivered to the Democratic State Convention of Vermont in May, 1851: "As for myself," he declared, "I am free to say that I look with detestation upon the practice of buying and selling live bodies. *Within the limits of the Constitution,* hostility to human slavery is the predominant sentiment of my heart. It is as natural to me as the air I breathe, and will perish only with my life."[51] That this was also the sentiment of the political gathering he addressed is evidenced by the applause which greeted his declaration; the prominent *Evening Post* of New York printed the entire speech on its front page, reporting that "as the speaker closed his remarks, three tremendous cheers were given for John Van Buren."

Yet, ten years later, in the midst of the Civil War, this son of ex-President Martin Van Buren opposed the abolition of slavery by proclamation. He considered that an unconstitutional way. He did not hate slavery less, but he was devoted to the Constitution more. He opposed vigorously any infraction of established legal procedure. Ardent abolitionists in New York urged the arrest of all those who criticized Lincoln's plan to free the slaves as a military necessity; John Van Buren declared he would obtain the arrest of any official who attempted to imprison New York citizens. There was an outcry against him and a demand that he himself be jailed; he publicly defied his enemies. Federal authorities did not come to New York, so he went to Philadelphia, to Baltimore, to the White House in Washington—challenging the Government to deprive him of his Constitutional right to express his views. "I kept inside the Constitution and the law," he proclaimed at a political meeting, "for though I am a moderate lawyer, I know enough not to violate it."[52]

While John Van Buren won a national reputation in political conflicts, he was equally famous for his battles in courts of law. His knowledge of legal principles, his keen analysis of evidence, his eloquence in presenting conclusions to juries had won him the respect of the bar and the admiration of the public. That astute politician, James Buchanan, considered him in political debate "able, eloquent, witty and eccentric";[53] in legal arguments he was persuasive, unrelenting, and clever. Many prominent and wealthy clients engaged him to advise or to defend them; but his renown as a lawyer spread from ocean to ocean in the Forrest divorce case in which he was counsel for the actor, Edwin Forrest.

Edwin Forrest was a truly great tragedian who had won acclaim as well as animosity not only in America but also in England.[54] His admirers were fierce partisans whose fury at any rivalry burst into physical violence. Particularly bitter was the dispute between him and the English actor, William Charles Macready, whom most critics regarded as the foremost Shakespearean actor of that day. Edwin Forrest had played Shakespeare in England, and the resentment of Macready followers drove him from the London stage in 1845. Four years later Macready came to the United States and his appearance on the New York stage kindled the indignation of the Forrest faction. At first Edwin Forrest and William Macready exchanged recriminations through the newspapers, and Macready also gave vent to his feelings in tactless curtain speeches. The bitterness between them and their respective cliques increased, particularly when either played the part of Macbeth which each considered his own peculiar role; then verbal onslaughts against Macready changed to a deluge of rotten eggs, stench bombs, and vegetables.[55] Leading citizens of New York became alarmed, and advised both actors to make peace; the newspapers, too, criticized the partisans of both sides. But the animosities were now beyond control, and on the night of May 10, 1849, there was a clash between Forrest and Macready followers at Astor Place. The militia, called out to quell the disturbance, fired on the mob; twenty-two persons were killed and twice as many were wounded.[56] William Charles Macready returned to England, and Edwin Forrest continued to be the idol of the American stage.[57]

But even though Edwin Forrest was regarded by his adherents as triumphant in the theater, he was to meet defeat in a drama of far greater personal moment to himself. The stage was in a courtroom; the other principal player was his wife. Edwin Forrest, claiming Philadelphia as his home, attempted to obtain a divorce from her in Pennsylvania, but his failure to establish citizenship in that State ended the legal proceedings. He had accused her of adultery; [58] and now Mrs. Forrest countered with a suit in New York, charging her husband with numerous infidelities. Edwin Forrest engaged John Van Buren as his counsel, while Mrs. Forrest had as her lawyer Charles O'Conor.

As revealed in the opening testimony of the trial, Edwin Forrest, while performing in England became acquainted with a singer, John Sinclair, and fell in love with the latter's nineteen-year-old daughter, Catherine. He married her; and the following year Forrest brought his wife to New York.[59] The couple lived together happily for twelve years, then they suddenly parted. During the separation, however, they carried on a prolific correspondence even though later at the trial each claimed that during this period the other had constantly broken the marriage vows. Mrs. Forrest's attorney called many witnesses to prove the husband's numerous intimacies with other women. Forrest countered with the accusation that his wife had carried on an affair with a fellow actor, George Jamieson; as proof of these transgressions he claimed to have found in his wife's effects a letter in Jamieson's handwriting which, though not specifically addressed to her, embodied many references to passionate episodes and illicit relationships. The wife's attorney admitted that the letter had been received by her, but claimed that it should be interpreted as an impersonal expression of a man who indulged in poetical fancy. John Van Buren's opening speech to the jury is typical of his courtroom strategy: innuendo, biting irony, relentless logic. Said he:

> Mr. Jamieson addressed a letter to Mrs. Forrest and we will prove it. It will be found that in that letter he addressed her in the language of deep affection, and that it contained admissions of criminality. It will be found that that letter speaks of the realization of a voluptuous enjoyment. It states that ecstasy is not affection; it contains intense appeals to the party to whom it was addressed to give him the benefit of her experience; that letter will speak of their enjoyment and the bliss attending it . . . it speaks of their adoration and love without being earthly. . . . And it will conclude with a poetic picture, descriptive of when they lay enfolded in each other's arms in the enjoyment of a kiss. . . . You may say that an innocent woman might receive such a letter; that some imprudent person might have thrust it on her; but would a virtuous wife have treasured it or would she not rather have shown it to her husband and said, "Here is a man who has dared to address me in terms implicating my honor"? Would not any virtuous woman have taken that course? [60]

The case dragged on for thirty-two days; and John Van Buren summed up on January 21, 1852—the leading New York paper devoted its entire front page to his speech. But there were other papers which were shocked by the endless flow of testimony intended to prove innumerable infidelities of both husband and wife; and one paper exclaimed sarcastically, "We congratulate the Bench, the Bar and the Jury and the rest of mankind upon the termination of this most tedious and disgraceful trial. . . . The public is disgusted with the very name of the case, so redolent of filthy communications, so contemptible in its plots and counter-plots, so beastly in its developments and so black in its purchased perjuries." [61]

It was evident, as the trial progressed, that both the court and the public felt sympathetic toward the wife. The jury was perplexed on one point, and asked the judge for instructions: how many visits to a house of ill fame were proof of adultery! The judge leaving this decision to the discretion of the jury, they found Forrest guilty and awarded his wife three thousand dollars annual alimony. Edwin Forrest, accompanied by friends, stalked out of the room with disdain. As he descended to the adjoining park he was saluted with vociferous cheers from the assembled multitude, who continued to shout and cheer him for many blocks on Broadway.[62] There were no cheers for his attorney, John Van Buren. It was the opposing lawyer, Charles O'Conor, who won public acclaim; the newspapers throughout the trial reported that Mrs. Forrest was penniless and that attorney O'Conor without compensation was defending her good name. Perhaps astute John Van Buren knew this was not true; if so, he said nothing. Twenty-five years later the public learned that O'Conor had received ample fees.[63] The failure to win the Forrest suit decreased neither John's lucrative legal practice nor his political influence. Wealthy clients still regarded him as New York's ablest lawyer, and large crowds still flocked to his public speeches.[64] "Prince John," as had been his Presidential father, continued to be the idol of his followers and the dread of his adversaries.

While John Van Buren was winning nation-wide renown in the law courts and in the political arena, and his older brother Abraham was achieving high rank in a military career, the two younger sons of Martin Van Buren—Martin, Jr. and Smith Thompson—were progressing in less conspicuous roles. Martin, called Mat by his brothers, was born two years after John; but the disparity was far greater in their physiques and temperaments. Martin lacked the robustness and energy of his older brother, his habits were more sedate, he aroused no deep laudation or animosities. During his father's Presidency he occasionally acted as secretary, though the other brothers alternated in that post. There had been talk, when he was in his late twenties, of an appointment for him as recorder in the General Land Office;[65] but there is no evidence that he made any serious effort to obtain the post.

Like his father, Martin, Jr., delved into political history, either engaging in research or analyzing the treatises of other historians. Thus, he compiled a detailed synopsis of thirty chapters of a work on New York politics, made notes on his father's appointment as attorney general forty years earlier, and on the reminiscences of his contemporaries.[66] Even when his strength was ebbing he collected data and arranged documents to aid his father in writing his memoirs. But he did more: he was eyes and ears for his father when Martin Van Buren left the White House and was still deeply absorbed in politics. To Martin, Jr., at the family home in Kinderhook, New York, astute Washington politicians wrote frequent reports regarding his father's prospects in the conventions of 1844.[67]

It was the credo of Martin Van Buren that his sons would prosper by association with the wealthy and the influential, and he saw to it that his namesake won the interest and the friendship of prominent American politicians. Thus, during the winter of 1848, the ex-President induced Martin, Jr., to spend a few months at the home of Francis Preston Blair, then a political power in Maryland. In the spacious, historic home at Silver Spring, a few miles from Washington, the third son of Martin Van Buren became intimate not only with the Blair family, but acquainted also with other important personages who came there for party conferences and also for financial manipulations which profited by Blair wealth and prestige.[68]

Had Martin, Jr., possessed the vigor of the other Van Buren sons he probably would have become better known for his literary ability and political acumen. But his health was noticeably failing. Already, in the autumn of 1849, Martin, Jr., was seriously ill; nevertheless, he kept a deep interest in political affairs and carried on a wide correspondence with his father's friends.[69] American physicians failed to restore his health, and the alarmed father persuaded him to seek recovery in Europe. Martin, Jr., vainly tried the curative waters in France and Germany and consulted eminent doctors in Switzerland and England. The seventy-year-old ex-President, himself ailing, was unmindful of his own welfare but deeply concerned about his namesake; his letters to friends at home reflect his grief and apprehension.[70] It had been the boast of Martin Van Buren that he had been the first President of the United States born under the American flag; it was the destiny of Martin Van Buren, Jr., to be the first Presidential son to die under a foreign flag. He passed away in Europe during the summer of 1855.

To his fourth and youngest son the eighth President had given the name of a political intimate, Chief Justice Smith Thompson of New York's Supreme Court. The two cronies later became rivals for the Governorship and drifted apart; years afterward, in writing his autobiography, Martin Van Buren referred to the judge as "my quondam friend." [71] But this unforeseen future rift did not mar the deep affection which the godfather held for his namesake; neither did the jurist's exalted post excite in Smith Thompson Van Buren a desire for a judicial career. He was reared in an atmosphere of political maneuverings and controversies, and he preferred the sagacious talk of astute politicians to the dry arguments of lawyers.

Like the other sons of Martin Van Buren, Smith Thompson devoted himself to political affairs not to advance ambitions of his own but to further the interests of his sire. Usually political opponents restricted their partisan attacks to the Presidential father and the brilliant, aggressive John; but, occasionally, the youngest son was also the object of vituperation. Thus, when William Mackenzie wrote his scurrilous polemic denouncing the ex-President and John Van Buren, he also derided Smith Thompson for his frugality, sarcastically referring to his "liberally bestowing a five-dollar bill to set afloat a Democratic journal." [72]

Although he himself was never a candidate for public office, his enthusiasm at political gatherings was intense and his shouts rang out in conventions when the tide turned in favor of his distinguished father or of any cause he espoused. The letters still preserved among the *Van Buren Papers* in the Library of Congress are ample testimony that this youngest son of the eighth President was well informed on political happenings and intimately acquainted with the dominating party personalities.[73]

In addition to his political activities Smith Thompson gave much of his time to arranging and editing his father's accumulated papers. During his father's Presidential term he aided in the preparation of official documents, and probably contributed paragraphs to the Inauguration speech and messages to Congress. But it was after Martin

Van Buren left the White House, and especially after the death of Martin, Jr., that this son was most active in transcribing the voluminous records and rough drafts which the ex-President used in writing his memoirs.

It was Smith Thompson whom the aged ex-President appointed as the literary executor of his works; [74] first with John,[75] and then alone, he edited his father's treatise on the development of political parties,[76] and other manuscripts discovered after Van Buren's death.

Smith Thompson Van Buren passed away in 1876, fourteen years after the death of his Presidential father. To the last he, like all the Van Buren sons, labored to defend his father's career and to exalt his fame—proud that his sire had been the "Little Magician," the eighth President of the United States—Martin Van Buren.

4

Son and Father of Presidents

ONLY ONCE IN THE HISTORY OF THE REPUBLIC HAS IT BEEN THE destiny of one man to be the son of a President and also the father of a President. That was the singular lot of John Scott Harrison. His sire was the ninth President of the United States, William Henry Harrison; his offspring, the twenty-third President, was Benjamin Harrison. Both of these who attained the highest office of the Nation also won renown on fields of battle, the former in the War of 1812 and the latter in the Civil War; both had achieved general's rank. But John Scott Harrison, the link between them, never led soldiers, never captivated the populace with the glamour of a military uniform while he rode a prancing horse, never bivouacked upon a field of battle. This son of the ninth President preferred the pursuits of peace; and chose to dwell where the courage and fortitude of his mother's people had transformed the wilderness into thriving towns, and the generalship of his father had ended the dangers of marauding Indians. In the interval between the two Harrisons who rose to the Presidency with records of martial valor, John Scott Harrison turned from swords to plowshares and, proud of his four hundred acres, raised abundant crops—and thirteen children, among them a President of the United States.

The father of John Scott Harrison, William Henry Harrison, was born upon the eve of the American Revolution, in 1775. His own father, Benjamin Harrison, was a signer of the Declaration of Independence, pledging "his life, his fortune and his sacred honor" to free the thirteen colonies from British tyranny; [1] dying when his son was only sixteen years old, he left him a large plantation in Virginia, and appointed another patriot, Robert Morris of Philadelphia, as guardian of the adolescent William. A doctor's career was planned for the youngster; but, despite advice of Robert Morris, he enlisted in the

Army. He served under "Mad Anthony Wayne," famed for his daring as an Indian fighter, and that general made William Henry Harrison, then a lieutenant, his aide-de-camp; it was Lieutenant Harrison's plan that won a battle at the important site of Fort Deposit.[2] In 1811 Harrison won a decisive victory over the Shawnees; this momentous clash with the red men occurred along a small river, named Tippecanoe, in the northern part of Indiana; henceforth, William Henry Harrison was known as "Old Tippecanoe." Later, in our second conflict with England, the War of 1812, Harrison fought both the Indians and the British; despite the larger forces of the enemy, his skill and courage in leading troops brought him repeated victories.

But these were not his only conquests; years earlier he overcame obstacles in romantic fields, and, despite her father's opposition, married the daughter of the prominent Judge Cleves Symmes. Symmes had aided in financing Washington's army in its retreat through New Jersey; in return for his loans he received certificates of indebtedness. Unable to redeem these in cash, the Continental Congress accepted them in part payment for a million acres of land in Ohio. He selected the beautiful and fertile region between the Great and Little Miami Rivers, including the site of Cincinnati; he acquired the land for sixty-five cents an acre.[3] He brought with him from New Jersey, early in 1790, some fifty sturdy farmers and mechanics, thus taking the first steps in the settlement of the Northwest Territory. Upon the elevated plateau at the most northerly bend of the Ohio River he proceeded to lay out a village, and named it "Symmes City." There is a legend that here it was intended to build a blockhouse, but the army officer in charge of the troops became infatuated with the attractive wife of a settler who thought to end the romance by taking his spouse to the less important settlement at Cincinnati. Whereupon the army officer transferred his troops to the latter town and built the blockhouse there.[4] The city which Judge Symmes had hoped would be the metropolis, bereft of a protective blockhouse, was reduced to secondary importance, but the surrounding farmlands continued to yield large crops and the untrammeled forests were filled with game.

The judge built himself a large mansion and here Captain William Henry Harrison met his daughter Anna, radiant in the beauty of twenty summers. At first the judge regarded very favorably the young army officer but, hearing some whispered scandal about his affairs with another girl, he forbade young Harrison to pay further court to

Anna. The resourceful captain did not accept defeat; aided and abetted by the girl's mother, he waited until his prospective father-in-law had left the mansion for some business in Cincinnati, then calmly married Anna. Weeks later the irate judge met his son-in-law at a reception given by the commanding general, and thundered, "So you have married my Anna! How do you expect to support her?" The young husband replied, "By my sword and my right arm, Sir." Tradition has it that this apt retort captivated Judge Symmes, and he welcomed his daughter and her husband to his home. Anna must have been a girl of rare attractiveness; that roaming historian, Benson Lossing, tells us that, upon his visit to the Harrison homestead sixty-five years later, Anna Harrison, then in her 86th year, still retained much of her beauty.[5]

From this union sprang ten children. With unfailing regularity, every second year, a child was born in the Harrison household, and the biennial chronology of their births is as measured as the periodic appearance of the planets. Five of them were sons: John Cleves Symmes, William Henry, Jr., John Scott, Benjamin, and Carter Bassett. William Henry Harrison was a devoted father, spending much time and effort for his sons' honorable and successful careers. For the oldest, whom he called Symmes, he obtained an appointment in the finance division of the Government land office at Vincennes, Indiana. Symmes married the only daughter of General Zebulon Montgomery Pike, who combined exploring with soldiering, winning fame both as the discoverer of Pike's Peak and as a hero who led the attack on Toronto, Canada, during the War of 1812.

For his second son and namesake, General William Henry Harrison wanted fame in law; and, though his financial status was becoming weak, the father was determined that William Henry, Jr., should have adequate education. The boy, at seventeen, was sent to Transylvania College at Lexington, Kentucky, in April, 1819, and the father repeatedly wrote him letters of admonition and encouragement. "I hope," William Henry Harrison wrote to his young son shortly after the latter's arrival at college, "you will exert yourself to the utmost before the examination takes place so you may pass a good one & be received with some éclat in the Sophomore class."[6] The boy became discontented and homesick; he wanted to transfer to a college in Cincinnati a short distance from the family home in North Bend; he yearned at least to come home for the Christmas holidays but his father disapproved; in November he wrote to William, Jr., "I cannot think of your changing your situation for Cincinnati—I do not believe the college at the latter place can compare with the University of Lexington. . . . We certainly want to see you but I cannot consent for your return at Christmas. . . . The present period is the most important of your whole life, and your conduct in it will fix your entire destiny." [7]

We do not have the letters which William Henry, Jr., wrote to his father at this period, but the communications of the elder Harrison leave no doubt that the son did not share his father's opinions regarding the importance of this educational preparation. A year after young Harrison entered Transylvania College we find the father pleading with him to continue his studies:

> My dear Son:
>
> I have received your letter of the 30th Inst. and have read it with much regret because you manifest in it a disposition to abandon the pursuit of that complete education which it is my great object to give you & with the importance of which I had hoped you were fully impressed. If you possess talents to distinguish yourself with the education which you have acquired nothing can be more certain than that you will by persevering in the course you are in be enabled to occupy a stand at some future day either at the Bar or in the Councils of yr Country to which it is the lot of very few to attain. Is not this a sufficient motive to induce you to strain every nerve to make every exertion to arrive at that goal when a reward awaits you. An indulgent parent is willing to furnish the means [for using an] opportunity which those who possess it estimate as the greatest advantage of their lives & those who do not (and possess proper judgment) lament the worst of misfortunes.
>
> But it shall not be—I will certainly keep you at school. It will be yours to take advantage of or not & if you have not the Perfect Education which I design for you, you shall in yr future life blame yourself for the misfortune.[8]

Two years later William Henry Harrison, Jr., now twenty-one, was pursuing his law studies in Cincinnati, and complaining that members of the family, when they came from nearby North Bend, made little effort to visit him. Though his lack of studious habits grieved his father, young Harrison's letters to his parents reflected filial devotion and concern. When his mother upbraided him for writing her infrequently, he replied, "Could I have supposed that it would have afforded you any satisfaction to hear from me by every opportunity I should certainly have very often written you. Very often I could only say that I was well, & give assurance of my affection—I have no doubt the first would have offered you pleasure—& I hope it is not necessary for me to assure you of the other." [9]

While his numerous children were growing older, William Henry Harrison was advancing in position and public esteem. He had risen to the rank of general; in 1816 he had been elected to the Congress of the United States. In 1824 he attempted to obtain an appointment as Minister to Mexico, and William Henry, Jr., was his emissary to Washington. Though only twenty-three, this son conducted the mission with the skill of a veteran: in a single week he had enlisted the support of prominent politicians and influential newspaper editors; he obtained pledges from General Scott; he dined with Henry Clay; he even attempted to sway the supporters of a rival candidate. General Harrison did not receive the post; but, in 1828, President John Quincy Adams appointed him Minister to Colombia. To this post he took with him, as his private aide and Legation attaché, the younger son, Carter Bassett, then seventeen. The fact that the boy did not have any training did not trouble Minister Harrison, because the father stressed only the importance of being properly attired in the regulation garb of his Legation staff—"a plain coat with the Diplomatic buttons, which can only be got in Philadelphia, is all the uniform he will require . . . the button has an Eagle with an olive branch in one talon, with a thunderbolt in the other." [10] An olive branch or thunderbolts! Foreign nations, not always friendly to the fifty-year-old American Republic must have pondered upon the meaning of the emblem; possibly, nearly a hundred years later, President Theodore Roosevelt had it in mind when he defined effective diplomacy as "tread lightly, and carry a big stick."

General Harrison and his young son did not remain long in the South American nation; there were contending political parties, and a revolution broke out. The Harrisons were accused of taking sides, and the Minister was recalled. Ten years later William Henry Harrison was elevated to the highest place in the United States—being elected President in 1840. Inaugurated on March 4, 1841, he lived only a month.

But these successes of "Old Tippecanoe" in military and political spheres alternated with hardship and bitter disappointment in private life. When he did not hold office he was beset with financial difficulties and family troubles. He devoted his energies to the farm at North Bend; but taxes, expenses, and burdens thrown upon him by several of his sons darkened the old age of General William Henry Harrison. "To the distress produced by the destruction of my hopes in relation to two of my sons, is added that of increasingly embarrassed circumstances," he wrote to a friend at the end of 1832. "I never felt so much despondency in all my life."[11] The sons to whom he referred were John Cleves Symmes and William Henry, Jr. For more than ten years John Cleves Symmes Harrison had held the post in the Government land office at Vincennes, Indiana, and there he handled large sums of money. He was accused of embezzling nearly thirteen thousand dollars; the Government obtained a judgment against him and against his father as his surety. Despite this act, which brought both a pecuniary burden and sorrow to the father, General William Henry Harrison loved his son; in a letter to James Findlay, father-in-law of his second son, he voices his grief and his burden: "The morning I left you I barely got down in time to see my beloved son expire. It almost broke my heart. . . . Never was a man taken away whose life was more necessary to his family . . . six orphan children, four ill. . . . I was served with a summons to answer to a claim of the United States against me as security of my son of $12,803. . . . The above sum is the supposed amount of his defalcation."[12] This son had died at the age of thirty-two.

William Henry Harrison, Jr., had married the daughter of a Congressman, James Findlay, a devoted friend of General Harrison. To his wife's father William Henry, Jr., assumed an air of exceptional courage and patriotism. When, in 1832, the State of South Carolina threatened to nullify the Tariff Act which had been passed by Congress, young Harrison, enfeebled by dissipation, and his wife and children were living on the North Bend farm. But he writes his father-in-law a ringing challenge, without a single word to reflect his unfortunate condition: "Born and raised a free-man, and my ancestors having contributed freely and risked much to gain, maintain and support our happy government, I feel an indignation I cannot express against those who are now raising the standard of Nullification, which I consider a decent term for rebellion and treason. Should the South really rebel—I will thank you to recommend me to the President as a fit and proper person to command a Regiment of volunteers from this part of the country. I will guarantee that in one month from the time we march, I will ride through the streets of Charleston." [13] And he closes his letter with the remark, "I have spent this 4th of July like a gentleman, making hay."

His allusion to his farming activities indicated that he had abandoned the practice of law for which his father, despite decreasing resources, had had him trained. Impeded by intemperance, his efforts at farming did not prosper. This son of the Indian-fighter who became President, who proclaimed blithely that he could conquer a state, could not master his craving for drink. Six months later, his despairing father writes to the father-in-law of William, Jr.: "I am sorry to tell you that there is no hope of William's reformation if he remains here, and I know of no place where he could be out of the reach of temptation but in one of our remote posts on the frontiers. I think I could prevail on him to go to one of them and remain ten or twelve months. I would sell anything I have to raise money for his journey." [14] But the son never completely conquered his weaknesses; to the end of his days he was a source of deep concern to his aging father. He died in 1838; and his widow and children continued to live at North Bend.

With one exception, all the sons of William Henry Harrison preceded their father in death: Symmes, whose last days were troubled by judgments which the Government won to reimburse the public treasury for his alleged embezzlements; William Henry, Jr., whose dissipations not only ruined his own career but burdened his father with grief and monetary losses; Benjamin, who studied medicine and established a fair practice; the youngest son, Carter Bassett who, after his experience in the Colombia Legation, remained inconspicuous.

Only one son outlived the ninth President of the United States—the third, John Scott Harrison. He was born in the little town at the north bend of the Ohio where his mother's father and the adventurous men who accompanied him cleared the forest and constructed from the virgin timbers the first homes ever erected by white men in the Northwest Territory. Here his mother, before her marriage, roamed the clearings on horseback, and witnessed thefts and murders by unfriendly Indians. When John Scott Harrison had grown to manhood, he recalled many absorbing tales of the fortitude and courage of the men and women who had brought the white man's civilization to this wilderness—stories he heard from the pioneer's widow who was his mother's companion when his father was on the battlefields in the War of 1812, stories of how the women in the fort molded bullets and carried them to their husbands, fathers, and brothers, to be hurled at the savage foe. John Scott Harrison was proud of the men and women who, with his grandfather, established the settlements along the Ohio; often he contrasted them with the generations which followed:

The settlers of this whole Western country were men of peculiar characteristics. Brave, generous, and single-minded, they knew nothing of that debasing passion of avarice so common in our day—a passion that grows with our growth, and strengthens with our strength—sapping and drying up all the nobler impulses of the heart. Our pioneer fathers were strangers to such a passion. Nor was it long before the educated and retired scholar of the East turned his attention to these Western wilds, as offering a broad road to wealth and distinction. . . . They have generally outstripped the natives of the West in the acquirement of wealth and position. And to this there is no objection. . . . But we may say, without offense, to these prosperous, fair-weather emigrants, that while they remember with reverence their Puritan fathers, they should not forget the memory and services of those brave men (of the West) who macadamized with their blood the highway to this land of milk and honey.[15]

John Scott Harrison did not aspire to political honors; he preferred to remain upon the fertile acres, and to join with some of his neighbors in loading the products of his farm upon flatboats, which were floated down the broad Mississippi to New Orleans. Once a year they made this river pilgrimage; the perils of the currents required skill in navigation, but he and his neighbors were familiar with the Father of Waters.[16] He enjoyed the comfort of his home. When business affairs did not require his time, he liked to gather with his neighbors, the dwindling number of the pioneers, and to chat with them about the thrilling events of the past. He liked to delve into the chronicles of the past, to retell the story of his forebears and their worthy deeds. That, he asserted, was a duty of the living to the dead: "To preserve a record of such acts, and the history of the men who performed them, is not only praiseworthy in itself, but is an absolute duty imposed on posterity. . . . Nor is the observance of this duty confined to civilized life. The wild and untutored Indian cherishes with reverence the memory of his forefathers; and chants at his campfire their deeds of savage daring . . . and shall not we, educated and enlightened, cherish with yet deeper reverence the memory of our fathers, distinguished not for deeds of violence and blood, but for patriotism and humanity?"[17]

The political views to which John Scott Harrison adhered were not those of the party which was decisive in the local or state elections. Nevertheless, regardless of political affiliation, his neighbors regarded John Scott Harrison with confidence and respect, and he became their Representative in Congress, serving from December, 1853, to March 3, 1857. As a member of the House of Representatives he took no part in the acrimonious debates which marked that period. As he himself told his colleagues, he was "but little skilled in the mazes and mysteries of politics—knew little of the plots and counterplots resorted to by politicians to keep on the wave of public opinion."[18] Only on one occasion did he arise to voice his opinions, and that was in opposition to the bill to organize the territorial governments of Nebraska and Kansas, which was likely to extend slavery. Even then he was ready to content himself with the fifteen minutes allotted him by the presiding officer, even though he was entitled to an hour. Other members protested at this restriction of time, and there was much excitement in the House of Representatives. But John Scott Harrison considered it "a particular act of courtesy on the part of the Chair" to grant him even a portion of the time which was his right. His sole object in giving vocal expression to his views on this legislation was to inform his constituents publicly how he would vote and why, so that his neighbors might elect another man if they did not agree with him. He desired, he said,

to submit a few brief reasons which will govern me in my vote on the Kansas and Nebraska bill, now under consideration. The peculiar position in which I stand to my constituents seems to render this course not only proper but necessary. . . . The position, Mr. Chairman, to which I have alluded as peculiar, consists in the fact that the district which I have the honor to represent is largely Democratic, as was clearly indicated in the gubernatorial election preceding my own as well as at the Presidential election which immediately succeeded it. This being the case, sir, I desire to express my views upon the questions of policy involved in the bill, and thus afford my constituents an opportunity to compare my views with their own; and if, unhappily, they do not accord, to give them an opportunity to send another here who will more faithfully reflect their wishes and their will—believing, as I do, that it is the duty of the Representative to surrender to the people the power delegated whenever he may find that he cannot, consistently with his own conscience and honor, carry out clearly the expressed will of his constituents.[19]

John Scott Harrison felt deeply on this subject; he was an ardent opponent of slavery and any schemes to extend the territory in which it was legal. Even after he himself was no longer in Congress, we find him writing letters of praise to other legislators who argued against new states for slave-owning.[20]

After serving nearly four years in Congress, John Scott Harrison inconspicuously continued his pursuits of peace. His large home afforded shelter and hospitality for many who made pilgrimages to the nearby tomb of his famous father, William Henry Harrison. His own son, Benjamin Harrison, was a rising political figure in the adjoining State of Indiana, but John Scott Harrison shunned further public office. As with the patriarchs of old, his flowing locks of white hair and beard were symbols of tranquility. Possibly he recalled the rancor and bitterness which had come into the lives of his forebears. A political enemy had applied a flaming torch to the costly home of his grandfather, Judge Symmes, and it was entirely consumed. A vengeful servant girl set on fire the home of his father and the building burned to the ground.[21] John Scott Harrison wanted to live in peace and to die in peace. But it was not to be.

On May 26, 1878, John Scott Harrison died suddenly of a mysterious disease. The newspapers of nearby Cincinnati made no mention of his death until May 28. Then, on the editorial page of the leading paper, without any heading, there appeared an item of fourteen lines:

Hon. John Scott Harrison, son of Wm. Henry Harrison, and father of Hon. Ben Harrison, now prominent in Indiana politics, was found dead at his residence at Point Farm, Indiana, on the morning of the 26th. inst. Most of those who will hear of his death did not know that he was living. An impulse, a cultural wave, sent his father to the White House for a month, but no member of the family has given proof of the possession of talents of a high order. In so far as it is a family of renown it is a family of happy accidents. It is only just to say that it is also one without reproach.[22]

Political antagonism stooped to belittle the dead lest a eulogy would help his son who had now become a political figure in Indiana; this

THE CINCINNATI DAILY ENQUIRER, FRIDAY MORNING, MAY 31, 1878.

HUMAN HYENAS.

Hon. John Scott Harrison Torn From His Grave.

The Gray Old Man Found Dangling in a "Dead-Shaft."

Naked and Mutilated, Awaiting the Dissector's Knife.

The Foremost of Our Medical Colleges the Scene.

Futile Efforts to Guard the Resting-Place of the Son of a President.

It Is Violated in the Very Shadow of Tippecanoe's Tomb.

A Son Suddenly Confronted With the Corpse While Looking for That of a Friend.

Another Son Simultaneously Discovers the Desecrated Grave.

The Chute, the Shovel, the Shaft, and the Windlass.

Interview With General Ben Harrison and With Leading Physicians.

Arrest of the Janitor of the Building.

Chicago Detectives Summoned and Every Clue to Be Followed to the Bitter End.

Great Excitement Among All Concerned.

Full Details of the Most Horrible Episode in the History of the City.

JOHN SCOTT HARRISON.

Further Details of Thursday's Horror.

Efforts to Overtake the Perpetrators of the Crime.

The Sons Determined to Continue the Search Until Successful.

The Body Entombed at Spring Grove.

Opinions of Prominent Physicians.

Probability That the Remains of President Harrison Will Be Removed to Spring Grove.

An Arrest and a Clue at Midnight.

John Scott Harrison.

The Shaft.

A PRESIDENT'S SON, INCONSPICUOUS IN LIFE, MAKES HEADLINES IN DEATH

John Scott Harrison, son of the ninth President, was ignored by newspapers during his lifetime; when his body was stolen from its grave, his name was blazoned in large type, and entire pages described the ghoulish episode. (Cincinnati *Enquirer*, May 31, 1878)

begrudging obituary implied that the American people had elected William Henry Harrison President merely for a month, when it was death which ended his career at the White House after so brief an occupancy. Four days later several of the Cincinnati papers printed an account of the "funeral of Hon. J. Scott Harrison," but this notice was written by a reporter and not by a politically-minded editor. The article described the gathering of friends, "old pioneers who had known him from boyhood." It mentioned that "the blind Presbyterian Minister pronounced a eulogy; the funeral sermon was a little out of the stereotyped style, was delivered in a conversational way, and was directed more to the living than to the dead." It stated also that the son of the ex-President was buried in the family plot "not far removed from the tomb of his illustrious father." [23]

The leading paper had stated that "most of those who will hear of his death did not know he was living." That prophecy was verified far beyond any anticipation of the editor who penned the obituary. Several days before John Scott Harrison passed away the community discovered that a body had been stolen from the cemetery—that of his young nephew, named Devin. To discourage a similar desecration, the grave of John Scott Harrison was dug to an unusual depth, carefully walled up with brick, and when it was partially filled there was placed over the metallic coffin an immense stone so heavy that the strength of sixteen men was required to move it. Then the grave was covered with cement.

The day following the funeral of John Scott Harrison his son John, accompanied by several neighbors, went to nearby Cincinnati to search the medical dissecting rooms for the body of his cousin Devin which, as has been noted previously, had been stolen from the North Bend cemetery. The quest went on all day, and their final call late in the evening was at the Ohio Medical College. A local constable joined the searchers, but Devin's body was not among those they found. Just before they left, it was discovered that a body was hanging in a shaft, and the constable pulled up the corpse by the rope which had been tied around its neck. The face had been covered with a burlap bag, and John pronounced the body as larger than the emaciated remains of his cousin Devin, who had died of consumption. However, in a perfunctory manner the sack was removed, and to his horror John discovered that the body was that of his own father, John Scott Harrison! [24]

The Cincinnati newspaper which had noted his passing with the scant appraisal that "no member of the family has given proof of the possession of talents of a high order" now referred to John Scott Harrison as "the son of a President and honored citizen of the Ohio Valley and beloved member of society," and spoke of "his President father whose name the great country delights to revere." [25] The ghoulish event became the general theme of conversation on the street, on the stock exchange, in business circles, in homes, everywhere. In contrast to the meager untitled paragraph which told of his death, the Cincinnati *Enquirer* now devoted three full columns to the sordid details of the stealing of his body, with an engraving showing his long locks and flowing white beard, and pictures of the implements which the grave desecrators had used in their horrible work. The newspapers spoke of the distinction and generosity of John Scott Harrison, who was "an honored citizen whose life of good works had entitled his memory to honor and respect. More, he was the son of a President, the last son of one whose memory the Nation holds in reverence, whose name and deeds are sacred in the hearts of his countrymen." Once again the body of John Scott Harrison was moved to a grave near the tomb of his President father, William Henry Harrison. At the bier stood his three sons—the eldest, Benjamin Harrison, destined to become President of the United States.

5

Sons of John Tyler

In the national campaign of 1840 the Whig Party emerged victorious with the slogan, "Old Tippecanoe and Tyler too"—electing as President the rough William Henry Harrison whose triumph over the Indians on the Tippecanoe River gave him the popular sobriquet, and as Vice-President the genteel John Tyler who resigned a captain's commission in 1812 because there was no battle to fight where he was stationed. Harrison was sixty-nine; Tyler, fifty-one. The former had acquired his soldierly crudities fighting crafty red men in the Western wilderness; the other had attained culture and scholarship in a stately mansion on a Southern plantation. Yet the origins and careers of these two men were singularly similar. The sires of both had played important roles in the establishment of the Republic—the father of William Henry Harrison had been a signer of the Declaration of Independence; John Tyler was the son of a Revolutionary judge who had supported and counseled Thomas Jefferson.[1] Both sons had been members of the Virginia Legislature; each had served in the House of Representatives and in the Senate of the United States—part of their terms at the same time; and each had been Governor: William Henry Harrison of the newly created Indiana, not yet a state; John Tyler of the Old Dominion, the State of Virginia. But what is most startling is that these two men had been born in the same locality—Charles City County in Virginia! Never before in our history, and never since, have there been elected at the same time to the two highest positions in the American Government two men born within the boundaries of an identical county. But Fate went further.

Harrison and Tyler were inaugurated President and Vice-President on March 4, 1841. On April fourth of the same year William Henry Harrison was dead. The Vice-President, John Tyler, was thereupon sworn in as President of the United States.

Thus, John Tyler of Virginia became the first "accidental" President—a new event in the history of the Republic. He was not elected Chief Executive, but reached that exalted place through the death of another man whom the voters had chosen President.[2] John Tyler was the only President who had served in the Congress of the United States and also was to serve, later, in the Congress of the Confederacy. It was during his Administration that the independent Republic of Texas became the largest state in the American Union.[3] But these were not the only exceptional events in the career of this tenth President. John Tyler surpassed all other Presidents in the number of his progeny—he was the father of fourteen children, eight of them boys. The record of this President's sons constitutes a very intriguing story.

The saga of the Tyler progeny was the story of the life of Robert Tyler, the eldest son. John Tyler had once exclaimed, "God forbid that any son of mine should prove recreant." None of them did, but Robert above all embodied the pride, the courage, and the honor of his father. His is a remarkable story of freedom of spirit, of undeviating loyalties, of deep-rooted friendships, of dangers and poverty endured for the ideals to which he held steadfast. This President's son experienced all the vicissitudes of a capricious fate. A political power and President-maker, he was idolized by a populace which later became a frenzied mob that sacked his home and drove him from Philadelphia. A writer of verse, this poet became a master political craftsman. Counseling peace, he became a soldier to battle for what he deemed a righteous cause. From a position of comfort and influence in the White House, he descended to a barren room in which he cooked and scrubbed while he practiced law. And from penury and despair he rose again to political power and popular acclaim. In him the delicate spirit of the poet vied with the more realistic concepts of the astute politician and, above all, the uncompromising crusader.

Robert Tyler was born in 1816, the first of the fourteen children. That was twenty-five years before his father became President of the United States, thirty-seven years before his father's youngest son was born. His mother was Letitia Christian, the daughter of Colonel Robert Christian; she was reared in the sheltered environment characteristic of Southern plantations in the first quarter of the nineteenth century. She must have been extremely attractive in her girlhood; three decades later, as she lay dying, her daughter-in-law observed, "Letitia Christian Tyler was beautiful to the eye, even in her illness;

her complexion was clear as an infant's, her figure perfect, and her hands and feet the most delicate I ever saw." John Tyler was twenty when he began courting this Virginia girl, and their engagement continued for nearly five years before they married. During that long period he was never permitted to see her alone, and never mustered up courage to kiss his sweetheart until three weeks before their wedding. When he came to see her at her father's home, the whole family gathered in the spacious drawing room; when they went out, John Tyler did not sit at her side in the carriage where she was accompanied by one or two older ladies as chaperons, but he rode alongside on horseback.

Such was the etiquette of the chivalrous South when the future President won his bride. But, if he had little opportunity to voice words of ardent affection in the presence of chaperons, this future President told of his fervent love in the letters which he wrote to her when they were separated. He was happy that he was poor, because he knew then that it was his personal worth and not the glamour of wealth that won her; for himself, it was "love at first sight." He wrote Letitia, "From the first moment of my acquaintance with you I felt the influence of genuine affection; but now, when I reflect upon the sacrifice which you make to virtue and to feeling, by conferring your hand on one who has nothing to boast of, but an honest and upright soul, and a heart of purest love, I feel gratitude superadded to affection for you. Indeed, I esteem myself most rich in possessing you." [4] The long courtship ended in marriage in 1813; three years later Robert was born.

Even in his youth Robert Tyler was characterized by two predominant traits: shyness, and a proud disregard of the opinions of others. John Tyler was deeply attached to his sons, and concerned about their preparation for successful careers. He strove to encourage Robert to seek public approval and to be tactful in his associations. When Robert went to college he was willing to forego graduation rather than speak to a public audience, and we find John Tyler writing to his nineteen-year-old son:

I am sorry to learn, through your last letter, that you entertained difficulties about graduating, in consequence of the necessity which it would impose upon you to make a speech publicly. For this to produce any difficulty is what I had not anticipated. The very circumstance of your being the only graduate, and yours the only speech to be delivered, should be a circumstance rather for gratification than otherwise. The undivided honor is certainly calculated to render it more distinguished. . . . The report to be given the occasion for the newspapers will distinctly present you to the public. . . . I hope, therefore, that you will attempt no compromise with the professors, but press forward to the full and complete discharge of the whole task.[5]

The parental advice continues. John Tyler had steadily achieved political success and had become a member of the United States Senate; he desired that his first-born, like himself, should devote his life to law and politics. We find him, in January, 1836, counseling Robert in the rudiments of a successful career:

My son, I hope you are now engaged in your law studies. You should set in regularly to work and prepare yourself for the active concerns of life, so that if anything should befall me, you may be ready to take my place. You are too regardless of small affairs, and overlook the thrifty maxims of life; rely on it that a knowledge of the minutest circumstances connected with the everyday experience of life is essentially necessary to success. . . . You have intellect enough; add to it method and system and all will be well. . . . Destined for the profession of law, the acquisition of popularity is important. . . . Never give way to bad temper; restrain it and keep it in subjection.[6]

John Tyler could not suppress the fear that this son would not curb outspoken views which might offend others; and even though this was the year when he himself resigned his seat in the Senate rather than vote as the Virginia legislature instructed him, he wanted Robert to accede to the viewpoints of others. Four days after his letter to Robert, the father writes to Robert's sister Mary:

Tell Robert his only chance is the law. He should go to it at once, with all his heart and soul. That profession is the high road to fame; but he should set in at once to reforming himself in all that needs reforming. He should read Lord Chesterfield; half success in life depends on manner, and the first and highest conquest is for him to obtain mastery over his passions. I have no fear of him if he will study to be polite to all, learn to sacrifice his own wishes to the wishes of others, and restrain his temper. His talents ensure him success with these prerequisites. Without them, his life would probably be unhappy.[7]

And two weeks later, John Tyler again pleads with Robert:

My son, be in haste to prepare yourself for the bar. John will follow you; and, if our lives are spared, the father and two sons may still run a career of renown together. By uniting our exertions we may obtain an ample competency. Learn to make yourself popular by accommodating yourself to the feelings, nay whims, of others; we are put into the world, and it is our duty to *use,* while we abstain from *abusing* it.[8]

Despite this counsel, Robert did not court the good will of his classmates, or of others. He was challenged to a duel, but refused to turn to weapons when he was superior in logic. The father approved this decision to abstain from physical combat.

If Robert did not evidence outstanding erudition in his legal studies, it was not for want of mental capabilities. His interest was in verse, and he wrote a book of several poems—on the sombre theme of Death. Robert anticipated that readers might detect a similarity to the verse of Shelley; therefore, in the preface to his book he asserted disdainfully that his versification was in imitation of no other poet, but was in his own style.[9] The father, with the finesse which contributed so much to extending his friendships, used the poem to bring Robert to the attention of political personalities; sending the booklet to General Thompson, a Senator, he wrote: "My son Robert . . . has recently had published a small poem, a copy of which at his request I now forward you. If it has no merit, it will at least serve to apprise you that I have often spoken of you to him and that he has found a just estimate of you—and I obey his request which furnishes me an opportunity of renewing to you assurances of my high respect and regard."[10]

After completing his studies, Robert went to Philadelphia to engage in the practice of law. There he met Priscilla Cooper, the daughter of a well-known actor. Her character, her beauty, and her talent charmed the novelist Washington Irving, and he gave to posterity his delineation of her in Sophie Sparkle in *Salmagundi*. Like his father, Robert was an ardent suitor and soon Priscilla became his wife.[11]

When John Tyler suddenly became President of the United States, Robert became his father's private secretary; and, his mother being in delicate health, Robert's wife became mistress of the White House. These were momentous days in the history of the Nation, with many vexing political issues, including that of the annexation of Texas. Great orators, among them Daniel Webster, Henry Clay, and John C. Calhoun, filled the Senate chamber with their eloquence; sectional differences were becoming more acute. John Tyler matched his wit, his resourcefulness, and his independence with all of them; at his side was Robert, who was already developing political acumen. The closing years of the Administration brought tragedy and discord into the Tyler family, and these were aggravated by partisan politics. Letitia Christian Tyler had passed away in the White House in 1842, and two years later John Tyler took a second wife. We shall see later how, as ex-President, Tyler reared another family.

A year before his father's Presidential term ended, Robert Tyler with his wife and child returned to Philadelphia to resume the practice of law. He became active also in politics. At the outbreak of the Mexican War he raised a volunteer regiment; however, the Army already had sufficient troops and the Government declined his offer. In 1847, he was appointed solicitor to the sheriff of Philadelphia; three years later he was made prothonotary of the Supreme Court of Pennsylvania. Year after year Robert Tyler increased his political prestige, and was soon recognized as a dominating power in the Democratic Party of that State.[12] It was characteristic of Robert Tyler that, despite his aristocratic ancestry and inherited prestige, he should become the champion of the poor Irish immigrants; he taught them to exercise the freeman's rights in their adopted country, and they became a factor in political contests.[13] In 1859, he became chairman of the Democratic State Central Committee.

During all this time he was using his energies, his influence, and his political position to pave the path of another man to the White House; it was Robert Tyler, more than any other individual, who helped bring about the nomination of James Buchanan as the Democratic candidate for President in 1856, and his subsequent election. Scores of letters passed between these two men; and the astute James Buchanan, with his long experience in political affairs, accepted the younger man as his mentor. Robert Tyler indulged in poetic fantasy, but in the realm of politics his appraisals were realistic and incisive. His letters to Buchanan stressed a single goal: a definite, decisive program would make Buchanan President of the United States. We find him writing to Buchanan in the spring of 1848: "Would that I were in the Convention. I feel assured that one strong, determined, bold man could carry the day." And ten years later he gives expression to the identical theme, writing to Buchanan, "Should you, with your accustomed grip, seize this question with a strong & resolute hand the country I am sure would rally to you."[14] In the intervening period his program and his counsel were always the same. And during all these years Robert Tyler and his father were constantly exchanging views on political events; James Buchanan was his idol, but even he was second to John Tyler, the ex-President of the United States, in Robert Tyler's esteem and affection.

Robert Tyler's political activities were not motivated by any thought to reap personal advantage for himself. He resented the implication that he was an office seeker expecting rewards from those who owed to him their own political success. James Buchanan did become President of the United States; some historians believe that only political expediency kept him from appointing Robert to a Cabinet post, but he and other political leaders in Pennsylvania did endeavor to find a lucrative position for Robert, whom they knew to be in financial straits. Robert Tyler's pride of name and independence are reflected in a letter which he wrote to Buchanan in May, 1858:

My dear Sir: I believe I have mentioned to you that Judge Cadwalader has offered me the clerkship of the United States District Court. I declined the offer as a matter of course under the circumstances. Since his return from Washington he has given me certain hints of a conversation he had the honor to hold with you in which my name was utter'd. I do not know precisely what his kindness led him to say; but I desire to observe that neither my friend Cadwalader nor any other has ever been authorized by me, directly or indirectly, to place me in the position of an applicant, or expectant of office at your hands. I say this now in order to avoid all misconception. There is no man (except my Father) for whom I entertain greater regard & respect than I do for yourself, but I am distinctly my own master & no office seeker; and well knowing what is due (notwithstanding my Gorgon's head of debt and poverty) to my name, education & antecedents I ignore and absolutely repudiate the idea of being an expectant of official favors from anyone. . . . While I am by no means insensible to political honors and advancement I do not want them unless they come to me unsolicited and unquestioned.[15]

Living in Philadelphia, usually at Robert's home, was his brother, John Tyler, Jr., three years younger than Robert. He too had studied law; and, during their father's term as President, young John helped his older brother in some of the tasks which fell upon the President's secretary. He had a flair for writing political tracts which his father

Sherwood Forest
Dec 23. 1859

My Dear Robert:

I return the enclosures of your last letter rec'd yesterday. The tributes of respect you received at York and elsewhere are certainly flattering. Your speech at Philadelphia has been read by many in this part of the country and is much applauded. It was published in the Washington Star which John has sent me. Miss Brown's letter you can answer very briefly and readily. Waller's, John's, your own, Jones's, Tazewell little girl and Bessie Dennison are all familiar. My wife here, David Gardiner, John Alexander, Julia, Lachlan, Lionel, and FitzWalter will be added to your list. Your mother's ancestors (if necessary) you can trace back to your Great Grandfather William Christian. and your grandmother's to the Brown's and Pierce's of James City. and that is as far as I can go. Julia's runs back to Lion Gardiner, who was, and whose descendants are the possessors of Gardiner's Island. and on her mother's side to the Mc

AN EX-PRESIDENT ENUMERATES HIS SONS

John Tyler, President from 1841 to 1845, fathered fourteen children—eight of them sons. Forty years elapsed between the birth of Tyler's first son and that of his youngest. In this letter, addressed to his oldest son Robert, the ex-President enumerated his progeny. (*Papers of John Tyler,* Library of Congress)

Lackland who led the Clans McLachlan and McLean in the battle of Culloden where he perished. But I do not believe that the good lady wants any thing but the names with out previous geneology— so a few lines will suffice. I have just finished and despatched an Historic & Genealogical acct of my ancestors on both sides, paternal and maternal to the Society in Boston of which I am made an honorary member. They requested the sketch and it is briefly given. It will appear in their Register. I am very sorry to hear of Priscilla's indisposition, but am pleased to learn that she is better. I have been under the weather for sometime with a return of my old annoying complaint which, after an intermission of 12 months returned upon me. I nevertheless stir about the house and farm. Increasing years bring on increasing infirmities, and doubtless it is all right.

I do not doubt the overthrow of the Republicans— if your folks are firm but temperate [illegible] which is good. He has [illegible]

suggested the idea of a confederacy of the Mississippi valley States in the event of a dissolution. If broken up the fragments would collect around three centres, the North, the West, and the South. You may rely upon it, that Virginia will prepare for the worst. If there is a rally thro' the North, around the Democratic flag, I can not doubt its success— but is not a new element of discord spread at N. York in the nomination of Genl. Scott. The conservative men may rally to him in place of uniting with the Democracy. *Nous verrons.* What means this numerous body of Southern Medical Students proposing to leave Philadelphia for Richmond? As many as 150 the papers state are likely to be en route for Richmond.

With love to P. and children in which Julia unites.

Yr Father

J. Tyler

Ro: Tyler Esr

regarded very highly. As early as May, 1845, we find the elder Tyler writing to a friend who had requested the ex-President's views on a political question, "I do not know that I can do better than send you some of John's speeches embodied in pamphlet form; . . . the facts are so succinctly and at the same time so lucidly set forth as pretty much to cover the whole ground." [16]

This second son and namesake of President John Tyler not only defended his father's policies with literary weapons, but he was also ready to vindicate them in physical combat. The editor of a Richmond paper had criticized Tyler's official acts; John Tyler, Jr., answered him vehemently with a newspaper article and in addition challenged his father's detractor to a duel. A spot in North Carolina was selected for the "field of honor"; and impetuous John left Washington to meet his adversary.[17] Unfriendly newspapers indulged in no eulogies of the President's son; instead they printed paragraphs either criticizing him or insinuating that the challenge would not go beyond the verbal state. Heading its editorial "Another Silly Affair," the Norfolk *Herald* observed that "we must say that we think Mr. John Tyler, Jr., lacked philosophy, if not judgment, in provoking a duel in this case. If he was stung and maddened by the caustic remarks, he might have seen, if he had taken the trouble to read, that they were all cakes and sugar plums to what had been said of his father in speeches by members of both Houses of Congress." [18] This journal intimated that the duel had been canceled; but, after the type had been set, the editor discovered that John, Jr., had actually left for the dueling grounds and, in a postscript, added the information that the encounter would take place. The sequel of the affair was noted in the Washington *Globe* a few days later: the President's son had gone to the appointed place in North Carolina, but the challenged critic did not appear; "after waiting a considerable time for his adversary, John Tyler, Jr., was about preparing to retire when a messenger arrived stating that the other duelist had not known of the hour appointed and was now ready to come to the field if Mr. Tyler would wait. . . . Mr. Tyler, however, being satisfied that he had fulfilled his part of the contract, immediately returned to Washington." [19]

With such eagerness to become a political figure it was not surprising that, when later John, Jr., joined his older brother in Philadelphia, he was ambitious to parallel Robert's prominence. Thus, while Robert Tyler was advancing the interests of James Buchanan, his younger brother was covertly attempting to play a similar role on behalf of Henry A. Wise, then United States Senator from Virginia, and later Governor of that State. Secretly he carried on a lengthy correspondence with Wise, in one note warning that "Robert knew nothing of my letter to you, or of my private views on the subject. He has been and will be all the time first and last a Buchanan man." Then, implying that Robert was selfish whereas he himself was prompted by nobler motives, his letter to Wise continued, "It is to his interest to be so and is a part of his policy looking to his *own* future. I was prompted to write you as I did because I wish to see justice done." But John stood in awe of Robert and concluded, "There is one thing you may rely on, and that is this: I shall be perfectly content with the man that Robert and you prefer. Robert is by far the best man for you here. He has more strength than any other dozen men in the Party, in the City and County of Philadelphia. In truth, the Party here is on his own shoulders."[20] Haughty and self-confident John, Jr., boasted that he had access to important papers in New England and in New York, and that "I have my own mode of probing men." However, in contrast to his boastings John, Jr.'s advancement, either in law or in politics, was extremely slow. In 1857, he obtained a subordinate position in the Attorney General's office in Washington. He still corresponded with Wise, and declared, "As for myself you know I would fight six duels for you and think it fine sport."

But the Government post did not last long; and the aging father became alarmed because John, Jr., despite his literary talent, failed to make material headway. Worried, the ex-President wrote from his Virginia plantation to Robert in the early summer of 1858:

> What is he to do? The people in Washington seem to be resolved to give him nothing and I am much concerned about him. . . . That a man of his fine talents and accomplishments should not be able to earn his daily bread or should fail to set about the task of doing so, is to me incomprehensible. . . . I had rather see him following the plow than doing nothing; and yet I feel persuaded that all the honors and emoluments of the profession are before him, if he would pursue it steadily. His course is an enigma which I cannot solve.[21]

In the interval preceding the Civil War, when the outstanding controversial themes were slavery and secession, the second son of ex-President John Tyler wrote numerous articles for the newspapers and engaged in a very voluminous correspondence with political leaders, especially with Henry A. Wise, who had become Governor of Virginia. When John Brown, following the raid at Harper's Ferry, was sentenced to be hanged, John Tyler, Jr., endeavored to persuade Governor Wise to commute Brown's sentence to imprisonment; this plea for a milder punishment was not actuated by sympathy with the Abolitionists, but by a desire to show that his native State of Virginia was merciful, and to offset public sentiment favorable to the Abolition cause, should Brown be executed.[22] This flair for rhetoric was later utilized in penning official documents for the Confederate Government.

Somehow, it was not the destiny of John Tyler, Jr., to achieve fame or wealth; neither his loyalties, the prestige of distinguished ancestry, nor his talents ever won him more than a meager return. Three decades later, in reduced circumstances in a very small home near Washington, this son of John Tyler was ending his days reminiscing about his residence and influence at the White House when his father was President of the United States.

If ex-President John Tyler was then concerned merely about the career of his second son, two years more brought still greater reasons to be alarmed about the future of his eldest son. Robert Tyler had reached a high place in law and politics in Pennsylvania; he had become the recognized leader in the Democratic Party of that State.[23] However, it was not his fate to enjoy the fruits of his talent and his efforts. During the fifteen years following the Presidential term of John Tyler a political storm had been gathering which, in its unforeseen fury, was to drench the Nation in blood. Five Presidents had occupied the White House; in 1860, James Buchanan was the Chief Executive and, in November of that year, Abraham Lincoln was elected President to succeed him. With every passing month there was increasing clamor in the slave-owning states for secession from the Federal Union. In his retirement at Sherwood Forest in Virginia ex-President John Tyler was hoping there would be a peaceful solution which would satisfy the exponents of "States' rights" and avoid a disruption of the Union; or, if that were impossible, that the Southern States would be permitted to go their way in peace. Robert, in Pennsylvania, ardently shared his father's views. But the compromises of the preceding half century no longer satisfied either the Abolitionists in the North nor the slaveholders in the South. A large majority of the Southern leaders believed that only withdrawal from the Union could safeguard the political and property rights which they claimed, and most of the Northern statesmen admitted, had been guaranteed them under the Constitution.[24]

Events moved rapidly: in April, 1861, the Federal fortress at Sumter was forced to lower the stars and stripes, to surrender to the troops of South Carolina. Abraham Lincoln, now President of the United States, called for volunteers to put down the "insurrection" with arms. The call was for three months' service—neither he nor other political leaders believed that any clash between the North and the South could last longer.[25] But the South was aroused to furious resistance, and the North seethed with violent animosity against all who came from the South and all that was Southern. Robert Tyler did not escape the engulfing resentment. A hooting mob looted his home and he was forced to flee from Philadelphia. In a single day, as he himself wrote years later, he lost all—office, home, friends, and property—for which he had toiled for years. Penniless, he returned to Virginia in May, 1861. The Government of the Confederacy had already been established. Robert Tyler was appointed Register of the Confederate Treasury. But he was not content to enjoy shelter and safety at an office desk. He wanted no exalted rank, no military honors; but when the Union forces approached Richmond he fought as a private.

For four years Robert Tyler, with the application, ability, and thoroughness which had characterized his achievement of high place in Pennsylvania, devoted his time and his energies to the finances of the Southern Confederacy, leaving his office of Register of the Treasury only to shoulder a musket against the Union troops which made incursions around Richmond. The war over, he again moved, beginning life anew in Montgomery, Alabama. There, in a single upstairs room, unknown and without a single client, he resumed the practice of law. He cooked his own meals, washed his own clothes, scrubbed and cleaned his miserable habitation. James Buchanan, retired from the Presidency, heard that Robert Tyler was in financial straits and sent him a thousand-dollar check. But, with the same proud independence which prompted him to decline political advancement at the hands of the man whom he had raised to the highest post in the land, Tyler returned the proffered aid. He wrote:

The conflict is ended, and I bow in submission to the inscrutable will of God. My political race is run, and my destiny is fixed. I only want to devote the rest of my life to work, and to dedicate my remaining energies exclusively to those dependent on my exertions. The war has left me literally nothing except an unstained honor that has triumphed over many temptations and many weaknesses in my character, and a resolute will. And verily it requires a great mental fortitude and a resolute temper to look out on the prospect with an unblanched cheek. But God in the hour of calamity helps me to do that.[26]

Robert Tyler was mistaken in one conclusion: his political race was not run, and his destiny was to achieve again the successes of earlier years. In Montgomery, as in Philadelphia, he succeeded both in law and in politics. Within a decade he became in Alabama what he had been in Pennsylvania: the chairman of the Democratic State Central Committee. One of the most prominent newspapers in the state, the Montgomery *Advertiser,* made him its editor. To the end of his days he held the admiration, the respect, and the affection of the entire Southland. He died in December, 1877. Numerous and lengthy obituaries paid tribute to his character and his abilities; all of them may be summed up in the single sentence of one editorial which said of this President's son, "No man was ever more unselfish. He devoted his time and talents to the cause of his People without reward or expectation of reward."[27]

The career of Tazewell Tyler, the third son of the President, was not noteworthy. Diligent search reveals only that he studied medicine, and that he served in the medical corps of the Confederate Army. Apparently, his life was little influenced by the prestige of his Presidential father.

As was noted, the mother of Robert, John, Jr., and Tazewell, Letitia Christian Tyler, had passed away at the White House three years before the end of her husband's Presidential term. President John Tyler had loved dearly this devoted wife who had borne him seven children, and his attachment to these sons and daughters became deeper with each passing month. However, two years later he took a second wife. The romance began in the midst of devastation and death. In February, 1844, President John Tyler with a party of Cabinet officers and political leaders sailed down the Potomac River on the gunboat Princeton. A gun exploded, killing a score and wounding twice as many. Among them was one of the President's most intimate friends, ex-Senator Gardiner. His forebears were the first proprietors of Gardiner's Island, near the head of Long Island Sound; and one of them, Lyon Gardiner, had been Commandant of Fort Saybrook, Connecticut, in pre-Revolutionary days.[28] This victim of the Princeton explosion left a large fortune and two beautiful daughters. Tyler had already been entranced with the elder, Julia. Had she lived in the days of soothsayers, they probably would have prognosticated that it was her predestined lot to meet Presidents; she herself tells us that, on a train journeying to Washington, an attractive man "cast furtive glances in her direction"; that man being the future President of the United States, Millard Fillmore.[29] But now the actual occupant of the White House fell in love with Julia Gardiner and married her in the summer of 1844. Some of his political opponents criticized this event as vehemently as they had attacked official acts of the President. Aging John Quincy Adams gave vent to the typical opinion of Tyler's enemies:

Captain John Tyler and his bride are the laughing stock of the city. It seems as if he was racing for a prize banner to the nuptial of the mock heroic—the sublime and the ridiculous. He has assumed the war power as a prerogative, the veto power as a caprice, the appointing and dismissing power as a fund for bribery; and now, under circumstances of revolting indecency is performing with a young girl from New York the old fable of January and May.[30]

Friends, too, endeavored to discourage the marriage. When Tyler confided his intentions to Henry Wise, the Virginia Governor, the latter told the President he was too old for a union with the youthful, vibrant Julia Gardiner. "Pooh," exclaimed John Tyler, "I am just full in my prime." [31] But there were some prominent statesmen who viewed Tyler's marriage with more sympathetic understanding. Among them was the lifelong bachelor James Buchanan—destined himself to be President of the United States—who commented: "The President is the most lucky man that ever lived. Both a belle and a fortune to crown and to close his Presidential year." [32] At any rate, Washington society welcomed the bridal couple with considerable acclaim. A party was given at the White House at which "a most magnificent bride's cake and sparkling champagne awaited the guests, and the distinctions of party and opinion were all forgotten and kind feelings and general impulses seemed to gladden the hearts of all." [33] The crowds thronged about the White House gardens, eager to obtain a glimpse of the bride as she and the President emerged upon the balcony while the Marine band played lively airs. A Washington journalist reported to his paper, "I have returned from the White House most pleasantly impressed with the beauty, grace, and elegance of the new ornament which has been added to it";[34] and the New York *Herald* reprinted accounts of the Presidential reception and the eulogies on the "beautiful and accomplished lady who is hereafter to preside at the Executive Mansion."[35]

The second Mrs. Tyler had but a few months of exalted position and deference as a President's wife, because John Tyler's term of office ended on March 4, 1845. For this glamour and glory she paid dearly: she suffered the resentment of her step-children who either could not forget that she came to occupy the place of their dead mother or did not relish her displacing them in directing the social affairs of the White House. There is ample proof, however, that Robert Tyler and his step-mother held each other in mutual regard; years later her letters to her mother reflected genuine concern for his welfare; and when he was driven from Philadelphia he, his wife, and children were made welcome at the Virginia Plantation where the ex-President and Julia Gardiner Tyler lived after the end of the Presidential term.[36]

But it was not family discord which saddened the life of Julia Gardiner Tyler. Bitterness between the North and the South was growing as the years passed. Many people in Virginia resented this woman who came from the North, where Abolitionists were plotting to destroy the rights of Southerners to own slaves; and even the merchants, who profited by her trade, made no attempt to disguise their feeling that, at best, she was an interloper. Despite this antagonism toward her, Julia Gardiner Tyler espoused the Southern cause, and her letters to her family in New York always defended her adopted State. In this beautiful woman from the North, the proud Virginian, John Tyler, found a mate devoted to him in speech, thought, and action, and the letters which the ex-President wrote to Robert and his other children are filled with tributes to this second wife. She continued to live at Sherwood Forest until John Tyler died, in January, 1862; she returned to New York when there was no longer any hope that the conflict between the North and the South could end until one or the other became victorious by force of might. Union soldiers ransacked her mansion in Virginia, but she fared no better in the North. There she was despised as an adherent to the Southern cause. Typical of this attitude toward her was the invasion of her home in Castleton, Staten Island, where a crowd of men tore from the mantelpiece what they claimed was a "rebel" flag, and sent it to Major General Dix, Commander of the Department of the East. An official inquiry was made, and it was proven that the flag had been made for one of her children eight years previously, "before the Rebellion." [37]

Julia Gardiner Tyler bore all these attacks with poise and pride; she gloried in the recollection that she had been the wife of ex-President John Tyler of Virginia. Even though she took with her to New York her younger children, when they grew to maturity their fierce love for the land of their father was proof that she had instilled in their minds a deep affection for the Southland. Long after the Civil War had ended, we find this widow of President Tyler living in Virginia, and on her trips to Washington maintaining the same dignity and hauteur which marked her when she was mistress of the White House. President Ulysses S. Grant invited her to a State dinner, and assigned to her the place of honor; and she would not visit the wives of Senators and high officials unless they first called on her. Even then, she was a beautiful and fascinating woman.[38]

Such was the second wife of ex-President John Tyler, mistress of the White House during his last year in office and then of the large mansion at Sherwood Forest, Virginia. She, like his first wife, bore him seven children—among them, five sons: David Gardiner, John Alexander, Lachlan, Lyon Gardiner, and Robert Fitzwalter. Her eldest, David Gardiner, was born in July, 1846; thirty years had passed since the birth of John Tyler's first son, Robert. Julia Gardiner Tyler was devoted to her little son, and her letters to her mother and brother in New York were filled with glowing descriptions of the infant. She had been so enthusiastic about her Southern home, so intrigued with the growing things on the land at Sherwood Forest, that her latest letters startled her brother, Alexander Gardiner, and he exclaimed, "You do not seem to have interested yourself much in the farm of late. Indeed it is quite obvious that your ruling attraction is now Mr. D.G.T. respecting whom you induce me to form so exalted an idea, that I am almost afraid to see him, lest I should be doomed to disappointment." [39] Less than two years later the second son, John Alexander, was born. The outbreak of the Civil

War found the two boys studying at Washington College; David Gardiner was sixteen and his brother fifteen. Both of these Tyler sons immediately joined the Confederate Army. David Gardiner Tyler served throughout the War, first in the infantry and later in the artillery.

At the end of the War their mother, now a widow, sent these two sons to Germany and there they studied for several years. John Alexander Tyler served in the German Army during the Franco-Prussian War, and the Emperor of Germany decorated him for bravery.[40] Upon their return to the United States, Alexander became an engineer and settled in New Mexico. In 1883 he died. David Gardiner, like his father, began a career of law and politics. He was a Presidential elector in 1888, and served as State Senator from 1891 to 1892. In 1892 he was elected to the United States House of Representatives, and the family was elated that he was following in the footsteps of his famous father. His brother Lyon in Richmond wired the happy news to another brother, Lachlan, who was practicing medicine in New York, "Gardiner elected to Congress by over five thousand. State safe."[41] He served as Congressman for four years. His influence in party councils increased and, in 1896, he was made a member of the Executive Committee of the Democratic Party. Intermittently he practiced law in Charles City, Virginia; then he was again elected State Senator and served from 1899 to 1904. In the latter year he became the Judge of the 14th Judicial Circuit Court, and held that position for twenty-four years.[42] He died in September, 1927.

The third son, Lachlan, was five years younger than David Gardiner. He grew to manhood in a South that was struggling to repair the ravages of the Civil War; and, when he became a physician, he settled in the North, where his father was remembered not as a President of the United States, but as one who had brought about the secession of Virginia. Nevertheless, Lachlan established a lucrative practice. He alone, among the children of Julia Gardiner Tyler, was friendly with his half-brother, John, Jr.; letters passed between the two during the years when the older brother, in a suburb of Washington, was living in ill health and straitened financial circumstances.[43]

The most literary and scholarly son of John Tyler was Lyon Gardiner Tyler, Julia's fourth son. He was named after her ancestor,

Lyon Gardiner, who was the first proprietor of Gardiner's Island, near the head of Long Island Sound.[44] His brothers called him "Louie," a nickname probably acquired during his schooling in Germany. He was born in 1853; the exact date is not known, as the family records in the Southern home were scattered or destroyed when the Union troops invaded Virginia.[45] He was eight years old when his father died, and his mother took him and her younger children to her Northern home in New York. Here he remained while the Civil War was raging in his native Virginia; but, despite his adolescent years in the North, Lyon Gardiner Tyler became one of the most devoted and uncompromising defenders of the South's role in the Civil War. His older half-brothers, Robert and John—the sons of his father's first wife—were already in the service of the Confederate States; but it was not they who inculcated in him such a passionate devotion for the land of their father. In fact, throughout his entire life Lyon Gardiner Tyler never met or saw his brother, Robert. In later years, after Robert had passed away, Lyon Gardiner Tyler gave as a reason for his failure to know his brother personally the "difference in ages and the distances" between them.[46] This explanation is not convincing; during a part of the time when Robert was living in Montgomery, Alabama, Lyon Gardiner resided in Richmond, Virginia.

Lyon Gardiner Tyler received an excellent education, both in Germany and in the United States; he became a professor of literature and devoted much of his time to research in Southern genealogy and history. He wrote a number of books, and finally became president of William and Mary College. He was not a cloistered scholar disdaining popular acclaim or content with professional success in obscure institutions of learning. The shyness and modesty attributed to him in obituary tributes are not borne out by his letters that are still extant. On the contrary, he was aggressive, determined, and conscious of the benefits which result from acquaintance among the great and mention in the press. He carried on a correspondence with prominent and influential men, himself initiating correspondence after a single meeting. Like other sons of John Tyler, he disdained to obtain friendships at the cost of compromise with what he considered the truth—particularly when it related to his father. He was wary of every word written about the Presidential career of John Tyler. When the historian George Bancroft was writing about the

Tyler Administration, Lyon Gardiner argued about sentences, phrases, and even words. Impatient Bancroft replied on one occasion, "I see no difference between 'kept in the background' and 'kept in reserve,'" but Lyon Gardiner Tyler did induce him to change other expressions.[47]

Nor did this son of ex-President Tyler remain passive when there were opportunities for personal advancement; he did not wait for a spontaneity of popular demand or an acknowledged reputation to raise him to high place. When, in the autumn of 1888, there was need for a president for William and Mary College, he promptly wrote a formal letter of application for the post, sending with his note numerous letters of recommendation systematically separated into three files. To the Secretary of the Board of Visitors of the college, which was to make the selection of a presiding head he wrote:

> I am an applicant for the Presidency of William and Mary College and beg to refer you to the accompanying testimonials, in support of my application. They are divided into three small packages and are intended to illustrate three periods in my life as instructor—the first having reference to my election in 1876 as professor of Belles Lettres in your institution, the second to the discharge of my duties as principal of the Memphis Institute, and the third [to] my present fitness and qualifications for the office in question. . . . If I am elected, I can assure the Board that I will do all in my power to meet the Expectations of the public.[48]

He was the successful candidate, and under his able direction William and Mary assumed a distinguished and prominent place among the colleges of the United States.

Having established a reputation as a college president, Lyon Gardiner Tyler assumed the task of refuting Northern historians who did not give complete approval to John Tyler's Administration or who asserted that the Civil War was brought on by the action of the slave-owning states. In all of his prolific writings, Lyon Gardiner Tyler was moved by a passionate zeal to justify the actions of the South and to prove that, in the Civil War and in the events leading to it, the North was the aggressor, selfish in its aims, unjust in its attitude, inexcusable in its actions.[49] Even though he cited documentary evidence and set down incontrovertible facts, this son of President John Tyler was never impersonal in his review of history, seldom impartial in assembling data, or unbiased in interpreting the motives of those whose political concepts differed from those of his father. His knowledge of historical sources and his skill in marshaling phrases gave him weapons for answering historians who criticized the slave-holding states or praised Lincoln's policies. Lyon Gardiner Tyler did not regard Abraham Lincoln as a great man; he considered him of smaller stature than his own father. John Tyler, he argued, was a President who had maintained peace between the states; in contrast, Lincoln brought on a war. The former was elected by an overwhelming vote of the people; Lincoln, by a limited minority. Tyler was consistent always; Lincoln constantly admitted that slavery was protected by the Constitution but, as President, he freed the slaves. Tyler was a great man; he never sacrificed principle for political advancement; Lincoln repeatedly made "trades" to gain political power.[50] The South, Lyon Gardiner Tyler always contended, was ever willing to abide by the Constitution; it was Lincoln who disregarded it.[51]

Lyon Gardiner Tyler remained the head of William and Mary for thirty years. In 1919 he retired from the college presidency, but continued his historical writing. He became engrossed in genealogical research, and traced the origins and lineage of many Virginia families; their relationships intrigued him, though he would not travel a hundred miles to become acquainted with his own half-brothers! [52]

Lyon Gardiner Tyler outlived his numerous brothers. At eighty-two this Presidential son, big-bodied and six feet tall, still walked erect; [53] it was not merely his physique but also his aristocratic bearing that gave him impressive stature. Always conscious of his Southern birth and always proud that his sire had been John Tyler, he had spent most of his life championing and glorifying both his native State and his Presidential father; as a leading Virginia paper observed, "Historians in the North as well as the South knew him as the vigorous defender of the Southern tradition in statesmanship and in war." [54]

In February, 1935, he died at his plantation home, which he had named "The Lyon's Den." Although nearly a century had passed since his father had occupied the White House, newspapers in the South did not forget that he was a President's son. News columns and editorials, in city journals and country gazettes, noted his passing and eulogized his career. They remembered him also as an ardent historian of the Southland and as president of William and Mary.[55]

Said the Richmond *Times-Dispatch:* "Hundreds knew him as the genealogist who, perhaps more than any other man, aroused their interest in the collection and preservation of old Virginia family and county records, and thousands more remembered him as the lovable 'prexy' who first saved from abandonment the second oldest college in America and thus established it firmly as one of the best of the smaller colleges in the land." [56]

Such is the chronicle of the sons of John Tyler, tenth President of the United States. Between the first to be born and the last to die there elapsed one hundred and seventeen years!

6

Son of Old Rough and Ready

It was May, 1865. For four years the Civil War between the North and the South had dragged on, and the youth in blue and gray had bled and died on scores of battlefields. It was not upon Northern soil that the conflict raged, the Confederate army had been turned back in the Pennsylvania hills around Gettysburg in July, 1863; there were in those days no long-range cannon, no bombers, no rocket guns to threaten the security of cities or to devastate the fertile fields in the Northern States. On the contrary, the war had brought increased prosperity; mills, factories, forges, and furnaces were busier than they had been in the preceding days of peace. It was in the South that the clash of Union and Confederate troops brought destruction and poverty and fear. It was there that Sheridan received orders to "make the valley a barren waste"; [1] and Sherman's invasion gave fearful reality to his boast that even a crow would find no nourishment where his armies had passed.[2] Burned cities, devastated plantations, and looted homes were no longer uncommon south of the Mason and Dixon line.

It was an unequal contest from the first: the North had overwhelming resources in manpower and materials of war; yet the generalship and courage of the Southern armies forestalled conquest by the superior forces of the North. But now, in the fifth spring of the struggle, even the leaders of the Confederacy realized that there could be no victory for them. Robert E. Lee had surrendered at Appomattox, Virginia, on April 19; General Joseph E. Johnston, with a large force, had capitulated on April 26. Still the war was not over. Another general had now become senior commander of the remaining Southern troops east of the Mississippi.[3] Then came the news for which the North had eagerly hoped and waited—and, at last, the Civil War was ended:

New-York Times.

NEW-YORK, TUESDAY MAY 9, 1865. PRICE FOUR CENTS

The New Orleans Times, Sunday May 7, 1865.

BY TELEGRAPH.

SURRENDER OF DICK TAYLOR.

TERMS OF AGREEMENT.

OFFICIAL

[Special Dispatch by Telegraph to the N. O. Times.]

LAKEPORT, 9:50 A. M., May 6.—Capt. Block's compliments, with the following from Mobile:

May 5.—Major Gen. Canby, accompanied by Gen. Osterhaus, his Chief of Staff, Brig. Gen. Andrews, Provost Marshal General, Col. Christensen, A. A. G., and Capts. Barrett and Perkins, A. D. C., left the city yesterday morning at 8:30 for Citronelle for the purpose of completing the negotiations of the surrender of all the Confederate troops in

come out of the woods and asked for something to eat, offering to pay any sum for it. She being afraid told them she had nothing; that there was no white people around, and that they could get nothing to eat in that vicinity. The lame man then inquired the direction to the Great Swamp, which she gave, and the two went off. The shanty stands in a small clearing surrounded on all sides by dense pine woods, with the exception of one side bounded by the swamps. The 8th Illinois Cavalry and a regiment of colored troops were immediately sent through the swamps in every direction, searching every thicket, but without finding any trace of the assassins, the latter evidently having secreted themselves in the pine woods, and made their escape while the swamp was being searched on Sunday P. M. Booth and Harold crossed the Potomac at Swan Point, a short distance below Matthias Point, and passing through Port Royal, en route to Louisa Court-house, were captured as previously described. In the s ay at Garrett's place facts have come to light which show conclusively that Booth and his accomplices had, before carrying their plans into execution, decided upon the route to be taken in making their escape. Maps, understood to be in possession of the Government, and which are known to have belonged to those parties, bear distinct marks of the routes laid out by them. Booth and Harold were to escape to rebeldom, and seek Jeff. Davis' protection, who was finally to assist them in leaving the country. Harold, in conversation with an acquaintance of his who resides in Maryland, some time previous to the murder of the President, Lincoln made a remark to the effect that there was no extradition treaty between the United States and Spain, a remark that excited no special attention at the time, but in the light of subsequent events it would appear that Booth and

ANOTHER SURRENDER.

Dick Taylor Abandons the Rebel Cause.

No More Armed Enemies East of the Mississippi.

The Fag End of the Rebellion Vanishes to the Wilds of Texas.

All Guerrilla Warfare will Now be Outlawed.

The "Confederate States Confined to Jeff. Davis' Carpet Bag.

Special Dispatch to the New-York Times.

WASHINGTON, Monday, May 8.

Information was received at army headquarters to-day of the *final and complete surrender* of DICK TAYLOR'S forces in Alabama and Mississippi to Gen. CANBY.

It is a remarkable fact that this news and other dispatches from Gen. WILSON were received by telegraph direct from Macon, Ga., to this city.

AN EX-PRESIDENT'S SON SURRENDERS

General Dick Taylor, son of the twelfth President, surrendered the last army of the Confederacy—and the hope of the South was ended forever.

ANOTHER SURRENDER

Dick Taylor Abandons the Rebel Cause

> Washington, May 8, 1865.—Information has been received at army headquarters of the final and complete surrender of Dick Taylor's forces in Mississippi and Alabama to General Canby.[4]

Dick Taylor, although he was among the first of the Southern military leaders to grasp the meaning of Gettysburg,[5] held out even after the illustrious Lee acknowledged defeat; and, even though the Union armies were now able to exact sterner terms, he was accorded the same surrender conditions as had been granted to the Confederate commander-in-chief. Dick Taylor was Richard Taylor—the son of the twelfth President of the United States, Zachary Taylor.

The man who fathered Richard Taylor had gained the title "Rough and Ready" because he was a stern and efficient military leader, winning victories over Indians, British, and Mexicans with equal skill. Zachary Taylor, except for his sixteen months as President, always served his country as a soldier. As he himself had said, "For more than a quarter of a century my house has been a tent, and my home the battlefield." Born in Virginia, ten years after the Declaration of Independence, of a father who had fought with Washington throughout the Revolution, Zachary Taylor still hated the British when the War of 1812 broke out. In command of a group of fifty-two men, he was attacked by a larger group of British troops and his fort on the Wabash River was burned; but in the end his reckless courage and resourcefulness forced the retreat of the enemy. Raised to the rank of major, he was sent against the Indians, and they sued for peace. Step by step, he rose to the rank of general.

Then, in 1846, came our war with Mexico. Every schoolboy has read of his victories at Palo Alto, Resaca de la Palma, and Buena Vista. Always prepared to meet the enemy and to inflict defeat even though superior forces opposed him, "Old Rough and Ready" was acclaimed a hero, but he put on no airs. In all the Mexican campaigns, Ulysses Grant tells us, Zachary Taylor put on his general's uniform only twice, preferring the inelegant soldier's garb in which he fought Indians. "I can call to mind only one instance when I saw him in uniform, and one other when I heard of his wearing it. On both occasions he was unfortunate," Grant wrote in his *Personal*

Memoirs. The first episode, at Corpus Christi, occurred when he prepared to review his troops before starting on the march toward Mexico, but there was a dispute regarding precedence in rank among several breveted generals under him, and the review broke up with the resignation of a general who refused to attend. "The second occasion on which General Zachary Taylor was said to have donned his uniform was in order to receive a visit from the Flag Officer of the naval squadron off the mouth of the Rio Grande. . . . General Taylor, knowing that naval officers habitually wore all the uniform the 'law allowed' on all occasions of ceremony, thought it would be only civil to receive his guest in the same style. His uniform was therefore got out, brushed up, and put on, in advance of the visit. The Flag Officer, knowing General Taylor's aversion to the wearing of the uniform, and feeling that it would be regarded as a compliment should he meet him in civilian's dress, left off his uniform for this occasion. The meeting was said to have been embarrassing to both, and the conversation was principally apologetic."[6]

The American people were eager to bestow honors upon General Zachary Taylor, but he was indifferent. When he was urged to seek nomination for the Presidency, he wrote a single letter telling the Convention that, if they nominated him, he would not be the mere President of his own party, but would act independently of party domination. With the independence and honesty which later characterized his son Richard, Zachary Taylor spoke out his views on national problems. Nevertheless, he was nominated. Unique in the history of American politics, the Convention drafted no platform; it simply adopted the forthright letter of Zachary Taylor as its declaration of principles.[7] And the American people elected this rough soldier President of the United States. He was inaugurated on March 4, 1849.

It is one of the ironies of human existence that men often triumph over great dangers and succumb to small mishaps. Zachary Taylor had been inured to the rigors of the frontier, the hardships of army camps, the perils of the battlefield. But a glass of cold milk killed him! On July 4, 1850, the Nation's great gathered in the Capital to lay the cornerstone of the obelisk which was to honor the memory of George Washington. President Zachary Taylor was the principal figure at the ceremonies. The day was unusually hot, and he drank iced milk to quench a great thirst. Previously, he had eaten fruit.

Before the end of the day the Indian fighter was stricken, and five days later he was dead. The doctors diagnosed the mortal ailment as "cholera morbus." [8]

Zachary Taylor, in 1810, had married Margaret Smith, the daughter of an army officer and planter of Calvert County, Maryland. He was then a captain, and twenty-six; she was just twenty. The bride accompanied him to the frontier, and for thirty years shared the hardships and dangers of his army career, with only brief separations when he was ordered to Mexico. "My wife," said Taylor when in the White House, "was as much a soldier as I was." She was of distinguished origin; her ancestors had come from England in the middle of the seventeenth century, and had settled in Maryland, where one of them was appointed Attorney General by Oliver Cromwell.[9] A gentle woman, Margaret Smith Taylor was described by one of her own sex as "a modest retiring woman; her life, in its abnegation and wifely devotion, under every stress of privation and danger, on the Indian's trail, amid fever-breeding swamps, and on the edge of the battlefield, was more heroic than ever dreamed of by Martha Washington." [10] She bore three daughters; and then, sixteen years after her marriage to Zachary Taylor, their only son, Richard, was born. The daughters all married army officers of high rank; the second one became the wife of a graduate of West Point who, like her own father, won fame in fighting Indians; he was an outstanding leader, had served as Secretary of War and as United States Senator for Mississippi—Jefferson Davis.[11] It was his destiny to become President of the Confederate States; and years later this man, beholding the onslaught of the Union armies on the dwindling resources of the South, prayed for a miracle from the generalship of Richard Taylor whose sister he had married. When the telegraph ticked out the report that Dick Taylor had surrendered, Jefferson Davis knew that his own star had set, and that the Confederate States had been finally defeated.

Richard Taylor was born in 1826. Various cities have been named as the place of his birth, but he himself referred to New Orleans as "my native place and home." [12] At the age when most boys merely read about martial parades or indulge in mock battles with wooden swords, Richard was spending his days at army camps, watching military maneuvers, listening to the rough language of officers training frontiersmen. No wonder he acquired that forceful vocabulary which impressed recruits and effected discipline; twenty-five years later, when he had attained high rank in the Confederate Army, his troops stood in equal awe of his recklessness and his expletives. It was his fate to serve under that pious military genius, Stonewall Jackson, whose typical reports on his battles read, "To Adjutant General, God blessed our arms with victory at McDowell yesterday," "Winchester, During the last three days God has given us brilliant success," "Through God's blessing, the enemy near Fort Republic was this day routed." [13] It was this reverent general who heard Richard Taylor swear in the heat of an engagement because his men trembled when bullets shattered the earth near them; Stonewall Jackson put his arm on Taylor's shoulder and exclaimed, "I fear that General Taylor is a very wicked man."

But, if the commanding general disapproved, the men in the ranks showed still greater concern. Taylor himself recounts that riding away from camp he came upon some fifty men from the front, and reined his horse to speak to them. But, before he could open his mouth, he received a rebuke from one of the party who exclaimed: "General, if you won't curse us, we will go back with you." [14] Yet, when Richard Taylor died, even newspapers in the North against which he had fought praised his gentleness; the New York *Times*, which, a quarter of a century previously, had hailed the surrender of this "rebel," declared at his death that "personally, General Taylor had none of the roughness of his sire. He was of winning address, rather slight in figure, of courteous bearing"; there were no longer any brusque phrases in his speech, though the newspaper declared that "a slight dash of cynicism tempered his conversation." [15] We shall see later that Richard Taylor, through with the grim business of war, could indeed fashion words into phrases of unusual elegance.

Probably his parents foresaw the development of this habit of barrack speech and reflected that young Dick was absorbing too much of the crudities of unlettered soldiers who had been closer to nature than to books; probably his mother recalled that her forebears had been schooled in social graces and historic lore; probably she envisioned for him achievements in the arts of peace. So Dick was sent to Edinburgh, Scotland, to absorb Latin and literature. There he spent two years, and another year in France. Returning to America, he was privately tutored and Harvard, in 1843, found him qualified to enter the Junior class. For some reason, he preferred

Yale; transferring to that college, he graduated within two years. From the college campus he went to the Mexican frontier, where warfare was imminent. Texas had wrested its independence from Mexico ten years earlier when Sam Houston and other intrepid American settlers in that territory routed the Mexican Dictator, Santa Anna, and forced his recognition of Texas as a separate Republic. But, settled and freed by men who had been citizens of the United States, Texas preferred to end its status as a sovereign nation and become a State in the Union. Now arose the question of its southern boundary, and its relations with Mexico became the concern of the United States. We insisted on the Rio Grande River as the dividing line; Mexico contended that the Nueces River was the just boundary. General Zachary Taylor was in command at the border, and Dick became his father's military secretary and aide-de-camp. General Winfield Scott led the other American forces from Vera Cruz to Mexico City, but historians agree that the victories of Zachary Taylor brought the war to an end.

Dick Taylor was no "swivel chair soldier." He did not shirk difficult tasks or claim privileges because he was the son of the commanding officer. He was on the battlefield, sharing the discomforts and dangers of the men without rank. Time and again we find him mentioned in his father's official dispatches. He was present at the battles of Palo Alto, Resaca de la Palma, Monterrey. Courage was his badge. Only when he contracted a fever did he consent to leave the battle area and return to Baton Rouge to regain health. It was his belief that military science could best be mastered in actual practice, and he had no patience with amateur strategists who did not possess actual military experience. These "arm chair generals," he derided; declaring:

Although since the days of Nimrod war has been the constant occupation of men, the fingers of one hand suffice to number great commanders. The "unlearned" hardly think of usurping Tyndall's place in the lecture room, or taking his cuneiform bricks from Rawlinson; yet the world has been much more prolific of learned scientists and philosophers than of able generals. Notwithstanding, the average American would not have hesitated to supersede Napoleon at Austerlitz or Nelson at Trafalgar. . . . True, Cleon captured the Spartan garrison, and Narses gained victories, and Bunyan wrote the *Pilgrim's Progress;* but pestilent demagogues have not always been successful in war. As men without knowledge have at all times usurped the right to criticize campaigns and commanders, they will doubtless continue to do so despite the protests of professional soldiers who discharge this duty in a reverent spirit, knowing that the greatest is he who commits fewest blunders.[16]

After Taylor returned to his Louisiana home and recovered from the fever he had contracted on the battlefield, he devoted himself to his sugar plantation. But his father having been elected President, Richard accompanied him to the White House on March 4, 1849, and became his private secretary. Upon Zachary Taylor's sudden death, in July, 1850, Richard returned to Baton Rouge. A year later he married Myrth Bringier, a girl of French ancestry, who combined beauty and fortune. Her large estates increased his material wealth, and the influence of her family enhanced his own prestige and popularity. In 1856 he was elected a member of the Louisiana State Senate, and continued in that body for four years. Richard Taylor attended to his plantation; he did not aspire to higher political eminence. He had known the crudities of camp life and the precarious existence upon battlefields, but he had also known the elegance of cultured homes in Europe, the fashionable salons of New Orleans, the abundance and natural beauties of Southern plantations. He had what the poet Wordsworth called "that inward eye"—the capacity to recall scenes of beauty and to re-live the happy experiences of the past. Almost two decades after he had visited the Virginia home of his father, even though weary after battles, he thrilled as he remembered that

> flowery plants and rose trees, in full bloom, attended the glorious wealth of June. . . . A white-haired butler, holding a salver on which rested a huge silver goblet filled with Virginia nectar, mint julep. Quantities of cracked ice rattled refreshingly in the goblet; sprigs of fragrant mint peered above its broad rim; a mass of white sugar, too sweetly indolent to melt, rested on the mint; and, like rose buds on a snow bank, luscious strawberries crowned the sugar. Ah, that julep! Mars ne'er received such tipple from the hands of Ganymede!

Thus, in the spring of 1860, we find this ex-President's son enjoying his vast acres, hailed as a leading citizen of Louisiana, happy with a beautiful and accomplished wife. Five children had come; two sons had died in childhood, three daughters were blossoming into radiant girlhood. But now Richard Taylor was troubled; there were rumblings of discord, armed conflict, the disruption of ardent friendships, brother turning against brother as each espoused a different cause. The Southern States were fearful that the Northern abolitionists would end their Constitutional right to own slaves; in the preceding year John Brown had raided the Federal arsenal at Harper's Ferry with the object of freeing the blacks in western Virginia, and though he was hanged, there were others who would risk their lives to end slavery. The Southern States contended that they had entered the Union under a Constitution which clearly recognized their right to ownership of slaves; if the Northern States chose to ignore that compact, if the North intended to restrict slavery in territories not yet created into states, then it was the right of the Southern States to withdraw from the Union, and to form its own separate Confederacy. An election was impending, and the newly formed Republican Party was likely to have as its candidate one Abraham Lincoln of Illinois, who had declared that "the Nation could not survive half slave, half free." If he were elected, spokesmen for the South declared, the Union would be dissolved. In the Congress of the United States, the Senators and Representatives of slaveholding states made that clear; and the man who was most eloquent in defense of the South's constitutional right—to own slaves, to take them wherever their owners pleased, or to secede from the Union if that right were not recognized—was Senator Jefferson Davis of Mississippi, who had married Richard Taylor's sister, Sarah.

Richard Taylor was a delegate to the Democratic National Convention which met at Charleston, South Carolina, to select candidates for the office of President and Vice-President and to declare the principles which the Southern States considered their sovereign right. The meetings were marked by heated arguments and irreconcilable viewpoints. The clamor for secession was increasing in intensity; the delegates of Alabama and other states withdrew and met again in another city. Rival factions of the Democratic Party advanced divergent platforms and uncompromising leaders as their candidates; and in the ensuing election Abraham Lincoln, nominee of the Republican Party, was the victor. For fifty years the owners of slaves had endeavored to extend the territory where their rights to these human chattels would be recognized, and with equal zeal anti-slavery men in the North strove to make slavery illegal beyond the existing slave-owning states. But, apart from a comparatively small number of ardent Abolitionists, even those who deplored the institution of slavery admitted that, under the Constitution of the United States, slavery was entirely legal. Abraham Lincoln stated repeatedly that Congress had no power to abolish it; in fact, as a struggling lawyer, he once defended the right of a slaveowner to recover a runaway slave.[17] The mistaken notion that the North marshaled its armies to end slavery in the South is controverted by editorials in leading Northern papers which proclaimed that "what we are fighting for" was to keep the Union intact because a division into two separate parts would bring uncertainty to businessmen in collecting debts! [18] There were many Northerners, well versed in the history of the Republic, who granted the legal right of the Southern States to secede but believed that secession would not be the means by which the South could continue to hold slaves.[19]

The slaveholding states did not wait for Lincoln to be inaugurated. In December, 1860, South Carolina, in a State Convention, repealed its Act of 1788 which had ratified the Constitution of the United States, and declared that "the union now subsisting between South Carolina and other states, under the name of United States of America, is hereby dissolved." Mississippi took a similar step in the following January; Florida, Alabama, and Georgia in rapid succession also proclaimed their secession from the Union. The time now came for the State of Louisiana to take its stand. The General Assembly, of which Richard Taylor was a member, met in 1861. In the political conventions he had worked fervently to discourage secession, hoping for a solution which would not result in the disruption of the Union. It was Richard Taylor who carried from Jefferson Davis to Abraham Lincoln the letter which proposed a peaceful solution of the differences between the North and the South.[20] But now the conflict was inevitable. The states surrounding Louisiana had already declared an end of the Federal Union which they had joined under the Constitution of 1789. An overwhelming majority of the people of Louisiana were in favor of seceding; like the people of neighboring states they believed the risk small and the victory certain. "Northern writers have persistently declared that we of the South do not possess the elements of strength which would enable us vigorously to conduct the war," editorialized the Richmond *En-*

quirer, "but the truth is that in the South, and we may say in the South only, are found all the resources necessary for a protracted struggle." [21] And the Richmond *Express* likewise scoffed at any doubt of the South's triumph: "A foolish idea prevails in the North that the South cannot raise its own provisions, and will starve outright if the war is kept up. . . . In no manner can the South be disastrously affected by this war; in every manner will the North be." [22]

A State Convention was called by the General Assembly to decide whether Louisiana should secede; Richard Taylor was a delegate from Charles City parish. The ordinance for secession was adopted by a vote of 112 yeas, there being only 17 nays.[23] When, nearly twenty years after this event, Richard Taylor wrote his *Destruction and Reconstruction* he expressed astonishment that such momentous decisions could be made with so little consideration of the tragedies likely to follow in their wake. "At that time and since, I marveled at the joyous and careless temper in which men, much my superior in sagacity and experience, consummated these acts." The official report of the Convention records that as the names were called the delegates were permitted to express their reason for the vote they might give on the ordinance, but no remarks are embodied in the printed journal, and there is nothing to indicate that Richard Taylor raised his voice to counsel against secession; in fact, his vote is recorded in favor of the secession ordinance. One of the delegates introduced a resolution at the opening sessions providing that "whatever the action of the Convention whether or not this State ought to secede from the Union, it shall have no effect until the same shall have been ratified by the majority of the people at the ballot box; and, to this effect, an election shall be held." This proposal was voted down by a vote of 84 nays and 43 yeas; Richard Taylor voted against submitting the question to the people.[24]

The son of Zachary Taylor, twelfth President of the United States, forced to choose between allegiance to the National Government and loyalty to his native State, followed the path of Robert E. Lee and other great men of the South. The Governor of the State, recalling his military experience, appointed Richard Taylor as colonel of an infantry regiment; and, always believing that the sole duty of a soldier is to fight, he startled his superior officers by insisting that he be permitted to start immediately with his men for the battlefield. The first battle of Bull Run was being fought, and he hoped to reach the firing line in time to take part in the fray. He crowded his men into the available coaches, and the train started; but the engine proved to be of "the most weezy and helpless character, creeping snail-like on levels and requiring the men to leave the carriage to push it upgrade." Richard Taylor reached the battlefield at dusk, after the conflict had ended.

During the summer and winter of 1861 his regiment was fearfully smitten with virulent measles, and he spent his days in hospitals nursing the sick soldiers so far from home and friends. He himself was stricken with a persistent fever which sapped his strength and impaired the use of his limbs. The commanding officer ordered him off to a nearby sulphur spring, and there his sister nursed him back to health. Returning to the Army, he learned that he had been promoted to the rank of brigadier general, but he protested against this elevation because there were three other colonels who were his seniors. He felt that it would be charged that he had been promoted because of his friendship with President Jefferson Davis who, as we have seen, married Richard's sister; and he begged Davis to revoke his promotion. Despite his reluctance, the senior officers of the brigade enthusiastically supported his elevation to general's rank. Then came news that the Union troops were invading his home, that his wife with their children were fleeing at their approach. But before they reached their destination, Shreveport, scarlet fever killed the two boys.

With the passing months the conflict between the States increased in fury. The Federal Government sent larger armies into the field, and the South recruited greater forces to impress the world with its determination and its power to preserve its independent existence.

A year's warfare between the North and South still left the European powers unwilling to recognize the Confederate States as a separate and sovereign nation, and the Confederacy was in great need of more impressive military successes. Robert E. Lee had been given command of all the Southern armies, and his strategy inspired both confidence and encouragement, bringing a number of victories to the Southern forces in the closing week of May, 1862. In these operations Richard Taylor played an important part, and the Confederate Secretary of State, Judah P. Benjamin, called them "a series of triumphs which will at last have satisfied the most skeptical of foreign

Cabinets that we are an independent nation"; in a dispatch to the Confederate emissary in Paris, Secretary Benjamin enthusiastically noted that "in these battles Brig. Gen. Richard Taylor, of Louisiana, particularly distinguished himself and has been warmly recommended by his commander for promotion." [25]

For two years more Richard Taylor devoted himself constantly to the exacting tasks of training, leading and provisioning the ragged troops who had survived pestilence, hunger, and the overwhelming armies of the North. With only a respite of a few weeks to see his wife and surviving children, he was given command of all the Confederate forces west of the Mississippi River; but in the winter of 1864 it became evident to him that the South had lost the war and boldly he expressed that opinion to the President of the Confederate States, Jefferson Davis, and to other leaders. Nevertheless, he felt it a soldier's duty to continue the struggle even though he despaired of victory, and he was the last important general to surrender to the Federal forces. In his Order of Surrender he explains how the capitulations of the other ranking generals—Lee and Johnston—indicate the hopelessness of the Southern cause, and he tells of his own insurmountable difficulties in continuing operations: "With the Mississippi impassable for troops, it was impossible to withdraw toward the west, and we could accomplish no good by prolonging a useless struggle here, against overwhelming numbers. Once convinced of these facts, my duty, as Department Commander, was to stop further loss of life and devastation of States already impoverished by war; and, whilst still in my power to do so, make such terms for my troops as would preserve their honor and best protect them and the people generally from the further ravages of war." [26] The previous surrender of the commander-in-chief, Robert E. Lee, had filled the South with the realization of impending defeat for the Confederate States; the surrender of Richard Taylor, half a month later, meant that the struggle was at an end. The colonel in charge of exchanging prisoners at Vicksburg summed up the significance of Taylor's act: "I have received official information of the surrender of Lieut. General Dick Taylor," he said sorrowfully to his staff, "I am afraid the Confederacy is no more." [27]

To the end, in victories or defeat, Dick Taylor had the unwavering confidence of the entire Southland; and this faith in his devotion and ability was voiced in Southern papers large and small. Typical of this reliance on his judgment in the darkest hour was the editorial in a Mississippi newspaper, the Meridian *Clarion:*

Whatever the orders, policy and action of Gen. Taylor may be, we are well satisfied that his unwavering fidelity to the army and people of his Department will never be questioned. For some time past his situation has been peculiarly embarrassing. All information affecting our condition, and his resulting duties, have been derived from Federal sources. His purpose must now be to protect the people against the ravages of a foe whose destructiveness is comparable alone to their exhaustless resources. It is needless for him to protract a struggle when all other armies have been surrendered. If Lee and Johnston have yielded to the pressure of resistless numbers, Gen. Taylor could hardly be expected to sacrifice lives, property, towns, villages, in defense of a country utterly indefensible. It is not his wish to surrender. He is made of sterner stuff; but he has a thorough comprehension of his duties to the States over which his military jurisdiction extends, and we are inclined to believe that he will follow the example of Lee and Johnston.

God knows we wish it otherwise; but the doom, it would seem, is inevitable. If Gen. Taylor think differently we shall not dissent. We speak plainly of facts palpable to the dullest observer. Whatever the present policy and future fortunes of the Department Commander, whatever his personal peculiarities, the attachés of the *Clarion* have abundant reason to remember his honesty, his blunt truthfulness, his tireless energy, his sleepless labors, and, then, this people should not forget, nor this army fail to remember, that the course of the commander in chief, whatever it may be, is dictated by a degree of wisdom which overrides personal considerations; and by a courage as lofty as that which illustrated his deeds at Mansfield, and made his name immortal.[28]

After an absence of four years, Richard Taylor returned to New Orleans. His estate had been confiscated and sold, and he was penniless. But having cast his lot with the Southern cause, he neither sought nor accepted any restoration to citizenship or restitution of his property after the war; [29] he made no apologies for the decision he had made at the outbreak of the Civil War; long before, he had declared that he "had cut into the game with eyes wide open, and felt that in staking life, fortune, and the future of my children, the chances were against success." [30]

The war had left him in a very delicate health, the aftermath of the malignant malarial fever which had almost paralyzed his lower limbs. Admired and respected by Northern leaders, Richard Taylor spent long periods in Washington endeavoring to obtain for Louisiana a respite from military occupation and relief from the carpetbaggers who harassed and plundered the people of his native State. Ulysses S. Grant, who had served in the Mexican War under his father, General Zachary Taylor, now listened to the views of the son; the Secretary of the Navy, Gideon Welles, recorded in his diary that "General Dick Taylor was in Washington and has spent some time with General Grant. The two discussed very fully the condition of affairs." [31] But there were Northerners who could never forget the victories which this President's son had won over the Union armies, and when he attended a political convention in Philadelphia the newspapers lashed out in furious and scurrilous attacks.

Unable to obtain for Louisiana the considerate treatment to which he considered it entitled, he sailed for Europe in May, 1873, and remained there for some months as a representative of American business interests. Returning to the United States, he wrote a volume—*Destruction and Reconstruction*—describing the events which led up to the War between the States and the deplorable conditions in the South which followed the end of the unequal contest. Although the book is a serious analysis of political, military, and social trends—embodying scathing criticisms of inefficiency and lack of vision on the part of Confederate leaders—it sparkles with literary gems that are unexcelled in any book relating to the Civil War. We can see General Stonewall Jackson, constantly sucking his lemons, "a pair of cavalry boots covering feet of gigantic size, a mangy cap with visor drawn low, a heavy, dark beard and weary eyes filled with intense but never brilliant light"; we can almost imagine approaching us that "buxom, comely dame of some five and thirty summers, with bright eyes and tight ankles, and conscious of these advantages," or that "small, fairy-like creature, plucky as a Dandie Dinmont terrier, and with a heart as big as a massamutter"; and equally picturesque is the description of that statesman who, "over-educated, had retained but not digested the learning, and the beautiful flowers of literature were attached to him by filaments of memory as lovely orchids to sapless sticks."

In the last decade of his life Dick Taylor fought the recurrent ravages of the malignant fever he had contracted during the Civil War. But bodily ailments did not dim the vigor of his mind nor lessen his efforts to improve the condition of his beloved Southland. In New

Orleans, in New York, in the Nation's Capital, and in other places he sought the aid and influence of political and social leaders to erase the bitterness engendered in the conflict between North and South. Despite the warnings of his physicians he wrote his *Destruction and Reconstruction,* but the task taxed his ebbing vitality. Death waited at his elbow until he completed his book; he passed away on April 12, 1879.

In its record of graduates who had passed to the final source of wisdom, Yale University recounted his academic progress, his military achievements, and his prominence in the political affairs of Louisiana.[32] Newspapers which had watched his postwar efforts to reconcile North and South, said more: they wrote of his unswerving devotion to the region of his birth, and of his unselfish dedication to the improvement of the lot of his fellow men.[33] This President's son died as he had lived and fought—a man of ideals and honor.

7

Son of Millard Fillmore

One late afternoon in May, 1884, a lonely bachelor lingered at his desk in a Buffalo courthouse and made his last will and testament. It was not the disposition of his money or property which was of concern to him; it was the fear that death would overtake him before he himself could accomplish a task which he was eager to perform. He wanted to make certain that, if he did not see that end achieved during his lifetime, others would definitely finish the work when he was in his grave. So he wrote:

> I, Millard Powers Fillmore, particularly request and direct my Executors at the earliest practicable moment to burn or otherwise effectively destroy all correspondence or letters to or from my father, mother, sister or me. . . . I hope to be able to do that before my death.

The man who penned that will was the only son of Millard Fillmore, the thirteenth President of the United States.[1] Millard Powers Fillmore lived on until 1889. We do not know whether this son himself consigned any of his father's papers to the flames; possibly the shade of his illustrious sire weakened that unfilial resolve. But, when the son passed on, his executors carried out his unequivocal instructions. In the words of the historian, James Grant Wilson, "A singular instance of literary vandalism occurred in the City of Buffalo early in 1891 when all the valuable letters and documents relating to the administration of Millard Fillmore were destroyed by the Executors of the ex-President's only son whose will contained a mandate to that effect. Why he should have wished in this way to destroy an important part of the history of his country as well as his father's honorable career . . . is entirely beyond the comprehension of ordinary mortals." [2]

How utterly different were the efforts of the other Presidents' sons to preserve the writings of their fathers. The son of John Adams patiently edited the papers of his father.[3] John Tyler's son compiled several volumes to record the history of his father's progress to the Presidency, and transcribed every available letter.[4] Ulysses S. Grant, in his *Personal Memoirs,* tells us of the aid his son rendered in the compilation of his biography.[5] The son of John Quincy Adams spent many years seeking out and publishing the letters and diaries of that President.[6] One son of Martin Van Buren spent his last days arranging his father's documents; [7] and after the death of that ex-President, his two surviving sons devoted themselves to the task of editing and completing his memoirs. Andrew Johnson's son, in the midst of the Civil War, gathered and arranged his father's correspondence and other papers.[8] A son of Rutherford Hayes collected the diaries and letters of his Presidential father, and erected a library to house them.[9] The adopted son of Andrew Jackson carefully recovered and preserved the papers of his foster father.[10] William Henry Harrison's son, beset with financial burdens and family tragedies, found time to search out the records of his father's people as "an absolute duty imposed on posterity." [11] The only other son of a President who had an intention of destroying any of his father's papers was Robert Lincoln, and his explanation was that he burned documents which incriminated one of the members of Abraham Lincoln's Cabinet.[12] Only the son of Millard Fillmore wished to wipe out the written records of his father's life.

What prompted this President's son in his singular behavior? Certainly there was no reason to be ashamed of his father's upward climb from menial tasks, half-illiteracy, and struggle for the bare necessities of life. Possibly Millard Fillmore had a premonition that this son would seek to blot out the story of all the father had suffered in childhood, for he himself gave to the Buffalo Historical Society a brief résumé of his youth, writing, "I believe that a humble origin affords no cause of concealment." No man rose to the Presidency with memories of a less joyous boyhood or a more despairing struggle for education. He himself tells us that, until he was nineteen, he had never seen a geography or history book. He trudged afoot a hundred miles to the mill of an employer who promised to teach the boy the tanning trade; instead, the future President was imposed upon to fell trees and chop wood and subjected to threats of punishment when he protested that he had not been employed for such labor. His reward for a year's toil was a diet of salt pork and fifty-five dollars in cash! In his eagerness to become a lawyer he undertook to serve seven years in the office of a man who professed piety and spoke in Biblical language. But again Millard Fillmore was deceived and imposed upon. Penniless, he earned two dollars in some work before a justice of the peace—a minor legal act he could perform before being admitted to the bar—but the pious lawyer insisted that this ambitious boy should devote all his time and energies solely to collecting rents and doing other tasks for his instructor. And, to escape this unfair servitude, Fillmore was forced to pay the lawyer thirty dollars! Not having so much wealth, he gave notes which he arduously paid off with a pittance he earned in teaching. There still exists the receipt which the young teacher, Millard Fillmore, gave to the school district trustees when they paid him in full for his season's services—the munificent sum of nineteen dollars and seventy-three cents.[13]

This was the father who became President of the United States. He had met Abigail Powers, a minister's daughter, and it was she who encouraged the eager Millard Fillmore to continue his quest for knowledge. She became his wife; and, two years after their marriage, their only son, Millard Powers Fillmore, was born. When this son came into the world, the elder Fillmore had already practiced law for five years and was about to be elected a member of the New York Legislature; another four years was to see him elected to the United States Congress. Millard Fillmore became a prominent member of the House of Representatives, and rose high in the esteem of his fellow Congressmen.[14] In appearance and demeanor he impressed all who saw him. Julia Gardiner, later the wife of President John Tyler, gives us a picture of Millard Fillmore as she saw him before she knew his identity. She had just returned from extended travels in Europe and, with her sister, was on a train en route from New York to Washington when "a handsome, portly gentleman came several times into the car in which we were seated and excited the interest of myself and sister by the self-conscious manner in which he looked into the mirror at the head of the car and adjusted his cravat, while he cast furtive glances in our direction. These glances were, doubtless, accidental. Soon after our arrival in Washington the gentleman alluded to called upon our parents with an old friend of my father. Then we found that the handsome stranger was no less a personage than Millard

Fillmore, the then chairman of the Committee on Ways and Means of the House of Representatives." [15]

After his service in Congress, Fillmore became comptroller of the State of New York and, in 1848, he was elected Vice-President of the United States on the ticket which made aged General Zachary Taylor President. Taylor died in July, 1850, and Millard Fillmore succeeded him to the Presidency.

When his father became Chief Executive, the son was twenty-two years old. Although he used his full name in documents, he came to be known as Powers Fillmore. The elder Fillmore guided Powers' education carefully, remembering the handicaps of his own youth. In his father's office Powers studied law, and his father not only instilled legal precepts but also trained him in cultivating the appearance which impressed judges and juries. Three other young men pursued their legal training with Powers Fillmore, and one of them long afterward recalled the admonition of Powers' father. Said Millard Fillmore to his son's companion, "Last evening I saw you and Powers walking out on Main Street and going as though you were walking on a wager; that is undignified and unprofessional." And he repeated the same criticism to Powers.[16]

Powers did not open a law office after he completed his legal studies; instead he became his father's secretary in the White House. Possibly in the papers which he destroyed we might have found evidence that his work was creditable and of value to the President; there is nothing in contemporary records to indicate that Powers Fillmore was prominent either in the political or in the social circles of the Capital. He did accompany his father on an extended trip West, in June, 1854, when the Rock Island Railroad extended its system;[17] but, while newspapers refer to the President's speeches and activities, the son was mentioned merely as a member of the Presidential party. After his term expired, Millard Fillmore returned to Buffalo and the son accompanied him.

Thereafter, the ex-President's son practiced law for a short period,[18] then obtained a position in the Federal Court as a clerk; [19] with the passing years he rose to higher posts, and finally became United States Commissioner. His mother had died in Washington in the spring of 1853; and, five years later, the ex-President married Caroline McIntosh. To her he pays warm tribute in his will. Millard Fillmore died in 1874; in his last will and testament, made ten years before his death, he expressed the hope that his son and his second wife would feel toward each other the affection he had felt for both. This document, leaving annuities to his two sisters and a farm to a brother, divided the residuary estate between the son, Millard Powers Fillmore, and the second wife:

First, I feel it my duty and pleasure to record my dying testimony to the noble qualities of my beloved wife Caroline; and if she and my son, Millard Powers, shall survive me, I hope and trust that they may love each other as I have loved them; and as they will both be orphans, indeed, I hope also that they will naturally render to each other every assistance due from a most affectionate parent to a beloved child and from a most affectionate and dutiful child to a beloved parent; and with this I shall rest in peace.[20]

The injunction of the former President was observed by the widow and her stepson—at least outwardly. For a while they continued to live in the Buffalo mansion where Millard Fillmore resided after his second marriage; then Powers moved to other quarters.[21] But, after her death, it became evident that it was not the son of her dead husband who was first in her thoughts when she wrote her will. In that document she attempted to leave to her own kin the Fillmore library, a costly silver set, and other valuable articles. She assumed that this was her right, based upon a pre-nuptial agreement which the ex-President had made, providing that "all the furniture, plate, carriages and personal property in use by the parties (the ex-President and his prospective second wife) at the time of the death of either shall vest absolutely in the survivor."[22] The ex-President's son opposed this disposal of what he regarded as his father's belongings, and he asked the courts to declare his own right to the property.[23] In the contest he particularly sought the ownership of a huge cask of Madeira wine which Commodore Perry had brought from Japan after his warships, in 1854, forced the Japanese to open their ports to American traders.[24] Millard Fillmore was President when Perry made his expedition, and, although the Madeira was brought back upon a warship, the Chief Executive insisted upon paying the lawful import duty. The cask remained unopened during the lifetime of the President, and the wine untasted; now its aging had increased its value. The legal proceedings dragged through the highest courts of the State; finally, Millard Powers Fillmore was declared the rightful owner. He sold the wine and the silver at auction. He also sold the magnificent collection of books which his parents had collected and prized.[25] And, as has been noted, he left for his executors to destroy the documents and letters which had been part of the library.

Millard Powers Fillmore survived his father for fifteen years. He continued to live in Buffalo. He never married. He resided in a Buffalo hotel, the Tift House, which in its earlier days had been the scene of lively and lavish parties staged by men of social and political prominence, among them the future President, Grover Cleveland.[26] Here in the lobby of the hotel, Millard Powers Fillmore would while away the evening hours with lifelong friends. It was after one of these nightly chats, on November 15, 1889, that he retired to his upstairs room and was later found unconscious.[27] Said the leading Buffalo newspaper, "Mr. Fillmore, son of the ex-President, was about fifty-five years of age, was unmarried, and at the time of his death had no living relatives. He had a wide circle of friends among whom he was highly esteemed and to whom the sad news of his death will be a heavy blow. Until a short time prior to his decease he had held the office of United States Commissioner, and in that capacity he performed his duties honestly, faithfully, and efficiently. He was a member of the Erie County Bar." [28]

At the home of a lifelong friend, the bishop and the rector of a fashionable church conducted the last rites over an elaborate red-cedar casket, bearing an engraved silver plate, and covered with floral tributes. But there were present neither the prominent statesmen nor the politicians who had eagerly sought the aid and influence of his Presidential father, Millard Fillmore. A telegram had been sent to ex-President Grover Cleveland, whose entire political career had flowered in Buffalo, but no reply was received.[29] Millard Powers Fillmore, son of a President, was buried beside his father.

8

Sons of Abraham Lincoln

WHEN ABRAHAM LINCOLN, IN THE CLOSING DAYS OF FEBRUARY, 1861, made his circuitous and guarded journey from Springfield, Illinois, to Washington to assume the office of President he was accompanied by Mrs. Lincoln and their three sons—Robert Todd, seventeen years old, William aged ten, and Thomas, two years younger.[1] Lincoln was always a very indulgent father, never reprimanding juvenile misbehavior which most parents often punished severely. William Herndon who, as Lincoln's law partner for two decades, had ample opportunity to observe the Lincoln ménage, tells us that Lincoln "exercised no government at all over his household. His children did much as they pleased. Many of their antics he approved, but he restrained them in nothing. He never reproved them or gave them a fatherly frown." When on Sundays, while their mother was at church, the boys came to the law office they played havoc with the furniture and equipment; and while they harassed Herndon to the extreme, Lincoln displayed no concern. "The boys were absolutely unrestrained in their amusement. If they pulled down all the books from the shelves, bent the points of all the pens, overturned inkstands, scattered law books over the floor, or threw pencils into the spittoon, it never disturbed the serenity of their father's good nature."[2] One of the amusements of the boys was to hide behind a screening hedge and, with a long pole, knock off the hats of passing gentlemen, including their father's.[3] And though this exuberance was somewhat subdued after their father became President, the two younger boys indulged in many tantalizing escapades during their residence in the White House.[4]

One of Lincoln's secretaries, John Hay, tells of their hectic activities. "During the first year of the administration the house was made lively by the games and pranks of Mr. Lincoln's two younger children, William and Thomas. Robert, the eldest, was away at Harvard, only coming home for short vacations. The two little boys, aged eight and ten, with their Western independence and enterprise, kept the house in an uproar. They drove their tutor wild with their good-natured disobedience; they organized a minstrel show in the attic; they made acquaintance with the office-seekers and became hot champions of the distressed." [5] Three decades later the playmates of the Lincoln youngsters still had vivid recollections of the goat which they drove into the White House drawing room while Mrs. Lincoln was entertaining the social elite of Washington, and of the hilarious circus they staged on an upper floor.[6]

The Lincoln family was not long in the White House before it became apparent that both with Abraham Lincoln and with the public Willie, the second son, was the favorite. He was born on December 21, 1850. While he enjoyed boyish pranks as did his younger brother, he was more studious. The trip East, his first railroad journey, left upon his mind a deep impression; he had a fancy for drawing up railway timetables, and conducted an imaginary train from Chicago to New York with a precision that startled more mature travelers.[7] He was scarcely eleven when the Civil War broke out, but his little heart was deeply touched by love for the country of which his father was President and by the sorrows which the battles brought. Among the first officers to lose their lives was Abraham Lincoln's close friend, Colonel Edward Baker. Willie Lincoln wrote a poem and sent it to a Washington paper, the *National Republican.* The editor published both the boy's letter and the verses with a few words of introduction:

Little William Lincoln, son of President Lincoln, has sent us the following verses, which are quite creditable for one so young. We insert them with pleasure, and hope that Willie's desire, as expressed in the last verse, will meet with a ready response from the whole country.

Washington, D. C. Oct. 30, 1861

DEAR SIR: I enclose my first attempt at poetry.

Yours truly,

WILLIAM W. LINCOLN

LINES

On the death of Colonel Edward Baker

There was no patriot like Baker
So noble and so true;
He fell as a soldier on the field,
His face to the sky of blue.

His voice is silent in the hall,
  Which oft his presence grac'd,
No more he'll hear the loud acclaim,
  Which rang from place to place.

No squeamish notions filled his breast,
  The Union was his theme
"No surrender and no compromise"
  His day's thought and night's dream.

His country has *her* part to play,
  To'rds those he has left behind,
His widow and his children all,—
  She must always keep in mind.[8]

But Willie did not live long to develop his poetic talents; in 1862 he sickened and died. Both parents were terribly affected by his loss; the passing years did not dim this sorrow in either Abraham Lincoln or his wife, and even two years later Lincoln's bodyguard, Colonel W. H. Crook, noted that "both the President and Mrs. Lincoln unquestionably felt this loss." [9] The death of little Willie brought an end to social entertainments at the White House; [10] Mrs. Lincoln never entered the room where he died or where the coffin stood.[11] Lincoln rarely spoke of his little son. The painter Carpenter tells us that during his six months at the White House the only allusion to Willie he ever heard the President make was when the White House stables burned and Willie's pony was destroyed.[12] There was a popular belief, which spread all over the Nation after Lincoln's death, that the President had had Willie's embalmed body disinterred twice so he could look upon it.[13] Willie's remains were placed in a vault in a Washington cemetery, and there they remained until Abraham Lincoln himself died. Then the little coffin of Willie whom the President loved so deeply was placed in the same funeral car that carried the assassinated President's body to Springfield, Illinois, and the millions who stood bowed as the funeral train rolled by unknowingly paid homage not only to the martyred President but also to little Willie Lincoln.[14] The bill of $7,458 which the undertakers rendered the Government for the funeral expenses of President Abraham Lincoln includes a pathetic little item: "removing remains of Willie $10." [15]

After Willie passed away, Lincoln's interest and affection centered in the youngest son, Thomas, known as Tad. Tad was born on April

NATIONAL REPUBLICAN.

LITTLE WILLIE LINCOLN, son of President Lincoln, has sent us the following verses, which are quite creditable, as a first effort, for one so young. We insert them with pleasure, and hope that Willie's desire, as expressed in the last verse, will meet with a ready response by the whole country. It should not be forgotten that the rebels gave Mrs. Jackson *one hundred thousand dollars;* Charleston alone giving twenty thousand:

WASHINGTON, D. C., October 30, 1861.

DEAR SIR: I enclose you my first attempt at poetry.

Yours truly, WILLIAM W. LINCOLN.

The Editor of the National Republican.

LINES

On the death of Colonel Edward Baker.

There was no patriot like Baker,
So noble and so true;
He fell as a soldier on the field,
His face to the sky of blue.

His voice is silent in the hall,
Which oft his presence grac'd,
No more he'll hear the loud acclaim,
Which rang from place to place.

No squeamish notions filled his breast,
The Union was his theme,
"*No surrender and no compromise,*"
His day thought and night's dream.

His country has *her* part to play,
To'rds those he has left behind,
His widow and his children all,—
She must always keep in mind.

A PRESIDENT'S SON WRITES POETRY

Eleven-year-old Willie Lincoln, son of Abraham Lincoln, wrote a poem upon the death of a family friend, killed in the early days of the Civil War. (Washington *National Republican,* Nov. 4, 1861)

4, 1853, being eight years old when he came to the White House. During the last summer spent in Springfield, Tad was stricken with scarlet fever; [16] it is possible that this was the cause of his inability later to speak distinctly. Colonel Crook tells us that "an unusual impediment in little Tad's speech made it extremely difficult for him to pronounce certain words, and really impossible for him to enunciate a name like Smith, for instance." [17] This affliction, as well as the loss of Willie must have endeared the child still more to Abraham Lincoln. Whenever it was possible, the President had the little fellow with him and very often the White House attachés would come upon them with Tad sitting on his father's shoulders while President Lincoln galloped up and down the long corridor outside their private apartments, the boy laughing and shaking with glee. Lincoln's secretaries loved little Tad, and without exception their memoirs speak of him in terms of deep affection and sympathy. John Hay described him as "a merry, warm-blooded, kindly little boy, perfectly lawless, and full of odd fancies, the 'chartered libertine' of the Executive Mansion. He ran continually in and out of his father's cabinet, interrupting his gravest labors and conversations with bright, rapid, and very imperfect speech. . . . He would perch upon his father's knee while the most weighty conferences were going on. Sometimes, escaping from the domestic authorities, he would take refuge in that sanctuary for the whole evening, dropping to sleep at last on the floor, when the President would pick him up and carry him tenderly to bed." [18]

The President gratified Tad's every whim; when the boy wanted to parade in celebration of Union victories, the President put aside important matters to write to the Secretary of War, "Tad wants some flags. Can he be accommodated?" [19] But Tad did not always need his father's help to effect his schemes. One day he went to the War Department and obtained from Secretary Stanton a commission as "lieutenant"; the Secretary of War considered it fun, but Tad regarded this military status seriously. Whereupon, this ten-year-old "lieutenant," exercising the authority of his rank, ordered to the White House a score of muskets, discharged the night guards, asembled all the gardeners and servants and gave them the guns. Then Tad drilled them, and put them on duty as guards. Robert Lincoln discovered the proceedings and complained to the President. But Abraham Lincoln did not reprimand the boy; he considered it a joke, waited until Tad had gone to bed, and then dismissed the nondescript army. That night, though a war was raging and plots against the President were brewing, the White House was without a protective guard.[20] Later, when the War Department gave Tad a sword and a uniform and jokingly raised his rank to "colonel," he obtained official stationery and sent out telegrams signed "Col. Tad Lincoln." [21] With deep seriousness the little boy adopted the military formalities of his father's generals; when he and his playmates as a court-martial condemned a doll named "Jack" to be shot for sleeping at his sentry post, "Colonel Tad" prevailed upon his father to lift the sentence in proper manner, and Abraham Lincoln solemnly wrote out an order reading, "The doll Jack is pardoned by order of the President. Signed, A. Lincoln." [22]

Tad Lincoln outlived his illustrious father; and to his mother, mentally unbalanced by the murder of Abraham Lincoln, he became still more the symbol of her shattered dreams and the link with a tragic past which she wanted both to remember and to forget. Her sister's diary records how Mary Todd Lincoln, clutching tightly Tad's hand, left the White House with the obsession that those two were alone in the world.[23]

Mrs. Lincoln took Tad to Europe and, as she traveled about, placed him first in one school and then in another. In February, 1870, the mother wrote that Tad had been placed in an English school with the expectation of remaining there a year; in May, her letters refer to "Taddie's new school quarters" in Obennsal, Germany; during the following September, she engaged a tutor for him in Leamington, England.[24] Mother and son returned from Europe, and Tad was stricken shortly after. He died in 1871. Of the sons of Abraham Lincoln, only one lived out a full life—Robert Todd Lincoln.

Robert Todd Lincoln, eldest son of Abraham Lincoln, was seventeen and a half years old when his father became President of the United States. In contrast to the strong attachment which the Emancipator had for his two younger boys, there was no close relationship between this son and the father; even when Robert was older he was not, as sons of his age were to other Presidents, either a confidant, a constant companion, or an aide. Immediately after Abraham Lincoln's death Robert could give to biographers no details of intimate events in his father's life, admitting that he had not known his father very well.[25] He explained that during Robert's boyhood his father was constantly away attending to his law cases in scattered courts of the circuit; and when Abraham Lincoln's presence at home could have brought a closer relationship between father and son, Robert went away to colleges far from home. Then, said Robert Lincoln, his father became President and was so absorbed in his official work that Robert seldom saw him for ten uninterrupted minutes.[26]

But the strain of the Civil War could not account for the absence of close ties between the President and Robert; Abraham Lincoln had the time and patience for the troubles and problems of strangers. Possibly he recalled that he himself, at Robert's age, was fatherless and self-reliant, solving without aid the perplexing questions which confront adolescent youth. But, as we have seen, not even the overwhelming and arduous tasks of the Presidency deterred Abraham Lincoln from listening to the lengthy stories of his younger sons, and romping and playing with them.

Robert Todd Lincoln was born in the Globe Tavern in Springfield, Illinois, on April 1, 1843, nine months after Abraham Lincoln and Mary Todd reconsidered their broken engagement, became reconciled after unhappy misunderstandings, and were united in marriage. In the following May Abraham Lincoln purchased from a clergyman a frame house of one and a half stories, and later enlarged it.[27] Here Robert spent the first sixteen years of his life. Abraham Lincoln thus appraised his first-born when he was three: "Bob is short and low; and I expect he always will be. He talks very plainly—almost as plainly as anybody. He is quite smart enough. I sometimes fear that he is one of those little *rare-ripe* sort that are smarter at about five than ever after." [28] He attended the public schools, but evidenced no exceptional scholarship; in after years his classmates recalled that he had been nicknamed "Cockeye" because of his aloofness, which was attributed by some to excessive shyness and by others to snobbishness.[29] As with his younger sons, Abraham Lincoln did not instill in Robert filial reverence; it is recorded that, when his father became engrossed in a game of chess and either did not hear or heed Robert's call to dinner, the boy knocked the chessboard from the knees of Abraham Lincoln and his fellow player.[30]

In the fall of 1859, Robert made an attempt to enter Harvard College; he was examined in sixteen subjects and failed in all but one of them. Thereupon, he was sent to Phillips Academy at Exeter, New Hampshire. Abraham Lincoln was much worried about his son's slow academic progress, and made a visit to the school to talk with Robert.[31] After a year's residence at Exeter, Robert did succeed in obtaining admission to Harvard. We do not know why this college, so distant from his Illinois home, was selected for him; at that period it was not usual for boys to make such long journeys in quest of academic training, but possibly Abraham Lincoln wanted his eldest son to have the prestige of attending a leading institution.[32] But after providing for his son's education, the President expressed no interest in his future, offered no counsel. When he asked Robert what he planned to do after his graduation from Harvard and was told that the son intended to study law, Lincoln's only comment was, "You should learn more than I ever did, but you will never have so good a time." And Robert in after years reflected sadly, "That was the only advice I ever had from my father as to my career." [33]

When Abraham Lincoln left his Springfield home to begin his Presidential residence in the White House he took his family with him to be present when he assumed the highest office of the Republic. Robert was granted absence from his classrooms at Harvard to accompany his father and witness the inauguration. It was still apparent that the son had not developed a sense of responsibility: entrusted with Abraham Lincoln's carpetbag which contained the draft of the Inaugural Address, Robert negligently lost baggage and speech.[34] After the Inauguration ceremonies, Robert remained at the White House for a short time, then returned to his college.

Robert Todd Lincoln had scarcely resumed his studies when his father in Washington was confronted with the greatest crisis in the Nation's history since the thirteen American colonies had established themselves as the United States. One by one the slaveholding states were seceding from the Union; the troops of South Carolina had fired their cannon against Fort Sumter in Charleston harbor, and that arsenal had surrendered. The Southern States were bent upon forming a separate Confederacy of their own—peacefully, if permitted; by armed force, if there was no other alternative. Civil war was inevitable.

In April, 1861, Abraham Lincoln called for 75,000 volunteers "to repossess the forts, places and property which have been seized from the Union." [35] From all sections of the North, from all trades and professions, men of all ages flocked to the recruiting offices; particularly, professors and students answered the call. "What an infusion of character went out from Harvard and other colleges," exclaimed Ralph Waldo Emerson, "scholars exchanged the black coat for the blue; a single company in the Forty-fourth Massachusetts contained thirty-five sons of Harvard."[36] In similar manner, young men deserted classrooms both in Northern and Southern colleges to enter the ranks of the Confederate forces. The Boston *Herald* reported that, in May, 1861, sixteen undergraduates had left Harvard College for the war, "ten of them are secessionists."[37] But Robert Lincoln, the President's son, continued with his studies. During his stay, forty men of his class left the campus for the battlefields, enlisting as privates, corporals, sergeants; six of them were killed in action.[38] Numerous alumni, some who, like Richard Jeffrey Cleveland, had graduated from Harvard thirty-five years prior to the war, declined commissions and served as privates. But Robert Lincoln was not among them. Friends of the Lincoln family said that Mrs. Lincoln had kept Robert from enlisting, that having lost her younger son Willie through disease in peace she feared to lose the elder through wounds in war. Those who disliked the President's wife hinted that her sympathies were with the Southern States, and that she did not want her son to fight against them. Herndon quotes her as saying, "If ever my husband dies, his spirit will never find me living outside the limits of a slave state."[39] It is true that her own three brothers were in the army of the Confederacy.

From the very beginning of the conflict the newspapers of the South gave prominent space to the enlistments of the Todd brothers whose sister was none other than the wife of the President of the Union States. In May, 1861, the Richmond *Enquirer* announced that "D. H. Todd of New Orleans, and brother-in-law of Abraham Lincoln, has been appointed first lieutenant in the Army of the Confederate States. Mr. Todd is a daring young man, of good character, fine talent, and an ardent friend of the South—his home by birth, education and choice."[40] He and his two brothers, as the war continued, died upon fields of battle. The eldest son of the President bore their family name, but he did not imitate his uncles' eagerness to risk life in an espoused cause. Robert Todd Lincoln remained on the Harvard campus; graduating in 1864 from the college courses, he enrolled in the Law School.

Possibly he himself had an inclination to enter the Army, but certainly there is no proof of any active effort to effect that purpose or of any fervent entreaties to persuade either of his parents of its propriety or inherent justice. Carl Sandburg, in his painstaking chronicle of Lincoln during the war years, refers to a conversation which Robert had with a friend in which he implied that his father opposed his enlistment; when Abraham Lincoln inquired what he intended doing after his graduation, Robert retorted: "As long as you object to my joining the Army, I am going to study law." [41] But there is evidence that the President entertained the belief that his son should assume the same obligation as the sons of other fathers not in exalted place. At that time Mrs. Lincoln's sister Emilie, the widow of a Confederate officer, was living at the White House and overheard a conversation between Abraham Lincoln and his wife; her diary tells us: "Sister Mary is on a terrible strain. She is frightened about Robert going into the Army. She said today to Brother Lincoln: 'Of course, Mr. Lincoln, I know that Robert's plea to go into the Army is manly and noble and I want him to go, but oh! I am so frightened he may never come back to us!' Mr. Lincoln said sadly, 'Many a poor mother, Mary, has had to make this sacrifice and has given up every son she had—and lost them all!" [42]

As the Civil War continued there was increasing and more widespread criticism of the fact that, while thousands of young men both in the North and in the South were bleeding and dying, the son of Abraham Lincoln was enjoying the safety and comforts of the Harvard dormitories. It was now the fateful year of 1865; the conflict had continued four long years and was approaching its end. On January 19, we find the President of the United States writing to General Ulysses S. Grant, commander of the Union armies:

Please read and answer this letter as though I was not President. My son, now in his twenty-second year, having graduated from Harvard, wishes to see something of the war before it ends. I do not wish him put in the ranks, nor yet give him a commission, to which those who have already served long are better entitled, and better qualified to hold. Could he, without embarrassment to you, or detriment to the service, go into your military family with some nominal rank, I, and not the public, furnishing his necessary means? If no, say so without the least hesitation, because I am as anxious and as deeply interested that you should not be encumbered as you can be yourself.[43]

Grant did not delay an answer; tearing off the blank part of Lincoln's note, he replied:

Your favor of this date in relation to your son serving in some military capacity is received. I will be most happy to have him in my military family in the manner you propose. The nominal rank given him is immaterial, but I would suggest that of captain, as I have three staff officers now, of considerable service, in no higher rank. Indeed, I have one officer with only the rank of lieutenant who has been in the service from the beginning of the war. This, however, will make no difference, and I would still say give the rank of captain.—Please excuse my writing on a half sheet. I have no resource but to take the blank half of your letter.

When General Grant made reference to the young officers on his staff, with rank no higher and even lower than he was so eager to bestow upon Robert Lincoln, one of those he had in mind was William Dunn who, in contrast to the President's son, ran away at sixteen to join the Union Army despite the objections of his father, the Judge Advocate General. The patriotism and determination of this youth must have been a topic of deep interest to General Grant after the Civil War had long ended, and he told his sons about it. Even at seventy, Jesse Grant recalled this young soldier: when President Lincoln issued his first call for volunteers Will Dunn was some few months over fifteen. He promptly left home and enlisted, and had served several months before his father located him and obtained his discharge. The youngster remained at home a few weeks, then ran away again and re-enlisted. Every effort was made to locate him, but more than a year elapsed and the boy had served through an arduous campaign, before he was again found. Grant told him he was to be discharged and sent home. Young Dunn faced the commander unflinchingly: "You can discharge me, General," he said, "but I'll find a way to get back. Nothing is going to keep me out of this war." Grant transferred him to his own staff and, after four years of service, he was a captain.[44] With this young officer near him, General Grant wrote his reply to President Lincoln urging a captaincy for Robert!

On February 17, 1865, Abraham Lincoln signed the commission which appointed Robert "Assistant Adjutant General of Volunteers with the rank of Captain." [45] Until his father's assassination, less than two months later, the President's son divided his time between Grant's headquarters and the White House in Washington. He did manage to be at camp around Petersburg, and at Appomattox to witness the surrender of Robert E. Lee. His name was carried on the Army rolls until June 20, when he resigned. It was these four months in uniform to which newspapers in the North, eager to advance his popularity,

Executive Mansion,

Washington, Jan 19th, 1865.

Lieut General Grant:

Please read and answer this letter as though I was not President, but only a friend— My son, now in his twenty-second year, having graduated at Harvard, wishes to see something of the war before it ends. I do not wish to put him in the ranks, nor yet to give him a commission, to which those who have already served long, are better entitled, and better qualified to hold. Could he, without embarrassment to you, or detriment to the service, go into your Military family with some nominal rank, I, and not the public, furnishing his necessary means? If no, say so without the least hesitation, because I am as anxious & as deeply interested, that you shall not be encumbered, as you can be yourself—

Yours truly

A. Lincoln.

A PRESIDENT ASKS RANK FOR HIS SON

The immortal Lincoln suggested that General Grant appoint Robert Lincoln an officer on his staff. (*Papers of John G. Nicolay*, Library of Congress) referred as "Robert Lincoln's distinguished service as an Army officer." [46] When his father's secretaries, Nicolay and Hay, wrote their monumental biography of Abraham Lincoln they bound themselves to submit to Robert for deletion or change every sentence of their work, and they were extremely desirous to portray Robert in the most favorable light; but all they ventured to write was, "The President's son therefore became a member of Grant's staff with the rank of captain, and acquitted himself of the duties of that station with fidelity and honor." [47]

Robert had come to Washington with General Grant on the morning of April 14, 1865; that night he was chatting at the White House when, just seven blocks away at Ford's Theater, the fanatical actor John Wilkes Booth fired the fatal bullets into Abraham Lincoln.[48] It was the destiny of Robert Todd Lincoln to be near the scene of every assassination of an American President. When Garfield and McKinley were assassinated he was not far away. Possibly these tragic events dimmed for him the lustre of the Presidency and prompted him to exclaim in later years, "It seems difficult for the average American to understand that it is possible for anyone not to desire the Presidency, but I most certainly do not." [49]

Shortly after his father's funeral, Robert T. Lincoln hurried to Chicago and there entered a prominent law firm, being formally admitted to the Illinois bar in 1867. Within a year the press reported that "Mr. Lincoln has a lucrative practice in the courts." [50] In September, 1868, he married Mary Harlan, the only daughter of the Senator from Iowa. The wedding was very private, at the Washington home of the bride's father, and was conspicuous by the absence of many prominent men or old family friends. Mrs. Lincoln, although her husband had been dead for nearly four years, was attired in severe black and without any jewelry. The wedding had been planned for a later date, but Robert's mother, with the impulsiveness and restlessness which had already become characteristic of her unbalanced mind, had suddenly decided to sail for Europe.[51] A special car, attached to the noon train, took the couple to New York on the morning after the wedding; Mary Todd Lincoln and little Tad accompanied them. Robert and his wife returned to Chicago, and there became the parents of three children, one of them a boy who died in London at the age of seventeen. This son, though christened Abraham Lincoln II, was always called "Jack" by his father; there was a legend that Robert had told his offspring not to use his grandfather's illustrious name until the boy's own deeds became worthy of the appellation "Abraham Lincoln." [52]

In 1876, Robert Lincoln was elected supervisor of the southern section of Chicago.[53] This was the only public office he ever held by virtue of the votes of his fellow citizens. Robert devoted himself to the practice of law until 1881, becoming not only the legal counsel of very large corporations but also a director or official of many prominent companies, among them the Pullman Company. In that year he entered the Cabinet of James A. Garfield, and upon Garfield's death he continued under Chester Arthur in the same post of Secretary of War. Robert Lincoln had been chosen a delegate to the Republican National Convention in 1880, but he yielded his seat to the son of his father's famous rival, and Stephen A. Douglas, Jr., became the delegate. The son of Abraham Lincoln did not possess the inspiring personality which had won for his father fervent popular support; and it is probable that it was not excessive modesty, but the realization that he could not win the votes of his fellow countrymen, that made him reluctant to seek elective office. But, in the eighteen-eighties, memories of the Civil War were still vivid and Abraham Lincoln's role in it still revived memories or awakened awe and reverence; political manipulators in the Republican Party capitalized the Lincoln name, and some urged that Robert Todd Lincoln become a Presidential candidate. His name was presented to the party convention in 1880, and he received four votes.

Four years later, agitation was renewed for the nomination of the eldest son of the slain President. The New York *World* led the opposition; in virile editorials the famed Joseph Pulitzer denounced the selection of candidates because their fathers had been occupants of the White House. "True democracy recognizes no claims of birth or name," exclaimed the *World*, "the merits of the man, not the accident of his ancestry, should be the passport to positions of public trust under a republican government. But rotten Republicanism has learned to revere things that savor of monarchy and aristocracy. It would transmit the Presidency as their fathers' successors to crowns." [54] Regarding Robert's capabilities, the journal insisted that "no one claims that young Lincoln ever uttered a word or performed a solitary act showing superior ability, character or fitness to entitle him to the Chief Magistracy of the Republic. . . . Robert Todd Lincoln is the son of his father . . . a candidate for his name only."

But abstract ethics did not deter the professional politicians. With the approach of the 1888 national campaign they again appraised the fame of the Civil War President, and considered Robert T. Lincoln as their candidate for the office of President of the United States.[55] Again the press debated the wisdom of nominating this President's son, his abilities and his accomplishments. "It is curious how some papers hang on to the name of young Lincoln in discussing Presidential possibilities," exclaimed a Nebraska newspaper. "There is more sentiment than sense in the suggestion. There are a hundred men in Omaha his superior. He is simply a cipher in the name. When Abraham Lincoln died the ciphers in his family were left without a figure to the front." [56] There were contrary views about Robert's abilities. "The principal objections likely to be raised against Robert Lincoln are that he is young, has not been in Congress, is not especially noted save as the son of an illustrious father," conceded a Vermont journal; but it considered this President's son a promising candidate because he had made no political enemies among party leaders, had antagonized no segment of the voting population.[57]

An important factor in the calculations of the Republican politicos was the "colored vote," particularly in several important Northern states where the Democrats had lately been victorious; in these close states the Negroes might cast the decisive ballots. "In popular estimation there is much in a name," observed a Negro editor, "one of the few immortal names is that of Lincoln. The second name of Lincoln is associated in the popular mind with all that is grand, heroic and patriotic in this country, and with the integrity of the Union and the preservation of the Government—Robert T. Lincoln. Again we say hurrah for the delegates who have declared for Bob Lincoln for President. He is a worthy, noble and distinguished son—Robert T. Lincoln." [58] The white Atlanta *National* spoke more pointedly: "From the mountains to the seaboard, from the lakes to the gulf, in city and hamlet, every colored man, woman and child would leave an old-time camp meeting shouting for Abraham Lincoln's great, worthy, and illustrious son. With Robert Lincoln as the nominee we will go into the fight with an unbroken front, a united party." [59]

Of course, Robert T. Lincoln heard of these proposals. He was outspoken in his refusal to accept a nomination for the Vice-Presidency. But, as regarded his selection for the high place his father had held, Robert indulged in what our generation has come to term "double talk." In an interview he spurned the Vice-Presidency as too great a sacrifice of his business activities, and similarly expressed indifference for the Presidency both because he regarded his chances as meager and also because he considered the office too arduous. Said he:

I simply could not accept the nomination to the Vice-Presidency. To take any office at all would be a great sacrifice to business interests. I most certainly should not accept the nomination of the Vice-Presidency were it tendered.

As to being a candidate for the Presidency, I regret the use of my name in connection with any public office whatever. It seems difficult for the average American to understand that it is possible for anyone not to desire the Presidency, but I most certainly do not. I have seen enough of the inside of Washington official life to have lost all interest for it.

The Presidential office is but a gilded prison. Its cares and worries outweigh the honor which surrounds the position. I don't think there's any likelihood of my receiving the nomination. The men who make the ticket would hardly do so without exacting certain pledges, and those pledges I would not give.[60]

Although he expressed a dislike of public office, Robert Lincoln continued to hold the post of Secretary of War until March, 1885, when a Democratic President, Grover Cleveland, succeeded Chester A. Arthur and the latter's Cabinet ended with his retirement. Robert then returned to his activities as counsel for corporations. But four years later another Republican, Benjamin Harrison, was elected to the Presidency, and Robert T. Lincoln was appointed Minister to Great Britain. George Frisbie Hoar, the eminent statesman, who knew Robert Lincoln while the latter was Secretary of War, entertained a high opinion of Robert's ability; when President Benjamin Harrison asked his appraisal of Robert Lincoln as the prospective Minister to England, he told the Chief Executive that Robert "was a very modest man indeed, never pressing any claim to public consideration or office, either on his own account or as his father's son, and never seeking responsibility. But I noticed that when he had anything to say or anything to do, he always said or did the wisest and best thing to be said or done under the circumstances." [61] But the two Senators from Robert's State of Illinois did not share this liking for him. In fact, they bitterly opposed the appointment; the resentment against President Harrison led one Senator to oppose Harrison's nomination to succeed himself and in the subsequent election Illinois voted against Harrison. Robert Lincoln's career as Minister to England ended with the close of Harrison's term in 1893.

But while these honors were heaped upon him, Robert Todd Lincoln experienced also great sorrows. His brother Tad had died; his son "Jack" had passed away just upon the verge of manhood; and his mother, the widow of Abraham Lincoln, had become insane and doctors advised that she be placed in a sanitarium. In Illinois, as in most states, the law required a strict inquest to determine insanity, and these proceedings were public. In 1875 a jury declared Mary Todd Lincoln insane, and she was confined in a private institution. In her lucid moments she felt a deep grief that Robert had consented to this designation of her as a lunatic, and once she voiced her surprise and resentment. Robert was censured for his failure to keep the legal proceedings secret; and he protested, in justification, that he could not control the legal mandates which required that his mother's insanity be proved in open court. He wrote to a friend: "Some of my Eastern friends have criticized the public proceedings in court, which seemed to them unnecessary. Against it there was no help, for we have a statute in this State which imposes a very heavy penalty on any one depriving an insane person of his liberty without the verdict of a jury. The expression of surprise at my action which was telegraphed East was the first and last expression of the kind she has uttered, and we are on the best of terms." [62] A year later, Mary Todd Lincoln was declared sane, and again sought forgetfulness in the changing scenes of European travel, seeking escape from the world's knowledge that she had been adjudged a demented woman. When she returned to the United States, she hid herself from friends. She died in 1882.

Robert Lincoln continued to increase his worldly wealth. He bought a large estate in Vermont and there found relief from the inquiring public which was curious about this son of a great President. Rarely did he appear at public functions, and seldom did he join in ceremonies honoring his father's memory. He did attend the dedication of the Lincoln Memorial in Washington and remained a short while at the unveiling of a monument in Kentucky.[63] But, though he toured the European continent and visited shrines in the Old World, he never journeyed to the farm where his father spent his boyhood. He had rounded out a most successful career in law and finance by becoming the president of the Pullman Company in 1897; he had now become a recognized member of that inner group of financiers and business leaders who symbolized the wealth and power of the United States; wherever such men of money and power met, Robert Todd Lincoln, son of the sixteenth President, was a welcome guest.

When, in the spring of 1902, the brother of the Emperor of Germany, Prince Henry of Prussia, visited New York a breakfast was given in his honor—attendance restricted to the foremost financiers and business potentates in the United States. A little booklet, bound in white leather, listed the names of the guests, and gave a brief biography of each, stressing his dominance in his particular field of commerce and the tremendous influences wielded by him either as an employer of huge numbers of workers, as controller of vast amounts of capital, or as director of a corporation of great earning power. Entitled "Captains of Industry," it was a memento for Prince Henry to remind him, upon his return to the *Vaterland*, that these were the men who directed the destinies of the United States of America. Among the names listed in this catalogue of prominent and influential Americans was that of "Robert T. Lincoln, Chicago, Illinois," and his important status among Captains of Industry was noted: "President of the Pullman Company. Its business is carried on over nearly every railway line in the United States, the operations covering, in 1901, 165,283 of railway miles, and the mileage of cars being 335,742,267. The number of passengers carried was 9,618,438."[64] In Chicago, through lanes of applauding thousands, Robert rode in an open carriage with Prince Henry when the latter went to lay a wreath on the Emancipator's statue.[65]

Thus the eldest son of Abraham Lincoln, sixteenth President of the United States, rose to high place—without the travail and disappointments which marked the life of his illustrious father. He had no need to overcome many obstacles to reach public office; successes in life came easily to Robert Todd Lincoln. Without risking the dangers of the battlefield, without service or exertion, he became Assistant Adjutant General of the Army. Without completing a law course he obtained membership in an outstanding law firm. Without any experience in military science he was appointed Secretary of War. Without any knowledge of diplomacy he became Minister to Great Britain. In these influential positions he undoubtedly drew to himself men of ability and prominence, and probably had close friends.

But he did not arouse the devotion which his father inspired. Those who had known him from boyhood spoke of him in terms lacking both in affection and in great admiration,[66] and others expressed bitterness. His father's old law partner, William Herndon, disliked both Robert and his mother, saying that "Robert has his mother's insane temper without his father's discretion. . . . He is a Todd not a Lincoln. . . . I have a tender feeling for the man, first because of the 'boy,' and second, on account of his father; yet I say Bob is a 'little wee of a man.' "[67] It is probable that this appraisal was colored by Herndon's resentment of Robert Lincoln's efforts to prevent Herndon from revealing episodes in Abraham Lincoln's career which the son did not wish to see published.[68] But even where there was complete absence of ill-will toward Robert—where there was intent to accord him favorable notice—the commendation was restrained. A typical example is the comment by Gideon Welles, who served as Secretary of the Navy under Abraham Lincoln and, in after years, was in frequent contact with Robert; it was at the home of Welles that Robert courted the girl who became his wife. Yet, in Welles' diary there is but a single sentence of faint praise: "Robert Lincoln was married today. . . . His deportment and character then as always, impressed one favorably."[69]

How limited had become the popular interest in and esteem for Robert Todd Lincoln was reflected in the attitude of the nation's newspapers when he died, at the age of eighty-two, in the summer of 1926. Although the press associations sent out the report of his death and a résumé of his career, comparatively few papers printed the news. A few journals, in the cities where Robert had been active, published short reviews of his life, or voiced editorial comment. Most of the papers relegated an abbreviated press dispatch to the sixth, eighth, or fifteenth page.[70] The extremely few journals which regarded the passing of the President's son as of sufficient interest to their readers to warrant editorial comment interpreted Robert Lincoln's reluctance to mingle with the "common people" as an indication of his refusal to capitalize on the prestige of his famous father. Said the Chicago *Tribune,* "Robert Todd Lincoln had no more distinguishing characteristic than his refusal to trade on the greatness of his parent, in spite of which his career was noteworthy, for he attained positions of trust and power." [71] This opinion was shared by the St. Louis *Post Dispatch,* which declared that "it was a difficult heritage to which Robert Todd Lincoln was born. As the son of Abraham Lincoln he necessarily lived in the shadow of overpowering greatness. Nobody will claim for him that he inherited his father's genius. But he did inherit a liberal complement of admirable qualities—good ability, industry, a fine sense of proportion, a rare degree of personal charm." [72]

Perhaps the keenest appraisal of the eldest son of Abraham Lincoln was the short obituary in the columns of a Texas paper—the San Antonio *Express:* "There was a contrast in the characters of father and son: Robert Todd Lincoln inherited Abraham Lincoln's melancholy, brooding nature without his occasional relaxation in fun and his keen relish for sprightly humor. The son was not a born crusader and had little talent for mingling with his fellows; rather, he was exceedingly shy and shrank from contacts. The mother's aristocracy dominated the father's native democracy in his makeup." [73]

9

Sons of Andrew Johnson

On the morning of April 15, 1865, in his rooms at the Kirkwood House in Washington, Andrew Johnson repeated the oath administered by the Chief Justice of the United States and became President in succession to the assassinated Lincoln.

Andrew Johnson had been in public life for thirty-five years, beginning in 1830 as the mayor of a town in the mountains of Tennessee. In 1835, at the age of twenty-seven, he became a member of the House of Representatives of that State. He was re-elected in 1837 and 1839, and two years later the voters made him a member of the upper house of the State Legislature. To this office he was re-elected four successive times, serving until 1853, when the people of Tennessee made him Governor. They kept him in the Governor's chair until 1857, and then they sent him to Washington as the Senator from Tennessee in the Congress of the United States.[1] The legislation he sponsored was constructive; he was motivated by zeal to serve his country and not by eagerness to advance his own political fortunes; he fought to lighten the lives of the "forgotten men" of his times. His term in the Senate was during that crucial period when the slave-owning states threatened to withdraw from the Union unless they had assurance that neither Congress nor President would interfere with Negro slavery; the representatives in Congress from the South were outspoken in the prediction that, if Abraham Lincoln were victorious in the election of 1860, their states would secede. Andrew Johnson condemned this challenge to the Federal Government; he denounced those who counseled it.

Chief Justice Chase preserved the Bible upon which Johnson, becoming President, swore to "preserve the Constitution of the United States," and marked the spot where Johnson's lips touched the open page in token of his solemn covenant—it was the twenty-first verse of the eleventh chapter of Ezekiel: "But as for them whose heart walketh after the heart of their detestable things and their abominations, I will recompense their way upon their own heads, saith the Lord God." [2] This Biblical anathema epitomized Johnson's hatred, while he was still a Senator, of those who aided or acquiesced in the dissolution of the Union formed under the Constitution of 1789. Alone among the Senators from the Southern States he denounced the secession movement. In a fiery speech, a few days before Lincoln delivered his Inaugural Address on March 4, 1861, Johnson was so vehement in his castigation of those contemplating the dissolution of the Union that the New York *Post* regarded Lincoln's declaration as unimpressive in comparison, demanding, "Has he expressed himself even so decisively . . . as Andrew Johnson in the Senate?" [3]

It was not long before Lincoln recognized in this Southern statesman a great aid in keeping at least one "border state" from adding its military strength and productivity to the resources of the Confederacy.[4] Tennessee, by mandate of its Legislature, had held a special balloting to determine whether the people wanted to "separate" from the Union. An overwhelming vote was in favor of taking the step. Toward the end of June, 1861, the Governor of Tennessee had announced to the State Legislature that "the people of Tennessee, acting in their sovereign capacity, and in the exercise of their inalienable right have in the most solemn and deliberate manner dissolved their connection with the Government of the United States and, by the adoption of the Provisional Constitution of the Confederate States of America, have made Tennessee a member of that Government"; [5] on the 24th of June he issued a Proclamation "to make it known and declare all connection by the State of Tennessee with the Federal Union dissolved, and that Tennessee is a free, independent Government." [6] Gladly, on July 2, Jefferson Davis, President of the newly formed Confederate States, publicly announced "Tennessee a member of the Confederacy." There was little hope that this state could now be kept within the Federal Union. Abraham Lincoln turned to Andrew Johnson, appointing him Military Governor with the rank of brigadier general; and Johnson brought the State of Tennessee again under the control of the Government at Washington.[7]

When Lincoln was seeking a second Presidential term in 1864, he selected Andrew Johnson as his running mate. They were victorious in the ensuing election, and Johnson was inaugurated Vice-President on March 4, 1865. The North regarded him with respect and admiration, and the press echoed the praise of the New York *Times* that "in his highest position at home and in Washington Andrew Johnson was a man of frugal, economical habits. In this he was consistent with his early life as an industrious hard-working mechanic. . . . He had no professional training; was ambitious of none. He was never a lawyer. He was never a huckstering politician, . . . he was and is devoted to public service." [8]

No man who reached such high station ever had less promise at birth. Other men rose from modest beginnings, and overcame obstacles to achieve the Presidency; but, with the possible exception of Millard Fillmore, none who became President had trudged the path to the White House so painfully, so courageously, from a childhood of penury and illiteracy. Following the conspicuous greatness of Abraham Lincoln, accentuated by the drama of the Civil War and martyrdom by an assassin's bullet, Andrew Johnson dwelt in a shadow of public disdain and was faced with problems which Lincoln had not yet been forced to solve.

Unschooled, Andrew Johnson spent his boyhood in toil and want. For meager subsistence and scant clothes he became "indentured" to a tailor—his status being little more than that of a white slave. His lot was hard, and he ran away—his master advertised a reward for his return. He began life anew in Greeneville, Tennessee—earning a bare livelihood as a tailor. There still stands in that East Tennessee town the two-story brick house where he plied his trade; during the Civil War both Union and Confederate forces used it at different times as hospital, barracks, or cavalry headquarters. The cavalrymen would lead their horses in at the front-hall entrance and out, through the rear door, into the large lot behind the house. But, whether occupied by soldiers of the North or of the South, over the door of the building swung the signboard lettered: "A. Johnson—Tailor." [9]

It was in Greeneville that this unlettered tailor met a shoemaker's daughter, Eliza McCardle, who became his wife. With remarkable patience she taught him how to write, encouraged him to read. He never forgot these humble beginnings. When he had become President, friends in New York offered him a carriage and horses; knowing his scrupulous refusal to accept any courtesies from men likely to seek official favors, they "carefully excluded from the list of subscribers the names of politicians." [10] Still, Johnson declined the gift which the donors assured him was "a token of their high appreciation of his fidelity to the country," and the New York *Times* commented that "they were deeply impressed with his high concepts of public office." [11] And the House of Representatives, despite the increasing antagonism of its members, publicly praised him, passing a Resolution commending the action "affording an example to others, . . . with the unqualified approval of the House." [12]

There was a tradition in Tennessee that, while he was Governor, a political opponent posted placards around Nashville warning Andrew Johnson that he would shoot him on sight. Friends of the Governor gathered at his home to surround him when he went to the State Capitol. But he dismissed them, remarking, "No, gentlemen, if I am to be shot at, I want no man to be in the way of the bullet"; and he walked alone with cool deliberation through the streets.[13] But Johnson had more than physical courage, he possessed also that moral fearlessness which prompted him to risk the antagonism of powerful politicians. A Democrat before the Civil War, he supported Lincoln in his plans to maintain an undivided Union; a Southerner, he stood in opposition to the secession of the slaveholding states. And, when impeachment threatened to end his career as President, he defied the rabid Northerners because he believed it wrong to adopt their plan to punish further the Southern States after the War had ended.[14]

There were many, like his secretary, Frank Cowan, who were impressed with the grim severity of Andrew Johnson and observed that the grimness was not only personified in him but seemed to pervade the atmosphere about him.[15] A hard fate had molded him that way. A physical ailment brought him excruciating pain; the fierce hatred of ambitious politicians—determined to humiliate and to drive him from the Presidential chair—embittered him; the death of one son and the intemperance of another added still greater anguish to his troubled days. Yet neither family tragedies nor political defeats could mar his determination to achieve what he deemed right.[16]

In his rise to greatness, Andrew Johnson had the unfaltering encouragement, counsel, and devotion of the wife who inspired him to study and persevere. Eliza Johnson did not possess the brilliant intellect of Abigail Adams, nor the intriguing wit of Dolly Madison. Providence did not favor her with the distinguished ancestry of Lucy Webb Hayes nor endow her with the beauty of Letitia Tyler. Nevertheless, she did keep pace as her husband successively rose to higher public office; and with equal serenity she shared with Andrew Johnson his hardships, his disappointments, and his triumphs. In twenty-five years of happily married life there were born to Andrew and Eliza Johnson five children—three of them sons: Charles, in 1830; Robert, in 1834; and Andrew, in 1853.

At the outbreak of the Civil War, in 1861, Andrew Johnson was absent in Washington. His family was at Greeneville. Andrew, Jr., was attending school. Charles, educated in pharmacy and medicine, was a physician and also a partner in a drug store. Robert was a member of a law firm. President Lincoln appointed Johnson Military Governor of Tennessee, and the Confederates adjudged him a traitor, confiscating his property. The Southern troops had overrun East Tennessee, and ordered Mrs. Johnson, her daughters and the youngest son to leave Greeneville. Charles escaped to Nashville and there enlisted in the Union Army, as Assistant Surgeon in the regiment of the Middle Tennessee Infantry, and served throughout the war. Two weeks before Lee's surrender, Dr. Charles Johnson was riding a spirited horse to camp when the animal reared and Charles was killed. The accounts of the accident are confused and conflicting; one relating that he was thrown from the horse, the other story asserting that the horse fell on him.[17] The editorials in all the papers described him as an educated and generous man, with many friends. His funeral cortege was escorted by his own infantry regiment and also by the cavalry regiment commanded by his brother Robert.[18]

Robert was twenty-seven at the beginning of the War between the States. He was an uncompromising "Southern Unionist"; and delivered stirring speeches against secession. He had been a member of the State Legislature. At the first call for men to put down what the North regarded as "rebellion," Robert had organized an infantry regiment of volunteers, and was commissioned a colonel. The men were ill-fed, poorly equipped, and badly clothed. Colonel Robert Johnson entreated the superior military authorities to help; he wanted to change the regiment from infantry to cavalry. Again and again we read his despairing pleas on behalf of the horde of nondescript men, proud of being soldiers in the Union cause. "My men are exiled from home," he wrote to the Adjutant—"have never received any pay: my Official Instructions have been intercepted from the Secretary of War changing my Regiment from Infantry to Cavalry. I have been in the Mountains for three months—my men are naked, hatless and shoeless;—in the name of Heaven can you not

My men are exiles from their homes—
have never received any pay;— my Official Instruct-
-ions have been intercepted from the Secretary
of War changing my Regiment from Infantry
into Cavalry. I have been in the Mountains for
3 months— my men are naked, hatless and shoeless;—
in the name of Heaven can you not relieve them?
Answer me at this or whatever point our Brigade
may be ordered.

Robert A Johnson
Col. Comdg.
4th Regt. Tenn. Vols.

A PRESIDENT'S SON PLEADS FOR HIS REGIMENT

Robert A. Johnson, eldest son of the President who succeeded Lincoln, organized a regiment to fight for the Union cause. In this letter he pleaded for supplies for his "naked, hatless and shoeless" recruits. (*Johnson Papers,* Library of Congress)

relieve them?" [19] To his father, from Camp Spears, near Portland, Ohio, he wrote a lengthier description of the hardships borne by his men: "After a toilsome march of 18 days from Cumberland Gap through a dry, sandy and wilderness country we arrived at this place on the 5th inst. and are now encamped without tents, clothes or anything else. . . . There is satisfaction in having the best and largest Regiment in this Division of the Army. The men, without exception, love and respect me, and will follow wherever I lead, and will have no other commander, and what I say for them to do—they will do, with cheerfulness, but will not submit to any other officer." [20] Colonel Robert Johnson was proud that his men were so attached to him, and there is ample proof that he did not misjudge their devotion. There still exists a smudged petition drawn up by the officers of his regiment when they heard he was planning to resign. No army officer ever was accorded a more impressive declaration of confidence. Dated July 26, 1862, and interspersed with erasures and corrections, it reflects the deep feeling of those who penned it:

Dear Colonel—It being announced to us that you intend to resign your command as Col. of this Regiment, We the undersigned being perfectly satisfied with you as our Commander and fully and heartily endorsing your entire past conduct as our Commander, We the undersigned officers composing your command asks you in tones of love and kindness and in view of future oppression, usurpation and acts of Tyranny to hold your Commission as Colonel of this regiment, believing as we confidentially do that not only the officers but the entire private [corps] are perfectly Satisfied with your past Strict adhearance to your Military duty, Lenity and kindness to all of us as your Subordinates. We ask you only to remain as our Commander and we feel perfectly relieved of all future Acts of oppression.[21]

These hardy mountaineers from Tennessee had experienced the kindliness and consideration of Robert Johnson, and they were fearful that another commanding officer might prove arbitrary and indifferent to their needs.

The letters which Robert wrote to his father and the reports which he made to the higher military authorities are catalogues of the difficulties which beset him. Andrew Johnson, then Military Governor of Tennessee, tried to help his son to obtain arms and equipment for the infantry regiment which was Robert's first command, and later, horses for the cavalry brigade which his son was organizing. And when Robert despaired because the Washington authorities let the months pass by without responding to his pleas, Andrew Johnson wired him, "Do your duty, and all will come out all right."

Robert's concern for his soldiers did not manifest itself merely in communications to the War Department, or in the letters to his father; he made material contributions to the regiment. When a bugler was needed, Colonel Johnson and his staff raised a fund to engage one, but Robert gave ten times as much as any other officer.[22] When privates, unpaid for long periods, made purchases in towns near their camp, the merchants called upon Colonel Johnson to satisfy their claims; when a burial suit was supplied for an officer, the clothier asked Robert to pay because he "had no one else to look to."[23]

For four years Robert Johnson was tireless in organizing, equipping, and training recruits. In August, 1865, he resigned his colonel's commission and came to Washington to become his father's private secretary. He devoted himself wholeheartedly to the White House tasks, and his burden was increased by numerous appeals from former members of his regiment for jobs and aid—his reply always was that "he would not forget a friend." Gideon Welles, then Secretary of the Navy, noted in his diary that Robert began drinking in the spring of 1866, resuming a habit he had acquired in earlier years; he says that the President was deeply concerned about his son, and requested Welles to confer with the White House physician regarding means of remedying Robert's weakness. The diary relates a number of conversations of Welles with the doctor, and talks with Andrew Johnson. The physician attributed the infirmity to Robert's sociability and friendly disposition; Welles says that Robert himself had spoken of his intemperance in a manner that aroused sympathy in his behalf. The doctor believed that he could be cured, but Welles did not share this hope. In March, 1866, it was decided to send Robert on a long sea voyage.[24] A cruise was being planned to the East Indies, and it was arranged with Secretary of State Seward to assign to Robert the task of investigating the slave trade at the Cape of Good Hope and on the African coast. There were many conferences, and repeated changes in the original itinerary of the vessel which was to take Robert on the proposed mission. Months dragged by, and finally Robert refused to accept the assignment that had been offered him.

Either the alarm felt by Welles was unduly exaggerated or the President's son managed to control or conceal from the public his insobriety; there is ample evidence that, in the succeeding months, Robert Johnson was giving close attention to his secretarial tasks, and numerous documents addressed to him by various Government bureaus make reference to conversations between him and officials.[25] We have, too, the comments of an observant press in Washington: the *Star*, a critical newspaper, editorialized, a year after Gideon Welles made his diary notation, that the White House secretariat, headed by Robert Johnson, was alert and efficient. Said the *Star*, "More courteous, or more intelligent officers could not readily be found, as all appreciate who have business to transact at the White House." [26] The paper commented that "the only possible fault to be found" was that ladies claimed that Colonel Robert Johnson and his assistant "perversely, obstinately, and most unreasonably, shy, shirk, and dodge the matrimonial harness" and it called upon "Col. Johnson . . . to attend to this matter." [27]

Andrew Johnson's term as President ended in March, 1869. He returned to Greeneville, and again plunged into politics. In the third week of April the ex-President was touring the State delivering speeches, and when the train pulled in at the little town of Decatur, Tennessee, he was greeted with great cheers. He did not deliver the scheduled talk; a telegram was handed him announcing the sudden death, at Greeneville, of his son Robert.[28]

The newspapers of Tennessee praised the good qualities of Colonel Robert Johnson, his sincerity, his courage, and his loyalty. "He had his faults and his weaknesses, like other men," editorialized the Nashville *Banner,* "but he was ever generous and chivalrous, a true friend." [29] But some could not repress their hate of the father: the Chicago *Post,* in reporting Robert's death, commented that "the devil came for the old man, and not finding him, took the son," to which the New York *Times* retorted, "We suppose the *Post* considers this smart. It is cruel and cowardly." [30]

Andrew Johnson's youngest son and namesake, Andrew Johnson, Jr., grew to manhood after his father had left the Presidency. He was an ambitious young man, extremely fond of his father and eager to measure up to the ex-President's expectations of him. His letters to Andrew Johnson are filled with affectionate terms. We find him writing on the first day of 1873, sending his father belated birthday greetings with the comment, "Your birthday just passed, completing sixty-five years of a life devoted to the interest of the people, who seem little to appreciate it"; and he closes the letter with "My fervent, heartfelt wishes for your success, and believe me to be devotedly your son." He tells his father of his own New Year's resolutions: "I am resolved upon changing some things if I do others worse. One of the things I intend to do, is to apply myself diligently to my books and make something of myself. It's true I have rather exalted ideas of what I *can* do, but I believe to aim too high and miss the mark is better than to aim too low and hit." [31]

He does make some progress, and develops a taste for books; we find him writing, eleven months later, "I have not got myself down to earnest hard work yet as I have been fixing my things up. I have been reading however every day, and to my surprise find I read with more understanding than I could have first expected."[32]

At the beginning of 1874 he returned to the family home at Greeneville. His father was then touring the State as a candidate for the United States Senate, and Andrew, Jr., writes him advice on the ex-President's plans; he tells his father to make a deal with his most potent rival. "Select your strongest opponent," writes Andrew, Jr., "and offer your influence for him four years hence."[33] Andrew, Jr., has now embarked upon a career of journalism, organizing a new paper, the Greeneville *Intelligencer;* and he writes his father of his ambitions and his hopes to outstrip the rival newspaper, the *American.* "I am determined the *Intelligencer* shall be a paper when the *American* is no more, . . . our circulation is steadily increasing and we hope by the 1st Jan'y, '76 to have a circulation of at least three if not five thousand. I know you will smile when you read this, but perseverance and hard work have accomplished more than this from equally as small beginnings."[34]

Andrew Johnson, Jr., was twenty-one years old when he blossomed out as a newspaper man, and his head was filled with many novel and aggressive plans. To dealers in organs, pianos, and sewing machines he arranged to give advertising space in return for these much wanted pieces of furniture, which he intended to give as premiums to persons obtaining 75 to 150 subscriptions for the *Intelligencer.* The newspaper was a weekly, and Andrew Johnson, Jr., was proud that he had 800 subscribers within less than three months. In the ninth issue he published an announcement to the merchants of Greeneville: "Advertisers take notice—this is only the 9th issue of the *Intelligencer,* and it can boast of 800 actual subscribers, and 1000 circulation. Subscribers coming in every day. 2000 copies will be issued on Friday the 25th, the last day of the County Fair, and distributed gratuitously."[35] One of the columns on the front page of the *Intelligencer* blazoned the merits of the paper:

> Now is the time to subscribe for a LIVE, WIDE-AWAKE, PROGRESSIVE newspaper. No pains shall be spared to make it the WEEKLY JOURNAL of East Tennessee, and fully up to the movements of the Political World.

ITS COLUMNS

shall be devoted to the discussion and presentation of those subjects which most nearly affect the general welfare and prosperity of our people.

ITS EDITORIAL COLUMNS

shall be interesting and valuable, because containing nothing but matters of vital importance to local or national interests.

ITS LOCAL DEPARTMENT

shall not be excelled. It shall be one of NEWS and VIVACIOUS reading matter. Its News, Literary and Agricultural Columns shall be replete with interesting and valuable information to The Family,

The Housewife,
The Mechanic,
The Farmer and
Patron of Husbandry.[36]

We have no data to tell us to what extent the *Intelligencer* outstripped its rival, the *American;* but we do know that the paper of Andrew Johnson, Jr., continued only until 1876, and that the competing newspaper, consolidated with another, likewise had an early demise.[37] During its brief career Andrew's paper recorded family triumphs and family tragedies. Ex-President Andrew Johnson, adored by this son, was elected to the United States Senate in 1875. He did not live to be sworn in as a member; on the last day of July in that year he died. Of the Johnson family only Andrew, Jr., and two sisters remained. In the summer of 1878, they erected a monument to the honor of their illustrious sire.[38]

Andrew survived his father four years. He had married, but left no children. He was buried near the tomb of his father and two brothers.

Thus ended the careers of the sons of Andrew Johnson, seventeenth President of the United States. They did not reach the high station he had attained, but in their hours of frustration and tragedy, each of them could say with justice what Andrew Johnson had written a few short years before his own death, when he was stricken with cholera:

All seems gloom and despair. I have performed my duty to my God, my country, and my family. I have nothing to fear. Approaching death to me is the mere shadow of God's protecting wing. Beneath it I almost feel sacred. Here I know no evil can come; there I will rest in quiet and peace, beyond the reach of calumny's poisoned shaft, the influence of envy and jealous enemies, where treason and traitors in State, backsliders and hypocrites in Church, can have no place, where the great fact will be realized that God is truth, and gratitude is the highest attribute of man.[39]

10

Sons of Ulysses S. Grant

Ulysses S. Grant, President from 1869 to 1877, was "a jack of all trades and a master of none"—until Destiny set the stage for the role in which he excelled. He had no distinguished ancestors to give him the glamour of inherited prestige, and his parents acquired no great wealth to afford him pampering comforts on a college campus. His grandfather, Captain Noah Grant, had endured the privations of a soldier in the Revolutionary War; rich only in progeny, he settled first in Pennsylvania, then migrated to Ohio. His second son, Jesse, mastered the trade of tanner, married a farmer's daughter, built a small cabin of wood, and became the father of three sons, the second being christened Hiram Ulysses Grant.

This boy, known as Ulysses S. Grant, forty-seven years later became the Chief Executive of the United States. He was not the only American President who became famous under a name different than that given by his parents at the baptismal font—Stephen Grover Cleveland was inaugurated as Grover Cleveland, Thomas Woodrow Wilson entered the White House as Woodrow Wilson, and John Calvin Coolidge became President Calvin Coolidge.[1] Hiram Ulysses Grant foresaw that the initials "H. U. G." would arouse merriment; he himself transposed the given name to Ulysses Hiram Grant. But his Congressman, appointing him to West Point, put his name upon the official records as Ulysses Simpson Grant. Eagerly, the youth adopted that appellation.[2]

In his boyhood Ulysses S. Grant worked on the farm which his father cultivated to supplement the insufficient income from his tanner's trade. Between father and son there was a strong attachment and Ulysses continued to rely on his father's judgment even after he himself had sons, writing to his father regularly for counsel.[3] Jesse Grant did not let plowing and chores on the farm interfere with the boy's education; Ulysses was encouraged to attend school and acquired the academic requirements which qualified him to enter the United States Military Academy when he was seventeen. In June, 1843, he graduated, and obtained a lieutenant's commission in the regular Army. Grant was always proud of his West Point training; when he had a son of his own he sent him to that military academy, and even for his grandson he planned a West Point career: shortly before his death Ulysses S. Grant penned a note to some future President of the United States requesting that, when his son's son reached the required age, an appointment be given him to the institution where the grandfather had learned the science of war.[4]

Upon completion of his studies at West Point, he was ordered to Jefferson Barracks at St. Louis. A few miles distant was the home of a West Point roommate and, upon one of his visits to his friend's home, Grant met a sister, Julia Dent, then seventeen. "After that I do not know but my visits became more frequent; they certainly did become more enjoyable," he tells us in his *Personal Memoirs*. The couple went on long walks, or on horseback to visit neighbors; with a brother or younger sister accompanying them as chaperon.[5] Julia Dent never overcame the tradition that it was improper for unmarried women to go about unescorted by some relative; when her own daughter was grown, the rule was still enforced. Her son Jesse Grant tells us that "to Mother it was unthinkable that sister should go out in the evening, no matter who constituted the party, unless also accompanied by a male of the family." [6] When his regiment, during one of his furloughs, was transferred to Louisiana, Grant on horseback rushed to see his sweetheart; the stream he had to cross was swollen by sudden rains, but he swam to the opposite bank despite a strong current, and reached the Dent home soaked. But his romantic ardor was not dampened; he proposed to Julia Dent, and she accepted. This was in May, 1844. It was not until four years later that they were married.

In 1846, the United States resorted to war to force from Mexico the recognition of the Rio Grande as the boundary of Texas. Ulysses Grant joined the army of General Zachary Taylor, who later became the twelfth President of the United States. At that old commander's side was his son, Richard Taylor, who was, in years to come, to oppose Grant on the battlefields of the Civil War—Grant as the commander in chief of the Union forces, Dick Taylor as the last Confederate general to surrender. Long after the end of the Civil War, when Richard Taylor was appraising the leading personalities in that struggle, he recalled his impressions of Grant in the Mexican War, saying that he remembered him "as a modest, amicable, but by no means promising lieutenant in a marching regiment."[7]

At the end of the Mexican War, in 1848, Grant married Julia Dent. They set up housekeeping, but their home was disrupted when Grant, then a captain, was ordered to the Pacific coast, then to Panama, and forced to leave wife and child. Away from home, Grant became a heavy drinker. In 1854 he resigned; it was the whim of fate that the Secretary of War who approved the resignation was Jefferson Davis who, seven years later, became President of the seceding Southern States. It was to be Grant's lot to command the Northern armies which ended the Southern Confederacy. Grant found himself stranded in San Francisco with no place to sleep, no food to appease his hunger, and no cash to procure transportation to his home in the East. In desperation he went to the office of the Army quartermaster, and the diary of the officer then in charge describes his penury and discouragement. Late one evening, as the office was closing, a captain inquired for the quartermaster; he wanted cash for an Army warrant of forty dollars, for services on a court martial. The certificate was incorrectly drawn and virtually void. The stranger asked permission to sleep on the old lounge in the office, announcing that he had not a cent to his name, either for lodging or food.[8] The applicant was Ulysses S. Grant—destined, with passing years, to become President of the United States. Cash was advanced and Grant obtained steamer passage home—in the steerage.

Rejoining his family in St. Louis, he tried various means to earn a livelihood. He failed in farming, was unsuccessful as a real estate agent. He applied for a teaching position at West Point, but another was appointed; his hope for a post as county engineer was unrealized; and he was equally unsuccessful when he attempted to obtain a clerkship in the custom house. He went back to Galena, Illinois, to clerk in his father's store, but no great success was his. Thus, in the nine years since he had left the Army Ulysses S. Grant shifted from one trade to another; and, even with the assistance of his father and father-in-law, was unable to earn the means necessary to support a family which had grown to two daughters and three sons. The year 1861 found Grant in St. Louis, Missouri, despairing of success, and writing to his father in Illinois for advice regarding his contemplated plans to move to the parental home.

Then came the Civil War, and Abraham Lincoln called for volunteers to overcome the armies of the seceding states in the South. Grant was not among those who responded with spontaneity. He wrote to his father for counsel, realizing that the growing cleavage in opinion and action would soon make it necessary for him to take sides in the conflict. He felt, too, as he had been trained at West Point at Government expense, it was proper that he should re-enter the Army now that there was need for qualified officers. So he wrote to the Adjutant General in Washington: "Having served for fifteen years in the regular Army, including four years at West Point, and feeling it the duty of every one who has been educated at the Government expense to offer their services for the support of that Government." [9] He expressed the belief that, in view of his age and length of service, he was competent to command a regiment. By the time he decided to enter the Army, the ranks of the volunteers were already filled. However, the Governor of the State called Grant to muster in the trained troops; and once again Ulysses S. Grant was an officer in the Army of the United States. It cannot be said that he was prompted by a crusader's zeal to free the slaves; in fact, Ulysses S. Grant had himself been very willing to profit by the system: his father-in-law gave to Grant's wife a young boy, and we find Grant writing to his father that here was a chance for him to sell the lad's services for three dollars a month, and more when he grew older.[10] Grant at that time had no deep-rooted social or political philosophy; probably his concept of soldiering was summed up in his proclamation to the citizens of Paducah when, as commanding general of the army capturing that city, he announced, "I have nothing to do with opinions, I shall deal only with armed rebellion." [11]

As a brigadier general in 1861 and 1862, his record was one of alternating small victories and somewhat larger defeats; but in the following year his military skill was crowned with a momentous success, and his capture of Vicksburg on July 4, 1863, moved Lincoln to appoint Ulysses S. Grant commander in chief of all the Union forces.[12] Now, undisputed master of his own concepts of strategy, Grant speedily conquered the Confederate forces; Robert E. Lee surrendered at Appomattox, and the other Southern generals laid down arms within a few months. Ulysses S. Grant was hailed the savior of the Nation.[13] The Republican Party nominated him for the Presidency; he was elected in 1868 and re-elected for another term in 1872. Inherently honest, Grant did not suspect the schemes of the calculating men about him, and his Administration was a heyday of political corruption and fraud. Similarly, as we shall see, after he ceased to be Chief Executive wily financial manipulators made use of his name and fame, intriguing him into Wall Street ventures in which he lost all the material wealth which he had patiently accumulated.

When Grant entered the White House in 1869, three sons accompanied him. Frederick Dent, the eldest, was then aged nineteen; Ulysses, Jr., two years younger; and the youngest son, Jesse, eleven. All of them survived their father, and their careers owed much of their success to the fame of their sire and the magic of his name.

Frederick was born in 1850. Even though older than his brothers when his father was President, Fred was jovial, happy, and boyish as they were.[14] And yet no White House boy had ever shown more self-reliance or had seen more of the serious aspects of life. Even when he was much younger both his parents had complete confidence that this lad could "take care of himself." Grant records in his *Memoirs,* "When I left Galena for the last time, to take command of the 21st regiment, I took with me my oldest son, Frederick D. Grant, then a lad of 11 years. On receiving the order to take rail for Quincy I wrote to Mrs. Grant, to relieve what I supposed would be her great anxiety for one so young going into danger, that I would send Fred home from Quincy by river. I received a prompt letter in reply decidedly disapproving my proposition, and urging that the lad should be allowed to accompany me. It came too late, Fred was already on his way home."[15] But later young Fred did go into the danger zones; Ulysses S. Grant tells us, "My son accompanied me throughout the campaign and siege at Fort Gibson, and caused no anxiety either to me or to his mother, who was at home. He looked out for himself and was in every battle of the campaign. His age, then not quite thirteen, enabled him to take in all he saw, and to retain a recollection of it that would not be possible in more mature years"; Fred was also present at other decisive battles of the Civil War, particularly during the Vicksburg campaign and siege and there he contracted a fever and became so violently ill that he was removed to St. Louis, where his father went to visit him, hardly expecting to find him alive upon his arrival.[16] Thus, when Fred entered West Point as a cadet he had personal knowledge of many topics discussed in the textbooks, and when he completed his courses at the age of twenty-one he was a soldier both in education and in experience. Upon his graduation from the Military Academy, in 1871, Frederick D. Grant acquired still more practical knowledge in engineering, transportation, and terrain problems, working with a railway construction company during the customary leave following the West Point training.[17] Then he obtained a leave of absence for eighteen months, and accompanied General Sherman on a tour in Europe. Upon his return he joined his regiment in the West, with the rank of second lieutenant; but, after a few months, this eldest son of President U. S. Grant was made an aide to General Philip Sheridan, and his rank was raised to that of lieutenant colonel; he continued to hold that "temporary" rank for nine years, drawing the full pay of that classification.[18]

In the summer of 1874 there were rumors that twenty-four year old Lieutenant-Colonel Frederick D. Grant was engaged to a Chicago heiress, Ida Marie Honoré. She was of French extraction, of a family which was prominent in the Illinois metropolis for several generations. There were various stories regarding their first meeting, but all reports agreed that she possessed beauty, culture, and wealth. The wedding took place at her father's luxurious home on October 20, 1874. "Fred Grant is at last married, to the relief of the fashionable world and the infinite injury of society reporters," exclaimed the New York *World,* aware that the event and the preparations for it had afforded columnists and editors a topic for prolific literary output.[19] A few dailies, like the New York *Times,* tinged with dislike of the Presidential father, scorned to print more than half a column of wedding news, sarcastically noting that "the marriage of the President's son afforded an opportunity to some of our dear brethren of the press which they turned to good account."[20] But other newspapers, in large cities and in smaller towns, recognized the public interest: the President of the United States was present at the wedding, the President's eldest son was the groom—this affair intrigued readers, thereby increasing circulation, resulting in more advertising linage and augmented revenue for the papers. Said the Chicago *Daily Tribune,* in journalistic rejoinder to the chiding of the *Times,* "The interest taken is due in part to the rank of the groom, to the halo which encompasseth one so closely related to the Chief Magistrate of the United States"; and, after devoting two pages to a minute description of the wedding ceremonies, this prominent journal editorialized, "This general sentiment forms a sufficient reason for the space devoted to this wedding, and the account given of it will be read with more interest than any other intelligence, political, religious, or miscellaneous, that the paper may contain." [21] Earlier in the same week, in Cincinnati, another couple had married in a balloon a mile above the city but, as the *Tribune* contrasted the interest in the "two weddings in high life," it was greater in that of the President's son who was married in Chicago. Thousands of words were used in portraying the President's son; he was described as "good size, not over medium height, but broad shouldered and massive in build. His face is not striking, but is like his father's—a good, shrewd face. The eyes are gray, and do not easily light up; nor does he use them much, speaking generally without using them. But, in the *tout ensemble* of his features, there is an impression that pleases and fascinates." [22]

The more astute editors bethought themselves of their women readers and their Chicago correspondents viewed the wedding from the "feminine angle," describing the bride, her trousseau, the ritual, and the bridal gifts. "There is not a feminine person in America who is not today scanning the columns of her daily paper for some account of the event," declared the Chicago *Inter Ocean* on the morning following the wedding.[23] Its rival, the *Tribune,* devoted twelve columns of small type to detailing the bride's attractiveness, the guests, and the wedding feast. By all accounts, in choosing Ida Marie Honoré, the President's son had won a wife of rare charm.[24] "Miss Honoré is according to public and private report as good as she is lovely," said the *Daily Graphic* in printing a full-page picture of the bride, "she is gifted not only with grace, refinement, and beauty, but high intelligence fostered by careful cultivation." [25] "In form, the new Mrs. Grant is smaller than the medium size; a lithe, girlish form, with drooping shoulders artists so much admire, and with a round, beautifully-modeled bust that leads to the symmetrical proportions of a tiny waist, that small and loving hands might span," enthused one Chicago writer.[26] "She is such a marvel of perfection, one thinks on seeing her, from the small, oval, pink-edged ear to the

The Chicago Daily Tribune.

CHICAGO, WEDNESDAY, OCTOBER 21, 1874—TEN PAGES. NUMBER 59.

GRANT—HONORE.

The Great Fashionable Wedding of Chicago.

The Prominent Parties in the Important Event.

How They Met, and Their True Love Ran Smoothly.

Superb Decorations of the Honore House.

An Unparalleled Profusion of Floral Decorations.

The Ceremony—Remarks of the Officiating Clergyman.

The Supper-Room—Its Decorations and Dishes.

The Bridal Dress—Costumes of Prominent Ladies Present.

Detailed Account of the Costly Trousseau.

Costly Presents Lavished on the Bride.

The Scenes Outside During the Ceremony.

The Departure.

A PRESIDENT'S SON TAKES A WIFE

Frederick D. Grant, eldest son of President Ulysses S. Grant, married—and the newspapers described the lingerie of his bride! (Chicago *Daily Tribune*, Oct. 21, 1874) dainty little foot that nestles like a bird in its kid boot, to the tiny hand with the diamond engagement solitaire gleaming on its tapering index finger," read another report.[27]

The bridal wardrobe was catalogued: the wedding gown, the traveling costume, the gorgeous gowns for social functions, stockings which cost twelve dollars a pair, and ballroom slippers for which forty dollars were paid. But the descriptions did not end there; reporters vied with one another to delineate the bride's intimate boudoir apparel. "It would be vain to attempt a résumé of the whole process," sighed one writer in narrating how scores of Chicago seamstresses transformed costly fabrics into the luxurious negligee, "the delicate embroidery all done by hand, the fine tucks and circumspect puffing, the minute cordings and diagonal plaitings, the rouchings of filmy white gossamer, and ruffles of daintiest cobweb-like lace, the folds upon folds of white fine linen, the shirrs of softest, daintiest illusion—fit garb for a petted child."[28] And, in an afterthought that humanity demanded a complete record, the individual boudoir garments were described to the last tuck, shirr, and frill.

In the national Capital society awaited impatiently the end of the honeymoon and the arrival of the wedded pair. A Washington paper reported that "the White House, which is whiter than ever by two fresh coats of paint, is all ready for the reception of the bride and groom. Mrs. President Grant has given up her own room for the use of the young couple."[29] Contemporary accounts indicate that the President's son and his attractive wife became popular among the social set; although, as related long after the event by Jesse Grant, one columnist spoke disparagingly of the young wife. Whereupon, Fred went to the newspaper office and administered a beating to the offending writer, for which the angered husband paid a hundred-dollar fine.[30]

Fred divided his time between Washington and Chicago. For several years following his marriage, there were innuendoes that he was implicated in questionable transactions at the expense of the taxpayers; these insinuations Washington correspondents of New York papers branded malicious and false, and an attempt of antagonistic politicians to strike at President Grant through his son.[31]

While this eldest son of President Ulysses S. Grant was receiving widespread publicity, his two younger brothers had grown to man's estate. The second son, Ulysses, Jr., was nicknamed "Buck" because he had been born in Ohio, the "Buckeye" State.[32] Sixteen years old when his father entered the White House, Ulysses, Jr., did not have the thrilling experiences near battlefields which marked the boyhood of his brother Fred, two years his senior. A contemporary historian of the White House who had daily opportunity to observe Ulysses, Jr., described him as a "modest, retiring lad, as sensitive and kindly as a girl; but not lacking whatever in virility or manly spirit. 'Buck' Grant was an unusual lad, and in spite of the high position and great fame of his renowned parent, he never put on any 'airs' whatever. At school 'Buck' was very popular—quiet, calm, absolutely fair and square, and withal so sensitive that a cross word was more of a punishment to him than a severe chastisement would be to most boys."[33] The timidity and retiring nature of the boy characterized him also in his mature years, and thirty years later probably cost him political success, for reporters noted that a prominent trait was that "Grant does not win friends easily."[34]

Ulysses, Jr., was prepared for college at the Phillips Exeter Academy, and later entered Harvard. His junior year was spent in Germany where he attended the University of Göttingen; for this he received due credit at Harvard and was graduated from the latter institution in 1874. In the fall of the year he began studying law in the office of a prominent firm in New York, at the same time attending lectures at the Columbia Law School. Graduating in 1876, he was admitted to the New York bar, but did not begin practice. For a year he was at the White House, serving as his father's secretary; subsequently he became the junior partner in a large firm whose senior members had long experience in the legal profession. Then followed a year's appointment as Assistant United States Attorney for the Southern District of New York. How this President's son, with practically no experience in the courts and no signal honors as a law student, achieved partnership in an outstanding law firm and an important post in the State, no one seemed to inquire. In the meantime he became actively interested in mining enterprises in the West; this was not unexpected, as he had married a Senator's daughter whose father was prominent in the State of Colorado both in politics and in finance. Thus far the newspapers took little notice of this second son of President Ulysses S. Grant.

The youngest of the three Grant sons, born in 1858, was named

Jesse after his grandfather. During the Civil War, Grant's aide-de-camp later recalled, Mrs. Grant often brought the toddling Jesse to her husband's headquarters, and the General became attached to his little son.[35] Of school age when his father became President, young Jesse received elementary instruction in the Washington schools, and at sixteen enrolled in the engineering school at Cornell.[36] The Presidential father was justly proud of this academic feat, writing to his friend General Badeau: "Jesse entered Cornell University, without a condition, although he has never attended school but three years." [37] There is no record that Jesse continued after his freshman year. He himself, with the aid of an admiring collaborator, narrated the story of his career, in a book entitled *In the Days of My Father;* but he was nearing seventy when the recollections were written and the passing years had given intriguing color to the incidents related.

By his own account, as a youth his sensibilities were easily ruffled. He grew self-centered, determined, and defiant; those who knew him intimately liked him, but he alienated strangers. An example may be cited: when his father ended his Presidential term in 1877, and made his extended journey through Europe, Jesse accompanied him. Queen Victoria, Jesse's book relates, had invited his parents to dine with her at Windsor Castle, but the Palace Master of the Household informed Jesse that he and General Badeau were not to sit at the Queen's table but were to dine with the lesser personalities of the royal ménage. Jesse threatened to leave London and, after protracted negotiations, he was finally invited to join ex-President Grant and his mother at the table of the monarch.[38] General Badeau, who had been Grant's military secretary and had a reputation as a writer, accepted the situation and dined with the lesser nobility.[39] Newspapers reported that the ex-President's youngest son was tactless and aroused criticism. The European correspondent of the New York *Herald,* who accompanied Grant on his journey and recorded the journey in two absorbing volumes, was prompted to write, "About Jesse there has been so much said in a satirical way, that I am tempted to do him justice by telling you how manly, original, and clever he is. But the young man is only a boy after all, and I hope he has many years in which to learn that praise or dispraise are to be heeded as idle words." [40] "Jesse Grant was always considered the favorite son of General and Mrs. Grant," said another New York paper.[41] This preference was not shared by the public or the press. The eldest son, Fred, still made headlines.

Fred remained in the army until 1881. But designing men knew that there was magic in the family name, and Frederick D. Grant was enticed into financial transactions of which he knew very little. We find him, in the spring of 1882, then a colonel, elected president of a Massachusetts electric-light company which became involved in complicated financial transactions that were criticized by the press. Frederick Grant protested that he was not aware of these manipulations, that his stock ownership was a formality foisted upon him. "I know nothing of the affairs of the Massachusetts Company, and I do not know whether I am still President," he pleaded. The five shares of stock, he said, were given him to qualify him for the office, and he had returned the certificate. Nevertheless, he found himself involved in protracted litigation, and he realized the possibility of monetary loss. "I may lose a little money," he told reporters, "but I feel much more deeply the humiliation of having my name connected with a failure."[42] The failure which startled the continent was yet to come.

Thus, in the spring of 1884, the three sons of Ulysses S. Grant were residing in New York. Frederick and Ulysses, Jr., as has been noted, had married daughters of wealthy men; Fred was now thirty-four, his brother two years younger. There were recurrent reports that they were wealthy men, that they occupied luxurious homes, and entertained lavishly. Jesse, twenty-seven, lived with his parents, whose brownstone house was in an exclusive neighborhood. At the end of his Presidential term General Grant had toured the world; he was acclaimed everywhere and feted by kings, queens, sultans, and emperors. Rich friends had created for him a trust fund of a quarter of a million, which yielded an annual return of fifteen thousand dollars. But his lavish expenditures, and those of his sons, were made possible by a greater source of income—the banking and brokerage firm of Grant & Ward. Much has been written about this enterprise; and, even after the lapse of seventy years, the researcher is confronted with a confusion of documentary data.[43]

At any rate, shortly after Grant's return from his triumphant sojourn across the seas the office stationery bore the names: General U. S. Grant, James D. Fish, Ulysses S. Grant, Jr., and Ferdinand Ward.[44] Fish was president of the prominent Marine Bank in which Grant & Ward deposited its funds. Ward had been an inconspicuous broker who joined Ulysses, Jr., in some profitable mining enterprise. The ex-President invested one hundred thousand dollars in the partnership; Ulysses, Jr., half as much. Frederick, though not a partner, loaned to the enterprise about a million dollars, and Jesse deposited with the firm about eighty thousand dollars.[45] In its banking and brokerage operations Grant & Ward became agent for prominent railroads in marketing their bonds; the City of New York made the firm a depository for a million dollars; wealthy men entrusted to the firm or to the individual partners huge amounts of negotiable securities. The firm name became a byword for soundness and monetary success. There was talk in financial circles that Grant & Ward made huge profits in Government contracts. Large sums were drawn by Ferdinand Ward, and substantial dividends were paid to the Grants. Upon the firm's ledgers the partners were credited with their shares of reputed gains. The ex-President and his sons considered themselves potential millionaires. All of them had their entire funds in the safekeeping of Grant & Ward.

May, 1884, began with important events in financial circles. In New York the Produce Exchange had moved into a magnificent new building, and the famed orator Chauncey M. Depew in an outburst of eloquence proclaimed that commerce and stock exchanges were the pioneers and bulwarks of civilization and freedom.[46] From Washington came word that the United States Supreme Court was restoring to its rightful owners an important railroad which had been stolen by Jay Gould and fellow manipulators through faked foreclosure suits.[47] And Jim Keene, whom the New York *World* called "one of the most brilliant speculators of today," was suspended from the Stock Exchange.[48] Thus it was that Wall Street had many exciting topics for discussion. But the news which eclipsed all this exploded during the second week in May.

On Tuesday, the seventh of May, newspaper headlines blazoned: "Panic in Wall Street. Grant & Ward Fail for Million Dollars." [49] The day had begun with the closing of the Marine Bank during the morning. That had stunned even the bank's directors themselves. They had held their customary weekly meeting at the bank's offices, without an inkling of impending events. Half an hour after they left the building the bank's president ordered that the door be shut. Ferdinand Ward had deposited a large amount of worthless checks, and had withdrawn larger sums in cash, leaving the Marine Bank without funds to meet legitimate demands of depositors. Ferdinand Ward disappeared with the keys to the Grant & Ward vaults, and no one knew whether the securities of the firm's customers remained. Of course, the firm's deposits in the Marine Bank were impounded. Yes, it was true! Grant & Ward had failed—their ledgers were confused, their assets dissipated.

The crash of Grant & Ward was followed by numerous court actions in which clients of the firm attempted to recover the securities they had deposited and the funds they had loaned. In this wild scramble there were unearthed all the seductive schemes and frenzied manipulations which characterized Wall Street speculators in that period and inveigled credulous investors. "The story of the failure of Grant & Ward becomes worse every day," commented the *Times*.[50] The effects of the crash extended beyond New York; public confidence was shaken, and there were bank failures in every part of the country. The Grant & Ward failure trapped not only the unwary, but also shrewd financiers of wide experience. It was evident that, as a prominent New York paper said, "the name of General Grant was used as a talisman to cover up the recklessness of the firm's business." [51] The Savannah *News* referred to the Grants as "these reckless gamblers"; [52] but the majority of American newspapers strove to shield the ex-President. The Boston *Transcript* argued that Grant had become involved because of a parent's interest in his sons, that "he had given his name to the firm more for the sake of helping his two boys than to add to his own fortune." [53] A small number of journals did not share this view; the San Francisco *Call* voiced its opinion that "as the misfortunes of Grant are owing to his being a speculator in stocks, the country will not feel for him the sympathy it otherwise would have had." [54] But the country did feel sympathy, believing, as did the Boston *Post*, that "people are prepared to forgive almost everything to a man to whom the country owes so much as to him." [55] This was Ulysses S. Grant whose military skill had saved the Union, and the Nation could not forget its gratitude, no matter what was his role in the unsavory failure of Grant & Ward. Congress restored him to a general's rank in the Army, with an annual pay of $17,500.[56]

As regarded the sons of the ex-President, the press was more critical. In scathing editorials the New York *World* and other prominent journals derided their incapacity and scorned their claims that they were unaware of the manipulations of the firm's member, Ferdinand Ward. "As to the affairs of the firm, I knew nothing more than has been published," protested Fred Grant to a newspaper reporter, adding that every penny he possessed had been invested in Grant & Ward.[57] Ulysses, Jr., who was a partner, pleaded the same ignorance of his firm's transactions. To which the *World* retorted angrily: "To assume that the Grant sons, who devoted their entire time and fortune to the swindling firm, knew nothing whatever of their own firm's operations for years past, is to assume that these sons of ex-President Grant must be idiots." [58] The Boston *Transcript* was milder in its censure, commenting, "The history of the concern is a history of a venture projected and managed by inexperienced and untrained hands." [59] And the *World,* still dubious that they were ignorant of the manipulations by the junior partner, agreed that "the Grant sons but for the accident of their father's Presidency might have been respectable dry-goods clerks in Galena. They have no qualifications as successful speculators. How much better for his sons if they had remained clerks or shopkeepers in a quiet Western town." [60] Only a year after the failure of Grant & Ward, ex-President Ulysses Simpson Grant was dead. The three Presidential sons separated and pursued their individual careers.

Frederick Grant returned to business activities, without great success. The prestige of his father's name was still great; and, despite the memory of the Grant & Ward scandal, politicians still believed that the son of the former President would prove a popular candidate for public office.

In 1887, Frederick Grant was nominated by the Republicans of New York as their candidate for the office of secretary of state. His selection to head the New York ticket aroused animated discussion far beyond the borders of his own State. "Every one knows," insisted the Washington *Sunday Herald,* "that it is only as the son of his father that he was given the place"; [61] and the Boston *Globe* expressed the same conclusion that "the nomination of Colonel Grant would never have been thought of had he not been his father's son." [62] Echoed a St. Louis paper: "Frederick Grant has not the slightest personal claim to the distinction, his sole merit is that he was born the son of General Grant." [63] And other papers, like the Atlanta *Constitution,* in milder terms reasoned that "if Colonel Grant's name is worth anything in this campaign it is because it carries the suggestion that the son may possess some of the virtues of his father." [64] But there were party journals which disputed these contentions. "Colonel Fred Grant, being the son of a distinguished father, probably will be told that he has nothing else to recommend him. Such a statement, however, is not true," asserted the Chicago *News,* insisting that "Colonel Grant has had much experience in public office." [65] "The magic of the Grant name has been invoked," conceded the Albany *Journal,* "and so long as the memory lasts of him who gave that name its meaning . . . so will that name be invoked not in vain." But the paper argued that "it would be manifestly unfair to the character of the nominee to convey the impression that Colonel Grant is nominated for his father's name alone. He is a man against whose ability, integrity, and reputation there has been and can be no objection. He was nominated for his own qualities as well as for the illustrious name he bears." [66] The leading Pennsylvania paper discounted the vote-getting power of the Grant name and derided the opinion that a President's son can win elections solely because of the father's prestige. "In all this," editorialized the Philadelphia *Journal,* "there is no sign that the American people have abandoned their old traditions and taken to worshiping the sons of great fathers. Much as they revere the memory of Grant and Lincoln they revere them for what they did and not for what their fathers did. And as their sons have done nothing remarkable they will be accepted for just what they are and no more. Colonel Grant may be elected secretary of state in New York, but if so it will be . . . not because he secured any considerable vote on the strength of his descent from America's greatest warrior." [67]

Thus the editors of the Nation's press debated whether the eldest son of Ulysses S. Grant owed his political progress to his own abilities or to the prestige of his Presidential father. Politicians watched eagerly the trend of public opinion and awaited the counting of the ballots in the impending election. The Republican Party had something more at stake than the election of a secretary of state in New York: if Frederick D. Grant emerged a conspicuous victor, they proposed to join him with another President's son—Robert T. Lincoln—as nominees for President and Vice-President in the forthcoming election.[68] These politicos had not long to wait for the verdict of New York voters: in November, 1887, Frederick Dent Grant was defeated for the office he was seeking.

In 1889, Benjamin Harrison, who had been a general in the Union armies commanded by Fred's father, became President, and appointed Fred Minister to the then existing Austro-Hungarian monarchy. He held the post at Vienna until a Democratic President, in 1893, succeeded Harrison.[69] Fred then returned to the United States, and soon another place was found for him as a member of the Board of Police Commissioners of the City of New York. The Police Commissioner then was Theodore Roosevelt who, in 1897, became Vice-President of the United States, and Frederick Grant succeeded him as Police Commissioner. But Grant aspired to higher political honors. William McKinley had been elected President of the United States, and Grant expected an appointment as Ambassador to Germany or Minister to Austria.[70] Colonel Frederick D. Grant had many friends; they pressed his appointment, but McKinley only offered him the post of assistant secretary of war. The President recognized the prestige of the Grant name, and accorded to this son of Ulysses S. Grant exceptional consideration when he came to Washington; he was singled out, and the press reported that "although the crush of callers at the White House was great when Colonel Grant arrived about noon, he was ushered into the Cabinet room by the private entrance and remained with the President about half an hour." [71]

In 1898, the United States declared war against Spain. Once again the eldest son of Ulysses S. Grant became an Army officer, and was soon made a brigadier general. He served in Cuba, in Porto Rico, and in the Philippines. At the close of the conflict, he had several assignments to organize civil government in the conquered islands; then he returned to command divisional areas in the States, retaining his general's rank. His peacetime duties were unspectacular, but occasionally he made headlines. In 1909, attired in full general's regalia, he led a prohibition parade in Chicago.[72] There was an outburst of criticism throughout the country; angry editorials accused him of "prostituting an Army uniform for a partisan purpose." Numerous protests were addressed to the War Department. But this was a President's son. "We do not expect severe reprimand for General Frederick Grant because he headed a Chicago prohibition parade in full uniform," prophesied the New York *Evening Post*.[73] The prognostication was correct. The Secretary of War replied that it was "not a prohibition parade, but a temperance and law enforcement parade"; that General Frederick Grant led the marchers as an individual and not as a representative of the War Department.

Frederick Dent Grant died in April, 1912. The news came to the public suddenly and unexpectedly; his absence from his military post and his last days were veiled in secrecy. There were rumors that he died of cancer as did his father; these surmises were denied emphatically by the family. The death certificate ascribed his death to "a blood-clot on the heart." [74] The press condemned the "mystery of Fred Grant's illness." "Why was it necessary to hedge about the fatal illness with such secrecy and deception?" demanded the New York *World;* and, forgetting its censure and derision of him when Grant & Ward crashed, the newspaper now referred to him as "a man of national reputation, a favorite General in whom the public felt a keen interest both because of his personality and inherited fame." [75] Numerous editorials commented on his passing, and there was now a feeling that his being a Presidential son had stood in the way of the greater success which his own talents could have achieved. "General Frederick Dent Grant was called upon to occupy one of the most difficult positions which falls to the lot of man," argued a Michigan paper. "As the son of his father, it was his task to support the honor of a great name without being afforded any real opportunity to prove to the world the extent of his own abilities." [76] And a Missouri editor voiced the opinion typical of other journals: "So far as a popular estimate of his ability is concerned he has labored under the not inconsiderable handicap of being the son of one of the greatest captains of the world." Nevertheless, it ascribed his popularity to the fact that "during the latter years of his life he has been in a peculiar way the object of the regard and affection of those who served under his distinguished father." [77]

It was to be expected that many newspapers in the North would express regret at the death of Frederick Grant: he was the eldest son of the military commander who defeated the armies of the South. But there were Southern papers, too, which spoke kindly. Said a Mississippi editor at Vicksburg where Fred's father had won his momentous victory: "The news of the death of General Frederick D. Grant excites especial regret in Vicksburg . . . on account of his intercourse with the ex-Confederate soldiers . . . his sympathy, and friendliness to the South and the Southern people." [78]

As the caisson bearing his coffin rolled along New York streets large crowds stood bareheaded to pay homage to the eldest son of the eighteenth President. He was buried at West Point.[79]

While Frederick Grant was pursuing his career in political and military fields, his two younger brothers were also rising from the financial ruin of Grant & Ward. Ulysses Grant, Jr., joined a New York law firm, but his practice was not conspicuous. Several years later he moved to California, giving as the reason the health of his wife.[80] He referred to the crash of Grant & Ward as a "suspension." This President's son had an easy manner of referring to his role in events which earned nationwide condemnation; later, when his effort to win nomination for Senator was tarnished by proven bribery, he proudly inserted in a biography sent to Harvard that he had been "a prominent candidate for election to the United States Senate." [81]

In California he took up residence in San Diego, where his brother Jesse had business interests. Here he prospered. He became active in politics, and was chosen a delegate to the Republican national convention in 1896. This brought him in contact with party leaders, and aroused in him the aspiration to follow in the footsteps of his wife's father as a United States Senator.

The fame of his own father, both as the triumphant commander in the Civil War and as President of the United States, was as great on the Pacific Coast as it was in the East, and the California politicians sponsored Ulysses S. Grant, Jr., as a candidate for the Senate of the United States. The selection of Senators at that time lay with the State Legislature, and both parties strove to obtain the support of its members. There were half a dozen aspirants, and the contest was exceedingly vigorous. Grant had no previous political experience, and his opponents sneered that he was merely trading on the renown of his father. But those who placed him in nomination argued that the son of the former President of the United States was entitled to the honor, and, moreover, that he himself was qualified. "It has been said by some that Mr. Grant is simply the son of his father and that was the sole reason for his candidacy," argued one of his sponsors in seconding his nomination. "Even if that were true it seems to me that loyal and patriotic Americans might do far worse than honor the dead captain, one of the most illustrious military leaders in the world's history and one to whom the Union owes its life, by bestowing upon his son the Senatorial toga. But Mr. Grant is much more than simply the son of his father. He is a gentleman of culture and education, of wide reading and observation, a gentleman of broad and liberal ideas. He is a practical and successful business man." [82] Others of his supporters argued that "if we elect Mr. Grant to the United States Senate, he will be no stranger to the lawmakers of our national Capital, for he is a man who has a personal acquaintance with most, if not all, the leading men in Congress and will need no introduction to the present Republican administration in Washington." [83]

The Call

VOLUME LXXXV—NO. 37. SAN FRANCISCO, FRIDAY, JANUARY 6, 1899. PRICE FIVE CENTS.

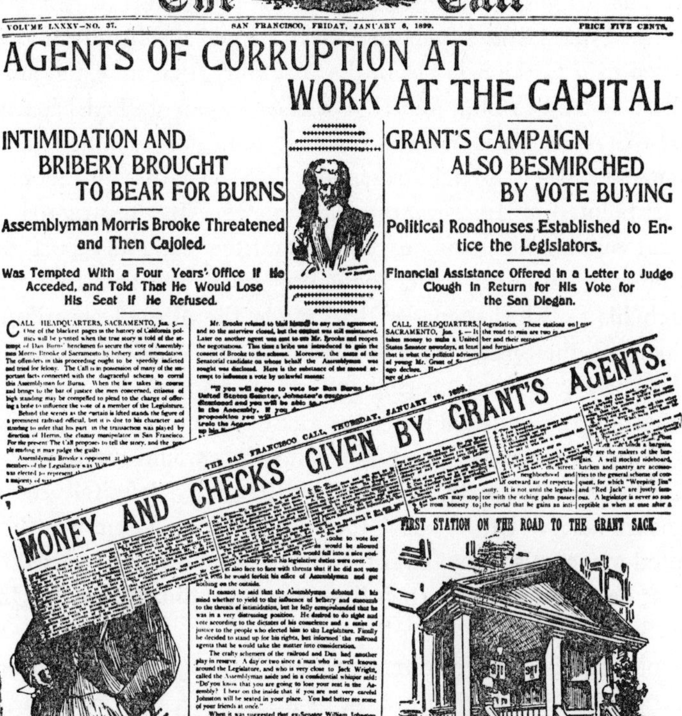

AGENTS OF CORRUPTION AT WORK AT THE CAPITAL

INTIMIDATION AND BRIBERY BROUGHT TO BEAR FOR BURNS

Assemblyman Morris Brooke Threatened and Then Cajoled.

Was Tempted With a Four Years' Office If He Acceded, and Told That He Would Lose His Seat If He Refused.

GRANT'S CAMPAIGN ALSO BESMIRCHED BY VOTE BUYING

Political Roadhouses Established to Entice the Legislators.

Financial Assistance Offered in a Letter to Judge Clough in Return for His Vote for the San Diegan.

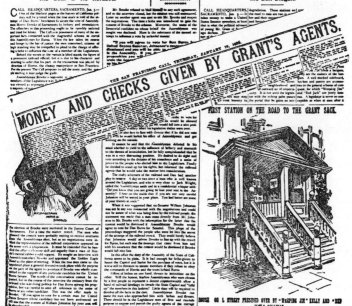

THE SAN FRANCISCO CALL, THURSDAY, JANUARY 19, 1899.

MONEY AND CHECKS GIVEN BY GRANT'S AGENTS.

FIRST STATION ON THE ROAD TO THE GRANT SACK.

HOUSE ON L STREET PRESIDED OVER BY "WEEPING JIM" KELLY AND "RED JACK" SULLIVAN.

AN EX-PRESIDENT'S SON IN POLITICS

The son of Ulysses S. Grant, in an effort to obtain the nomination for United States Senator, was accused of bribery to influence votes. (San Francisco *Call,* Jan. 6, 1899)

But before the balloting began the newspapers made charges that Grant was bribing members of the State Legislature which was to select the United States Senator; they charged specifically that $900 had been paid to the Speaker of the Assembly, that an equal amount had been loaned to him, and that similar payments had been made to other State Legislators. The scandal could not be stilled; and, in response to widespread public demand, the Legislature on January 16, 1899, appointed an Investigating Committee. After protracted hearings and voluminous testimony the Committee made its report eleven days later. Its findings were, that although it was true that Grant, through his political manager, had made the alleged contributions and loans to the Speaker of the Assembly and to other members, it was for their own electioneering and not improper in a political campaign, although Grant did expect as a natural consequence that when these Legislators were themselves elected they would support him for the United States Senate.[84] The Committee very definitely recorded its censure—not of Grant, but of the Speaker of the Assembly, who had accepted money also from Grant's opponents and had promised them too that he would advance their interests as candidates for the United States Senate! [85]

Despite charges and countercharges of bribery, the Legislature of California proceeded with its task of attempting to select a Senator of the United States. Ulysses S. Grant, Jr., vied for first place, and finally succeeded in obtaining a larger number of votes than any of his opponents. But he could not obtain a majority. After 104 ballots the Legislature adjourned, and Ulysses S. Grant, Jr., never again attempted to obtain membership in the United States Senate. The newspapers do not record what aid was rendered by his brother, Jesse Grant, who had proclaimed himself a Democrat. But, in a last attempt to win the Senatorial prize for a son of the former President, a plan was advanced to nominate Jesse Grant on the Democratic ticket and draw to him the Republican supporters of Ulysses S. Grant, Jr. "A Big Vote for Grant Family," "U.S. and Jesse to divide ballots," [86] blazoned the San Francisco papers; but the attempt gained no popular support.

Although high political office was denied him, this namesake of the eighteenth President achieved prominence in his community through financial successes. He was proud of his material progress; in his reports to the secretary of his Harvard class he detailed his activities in the affairs of large corporations, his monetary interest in financial institutions. In 1904 he was director in three banks; ten years later he was a director in six banks.[87] He had also acquired substantial stock in steel companies, and was successful in real-estate operations. At one time, said the Los Angeles papers, Ulysses, Jr., was the largest taxpayer in San Diego County.[88] And, as a "memorial to his father" he built at San Diego a large hotel which he named "U. S. Grant Hotel"—probably the only dividend paying "memorial" ever erected by a President's son.

Apart from his financial success, Ulysses Grant, Jr., found gratification in foreign travel. Yearly he made pilgrimages to other countries; to use his own words, he "passed the winter of one year in Europe, the spring of the following year in Mexico." He was proud that he "visited places not ordinarily seen by world tourists." [89] But it was his matrimonial venture that brought his name to the front pages of metropolitan papers.

His first wife, the Senator's daughter, died in 1909, leaving six children, all of whom had married. Four years later Ulysses announced that he would wed again; his bride was a widow, Mrs. America Will. Ulysses, Jr., was sixty, his bride thirty-six. Press dispatches spoke of his wealth; he was reputed to own properties valued at three million dollars. It was reported that he had made a prenuptial agreement whereby his second wife was to inherit two-thirds of this large sum.[90] His family bitterly resented this publicized arrangement, and friends were critical. Invitations to the wedding feast were scorned. Said a dispatch from San Diego, where the ceremony took place, "Tongues are wagging today over the large number who stayed away from the dinner. Of the sixty-five invited, only twelve attended." And two of the dozen diners were employees of the former Mrs. America Will.[91] Ulysses, Jr., and his wife departed hurriedly on a visit to Hawaii, and later followed the track of his Presidential father's trip around the world.

In the fifteen years following his second marriage, the name of Ulysses Grant, Jr., occasionally appeared in public print. Invariably the news was of some grandiose plan—the building of an Italian villa overlooking the Hudson, the development of large tracts of land, and other schemes which betokened great wealth.

In September, 1929, at the age of seventy-seven, this second son of Ulysses S. Grant died suddenly.[92] Sixty years had passed since his father had been President of the United States, and he himself had achieved no military or political successes. There were no editorial eulogies. Only his will and his estate were of interest: he had left all his estate to his wife—but it amounted to only ten thousand dollars. His testament stated that during his lifetime he had provided amply for his children. And once again the public was startled, as it had been in the days of Grant & Ward.

Far less frequently the subject of newspaper comment than his brothers, Frederick and Ulysses, Jr., the third Grant son reflected the independence and individualism of his youth. As was aptly said in one of the very few comments upon his death, "Jesse Grant went through life independent of any influence of the career of his illustrious father. He became a wanderer, covering much of the United States and Mexico."[93] For a while he was a mining engineer; finally he settled in California. He engaged in varied commercial enterprises and real-estate ventures, and there were rumors that he had acquired a very substantial fortune. In 1897 we find his name linked to successful negotiations with the Mexican Government for land surrounding the Hot Springs of Tia Juana across the boundary line in Southern California. The concession which was obtained in this Mexican territory included the privilege of running a lottery and gambling establishments, in addition to the right of colonization and the development of the mineral waters at the Springs. Jesse Grant told the newspapers that he himself would not operate the gambling casino which was to be built, but that the control of that enterprise would be turned over to an Eastern syndicate.[94]

But if readers of these dispatches concluded that Jesse Grant himself indulged in the reckless expenditures which characterized sportsmen at Tia Juana or that he entertained a disregard for money so evident at gambling tables, they were disillusioned when it was revealed that he would not attend the dedication of his father's monument in New York unless that city first sent him the funds with which to make the trip. One of New York's papers questioned the propriety of paying the traveling expenses of Jesse Grant and his family when the latter "has been reputed to be one of the richest land owners and citizens of Southern California." The Mayor of New York, whom Jesse's brother, Colonel Frederick Grant, had supported in a preceding election, replied that the "children and grandchildren of the great General were among the City-invited guests . . . and it had been decided that the City should furnish the transportation to and from New York and pay the hotel bills of all invited guests." [95] The Mayor refrained from noting that all the other invited guests came from Washington, a few hundred miles distant, whereas Jesse Grant was in San Diego, across the continent. Nevertheless, a hundred and fifty dollars were wired to Jesse Grant and he started eastward. It was reported that "Mr. Jesse Grant, while in New York, will be the guest of his brother, Colonel Grant, the Police Commissioner"; but upon his return to California, after the dedication ceremony, Jesse Grant sent to the City of New York a bill for $759 for traveling expenses, and this included $234 which he claimed for "meals, etc."

A few years later we find Jesse Grant again in New York, claiming voting privileges in that State. A heated election campaign for Governor was in progress and one of the candidates was the publisher, William Randolph Hearst. Jesse Grant wrote to Mr. Hearst's campaign committee that he would "vote for Mr. Hearst because I am a Democrat." [96] This assertion, of course, aroused a great deal of comment because Jesse's father had been elected President on the Republican ticket, and his brother, Ulysses, Jr., had been the Republican nominee for Senator in California. Apparently, the New York press had forgotten that Ulysses S. Grant himself had been a Democrat before the Civil War and that the Democratic Party would willingly have made him its candidate had not the Republicans put him upon their ticket. Even if Jesse Grant did not have this in mind, he could assert truthfully that the grandfather after whom he had been named had also been a Democrat.[97] At any rate, this President's son considered himself not only a Democrat, but an outstanding and popular Democrat as well. In 1908 he made political speeches in the West and South and, returning to New York, announced that he was an aspirant for the Democratic nomination as a candidate for President of the United States.[98]

It was his divorce actions which brought Jesse Grant's name to the front pages of the newspapers. The court pleadings revealed that he had married in 1880, but we know little of his marital affairs until the time when his wife charged that Jesse's mother had paid the wedding expenses and had given Jesse an allowance of $250 monthly, both during her lifetime and by her will. The couple had separated in 1902, and twelve years later Jesse obtained a divorce in Nevada.[99] This was later set aside. Then Jesse sued once more, and his wife interposed no objection. Whereupon Jesse, aged 61, married again—a woman twenty years his junior.[100]

Jesse died in June, 1934. The press associations, noting that he was a President's son, wired several short paragraphs to their member newspapers. But editors did not appraise the event as one of great public interest, and even those journals which printed the news devoted to it but one or two paragraphs. In death, as in life, Jesse Grant did not attract many friends. And his reputed wealth was revealed to be an estate of two thousand dollars.[101]

Thus lived and died the three sons of Ulysses Simpson Grant, eighteenth President of the United States.

11

Sons of Rutherford B. Hayes

On the evening of Friday, June 13, 1851, a young lawyer was rounding a corner of a Cincinnati street just as a runaway horse, dragging a carriage, came plunging along the pavement—in its path an attractive woman. Instantly, the young man clasped her in his arms and pulled her to safety. To onlookers it was a deed of gallantry and courage such as novelists often describe in tracing the beginning of a fruitful romance. But Rutherford Birchard Hayes did not thrill when he held the lady close, nor did he feel the throb of incipient love. We know—because Rutherford B. Hayes has described in detail his actions and his emotions on that occasion. He always wrote down in his diary exactly what happened, minutely describing joyful episodes and tragic events, analyzing his inner feelings, and concluding with his objective reflections. He freed the woman from his chivalrous embrace, apologized for his unconventional conduct and, without asking her identity, went on his way! One reason was that while he noticed her beauty he also saw that she wore a wedding ring; and this twenty-nine year old attorney adhered to a strict moral code which forbade flirtations with the wives of other men.

But the main reason for his indifference was that his heart had been enraptured by another girl. Why did he write of the occurrence? Because his unpremeditated act filled him with the confidence he needed to court the girl who was in his thoughts. The attractive wife went her way, and Rutherford B. Hayes hastened on. For him the evening continued to be eventful, and he himself tells us why in his diary:

I went on my way rejoicing, an inch taller for this feat—and naturally turned into the gate next house east of Dr. Priestley's church—a blessed vicinity forevermore in my memory—and soon was chatting gaily with my—since a goodly time—"received ideal" of a cheerful, truthful, trusting, loving and lovable girl who might have been the original in many points of Hawthorne's Phoebe—the sunbeam in the *House of Seven Gables;* or the fairy in Ik Marvel's revery over the anthracite, with the "deep eye" reaching back to the spirit; not the trading eye, weighing your purse; nor the worldly eye, weighing your position; nor the beastly eye, weighing your appearance; but the *heart's eye,* weighing your soul! An eye full of deep, tender, earnest feeling. An eye which looked on once, you longed to look on again; an eye which will haunt your dreams; an eye which will give a color, in spite of you, to all your reveries. An eye which lies before you in your future, like a star in the mariner's heavens, by which unconsciously you take all your observations.[1]

The conversation between man and girl touched many subjects; as the evening wore on they visited neighbors, then returned to the girl's home. Then something happened. But let Hayes tell it in his own words:

I listened carelessly, with a free and easy feeling to her talk "soft and low"—tones and voice just matching that otherwise matchless eye; not matchless for its brilliancy, or magnetizing power, or beauty even, but for its tenderness and goodness. . . . We spoke of different topics. I was sleepy from bad rest the night before, and told her so, but talked on. On a sudden the impulse seized me—unthought of, unpremeditated, involuntary, and (I was sitting in a rush-bottom rocking chair in front of her, she on a short sofa) I grasped her hand hastily in my own and with a smile, but earnestly and in quick accents said, "I love you." She did not comprehend it; *really,* no sham; and I repeated it more deliberately. She was not startled—no fluttering; but a puzzled expression of pleasure and surprise stole over her fine features. She grew more lovely every breath, returned the pressure of my hand. I *knew* it was as I wished, but I waited, perhaps repeated my declaration again, until she said, "I must confess, I like you very well." A queer, soft, loving tone, it stole to the very heart, and I without loosing her hand took a seat by her side, and—and the faith was plighted for life. A quiet, smiling, satisfied silence, broken by an occasional loving word followed. She said, "I don't know but I am dreaming. I thought I was too light and trifling for you." And so, and so—her younger brother Joseph came in, and after a short while I went home to dream of it all again and again.[2]

On the morrow he recorded this joyous engagement to Lucy Webb. He had considered Fridays as unlucky for himself, but now he burst forth in exuberance:

"Happy as a king," "a lark," "a clam," or any other of the happiest being animal or inanimate in this lower world. . . . Why this elation, elevation, hilarity of spirits, or rather quiet joyousness and self-satisfaction? . . . Last night, Friday evening—Friday no longer an ill-starred day in my calendar, (give me Fridays, such Fridays, or such Friday evenings for aye, and I'll not change them for the luckiest Thursday or Sunday, lucky days proverbially, that one lives through in an age!) . . .[3]

On the last day of the year 1877, the Marine Band was playing in the Blue Room of the White House at Washington. Ambassadors, statesmen, men prominent in politics and finance, and women famed for their wealth, beauty, and social position, crowded about a man and a woman: Rutherford Birchard Hayes, President of the United States, and Lucy Webb Hayes were celebrating their silver wedding.[4] Beside them stood their five children, four of them sons. Much had transpired in the quarter of a century since that June night when Rutherford B. Hayes saved a woman unknown to him and proposed to the woman he loved.

Born in 1822, this nineteenth President of the United States spent an uneventful boyhood, receiving an excellent education in the public schools and under private tutors, and completing his academic work at Kenyon College. He studied law at Harvard, and in 1845 he was admitted to the Ohio bar. Opening a law office in Cincinnati, he made rapid progress and his reputation both for legal ability and political astuteness spread beyond his own State. For a few years he was affiliated with the expiring Whig Party. Then, in 1856, the new Republican Party emerged; Hayes became a member of it, and from the very first he was regarded as one of its leaders in the State of Ohio. When the Civil War suddenly engulfed the nation in 1861, Rutherford B. Hayes left his law office and became a major in the Union Army. During the entire campaign, in barracks or battlefield camp, he continued to read the classics and current publications for which he had developed an insatiable appetite during his college days. Typical of this interest in literature is the record of his reading at Camp Flat Top, Virginia. Already a colonel, with added responsibilities, he wrote to his wife on June 12, 1862, "I have read 'Ivanhoe,' 'Bride of Lammermoor,' and one of Dickens' and one of Fielding's the last ten days"; and these he interspersed with reading newspapers till bedtime.[5]

While in the Army he was nominated for Congress, and his Cincinnati political supporters urged that he take leave and do some electioneering. The response of Rutherford B. Hayes was prompt and decisive; he wrote, "Your suggestion about getting a furlough to take the stump was certainly made without reflection. An officer fit for duty who at this crisis would abandon his post to electioneer for a seat in Congress ought to be scalped. You may feel perfectly sure I shall do no such thing." [6] Nevertheless, he was elected; and in after years this letter was used by his supporters in every campaign to prove his patriotism and devotion to duty. He emerged from the war with the rank of major general. In 1866 he was re-elected to Congress; two years later he became Governor of Ohio, and was elected for another two-year term in 1869. Retiring from the governorship, he devoted six years to practicing law; but in 1875 he was again elected Governor. His reputation transcended the boundaries of his own State, and soon the politicos who dictated nominations decided that Hayes' record and popularity would win him the Presidential office. In 1876 they made him the candidate for President, against Samuel Tilden, the Democratic nominee. In the November election both candidates claimed the majority of electoral votes; and, although the Constitution made no provision for such a determination, an "Electoral Commission" was appointed to decide who had won. Hayes was the victor. On March 4, 1877, he was sworn in as President.[7]

Moving into the White House, Rutherford Birchard Hayes and his wife soon won the respect of all who came in contact with them.[8] Colonel Crook, who had been bodyguard or Presidential clerk since the days of Lincoln, describes the impression they made: "Mr. and Mrs. Hayes brought with them to the White House an atmosphere somewhat different from that to which we had been accustomed. Almost all Presidents, during my experience of forty-six years, have attended church here and there in the City and in some sense have shown their acceptance of religious teachings. But Mr. and Mrs. Hayes actually lived their religion day by day, all through the week as well as on Sunday." [9] No wines or alcoholic beverages were served in the White House during the occupancy of the Hayes family except on a single occasion when a State dinner was given in honor of the Grand Duke of Russia. The President's wife became exceedingly popular not only because of her activities in church circles but also because of her kindliness and cordiality.[10] "Her expansive hospitality strained the capacity of the White House," the biographer Eckenrode records, and he quotes the younger Rutherford as saying, "In the old days I considered myself fortunate to sleep on the soft side of the billiard table; cots in the hall, couches in the reception room, billiard tables, and even bathtubs had to serve as beds. Even Father had virtually no privacy; I have seen him retire to the bathroom, lock the door, and prepare some important State papers." [11]

Newspaper correspondents and magazine writers liked this White House mistress, so friendly and lacking in ostentation, and they gave full rein to glowing phrases in their descriptions of her; one of these portrayals, later satirized by the New York *Tribune,* appeared in the periodical, *Graphic;* Lucy Webb Hayes was pictured thus: "Her nose is a finely moulded feature, bringing forward the sagacity which might else be embowered in such gracious sensibility, . . . her skin is a clear red olive, . . . her mouth is large, opens naturally and heartily at laughing, and shows behind a raspberry richness of lips full rows of natural teeth, which are attractive without being conspicuous." [12]

But long before her husband became President of the United States, Lucy Webb Hayes contributed to his success and to his happiness. She bore him eight children; five of them—a daughter and four sons—lived to round out successful careers. Lucy instilled in the boys her own deep convictions of ethics and modesty; and, when they became President's sons, they shunned the glare and glamour which come to occupants of the White House.

Like his wife, Rutherford B. Hayes was devoted to his progeny. Whether on the battlefield or in political campaigns, Hayes always found time to give guidance, encouragement, and counsel to his sons. The eldest, born in November, 1853, was christened Birchard. His eighth birthday found his father in a Virginia camp; but Hayes did not forget the little boy. Four days before the birthday he wrote Birchard a long letter, describing camp life, telling him what a flag of truce was. He admonishes the lad to do what is right:

And now, my son, as you are getting to be a large boy, I want you to resolve always to do what you know is right. No matter what you lose by it, no matter what danger there is, always do right. I hope you will go to school and study hard, and take exercise too, so as to grow and be strong, and if there is a war you can be a soldier and fight for your country as Washington did. Be kind to your brothers and to Grandmother, and above all to your mother. You don't know how your mother loves you, and you must show that you love her by always being a kind, truthful, brave boy; and I shall always be proud of you.[13]

At ten, Birchard went to Fremont to live with his great-uncle, Sardis Birchard, and there he prepared for college.[14] In all his letters to Birchard, Rutherford Hayes preaches a gospel of common sense and high ideals. We find him writing in March, 1870, when his son was undecided about what college to enter:

My dear Boy—You ask me about the college at Hudson. It has a good history—has turned out many able and successful men. I have no doubt you can get there all that is essential which any college can give. . . . The main thing is the student—his industry, his habits, character, and talents. The college affords him merely the tools.[15]

For a brief period Birchard attended a Michigan college, but was not satisfied. Finally, again consulting his father, the eldest Hayes son chose Cornell. His life at college was uneventful; other students attended dances at nearby towns, became engaged or married, were called to the Dean's office because of some escapades, or became active in sports—the college paper printed numerous items daily about Cornell classmen. But, regarding Birchard, there was a single entry: "Hayes, '74, denies that he has the measles." [16]

If there is evidence that Birchard shunned social prominence and athletic laurels, there is proof that he was concerned about his name when he did compete for honors and success. At the very beginning of his college career he altered the name his parents had given him at the baptismal font. Rutherford Hayes tells of his son's discontent and the change, noting in his diary:

Birchard came home from Cornell to spend the Christmas vacation. . . . We originally called him Birchard, with no other Christian name. . . . I now offered him for his choice as a middle name, Scott, Cook, Austin, Russell, etc., etc. He chose Austin, the maiden name of my grandmother Birchard. So Birchard Austin it shall be.[17]

Birchard Austin, as he was now called, graduated from Cornell in 1874. The courses must have been exacting; of the two hundred and sixty-one who entered in 1870, only seventy-two continued their studies during the entire four years, and of these seven failed to graduate.[18] But those who did complete their studies appeared content and happy on Commencement Day; the student paper joyously proclaimed that "the class day of '74 will be remembered as the most pleasant which it has ever happened to befall Cornell students, . . . 'one of those bright immortal days that was not born to die.' "[19] Birchard Austin won no scholastic honors; his father's diary expounds the reason:

Birch graduated at Cornell in July, visited the remaining kindred in Vermont, and is now at home, ready to begin law. His diffidence has kept him from improving his opportunity to learn to speak. He is an accurate, thorough student, not fond of books as I was, with an unusual fondness for statistics, especially for the preparation of tabular information.[20]

Birchard Austin Hayes entered the Harvard Law School. He graduated in 1877, just after his father had become Chief Executive. Going to New York, he became a member of a leading law firm; it is not improbable that, as a President's son, he acquired clients more easily than other young attorneys just beginning to practice. Two years later he moved to Toledo, Ohio; there he joined two sons of a Federal judge and began his successful legal practice which continued for thirty-six years.[21] His ability to analyze statistical data, so evident even during his college studies, led him to specialize in laws relating to taxation and in real-estate law.

Birchard Austin Hayes died in 1926. His passing was noted in a few papers; but not even the journals in Toledo, where he spent almost four decades, made editorial comment on his death. The quarter or half-column news reports were headed, "President's Son Dies";[22] they briefly noted his collegiate degrees,[23] his marriage, and his long residence in Toledo.[24]

The second son of the nineteenth President, born in 1856, was named by his parents James Webb. Like his older brother, he acquired his academic education at Cornell University; and to him the father similarly wrote regarding the moral ideals which he considered the essentials in a manly career. The counsel in his letter of September 28, 1872, is typical:

I was glad to get your first letter from Cornell today. . . . It was a genuine freshman's letter. A page or two of rushes and the like and a few lines about studies. But that is what I want. Letters that show me just what you are thinking of and what you are enjoying.[25]

In less than two weeks he writes to James Webb again:

Now, my son, I need not urge you to give solid and honest work to your studies. Whatever the line of business you pursue in life, training that hard study will give you will be of service to you. Try to understand fully whatever you go over. Thoroughness is a vital thing. More important than study, however, is honesty, trustfulness, and sincerity.[26]

Like Birchard, James Webb was not content with his baptismal name. The father noted this domestic incident:

Webb came Saturday. . . . He was named James Webb. He is called Webb, and preferring another family name we agree to drop the James and give him a middle letter, C for Cook. So Webb C. Hayes it shall be.[27]

Although in his diary, on April 13, 1874, the father observed that "Webb is not scholarly," [28] it was this second son whom Rutherford B. Hayes selected as his confidential secretary when he became President of the United States on March 4, 1877. In addition to the official duties which the President assigned to his son, his mother's excessive sociability burdened him with many tasks. Mrs. Hayes "would fill the White House with young ladies who had to be squired and beauxed on sight-seeing trips, and escorted constantly to social affairs. Often, when some impromptu expedition was gotten up, he had as many as eight girls to look after at one time." [29] Several White House chroniclers tell us of his inability to obtain much-needed sleep, because enraptured youths courting girls who were White House guests were blithely oblivious of passing hours. "Upon one occasion, when one of the lady guests had a caller who stayed overlong, Webb Hayes betook himself to a room above the Red Room, where the young people were chatting, and frightened them nearly to death by dropping the largest dictionary he could find on the floor just above their heads. The caller soon departed and the young secretary was able to see the mansion closed for the night and get his rest." [30] Despite these involuntary diversions and unofficial duties, Webb Cook Hayes performed very efficiently the numerous and arduous activities of Presidential secretary; President Hayes relied upon his son's ability, tact, and resourcefulness.

Webb was the only grown son of President Hayes who remained constantly at the White House during his father's four-year term from March, 1877 to March, 1881. At the expiration of his father's Presidential term Webb, then twenty-five, became an official of a small business enterprise; and again Rutherford B. Hayes wrote advice to his son:

Fremont, O.
7 July 1881

My dear Webb:

I have your note. The draft was duly honored by Burk. It now looks as if you were fairly embarked in an enterprise which may be successful. As an officer of the Company you are now a trustee for others. Honesty, good intentions, and industry you will have of course. Without these your career would soon end with a loss of your good name. But you must be ambitious to be a good deal more. Protect the interest of your employers by the greatest watchfulness.

AN EX-PRESIDENT GIVES HIS SON A LESSON IN BUSINESS ETHICS

Four months after Rutherford B. Hayes ended his Presidential term his son Webb embarked upon his first business venture. The ex-President outlined for him a "first lesson" in business ethics. (Hayes Memorial Library, Fremont, Ohio) and economy. Inform yourself fully as to Cost and Value — let there be nothing left half understood in bargains — beware of being hasty — keep full and accurate accounts — accurate to a cent. If you make mistakes, don't be afraid to face them. Conceal nothing — be careful not to brag, or talk too much — a common fault with all beginners. This is enough for the first Lesson.

All well — good luck to you

Sincerely

Webb C. Hayes — R. B. Hayes

It now looks as if you were fairly embarked in an enterprise which may be successful. As an officer of the company, you are now a trustee for others. Honesty, good intentions, and industry, you will have of course. Without these your career would soon end with the loss of your good name. But you must be ambitious to be a good deal more. Protect the interest of your employers by the greatest watchfulness and economy. Inform yourself fully as to cost and value. Beware of being hasty. Keep full and accurate accounts, accurate to a cent. If you make mistakes, don't be afraid to face them. Conceal nothing; be careful not to brag or talk too much—a common fault with beginners. This is enough for the first lesson.[31]

The third son, born three years after the second, bore in part his father's name; he was christened Rutherford Platt Hayes. Because he lacked the physical robustness of his older brothers, the father's concern for him was even more tender than for them. In June, 1870, we find the father writing jokingly to the boy's uncle, "Birch and Webb are at school at Fremont. . . . Ruddy is at home—treated like a stepchild because he is named after me!" One of his father's biographers characterized this son as "Rutherford, the Mild." [32] In his diary, several years later, Rutherford B. Hayes appraised all his sons, and noted that "Ruddy is our invalid. Tall and slender, at sixteen he is unfit for hard work or hard study. A bright, handsome, jovial boy. We are talking of trying a manual labor agricultural college." [33] When the boy was away at school there was periodic correspondence between the elder Rutherford and his namesake; the lad wrote postcards and the family, reading these open communications, often learned through the youngster of matters Rutherford B. Hayes preferred to keep unpublicized. The father kindly but firmly admonished the lad not to divulge all he knew:

You remember I sometimes make observations on the long tongue of one of my fine boys. Do you? Well, I fear I must repeat. What is put on a postal card is quite public. Other members of the family, at least, are likely to read it. Nobody here knew I had real estate in Columbus until your postal card came. Keep your wits about you, my boy. You must try to *know* a great deal. It is not necessary to *tell* it all.

"Aye free offhand your story tell
When wi' a bosom crony,
But still keep something to yoursel'
Ye hardly tell to ony." [34]

During his father's term as President, Rutherford was pursuing academic courses at the University of Michigan and Cornell, completing his work at the latter college in 1880. He then took graduate work at the Boston Institute of Technology, and returned to Fremont, Ohio, in 1882. There his uncle was prominent in financial circles, and young Rutherford became cashier in a savings bank; in later years he was credited with piloting the institution safely through the panic of 1893.[35] His uncle having founded the Birchard Library, Rutherford Platt Hayes was named one of the trustees, and here began his work in libraries which continued for thirty years. He inaugurated the first reading room for children, with small desks and chairs sized for their comfort and the shelves stocked with books particularly suitable for young minds. He also sent boxes of books to nearby towns and it has been said erroneously that he thus "anticipated" traveling libraries.[36] He was the moving force in founding the Library Association in 1895; and, after he moved to Chicago, he organized larger traveling libraries. In later years he became interested in real-estate projects, particularly in developing Asheville, North Carolina, as a health and pleasure resort. Thus his life reflected both his father's inordinate love of books and his uncle's flair for financial enterprises. He died at seventy in 1927.[37]

The youngest of the four surviving sons of Rutherford B. Hayes and Lucy Webb Hayes was named Scott Russell; he was born five years before the father became President. He was thirteen years younger than the third son, Rutherford Platt; two boys born in the interval had died in babyhood. As a tot he won the affection of all who saw him; and the proud father wrote in his diary, "Scott, almost four, is our handsomest. Interesting, too honest to joke, or to comprehend a joke readily. He talks with some hesitation when excited, and has many pretty ways. He says many queer things. He is fond of animals." [38] As he grew older and left home to attend college, he received letters of parental advice as had his older brothers. Wrote Rutherford B. Hayes to his son when Scott was twenty-one:

> Your welfare is very near to my heart. I am now happy in the thought that you will do well. First of all, keep your conscience at the helm. *Conscience is the authentic word of God to you.* Do not be uneasy for salary or promotion. But do strive to deserve it by fidelity and efficiency. I think of you very hopefully.[39]

And again, ten days later:

I want you to think with a purpose on the question of how to use your time, especially your evenings. At all times have on hand some solid reading. Either history, biography, or natural science connected with your present business. . . . Watch all workmen, learn all facts, be practical as well as a man of theories.[40]

The father wrote to Scott frequently—news of his own activities, of events at home, and of trips to New York and elsewhere. His letters bear varied postmarks: towns in Delaware and New York; and Fremont, Toledo, and Columbus, Ohio. Away from home, engaged in pressing conferences, he did not forget to pen a few lines or a lengthy letter to Scott; returning home, he searched through the accumulated mail and first read the communications from Scott, immediately replying, "Just home after two weeks' absence in New England; a pile of letters to notice. Yours come first." It was to Scott Russell that the ex-President, just before his death, wrote his last letter. He was planning to give him a watch which he himself had received from his own mother.[41]

Scott Russell did not fulfill prognostications that he would be "adventurous." After he had completed his education, he turned to business enterprises—especially those relating to railroad equipment. He was an official of a corporation dealing in railroad springs, and vice-president of a company manufacturing railroad air brakes. He died at fifty-seven in New York City, in May, 1923.[42] The newspapers printed brief paragraphs telling of his education and his business career; all of them noted that he was a President's son.

Of all the four Hayes sons Webb was most frequently in the public eye. His father's biographer called him "Webb, the Sportsman"; [43] but he should have applied to him the term he used for Scott, "the Adventurous"; the life of Webb Cook Hayes was truly filled with adventure.

Webb C. Hayes followed the sage business counsel of his Presidential father. The modest enterprise which he organized expanded, absorbed other plants, and grew into a business of national reputation—the huge Union Carbide Corporation. When he wrote his paragraph for *Who's Who* in 1928 Webb called himself a "retired manufacturer," but through the years he had often left the directors' rooms of his companies for the battlefields of the West Indies, Europe, Asia, and Africa. This son of the nineteenth President valued service to his country above the accumulation of dividends. In the tasks of war as in the endeavors of commerce Webb C. Hayes won respect and distinction.

In 1898 he was a major, leading troops against the Spaniards in Cuba and Puerto Rico. Crossing the San Juan River his horse was shot under him, and he himself was wounded.[44] Later we hear of him in the Philippines, again in the midst of combat. The citation which accompanied the Congressional Medal of Honor tells of his courage: "For distinguished gallantry in pushing through the enemy's lines alone at night of December 4, 1899, from the beach of our beleaguered force at Vigan, and returning the following morning to report the condition of affairs to the Navy to get assistance." Promoted to lieutenant colonel, he served until the end of the Spanish-American War. Even then his soldiering was not over. In 1900 the secret Chinese society of "Boxers" threatened the safety of white residents in China, particularly in the Capital city of Peking. The foreigners in that city, besieged in the British embassy, were in danger of violence by the aroused natives, and American troops joined the forces of other countries to put down the uprising and save their nationals. Webb Hayes marched with the American flag; the commander of the Relief Expedition, General Chaffee, made him his aide.

In the succeeding decade Webb devoted himself to his business enterprises. But again he put on his country's uniform: in 1911 and 1913 he served on the Mexican border, against the inroads of the Mexican bandits. That work done, he returned to the pursuits of peace.

In 1914 the German hordes began their first attempt to conquer the world, and three years passed before the United States became aware of its own peril and entered the conflict. Webb Cook did not delay in espousing the cause of Right. He preferred to fight under the American flag; but, until that banner was carried into battle, he served in British and French brigades, in Italy. Later he was transferred to the American Army and again was decorated for service in France and Africa.[45] Webb C. Hayes was as bold in his commercial ventures as he was courageous in his soldiering. His investments prospered, and he amassed a large fortune. Always adhering to the precepts which had been enunciated by his distinguished sire, he was respected for his integrity as he was admired for his business acumen. To the memory of his Presidential father who had guided his youth, he erected a magnificent library and museum; there, amid the records of the older Hayes, repose also the mementos of Webb's colorful career. Webb Cook Hayes died in July, 1934.

Such were the lives of the four sons of Rutherford B. Hayes, nineteenth President of the United States, and Lucy Webb Hayes—one of them attained military distinction as did the father; all of them achieved financial success.

12

Sons of James A. Garfield

FOUR SONS CAME TO THE WHITE HOUSE WHEN JAMES ABRAM GARfield was sworn in as Chief Executive on March 4, 1881. The oldest boy, Harry Augustus, was nearing seventeen; the youngest, Abram, was nine. The two others, James Rudolph and Irvin McDowell, were, respectively, fifteen and eleven.[1] Since they were Presidential sons, the nation was interested in their personalities, their tastes, and their scholastic attainments; newspapers sent to Washington their ablest writers to portray the Garfield youngsters. Colonel Crook, who was a White House aide, recalled in later years that "James and Harry were then preparing for college, and a small room at the northeast end of the White House was set aside as their study . . . there the boys studied every morning. . . . James and Harry were both of studious habits and paid close attention to their books." [2]

But contemporary reporters have left more detailed descriptions of these two boys and their younger brothers; the feature writer of the New York *Tribune* was especially intrigued by their individual characteristics. Harry, he reported, was a quiet, steady boy; very obedient and dutiful, particularly respectful toward his parents and grandmother. He and Jim were at school at Concord, New Hampshire, after their father was nominated for President. He wrote to his father that some of his schoolmates had manifested a great deal more interest in them since "Pa" was nominated; this he considered snobbish, and he said he didn't think that they were a bit bigger or better than they were before, and that he would respect his father just as much "even if he were nothing but a Congressman all his life." The sixteen-year-old schoolboy didn't regard a Congressman's status as being very lofty or important.[3] Jim, the reporter called "a rollicking boy." He was never known to be still except when he was asleep. Both physically and intellectually he was very strong and very quick. He mastered his studies almost without effort, and in an incredibly short time. At school he liked the gymnasium, and excelled on the trapeze and springboard; at home he stood on his head, walked on his hands, turned handsprings and somersaults, and jumped the fence in preference to opening the gate. He was good-natured, kind-hearted, and accommodating, but full of boyish devilment. The third son, Irvin, defied analysis, and the reporter merely called him "the queerest genius" of the family. "Abe," the youngest of the Garfield boys, diverted his energies into art. He was always making pictures, and seemed to prefer drawings of machinery. A train of cars was one of his favorite delineations, and he drew with remarkable precision the engine, the baggage and mail cars, the coaches, and the sleepers.

Such were the juvenile traits of the sons of the twentieth President; in their maturer years other characteristics brought them prominence. But it was not in the White House that their personalities developed, for their father's residence there was brief. Four months after he became President of the United States he was fatally shot by Charles Guiteau. Shrieked the murderer at his trial, "The Deity inspired me . . . the whole question in this case rests on the fact whether I was inspired by the Deity." [4] The untimely death of President Garfield by an assassin's bullet aroused unprecedented sympathy for his orphaned children. Never before, and never since, did the American people render so much material assistance to the family of a dead President. The mind of Abraham Lincoln's widow was beclouded with the fear of insufficient finances, and the obsession drove her insane; but no such anxiety haunted the family of the assassinated Garfield. A spontaneous outpouring of contributions made secure the future of the bereaved wife and the sons. Even before Garfield's body was lowered into its grave, a committee of prominent New York citizens raised a fund of over three hundred thousand dollars "for the benefit of Mrs. Garfield and her children." [5] The fund grew to half a million dollars, exclusive of payments voted by Congress and independent of the personal estate of the slain Chief Executive.[6] Thus the sons of the twentieth President, though their father had held the high office but a few months, became endowed even in youth with a large amount of worldly goods. In sharp contrast, their father's path through life had begun with a childhood of hardship and a youth beset with difficulties.

James Abram Garfield was born in a log cabin, on a cold November day in 1831.[7] In the words of his mother, written in retrospect forty years later, the future President was the largest baby she had ever seen. "He looked like a red Irishman, a very large Head and Shoulders & Body equal to the Head and Shoulders. He was a very good natured Child he walked when nine months old, when ten months old he would climb the fence, go up a ladder a dozen times a day he never was still a minute at a time in his whole life . . . always uneasy, very quick to learn, he was rather lazy, did not work the best that ever was." [8] The future President was the youngest of four children; his father, an industrious farmer who had worked on canals, died within eighteen months after the birth of this last child. It was the widowed mother who reared the young brood; she was a pious and resourceful woman who scorned outside aid—preferring herself to care for the farm and to perform a dozen other tasks for neighbors in exchange for clothing and supplies. Like Longfellow's blacksmith, she could look the whole world in the face, for she paid off her husband's debts even beyond the obligation legally imposed upon her. Yet biographers say that she filled the cabin with song, thrilled the adolescent minds of her children with tales of adventure, and inspired in them devotion to ideals and a longing for knowledge.

It has been a boon for historians that so many of our Presidents have set down in diaries their daily activities. James A. Garfield began his at sixteen, and his leading biographer quotes interesting passages which reveal how the lad worked for neighboring farmers to support himself and to increase the funds of his mother. Young Garfield chopped wood for fifty cents a day, cut grass for the same remuneration per acre, washed sheep, and plowed fields.[9] Then came the urge to be a sailor, but the drunken appearance of the ship's captain to whom he applied discouraged him temporarily. Thereupon, still intrigued with boats, he accepted a job on a canal barge of which his own cousin was captain. The accounts of his experiences, which involved encounters with brutal and bullying deckhands and near drownings, make interesting reading. This boy of sixteen, relying on brawn and brain, was observing the coarser phases of life. Within a few months, while on a visit home, he was stricken with malaria; his sailing career was at an end. During his illness he read borrowed books, which whetted his yearning for more schooling. Well again, he helped on his mother's farm, and her diligent saving from her meager income enabled him to enroll at an "academy" in a neighboring town; there he added to the rudiments of learning which he had acquired in the cabin school nearer his home. By alternating his studies with manual labor, he managed to remain for the entire school session, paying twelve dollars for his bare lodging during the term.

In those days the school curriculum did not include the manual arts or athletic activities. There was abundant physical exertion in earning the means of paying for tuition and subsistence. Education for the farm boy was a privilege, not an imposed routine. But there were diversions from studying. Of these, debating societies were the most popular. And in these mental and vocal contests young James Abram Garfield excelled. Here he had the practice in public speaking that made him prominent later in the halls of Congress.

Despite his limited preparation, this future President at eighteen himself became a teacher, receiving less than fifty dollars for four months' work dispensing wisdom in the district school of a village which had named itself Solon. Then followed positions in other schools, his own studies at Williams College.[10] And finally the principalship of a small college. At twenty-seven, in 1858, he married Lucretia Rudolph, the daughter of Zeb Rudolph, a prominent leader of the Disciple Church which Garfield had joined and a founder of Hiram College, of which Garfield had become the head. His bride had been his classmate and later his student, and his interest in her gradually developed into a sincere affection. Although his courtship was not as ardent as the romances of other Presidents, there is no doubt that their life together was very happy. In the year following their marriage he was elected to the Ohio Senate.

Then came the Civil War. Abraham Lincoln called for volunteers to force the Southern States back into the Union. James A. Garfield, in Ohio, began to enlist soldiers in the Federal cause. For this task he was peculiarly fitted: as succinctly expressed by an able biographer, "His power of debate, already ripe, increased by his efforts as a lay-preacher in his church, and his oratorical style made Garfield a useful agent in raising troops and stimulating enlistments."[11] He was made lieutenant colonel of the regiment he organized; later he was advanced in rank. Assigned to staff work, he gave to his tasks the minute analysis which throughout his life he accorded to every problem from arranging seats in a classroom to a Congressional debate on the tariff issue. He blueprinted army organization with skill and incisiveness, developed plans for assembling military information. He was promoted to the rank of major general.

In that era generals and political careers were inseparable: James A. Garfield was elected to the Congress of the United States. His popularity and reputation for integrity dispelled the charges by political rivals that he profited by using his influence and official position to advance the interests of corrupt financial manipulators; the scandals which involved and destroyed other prominent figures grasped at him but did not pull him down.

In 1880 Garfield won the highest prize the Republican Party could accord. The national convention met to nominate a candidate for the Presidency. The outstanding contestant for the nomination was Ulysses S. Grant—four years out of the White House after serving two terms as Chief Executive. Grant wanted a third term, and he was the choice of a larger number of delegates than were mustered by any of his rivals throughout many ballots. But he did not have a majority of the votes; and powerful party chieftains were determined that he should not be the nominee. However, the leaders of the "stop Grant" movement could not agree upon a single man to oppose him. James A. Garfield came to the convention to nominate the experienced statesman, John Sherman. But it was Garfield who became the candidate of the Republican Party.[12] In the following November he was elected President, and was sworn in as Chief Executive on March 4, 1881. In September of that year he was dead —the victim of the crazed Charles Guiteau.

Such was the arduous career of the President to whom Lucretia Rudolph bore four sons for whom, upon their father's death, the American people lavished abundant funds to save them from the hardships experienced by their sire. Let us review their success stories.

The two older sons, Harry Augustus and James Rudolph, entered Williams College in 1881, in the class of 1885. That became a famous class, the largest at Williams up to that time. Writing the college history half a century later, the journalist Auguste Babize explained why so many more flocked to its halls in 1881 than in previous years. "In 1880 James Abram Garfield had been elected President of the United States. In December, 1880, the newspapers of the country carried the announcement that President Garfield had two sons, aged respectively seventeen and fifteen years, who would enter Williams College with the class of 1885."[13] But the President's sons claimed no privileges; they entered wholeheartedly into college activities, and mingled without hauteur among their classmates. Thus when, shortly after they became Williams students, their Presidential father was killed and the White House was no longer the parental home, these Garfield sons had no need to adjust their attitude nor their associations.

Although James was two years younger, he and Harry were in the same classes. We have a detailed comparison of the two brothers in the "class statistics" compiled by the secretary of the graduating seniors; the data were supplied by the Garfield boys themselves. James, called "Kid" or "Jimmy" on the campus, weighed ten pounds more than his brother, was five feet eleven inches in height while Harry was only five feet eight and one-half inches tall, and Jimmy's biceps measured two inches more than those of the older brother. Both wore shoes of the same size, but Jimmy required gloves one size larger than his brother's. Harry claimed musical talent at the piano, the younger brother listed his skill with banjo and guitar.[14] Harry played football, Jim was on the basketball team; Harry was editor of the college paper, Jim vied in intercollegiate tennis. In ambition, tastes, and mental traits the two brothers also were dissimilar. The older of the two listed "College Church" as his religion, the younger was "undecided" about his religion; in philosophy Harry had "not decided," his brother had adopted none at all. That James, just nineteen, could not formulate a definite philosophy of life and had completed his academic courses without becoming a professed communicant of some church might have been due to the diversity of creeds championed by his classmates: the sixty-two graduates listed twenty faiths—among them Congregationalist, Methodist, Roman Catholic, Baptist, Presbyterian, Orthodox, Swedenborgian, Universalist, Episcopalian, Hard-Shell Baptist, Unitarian, and Christian. There were also those who boldly called themselves "Agnostics," "Boycotters," or said that their religion was "not heavy," or that they had "no preference." Williams College, even in the closing years of the nineteenth century, was a forum for many philosophies and many credos. A great teacher, Mark Hopkins, presided over Williams and inspired its youth to independence in thought, understanding, and tolerance.[15]

Together Harry and James received their A.B. degrees in 1885, and both then began the study of law at Columbia University in New York City. After graduating from that law school, the brothers opened an office in Cleveland. The younger brother continued in the legal profession, with short excursions into the field of politics; the older embarked upon a more diversified career.

Harry Augustus Garfield devoted his abilities in turn to law, business, public service, and education; in all these fields his endeavors were crowned with considerable success. While later he became a professor and a college president, Harry at the beginning of his career evidenced no extraordinary attachment to scholastic theories or to pedagogy; he was a practical man and, while he took an active part in civil affairs, his talents were devoted largely to business enterprises—he organized banks, water companies, and syndicates to develop coal mines.[16] The pattern of his career is a crisscross of alternating professions and varied activities. From 1891 to 1897 we find him a professor of law at the Western Reserve University; in 1898 he is president of the Cleveland Chamber of Commerce. Thus, from the analysis of abstract legal dictums he turned to the solution of concrete industrial problems. Four years later, this eldest son of the former President again took up professorial tasks, lecturing on politics at Princeton University.[17]

While professor of politics at Princeton, Harry Augustus Garfield was elected president of Williams College in Massachusetts, where he, his brothers, and his Presidential father had studied. He was installed as head of that institution on the one hundred and fifteenth anniversary of its founding, which fell on October 7, 1908. Elegant brochures of the occasion were printed, and they afford details of the impressive academic procedure. The ceremony, long in preparation, was outdrawn and elaborate; eloquence and gastronomic offerings left pleasant memories. Present were the heads of fifty other American universities, the Governor of Massachusetts, the British Ambassador, men prominent in education, the professions, and politics.[18] There were processions around the college campus, and many of the marchers were attired in the academic gowns bespeaking their rank in the scholastic world. There were speeches to welcome the incoming president; among those who spoke was the head of Princeton University, Woodrow Wilson, destined within five years to become President of the United States. Harry Garfield, formally declared president of Williams College, delivered an address on "What Is the Chief End of the American College?" His discourse was scholarly, and his thesis was summed up in a paragraph:

What is wanted in our colleges is an object that can appeal to every student, whatever may be the future lifework of each. This object must meet the requirements of the times, without sacrificing the rich heritage of the past. It must quicken and inspire men to new and higher conceptions of life, without rendering them less, but rather more, efficient members of society. Such an object is expressed by the word citizenship. America's greatest need is that the men and women of the United States comprehend all that citizenship imports, and live up to its obligations. Hence, I venture to assert that the chief end of the American college is to train citizens for citizenship.

Harry Augustus Garfield had been president of Williams College for nearly a decade when the United States became an armed participant in the First World War, and he played an important part in several phases of our preparation for and conduct of the conflict. Even before war was formally declared he organized, in the summer of 1917, a camp for the military instruction of Williams students. The college was proud of this foresight, and an editorial in the *Alumni Review* said: "To President Garfield is due the credit for the establishment of the summer camp. Only two other colleges in the East have been able to organize camps of this kind under Government organization." [19] And another college periodical praised his "tenacity of purpose and determination to promote the best interests of the college, as exhibited so clearly in this matter." [20]

In the summer of 1917 it became clear that there was need to regulate the price of wheat, and this eldest son of the former President of the United States was chosen to head the committee charged with this essential task. In the words of the proud editor who recorded the achievements of Williams College graduates, "When the Government at Washington reached the decision that conditions in the market for wheat required the fixing of the price of the 1917 crop, at the suggestion of President Wilson, Dr. Harry A. Garfield was appointed as Chairman of the Price Committee of the United States Food Administration." [21] The committee made a report to the President at the end of August. In the meantime Wilson had appointed Harry A. Garfield to another post—that of United States Fuel Administrator. He was charged with the conservation and equitable distribution of the coal output which was essential to the war effort. In this task he displayed ability as an administrator, although he was accused of using dictatorial methods to realize his objective. Said the New York *Times,* in retrospect two decades after his work had been done, "Under plans devised by Dr. Garfield and his associates, coal production during the first year of the Fuel Administration was increased 50,000,000 tons bituminous and 12,000,000 tons anthracite over the previous year. Conservation of the supply presented difficult problems. Some of the Fuel Administration's orders were unpopular, especially those that decreed heatless days and 'gasless' Sundays and the curtailed use of fuel for non-war industries. Protests were received from many parts of the country that the orders were too drastic, but Dr. Garfield insisted upon compliance to insure an adequate fuel supply for all essential war industries and activities." [22]

He held the post of Fuel Administrator for two years, until the middle of December, 1919. Whatever may have been the criticism by the industries which he regulated or the protests of the public chafing under wartime restrictions, his work impressed President Woodrow Wilson; [23] at the Chief Executive's command, the Distinguished Service Medal was awarded in February, 1921, to Harry A. Garfield, the citation reading:

> For meritorious and distinguished service in a position of great responsibility. During the progress of the war, by his conduct of the Fuel Administration, he stimulated the production, conserved the use, and supervised the distribution of those supplies of fuel necessary for the support and transportation of the Armies of the United States, the maintenance of industry, the production of war supplies, and the health and well-being of the civil population upon which the successful prosecution of military activities depended. This medal is awarded by the direction of the President of the United States.[24]

Ending his official tasks in Washington, Garfield returned to Williams College. Under his presidency, the college tripled its endowment funds, and increased greatly its facilities. But it was not the new buildings which increased the prestige and spread the reputation of Williams. Harry Garfield organized the Institute of Politics and at its annual sessions men of world prominence publicly discussed vital problems in political, social, and industrial fields.[25] This forum brought Williams to the forefront of American educational institutions. "Many institutes of politics have come into existence in the last ten years," commented the New York *Times* in 1930, "but the one at Williamstown still holds first place by the distinction and representative character of its group of lecturers and round-table leaders. . . . This is a phase of adult education most helpful to a democracy wishing to know its duty in a world which has left its fate so largely to the determination of public opinion." [26] The high plane of the forum was maintained during the succeeding fifteen years. But it cannot be said that its influence in molding world opinion, or even popular sentiment in the United States, fulfilled the hopes of its founders. Possibly, it was too much to expect any group of men, meeting in a single place once a year, to spread widely the theses evolved there. The Gospel was preached by itinerant devotees roaming the world. But, among the "intellectual class," the deliberations at Williamstown aroused much discussion.

The energies of Harry Augustus Garfield transcended the realm of his college functions. He roamed other fields as well. He might have said with the Latin poet Terence, "Whatever interests my fellow man, interests me." The diversity of his interests and the scope of his activities are reflected in the catalogue of organizations in which he held membership: American Historical Association, American Economic Association, American Political Society of International Law, American Bar Association, National Municipal League, National Institute of Social Sciences, League of Nations Nonpartisan Association, American Academy of Political and Social Science, and Council on Foreign Relations of the World Peace Foundation. He was also a member of the United States Constitutional Sesquicentennial Commission and the Washington National Monument Society, and president of the Outdoor Cleanliness Association of the District of Columbia.[27]

In 1933, Harry Augustus Garfield ended his career as head of Williams College; he had been its president for a quarter of a century. To the college trustees he wrote a formal letter of resignation, saying, "It is stated that at the time of his resignation in 1872, Mark Hopkins, when asked why he resigned, replied: 'I wish to resign that it may not be asked why I do not resign.' . . . After a prolonged and careful consideration, I have reached the conclusion that I should retire at the end of the present academic year. It is unnecessary to give expression to the reasons and sentiments that move me.

They are implicit in the reply made by Dr. Hopkins, which would be my reply."[28] Upon his retirement from the presidency of Williams College, the New York *Times* said in praise of him: "Heir to a distinguished name, trained in our best traditions, experienced in the rough ways of democracy yet keeping withal a fineness and gentleness of character, he might well be chosen as an ideal American type. The people of his own land have had reason to be proud of him as he has in recent years moved among the leaders in other countries. It has been the fortune of a generation of young men to have had the close association of college life with one whom his own generation would elect to represent it at its best."[29]

James Rudolph, the second Garfield son, was as mentally alert as he had been physically nimble. In the same class with Harry, he was a college freshman when his father died; the youngest member of the class, he was nicknamed "Kid."[30] In his junior year he was champion of the college in lawn tennis, and business manager of the baseball team. During the summer vacation he entered a law office in Cleveland, at the same time attending lectures on medicine. Like a gymnast undecided what test of skill would most likely prove his prowess, he was undetermined whether to become a doctor or a lawyer. Finally deciding to prepare for the legal profession, he entered the Columbia Law School, and graduated in two years. Thus, in March, 1888, he and Harry together opened a law office in Cleveland. But he was not content to live in a large city. Having married the daughter of a railroad president, Jim joined an uncle in purchasing two hundred acres of land near the smaller Ohio town of Mentor. There he not only built a home, but also conducted a stock farm. The sons of the twentieth President did not confine their energies to a single interest or profession; we have already seen how Harry organized business ventures, held Government posts, practiced law, became a college professor, and was elected president of Williams College. His younger brother practiced law and raised cattle. That was not enough—he wanted also to engage in politics.

His political career began before he was thirty, in 1895—fourteen years after his acrobatic stunts on the White House lawn. He wanted to be a State Senator, and the first hurdle was to obtain the Republican nomination. His rival was a former Speaker of the Legislature's lower house. The party convention for the two districts to be represented was held in Warren, and there was much excitement. A prominent Cleveland paper sent a reporter and devoted an entire column to the proceedings, saying, "Warren has had many political conventions, but few have exceeded in interest this meeting of Republicans. . . . It is also the fourteenth anniversary of the assassination of President Garfield, whose son is a candidate before the Convention." [31] The contest was lively, each candidate being eager to win the votes of the 196 delegates; but 106 preferred the son of the former President, and James Garfield became the nominee.[32] Upon his return home a band and "a large concourse of people" met him at the depot; there was a reception at the leading hotel, and James "spoke feelingly" in response to his neighbors' enthusiastic welcome. Nominated by the Republican convention, the election of young Garfield was assured because he was a candidate in two districts in which his party predominated. He served for three years.

Following the customary pattern, his father's successors in the White House appointed this President's son to Federal offices: James Garfield served as a United States Civil Service Commissioner, and also held a post in the Department of Commerce and Labor.[33] Theodore Roosevelt was then President, and was determined to curb the industrial trusts which were destroying smaller competitors. Garfield directed investigations of important industries accused of monopoly and price control, among them meat packing, oil refining, and coal mining. Popular approval of these efforts led the President to appoint James Rudolph Garfield a member of his Cabinet, as Secretary of the Interior. This post he retained until March, 1909. When, after retiring from the Presidency, Theodore Roosevelt reviewed the work of his former Cabinet officers, he singled out for high praise the integrity and ability of this son of a former President; he wrote in his *Autobiography* that "the appointment of James R. Garfield as Secretary of the Interior led to a new era in the interpretation and enforcement of the laws governing the public lands. His administration of the Interior Department was beyond comparison the best we have ever had. It was based primarily on the conception that it is as much the duty of public-land officials to help the honest settler get title to his claim as it is to prevent the looting of the public lands." [34] While this tribute was merited, it is not unlikely that when the ex-President wrote the eulogy about his former Secretary of the Interior the appraisal was colored with appreciation that James

Rudolph Garfield was one of the leading spirits who, in 1912, championed Theodore Roosevelt as the leader of the new Progressive Party and campaigned vigorously to elect the "Rough Rider" for a third term.[35]

The 1912 campaign was one of several national elections in which James Rudolph Garfield was a tireless worker for a lost cause. Theodore Roosevelt, in 1901, had been Vice-President when the assassination of the incumbent Chief Executive, William McKinley, raised him to the Presidency. In 1904 he was re-elected; at the end of his two terms he turned over the reins of government to the succeeding President, William Howard Taft, whose nomination he had dictated and in whose election he had played the dominant role. Roosevelt went on a hunting expedition in Africa; upon his return he became dissatisfied with the policies of his successor. Failing to obtain the nomination for a third term from the regular Republican Party convention which chose Taft, his enthusiastic followers organized the Progressive Party and made Theodore Roosevelt their candidate. James Garfield was prominent in conferences of the leaders of the movement, and active in campaigning. The Republican vote was divided; and the Democratic candidate, Woodrow Wilson, emerged the victor. "Since then Jim Garfield gradually has been retiring from active politics," was the terse but premature comment of the Williams College historian.[36]

While he did not hold conspicuous offices during the First World War as did his brother Harry, James Garfield did perform an important task. He became a divisional manager of the American Red Cross, supervising the work in Ohio, Indiana, and Kentucky. This post he held from June, 1917, to September, 1918.[37]

The year 1932 brought James Rudolph Garfield into the political arena again. Politicians had not forgotten that, twenty years previously, he had renounced affiliation with the regular Republican Party which had elected his own father to the Presidency; and that he had been active in organizing the Progressive Party, dedicated to nominate and elect Theodore Roosevelt as Chief Executive. That party had disintegrated, but Garfield still stood high among the liberal element which had returned to the Republican fold after the split of 1916. Now, one of the aspirants for the Republican Presidential nomination was the incumbent President, Herbert Hoover, and he enlisted the support of James R. Garfield. The strategy of the Hoover campaign manager in Ohio was to garner the delegation votes for President Hoover; and, as a safeguard against any possibility of their straying to another leading rival until they were ready to make deals, to tie them to James R. Garfield as a temporary alternative. Thus, as reported in the *Ohio State Journal,* "Hoover candidates to the national Republican convention were pledged to support James R. Garfield, Cleveland, as their second choice." [38] The shrewd political manipulators had plans other than this published declaration.

This President's son was Hoover's choice for the resolutions committee of the forthcoming convention—the committee which was to voice the party's views on the liquor question. Herbert Hoover was a "dry." Garfield was believed to hold similar views on the prohibition issue. But he refused to express himself.[39] Despite his taciturnity, he became Hoover's emissary in conferences with party leaders, possibly because there were more recent rumors that he was "a dry whose views have become more liberal during the last few years," and could therefore effect a compromise between the dry and wet factions among the Republicans.[40] At any rate, metropolitan papers devoted many columns to his meetings with political functionaries in Washington, in Cleveland, and in New York. He was then sixty-seven, described as "a tall, white-haired man with a bristling moustache." We find him called a "platform maker," [41] and an editorial writer of the New York *Times* stressed his qualifications as chairman of the resolutions committee because his stand on the harrassing liquor question was so indefinite: "He is reported to be 'a conservative dry,' a label which can mean almost anything. . . . A platform calls for facile command of the English language; it calls for a unique choice of words which will go around a point instead of making one. Now, Mr. Garfield has had the unusual opportunities to observe the process of platform-making." [42] The correspondent who watched him at the convention in Chicago corroborated still further the political diplomacy and resourcefulness of this President's son, reporting that he "has shown qualities which have won the admiration of the Administration and its spokesman. From the time he took over the post he has been tactful, discreet, and conciliatory with all who approached him." [43] When the text of the plank on the prohibition issue was published, it was evident that James Garfield and his associates were indeed master craftsmen: the phraseology meant all things to all men, with the predominant objective to persuade the voter that, no matter what views he held, his convictions should not prevent him from casting his ballot for the party! [44] James R. Garfield pleaded for party regularity.

There were those in the Republican Party, with more unequivocal and uncompromising convictions on the liquor problem, who repudiated the doctrine that, no matter what the platform was, there should be complete support of the party ticket at the ensuing election. One of these outspoken political figures was Hiram Johnson, the Senator from California who, in 1912, had bolted the regular Republican nominees and become the Vice-Presidential nominee of the Progressive Party, with Theodore Roosevelt as candidate for President. Johnson denounced the President's son who himself had left the Republican Party in 1912; said he: "I listened last night to a gentleman named Garfield read the Republican platform and I was particularly interested in the earnest and sonorous way he read the portion relating to party regularity and the duty of officials to a party. My memory goes back twenty years when I knew another Garfield—a man unafraid, who went forward in the glorious adventure of the Progressive Party under Theodore Roosevelt. No party tradition bound that Garfield; no loyalty to an organization as a mere organization then fettered his courage. That Garfield fought the good fight for high ideals and decent politics. At my age and with my memories I cherish the Garfield I knew in 1912." [45] Hiram Johnson's scorn for the plank conjured up by James Rudolph Garfield was eclipsed by the more biting condemnation of many influential papers. "In some paradise of politicians there may yet be devised a compromise more inclusive and vague," commented the New York *Herald Tribune*, a staunch Republican organ, "[but] to date it has no rival." [46] The Chicago *Tribune* called it "a product of political cowardice and hypocrisy"; [47] the New York *Sun* termed it "a pitiful example of ducking and dodging." [48] But there were also newspapers which considered the party declarations as the only practicable compromise of divergent views on the liquor problem.[49]

The avalanche of criticism of his handiwork prompted Garfield to issue a long explanation of the plank; and many newspapers reprinted it in full. He argued that it "was the fairest method possible for solving the prohibition question," and he answered in detail the charge that delegates to the national convention were office holders fearful of losing their Government posts if they had voted their own conviction and opposed his plank, which had been approved by the Administration.[50] Most of the Republican leaders praised his work, believing that it was the only way to win the largest number of votes. They had not long to wait for the verdict: in November the Republican Party was defeated decisively. Many impartial observers expressed the opinion that the plank drafted by James Rudolph Garfield destroyed every prospect of victory for the party he endeavored to serve. The election over, James R. Garfield returned to his legal practice in Cleveland. For the second time in a national election his efforts had merely split the voters of the Republican Party. He did not again play a conspicuous part in a Presidential campaign.

The two younger sons of the assassinated President Garfield—Irvin McDowell and Abram—also attended Williams College. Like their two older brothers, they were classmates, and with a similar two-year disparity in their ages they graduated together in the class of 1893. While they did not receive the newspaper publicity accorded Harry Augustus and James Rudolph, neither did these Presidential sons hide their lights under an obscuring bushel; short sketches of their lives, usually based upon their own résumés, have appeared in diversified "who's who" directories.[51]

The newspaper reporter who described Irvin in his boyhood called him "the queerest genius of the family," but his mature years certainly revealed neither idiosyncrasies nor outstanding talent to make headlines. Nevertheless, his career evidenced ability. He had studied law at Columbia in New York, and opened a law office in Boston. His clients were prominent corporations and wealthy individuals. He became chairman of boards of directors, he helped guide industrial enterprises, banks, and public utilities. His civic interest comprised membership on directorates of several hospitals.

Abram, who had whiled away the hours at the White House drawing railway cars and machinery, continued at the drafting board—designing buildings. He had studied architecture at the Massachusetts Institute of Technology; and, while other graduates reported to the class secretary that they were obliged for months and for years "to work for nothing" to gain experience, or to accept jobs at small salaries to prove their capabilities, the youngest son of the twentieth President prospered quickly as an architect in Cleveland.[52]

Later in his career, after he had become well known, he decried personal publicity, declaring that "achievement and success will bring about this desirable personal publicity but personal publicity may hardly be depended upon to bring about achievement and success."[53] Nevertheless, he maintained his office in a building bearing the Garfield name; and it is not improbable that, in Ohio at least, his name acquired additional lustre because he was the son of a former President—even in the professions where expertness and talent are essential the road to success is easier when there is family prestige and the influence of highly placed friends. Abram Garfield was elected to membership in the foremost professional organizations. From 1929 to 1942 he was chairman of the Cleveland Planning Commission. His father and his brothers having been prominent in political and Governmental affairs, it was to be expected that, when legislative problems arose, Abram Garfield would be chosen as spokesman for the architectural profession. He was active in the affairs of the American Institute of Architects, and was selected as chairman of the committee on practice. In this role he endeavored to correct abuses in the architectural profession.[54] He voiced opposition to a bill sponsored by the engineering profession for the reorganization of the Interior Department, lest public architecture be brought under the administrative control of an engineer. "The executive framework of the United States Government cannot be reconstructed to accord with engineering ideas and engineering training, to the exclusion of fundamental artistic considerations underlying the huge Federal building program," he argued.[55]

During the late nineteen-thirties the Garfield sons were seldom mentioned in the newspapers. Since they had been prominent in the councils of the Republican party, the incumbent Democratic Administration manifested no inclination to make them conspicuous even though they were scions of a former President. Harry Augustus died in December, 1942. Long eulogies of his work appeared in the leading newspapers. In these obituaries references were made to his association with his brother James Rudolph, and his closeness to the other brothers who survived him.[56] In the half decade following the death of the scholarly Harry Augustus, the names of the other three brothers disappeared from the columns of the metropolitan press. But, down to 1947, the leading biographical directory allotted a paragraph to each; noting, immediately after the date of birth, that the subject was a "son of James Abram Garfield, 20th President of the United States." [57] James Rudolph, in Cleveland, was still listed as practicing law; however, his name was not included in the legal register which named Irvin as a member of a prominent Boston law firm.[58] In business, too, Irvin remained active; at seventy-seven, he was still a director of large banks, public utilities, and land companies.[59]

Similarly, Abram progressed inconspicuously as an architect, in Cleveland. The press associations made no mention of him until the spring of 1947; then they took note not of his professional achievements but of his romance.[60] Now a widower, he wooed and won Miss Helen Matthews, the secretary to the president of Smith College. Abram was seventy-five; his prospective bride, much younger.[61] The brief accounts of the love affair made no reference to Abram Garfield's professional eminence or to his wealth, but did refer to him as the "son of the former President."

Such were the success stories of these four Presidential sons whose father toiled on farm and canal boat to earn tuition for his rudimentary education, and whose path to the White House was beset with sacrifices and hardships.

13

Son of Chester A. Arthur

WASHINGTON SOCIETY WAS BUZZING WITH WHISPERED COMMENTS—ladies with a taste for intrigue and romance were exchanging conjectures and confidences about the White House, which had been newly decorated and refurnished.[1] Only a few months had passed since an assassin's bullet had ended the life of President James A. Garfield, and now there was a new Chief Executive in the white mansion on Pennsylvania Avenue—Chester Alan Arthur. He had been elected Vice-President and, under the Constitution, succeeded to the Presidency when Charles Guiteau, claiming that God had directed him, fatally shot Garfield on the second day of July, 1881.[2] Official mourning and sympathetic thought for the Garfield family were now giving way to interest in the new President Arthur, a widower. A story went from lip to lip as punch was served in the elegant drawing rooms of the Nation's Capital: the President was enamored of a beautiful woman—he paid homage to her photograph every morning, placing before it, as did the ancient worshipers at the shrines of their goddesses, bouquets of flowers. Soon Washington changed the story: it was the portrait of Arthur's wife who had died before he had reached the Nation's highest office.[3]

If this particular rumor was merely the fanciful creation of romantic minds, it nevertheless reflected the public knowledge that Chester Alan Arthur was attractive to women. From George Washington to Franklin D. Roosevelt no American President was so tall, none more aristocratic in bearing. The contemporary newspapers described him, as did the New York *World,* as "a magnificent specimen of physical manhood. He was over six feet in height, broad shouldered and deep chested. His eye was clear, his skin fair, and his general appearance indicated a born athlete."[4] It was to be expected that he would set feminine hearts stirring and his admirers were numerous—society dowagers and debutantes, heiresses, women of beauty and talent. From New York, Newport, Saratoga Springs, and divers other fashionable resorts there came to Arthur short notes and lengthy letters, bespeaking admiration and regard. Cartoonists depicted the handsome Chief Executive at his White House desk, a fluttering cupid whispering in his ear, and spread before him crested invitations to dinners and dances, and a deluge of notes from matrons and maidens.[5] But the letters he treasured most were from a banker's daughter, Julia Sand, who, from her invalid's chair, wrote him frequently long before she met him. They were chiding, taunting, reproaching letters. She began writing when he was still Vice-President, entreating him to use his office for the Nation's good, condemning his passivity when some positive action on his part might correct a wrong; and, when some official act met her high concepts of public service, her missives praised him and voiced her unabashed joy that he had done good. At first Arthur ignored these letters, but their rare beauty of diction, their comprehensive grasp of political events, and their impassioned appeals for him to become a truly great statesman, finally prompted him to visit Julia Sand. And, when he became President, these missives of sage counsel came to the White House.

There was reason for Julia Sand's admonitions, criticisms, and entreaties.[6] Chester Alan Arthur, in his early political career, had become affiliated with the political machine which then controlled city and State government, and dictated New York's role in national elections. He had become Collector of the Port of New York; Rutherford B. Hayes, becoming President in 1877, removed him with the scathing accusation, "You have made the Custom House a center of partisan political management . . . with a deep sense of my obligation under the Constitution I regard it my plain duty to suspend you." The political bosses later dictated his nomination for Vice-President in the convention which selected James A. Garfield as candidate for President. They were elected, and were inaugurated in March, 1881. Garfield's assassination made Chester A. Arthur President of the United States in the following September.

The American people had been indifferent when Arthur, the product of a corrupt machine, was elected Vice-President—but President! The New York *World* later described the prevailing mood of the country: "It was not too much to say," it editorialized, "that the

Nation stood aghast at the thought, then for the first time presented to the public mind, that Chester A. Arthur might become President." [7] "Chet Arthur in the White House!" the journalist Henry Stoddard recalled two decades later. "The country staggered that September morning in 1881 as it read that Garfield was dead . . . and that at midnight Chester Alan Arthur had been sworn in as President." [8] And yet, despite the record of the past which warranted these dire misgivings, Chester Alan Arthur rose to the dignity of the Presidential post; and, as expressed by one competent biographer, "he left office with the respect, if not the affection, of the people." [9] The professional politicians, his former cronies, drifted away. He was reserved and maintained dignity. In fact, his closest political associates have claimed that Arthur always maintained aloofness, that no one ever applied a "nickname" to him, and that only his immediate family and very intimate friends ever addressed him by his first name.[10]

Nevertheless, Chester Alan Arthur brought to the Presidency an urbanity and cosmopolitan attitude not characteristic of his predecessors; contemporary writers sensed in his personality a new type of President. Said the Washington correspondent of the New York *Tribune:* "In Arthur we have a new type of man in the White House. There have been Presidents of all kinds. We have had stately Virginia gentlemen of the old school, and self-made men from the West. We have had soldiers of several varieties—the rough and honest and despotic soldier, the quiet and obstinate and sometimes wrong-headed soldier, the simple and docile soldier. We have had rural statesmen who were born to country seats and died upon them, after bestowing solemn political autobiographies upon an ineffective country. We have had one or two Presidents who grew up amid the healthful poverty of the frontier which, as Blaine aptly said, 'is indeed no poverty but the beginning of wealth,' and who in all their upward progress through the world never wore off their simplicity. But the 'city man,' the metropolitan gentleman, the member of clubs—the type that is represented by the well-bred and well-dressed New Yorker—the quiet man who wears a scarf and a pin and prefers a sack coat to the long-tailed frock coat that pervades politics, and a derby hat to the slouch that seems to be regarded in various quarters of this Union as something no statesman should be without—this is a novel species of President." [11]

When Arthur moved into the White House his sister, Mrs. Mary McElroy, assumed supervision of the household. It was she who, after Mrs. Arthur's death in 1880, reared the two orphaned children—a daughter, now about fifteen, and a son, Chester Alan, Jr. The latter, usually called Alan, was seventeen when his father became President. Colonel Crook, then a White House clerk and in daily contact with the President's family, describes him as "a tall handsome young fellow with piercing black eyes and white skin. He was very slender indeed, and bright and clever. Like his father, he was extremely fond of horses; although unlike the President in that he enjoyed driving them himself."[12] It was reported that he progressed well at college, but his studies were interrupted by sudden and frequent visits to Washington and other places where there were more diversions than the Princeton campus could offer. "He would suddenly appear in Washington without notice," Crook tells us. "President Arthur used to be surprised every once in a while by unexpectedly seeing Alan at the breakfast table when he supposed the young man to be delving away at his studies at Princeton. But that never bothered Alan to any extent. When the spirit moved him, he would simply step on a train at Princeton and bolt through to Washington as soon as he could get here. He had many friends in the city, among whom he was a great favorite; and it did not make any difference to him whether he arrived here at four o'clock in the afternoon or ten o'clock at night. The first thing Alan would do would be to order his team of horses from the White House stables. Then he would whirl to call upon some young lady, if it were not too late; or ring up some of his young men friends. He was of a happy disposition in those student days and when he was home on vacation he did much to add to the gayety at the White House."[13]

Alan Arthur graduated from Princeton in 1885. His class comprised the scions of rich families and also the sons of fathers who had no wealth. Some became ministers and, as one graduate later reported, were "fighting the world, the flesh, and the devil; big contract for small pay"; some reaped larger contracts and accumulated a great share of worldly goods. One of Alan's classmates was the son of John Wanamaker, who owned what was then the world's largest department store; upon graduation the younger Wanamaker, as he himself reported, "became a member of the firm and remained a partner ever since."[14] Other classmates went as teachers to Syria and Egypt; a few became doctors, engineers, bank officials, publishers, unimportant clerks. As the years rolled on the graduates of 1885 sent in to their class secretary accounts of their careers and their progress since leaving the Princeton campus; most of them were eager to keep in contact with their classmates and, at five-year intervals, they held reunions. The President's son was not among them. He neither attended class gatherings nor did he report his activities since his college days.

Alan Arthur was not absorbed in scholarly research nor eager for academic triumphs. He had other interests. Not only in Washington did the President's son enjoy the company of young ladies; observant Julia Sand reported him at Newport, and wrote to his father: "I saw your dear little boy at the Casino the other evening—he was talking to the ladies in front of me for quite a while." And she disputed a current opinion that Alan was a Beau Brummell, adding her comment, "By the way, he didn't seem silly and dudefied at all in spite of what you and some other men say about him." [15] Alan Arthur throughout his life frequented "exclusive" resorts and mingled with fashionable society. In a later period he would have been called a "playboy." Two decades after his graduation from Princeton classmates recorded his total endeavors and achievements: "Arthur was the Colorado representative on the committee for the Taft inauguration ball. He drives a four-in-hand, and otherwise lives the life of a gentleman of leisure." [16] Horses were his deepest interest. As was the mode in his day among the wealthy and leisure class, the son of the twenty-first President drove blue-ribbon steeds harnessed to elegant carriages, which he acquired in great number. Years later, at a resort in Colorado, he organized a procession of his famous carriages, mounted the box of the leading vehicle, and headed the long line to the grounds of an elite hotel.[17] Polo ponies, too, were in his stables, and he was recognized as an amateur polo player of high ability. At dances and teas handsome Alan was a welcome guest; everywhere he mingled with the socially prominent. In short, both in America and across the Atlantic, Alan Arthur was regarded as a social leader and a sportsman.

Whether Alan's Presidential father wholly approved his son's indulgence in social activities to the exclusion of more practical pursuits, we do not know; the papers and correspondence of the twenty-first President mysteriously disappeared.[18] Chester A. Arthur left the

White House in March, 1885; he resumed his unofficial life in New York, and died in November, 1886. Alan followed his father's coffin from the mansion where the ex-President had gaily spent the months following his retirement from the Presidency.[19] Alan was then twenty-two; by the ex-President's will he received the income from half his father's estate until attaining the age of thirty, then the principal was to be paid to him.

For nearly fifteen years following his father's death, Alan Arthur remained a roaming bachelor. In 1900, traveling in Europe he met a California heiress, Myra Townsend, and married her at Montreaux, Switzerland, in the summer of the same year. American newspapers had lost interest in this President's son, and there were only rare allusions to his activities as a "sportsman and clubman." In 1916 the couple separated; eleven years later the wife sued for divorce in the courts at Santa Barbara, California, charging desertion.[20] A brief press dispatch relating to the suit was printed in several Northern papers, but no reference to this domestic discord appeared in the prominent journals of California, where Mrs. Arthur had her residence.

When not sojourning in Europe Alan Arthur made his home in New York, in Philadelphia, and other metropolitan centers; periods of city life were alternated with residence at country estates and ocean resorts. Finally he migrated to the society colony at Colorado Springs; and, in that Colorado town in November, 1934, occurred his second marriage. The local newspaper, under the caption "Society Event," described the bride as "prominent in society, engaged in the real estate and insurance business"; [21] a Denver journal added that she was once a society reporter.[22] Generally, the press in the West gave little space to this episode in the life of the ex-President's son; but in the East, where there remained more vivid memories of Alan Arthur while his father was President of the United States, longer accounts of the marriage were printed. The New York *Times* recounted the event under a conspicuous heading:

C. A. ARTHUR MARRIED;
LATE PRESIDENT'S SON
Weds Mrs. Rowena D. Graves
of Colorado Springs, Col.
He is 69 and Bride 40

Colorado Springs, Col., Nov. 3—The marriage of Chester Alan Arthur, son of the former President, and Mrs. Rowena Dashwood Graves, prominent Colorado Springs business woman, was performed at noon today at the home of Mrs. Godfrey Kissel here by Judge John C. Young of the district court. The only attendants were Mrs. Kissel, prominent socially here and in Denver, and Joseph Stephens of New York, close friends of the bridegroom. The couple will live in Colorado Springs after a short trip. Mr. Arthur is 69 and Mrs. Graves is 40.

Mrs. Arthur, born in Colorado of English parents, conducts an insurance and real estate office in Colorado Springs. She has been active for years in civic affairs.

Mr. Arthur was born in New York and spent much of his early life abroad. He has been a resident of Colorado Springs six years.

Mr. Arthur formerly was president of the Cheyenne Mountain Country Club and the Cooking Club and is a member of the El Paso Club, the Cooking Club and the Country Club, the Travelers Club of Paris, and the Racquet and Knickerbocker Clubs of New York. He formerly was a notable figure in the polo world and brought many famous personages to Broadmoor, exclusive suburb of Colorado Springs. He once owned carriages and horses that were the pride of Colorado.[23]

Less than three years after his second marriage, Alan Arthur died in an environment which always was dear to him—a fashionable resort. It would have pleased him, too, if he could have anticipated that his social activities would receive mention in the obituaries, as they did in the New York *Times:*

CHESTER A. ARTHUR DEAD
EX-PRESIDENT'S SON
Sportsman and Connoisseur of Art
Is Victim of a Heart Attack

Colorado Springs, July 18, (AP)—Chester Alan Arthur, internationally known sportsman, art connoisseur, social leader, and son of the late President Arthur, died today from a heart attack at his home here. His age was 72.

He had been in poor health recently, but his condition had not been regarded serious. Born in Albany, N. Y., on July 25, 1864, Mr. Arthur came to Colorado Springs in 1900.

Among his close friends were James Gordon Bennett, the publisher of the New York *Herald,* and James McNeill Whistler and John Singer Sargent, the artists. He was active in polo.

He was a member of the El Paso Club, the Cooking & Country Club, the Travelers Club of Paris, and the Knickerbocker and Racquet Clubs of New York.[24]

14

Sons of Grover Cleveland

IN THE CLOSING DAYS OF SPRING, 1886, MEMBERS OF THE CABINET IN Washington and a half dozen other persons outside the Capital received a brief note:

Executive Mansion, May 29, 1886

I am to be married on Wednesday evening, at seven o'clock, at the White House, to Miss Folsom. It will be a very quiet affair and I will be extremely gratified at your attendance on the occasion.

Yours sincerely,

GROVER CLEVELAND

Thus, the President of the United States invited thirty guests, in addition to a dozen relatives, to attend his wedding. An official announcement of the impending marriage was made the preceding night; and the leading Washington paper discussed the event in a half column hedged in between four columns of want ads, three columns of reports relating to oleomargarine, a detailed account of attempted rape in adjoining Maryland, and diverse dispatches regarding river improvements, Indian uprisings, and a meeting of a "laryngological association." "The President's marriage," commented the Washington *Star,* "may be the absorbing topic in social circles, but it scarcely creates more than a ripple on the surface in legislative circles. Senators and Representatives naturally feel some interest in the event, but it only extended far enough to obtain assurance that the marriage is definitely settled." [1] But, even though the male politicos were indifferent, the feminine element in the Capital was alert. The report continues: "Among the earliest callers at the White House this morning were three ladies; one of them wanted an invitation card to the wedding, another wanted to bespeak some of the wedding flowers, the third came to preempt a slice of the wedding cake."

Grover Cleveland was not the first bachelor who became President of the United States. James Buchanan came to the White House in 1857, and was unmarried during his entire term. In his early manhood he was desperately in love with a beautiful girl, and the happy lovers planned marriage and a home together. Suddenly she wrote breaking the engagement; gossip had reached her ears, and she gave the youthful Buchanan no opportunity to deny or explain. Within a year she died; and in his poignant grief he wrote to her father, pleading for a last glimpse of his beloved.[2]

Grover Cleveland, too, was the victim of malicious tales. During the political campaign of 1884 which raised him to the Presidency, there was much vituperation regarding his "affairs with women," in particular his association with an attractive widow, named Maria Halpin. The episode had occurred a decade earlier, but just prior to election day the partisan press unearthed the story and published it nationwide. Maria Halpin had come to Buffalo from Pennsylvania and, in the spring of 1874, met Grover Cleveland, then unmarried. Her shapeliness and vivacious personality attracted him as they did other men prominent in political and social circles. In the following autumn she bore a son and named him Oscar Folsom Cleveland, the first two names being those of Cleveland's law partner, a married man. Mrs. Halpin charged Grover Cleveland with the paternity of her child. It was before the era of blood tests; and, although it was known that the mother had affairs also with other men, Cleveland agreed secretly to provide for the child. Later, the boy was placed in an orphan asylum, to which the mother objected. Soon her protestations became public, and the newspapers spread the scandal. When his campaign managers became fearful that this sudden exposure would result in Cleveland's political defeat, he merely told them to "tell the truth." Prominent churchmen investigated the facts: Maria Halpin had singled out Grover Cleveland as the father, but her charge was not conclusive; he assumed the monetary burden of supporting the child lest she involve married men.[3] Cleveland's political opponents failed in their efforts to make this affair the medium of his defeat; the voters elected Grover Cleveland President of the United States.[4]

But rancor and rumor seemed stilled when the election was over, and Cleveland came to the White House.[5] Now that he was to be married, there was interest in his wife-to-be. There was no hint that the President's respite from revilement was but temporary, or that later gossip mongers were to harass his private life with rumors that there was discord in his home, that he was brutal to his wife, that their first-born was mute.[6] No presentiment of all this beclouded the thoughts of Frances Folsom on the evening of June 2, 1886, when, leaning on President Grover Cleveland's arm, she came down the west staircase of the White House into the Blue Room, while the Marine Band played Mendelssohn's "Wedding March." In her gown of ivory-white satin, with a veil of tulle about five yards in length which completely enveloped her, she needed no flowers or jewelry to accent her own inherent beauty; and the newspapers remarked the absence of these accessories, noting as her sole adornment her engagement ring of a sapphire and two diamonds.[7] Grover Cleveland's bride was the daughter of his law partner, a distinguished citizen of Buffalo, who fell from his carriage and died when this little daughter was eleven. Her mother had been Frances' constant companion during her adolescent years, and now witnessed her marriage to the President of the United States.[8] But it was Grover Cleveland himself who had directed the education of this fatherless child, planning the schooling which alternated with extensive travel abroad. No mistress of the White House brought to it more culture, more grace, more charm.[9]

In the nine years following this marriage, Frances Folsom Cleveland bore three daughters. When the second was born, in the summer of 1893, newspaper writers indulged in surmises that Grover Cleveland had wanted sons. "The gossips say that the President is much disappointed," remarked the Brooklyn *Daily Eagle,* "because the new member of the family is not a boy, but there is no evidence of this in his demeanor." [10] Two years later the third girl was born, and there was so much public regret that Mrs. Cleveland lost no opportunity to voice the opinion that "little girls were exceedingly nice." [11]

It was not until Grover Cleveland had left the White House after his second term that his wife bore him a son. The event occurred in Princeton, New Jersey, where the ex-President had established his home and become a lecturer at the famous university. The boy was born in October, 1897. The entire Nation rejoiced with the ex-President that at last there was a son to bear his name. Prominent newspapers heralded the event on their front pages: "Mr. Cleveland Has a Son," headlined the New York *Tribune.* At Princeton University, where the ex-President had become extremely popular, the students staged several celebrations. Said the dispatches, "Princeton undergraduates have taken a great interest in the new Princetonian. The fact that a Cleveland heir was born was announced during the Varsity practice this afternoon. There was a big gathering of undergraduates on the field watching the game between the Varsity and scrub teams. When the announcement was made three Princeton cheers were given for the boy, three for the mother, and three more for the father.[12] On the college bulletin board was posted the notice:

> Grover Cleveland, Jr., arrived today at 12 o'clock; will enter Princeton with the class of 1916; and will play center rush on the championship football teams of '16, '17, '18 and '19.

This first son of the ex-President was not named Grover, Jr., as the Princeton students predicted; instead he was christened Richard Folsom Cleveland, and the father jovially gave the reason in his exuberant letter to his friend, Richard Olney:

> I wish I could write something satisfactory to the ladies of your household touching our new boy. This I cannot do on my own responsibility, for I agree with you that when they count but two weeks as the period of earthly existence, all babies are very much alike, both as regards their looks and their conduct. As sort of second-hand information, however, I venture to say that the female members of our household declare that this particular child looks like his father, that he has blue eyes, a finely shaped head, and bids fair to be a very handsome and a very distinguished man. . . . We have named him Richard Folsom —my father's first name and my wife's father's last name. Some good friends thought we ought to call him Grover, Jr.; but so many people have been bothered by the name Grover, and it has been so knocked about, that I thought it ought to have a rest.[13]

But, despite the name the parents gave at the baptismal font to this first son of Grover Cleveland, the students at Princeton for nearly a decade invariably spoke of him as "Grover, Junior." [14] The campus prophets were somewhat more justified in their prognostication of his gridiron career: two decades later Richard Folsom Cleveland did play on the Princeton football team, but only in his freshman year.[15]

Young Richard was exceedingly popular with faculty and students. At six, the press described him as "a sturdy fellow, wears Russian blouse suits and has his hair cut square across the back. He is a great chum of his father." [16] He was prepared for college at the Exeter Academy, and there he evidenced literary interest, taking part in editing the school monthly. This writing experience continued in after years. He was made a member of the Student Council, and chosen president of the Christian Association.

Five and a half years after Richard's birth, his brother Francis was born, in July, 1903. Recalling that three daughters had preceded the first son, the newspapers surmised that the public would be intrigued that the fifth child was a boy. Typical of the headlines was that on the front page of the New York *Tribune:*

CLEVELAND BABY NO. 5
Ex-President Has Another Son
Born at Buzzard's Bay

Buzzard's Bay, Mass., July 18—A son was born to ex-President and Mrs. Grover Cleveland at their summer home here today.[17]

Other papers also printed prominent captions; some journals, like the New York *World,* published pictures of the Cleveland summer home at Buzzard's Bay on the Massachusetts coast, and photographs of the ex-President, Mrs. Cleveland, and the older son Richard; the other Cleveland children were listed and it was noted that "Mr. Cleveland is in his sixty-seventh year." [18]

Grover Cleveland welcomed the arrival of this younger son in happy phrases, as he had the birth of Richard; to the wife of Princeton's president he wrote:

I sent you a telegram this morning that a tramp boy had trespassed upon our premises. He was first seen and heard at 10 o'clock A. M. (I hear him now), and I sent the despatch to you. . . . The shameless naked little scoundrel weighed over nine pounds. Richard was very much tickled as long as he thought it was something in the doll line, and was quite overcome with laughter when he found it was "a real baby." He and I have been planning for the amusement of the newcomer when he shall arrive at Richard's present age. He denies with considerable warmth any intention of taking him by the hair and throwing him down. In point of fact we have agreed upon no particular line of conduct, except an engagement on Richard's part to teach the young brother to swim if all goes well.[19]

Grover Cleveland lived only five years after the birth of his second son. He died in 1908. In February, 1913, his widow remarried, her second husband being a Princeton professor, Thomas J. Preston, Jr. Richard was then sixteen, living with his mother; Francis was a student at the Exeter Academy.[20] The eldest son of the ex-President later began his studies at Princeton. As an undergraduate he took part in the movement against the exclusive club system, a crusade which had brought fame to Woodrow Wilson, then president of Princeton.[21] Class president in his freshman year, he served also on the Student Council, and was secretary of several college organizations interested in political subjects. He belonged to the literary societies, and was on the board managing the college magazine. But his activities were not restricted to scholastic subjects; in his first year he played on the football team, won the Varsity "P," and was on the track team.[22]

Richard's academic career was interrupted in 1917 by our entry into the First World War. At first he contented himself with military drills on the Princeton campus, but in June he left college and enlisted in the Marines. From corporal he rose to first lieutenant, and in this uniform he was photographed for the *Class Book*. He served overseas, and at the war's end he held a minor post in the American Legation at Peking, China. Then he returned to Princeton, and was graduated with the Class of 1919. The senior record noted that "his father was until his death a lawyer and twice President of the United States." Called "Dick" by his classmates, he was voted the "most thorough gentleman," the "most respected," and also the student "who did most for Princeton." He was not included among "those most likely to succeed," but he was considered one of the six "having the biggest drag with the Faculty." [23] He continued his courses, and was awarded the degree of A. M. in 1921. He then took a trip to Europe and there met the daughter of Bishop Gailor, executive head of the Episcopal Church in America. Two years later, at Memphis, Tennessee, he married her.[24] "The nuptials were marked by the utmost simplicity," reported the Memphis *Commercial Appeal*, "only immediate members of the family and a few friends being invited. No formal notice of the time of the wedding had been made." [25] The bride, a teacher of English, was a graduate of Vassar and Columbia.

Richard Cleveland chose the legal profession as his career. After he left Princeton he had studied law at Harvard, graduating in 1924. During his Harvard years he spent his summer vacations in Baltimore, and wrote articles on political subjects for a leading newspaper there.[26] He liked the Maryland metropolis and there, after completing his law studies, he established residence. A year later he was admitted to the Maryland bar, and became associated with a law firm in Baltimore. His firm had important clients, among them banks, prominent distilleries, shipbuilding corporations, insurance companies, and large mercantile firms.[27]

Richard's father, through the votes of his fellow citizens, had achieved important public offices and finally was elected Chief Executive of the Republic; but the son made no great efforts to test his own popularity at the ballot box. Politicians in Maryland, recalling that he was a President's son, mentioned his name for Mayor, United States Attorney, and Vice-President; Richard Folsom Cleveland met these suggestions with a denial that he had political ambitions.[28] Nearly half a century had elapsed since Grover Cleveland had been a potent factor in national affairs; and it was almost three decades since his death. The public in general evidenced no interest in the Cleveland son. However, Richard did obtain several State offices by appointment. For a year he was General Counsel of the Public Service Commission in Baltimore.[29]

During the early nineteen thirties Richard was active in Maryland political maneuvers directed to the naming of a Presidential candidate to be supported by the Maryland Democratic delegation. In the presence of Governor Ritchie of Maryland, a contestant for the nomination to be made at the forthcoming Democratic national convention, a group of Democratic leaders met in Baltimore in May, 1932, and selected Richard F. Cleveland to present at the State convention meeting the following day a resolution binding the State delegates to cast their votes for the Governor.[30] Richard Cleveland performed his prescribed task exceedingly well; he presented the dictated resolution and made a speech eulogizing Governor Ritchie. Although the Baltimore *Sun* relegated to its twenty-sixth page the account of the meeting and quoted only several paragraphs of Richard's address, party leaders expressed complete satisfaction.[31] Another paper, however, was mindful that the speaker was a President's son, and headlined on its front page, "Son of Late Grover Cleveland Offers Governor's Name." [32] There were no impassioned phrases in the speech; on the contrary, the context was reminiscent of the direct language characteristic of his Presidential father, Grover Cleveland.

Said Richard: "Disillusioned Americans today are searching desperately for someone who will do his straightforward duty for the country without intimidation from any group. . . . We are mortally sick and tired of government by stuffed shirts. In this emergency, which is spiritual as well as economic, the Democratic Party must present a man who has not only a long record as an expert and trained administrator and forceful executive, but also one whose character stands forth as that of a thoroughbred." Having obtained the pledge that the Maryland delegates would support Governor Ritchie, Richard Cleveland was chosen to present Ritchie's name at the Democratic national convention. But this plan was changed when the delegation reached the convention city; Ritchie's name was placed in nomination by Millard Tydings, United States Senator from Maryland. However, Richard Cleveland had an opportunity to address the gathering; he seconded the nomination.[33] Ritchie failed to become the candidate.

In the election campaign of 1936 the eldest son of the twenty-second President joined the groups which were seeking to forestall the re-election of the incumbent President, Franklin D. Roosevelt. In Baltimore several influential papers, antagonistic to the Roosevelt Administration, gave prominent space to Richard's speeches, invariably noting in the headlines that he was a President's son. Thus the *News-Post* announced in blackface type, "Son of Cleveland to Hit New Deal," repeating in the text, "Richard F. Cleveland, a son of the onetime Democratic President of the United States, Grover Cleveland." [34]

While Richard Cleveland made no progress in the political arena, he did enhance his reputation by his endeavors for child welfare. In 1942 he was named as chairman of a commission to study juvenile delinquency. Sincere in his social objectives and forceful in his advocacy of methods he considered feasible, he was equally eager to adopt other measures when convinced of their greater effectiveness. In this he reflected the courage which had won for his father the respect of his fellow Americans and their choice of him as President. Richard gave careful thought to the problem of eradicating youthful crime; he submitted a report urging an amendment to the State Constitution which he deemed essential to permit the establishment of a court in Baltimore to deal with crimes committed by minors. When, a year later, another committee of judges declared that such courts could legally be established by legislative enactment, Richard Cleveland publicly called it "a sensible solution of the controversy over the amendment," and retreated from his previous contention that only a Constitutional amendment, ratified by the Maryland voters, could effect the desired result.[35]

Richard Cleveland was also interested in educational systems. Made secretary of the board of governors of St. Johns College at Annapolis, he not only obtained substantial funds to save that old institution from closing, but he also played an important role in modernizing the curricula. This latter activity brought him censure from the Maryland legislators, sitting in the Capitol not far from the campus; Cleveland retorted that "the college is only two blocks from the State House. Some members of the Legislature might even be encouraged to reread some of the great books in the college curriculum, many of which were intimately known to their predecessor statesmen who founded our American institutions." [36]

While Richard Folsom Cleveland was developing his law practice and making sorties into political fields, his younger brother, Francis Grover, was engaged in academic efforts and deciding what profession to make his career. A tot of five when his father died, and ten when his mother remarried, this second son of Grover Cleveland was sent to the Exeter Academy for his early schooling. Then he went to Harvard, enrolling with the class of 1925. However, he was not among the graduates of that year.[37] At the time his classmates were indulging in Commencement festivities, Francis was a groom. Like his brother, he married a minister's daughter. The wedding ceremony occurred on a Saturday afternoon; and, since few New Jersey papers then had Sunday editions, the event was meagerly mentioned in the press of that State, despite the fact that both Francis and his bride had lived in New Jersey most of their lives. One journal in the State Capital the day before the marriage headed a single paragraph: "Society Interested in Princeton Wedding," and noted that "the wedding of Miss Alice Erdman, daughter of Rev. Charles Erdman, and Francis Grover Cleveland, son of the late Grover Cleveland, will take place this afternoon at 4 o'clock in the First Presbyterian Church, Princeton. The ceremony will be performed by the father of the bride. A reception at the Graduate School will follow." [38] No later comment was printed, although, on the following Monday, the same paper devoted an entire column to a reception planned for the bride's father, who was Moderator of the Presbyterian Assembly.[39] In New York, where Francis' father had risen high in State politics before being elected President of the United States, several metropolitan papers printed short paragraphs about the wedding, but these reports, telegraphed from Princeton, stressed most the importance of the bride's father. The article in the New York *Times* was typical:

MISS ERDMAN BRIDE
OF F. G. CLEVELAND
Dr. Erdman Officiates at Marriage of His
Daughter to Ex-President's Son

Miss Alice Erdman, daughter of the Rev. Dr. and Mrs. Charles R. Erdman of Princeton, N. J., was married yesterday to Francis Grover Cleveland, son of the late President Grover Cleveland and Mrs. Thomas Jex Preston, Jr., of Princeton. The ceremony, which took place in the First Presbyterian Church, was performed by the bride's father who was elected Moderator at the session of the Presbyterian General Assembly last month. He is a member of the Faculty of Princeton Theological Seminary and Pastor of the First Church. . . . Richard Folsom Cleveland, brother of the bridegroom, who married Miss Ellen D. Gailor, daughter of Bishop Gailor, was best man.[40]

In the second year of their marriage a daughter was born; ten years later Francis reported, "I still have only one child, because I think that is enough." [41]

Francis returned to Harvard in 1926, and we find his name again on the college register for the year 1928 as a "candidate for a bachelor's degree, out of course." [42] Francis devoted himself to the study of drama; at that time Harvard was preeminent in courses pertaining to play writing and acting. Leaving Harvard, this younger son of Grover Cleveland became a teacher in a private school in nearby Cambridge.[43] But he had a deeper interest in the stage. Reporting to his class secretary in 1935, he noted that his occupation had changed from "education" to "theater": "At the time of the last report, I was teaching school. I like acting better," he wrote, "I am now in New York with a show." [44] Thus the son of the twenty-second President became an actor. Such were the epochal changes which had occurred in social concepts since the era of the second President, whose son held so low an opinion of the acting profession that he scorned even to talk to a child actress! [45] In the succeeding decade Francis Grover Cleveland continued his association with the stage, but neither the theatrical journals nor the public press mentioned him as an outstanding example of dramatic ability.[46]

Thus, in a generation which scarcely remembered that their father had been twice elected Chief Executive of the Republic, Richard Folsom Cleveland and Francis Grover Cleveland carved out their careers —President's sons without White House memories.

15

Son of Benjamin Harrison

A COLLEGE PRESIDENT'S DAUGHTER, CAROLINE LAVINIA SCOTT, STROLLED about the campus with a student named Benjamin Harrison; and, in 1853, married him. We have no eye-witness accounts of them then, but, thirty-five years later, he was described as "slightly under medium height, a figure broad and compact; his large head sets well between broad high shoulders as his neck is very short." [1] And the newspaper reporters wrote of her, "A little woman, plump, fresh and wonderfully young. As a girl she must have been exceedingly pretty. The regular features, bright eyes and abundant hair of the matron tell that. She has a beautiful little hand, every finger of which is straight and shapely." [2]

If these two were so diverse in physical characteristics, they were alike in a heritage of distinguished ancestry. We do not know whether Caroline ever dreamed that her husband would himself become President of the United States; however, she did know that he was the grandson of a President, William Henry Harrison; she did know that her husband was the great-grandson of that Benjamin Harrison who signed the Declaration of Independence, pledging his "life, fortune and sacred honor" to create a new Republic, the United States of America.[3] And he must have known that his bride was the offspring of distinguished ancestors—a lineage which later entitled her to become the first president of the Daughters of the American Revolution.[4] What neither of them then knew nor could foretell was that they would become the parents of a son, Russell Benjamin Harrison, who would be among the first to accompany his father into the White House and the last to follow his father's bier, long after Caroline Scott Harrison had passed away, when Benjamin Harrison, retired from the Presidency, had died with a second wife at his bedside.

Probably, in the early years of their married life neither Caroline nor Benjamin gave thought to their ancestors, for two children came to them—a boy and a girl—and there was immediate need for the young parents to think of this growing family. Benjamin Harrison was one of thirteen children, and he had no pampered childhood. His boyhood was spent on his father's farm at North Bend, Ohio, and he studied law in nearby Cincinnati. Immediately after his marriage he moved to Indianapolis, Indiana, and there began to build a legal practice which made him wealthy. When, in 1861, President Abraham Lincoln called for volunteers Benjamin Harrison accepted a commission. In after years, when he was a candidate for public offices, his campaign managers made popular the story that, when he was reluctant to leave his wife alone with a young child, she urged him to go, saying, "Your country needs you." Step by step, Benjamin Harrison rose to the rank of brigadier general; and when the Civil War had ended, he returned to his law practice. Thereafter, his career was typical of many able generals who combined law with politics: he was elected to the United States Senate in 1881, and seven years later he was nominated and elected President of the United States for the term 1889 to 1893.[5]

In the meantime his only son, Russell Benjamin Harrison, grew to manhood. As a boy he occasionally visited his father's headquarters, and in after years he alluded to his knowledge of the Civil War. "I was too young to know the causes which led up to the war, and the great forces which were factors in the intellectual struggle which preceded it, but I was with the Army for a time, and I know what it all meant," he told an audience in Atlanta when his father sent him as his representative.[6]

His early schooling was at a military academy, and later he went to Lafayette College at Easton, Pennsylvania, to study engineering. There he remained four years, until he was twenty-three. Russell Harrison was no honor student; however, he appears to have mastered the required courses. He was proud that he was the great-grandson of a President, but no snobbishness marked his attitude, and he joined in the collegiate activities of his classmates. His final month at Lafayette was crowded with the preliminaries and celebrations of graduation—the customary rites in the eighteen-seventies. On the last day in May, the seniors left the college town to hold their class supper at picturesque Delaware Water Gap in the Pocono Mountains. Leaving the environs of Lafayette, the class marched to the railroad station, accompanied by the college band and cheered along the way by groups of under-classmen. A special car was attached to the train, and the college journal described the seniors as being in gay spirits, and singing the college songs as the train started to its rustic destination in the mountains. When they arrived at the Gap, carriages took them to the famous Kittatinny House familiar to many succeeding generations. "The long piazzas were lighted up with Chinese lanterns . . . during the early part of the evening the band played several selections and all voices joined in the songs of Lafayette." [7] As was the vogue at banquets of that day, toasts were drunk and speeches were made. Russell B. Harrison's theme was "Statesmanship." The Commencement exercises were held during the closing week in June. Before the degrees were awarded, the graduating seniors were required to "read and defend their theses before the Board of Examiners of the Scientific Department." Russell Harrison expounded on a "Review of the Exploitation of Coal, Empire Shaft Colliery, Wilkes Barre, Pa." He satisfied the examiners, and the degree of Mechanical Engineer was conferred upon him at the public exercises, June 27, 1877.

After graduation Russell returned to Indianapolis, and immediately obtained a position as engineer with the local gas-light company. Within a year we find him appointed Assistant Assayer of the United States Mint at New Orleans. Thus far his activities were related to the engineering field, but we shall find him later engaged in other fields—journalism, publishing, soldiering, law, and politics.[8] How much of his success was due to his own talents and how much to the fact that he became a President's son is difficult to appraise. Certain it is that his progress fluctuated with the political fortunes of his father—and his father-in-law. Russell Harrison married the daughter of an influential Senator.

As a Senator, Benjamin Harrison was obliged to spend the winters in Washington during the sessions of Congress, living at a small hotel with his wife and daughter. Russell visited his parents occasionally, and on one of these trips he met his sister's friend, Miss Mamie Saunders, the only child of his father's Senatorial colleague from Nebraska, who was an important voice in the councils of the Republican Party. She was just home from a boarding school, and the press described her as "a young blonde beauty." Russell fell in love with her; and, after a long courtship, they were married. The couple moved to Helena, Montana, where Russell was transferred from New Orleans and promoted to be Assayer and, as he reported to his alumni recorder, also "Assistant U. S. Treasurer."[9] This post he held for eight years; but he did not restrict his activities to his Governmental functions. He became secretary of the Montana State Board of Stock Commissioners. He acquired an interest in the *Montana Live Stock Journal,* an organ of the cattle industry. He became president of the company, but his inexperience in publishing led to libel suits for articles which, in other periodicals, were left unchallenged.[10] Ending his work with the Mint, he was appointed State Recorder of Brands and Marks. Later he himself ventured into stock raising and feeding. In the meantime he became owner of the Helena *Daily Journal.* There were uncontradicted reports that neither the publishing venture nor the experiment with cattle proved profitable.[11]

When Benjamin Harrison, in March, 1889, was inaugurated President of the United States, Russell proudly escorted his father into the White House. He and his wife spent a few weeks with the President, but later returned to their Montana home; thereafter he was a visitor at the White House at frequent intervals.[12] Russell Harrison was "a good mixer," and he formed friendships easily because he managed to discover mutual interests. He had a liking for outdoor life, and the similar tastes of Theodore Roosevelt brought the two men together after Russell's father was elected to the Presidency. Both had been "roughing it" out West, and Theodore Roosevelt, himself destined to become President, was steeped in the lore of the woods and tales of adventure, and he related some of his stories to the President's son. Russell's favorite story was about his presence at the lynching of a horse thief and his subsequent summons to sit on a Grand Jury which was to investigate the sordid occurrence.[13] We have no record of how this President's son appraised horse-stealing in the West in comparison with the political manipulations in Washington which made inroads on the public treasury.

In 1890 we find Russell B. Harrison installed in the White House as his father's official aide. It was when he became his father's secretary and his wife assumed the direction of social affairs at the White House that his financial successes became noticeable, and there were hints that this conspicuous material prosperity was due entirely to his official position. In the fall of 1891 the New York *Tribune* reported that Russell Harrison had received a half million dollars' worth of stock in the Aransas Harbor City & Improvement Company which was organized in the expectation that Congress would authorize a project to secure deep water to the Aransas Pass, where the San Antonio & Aransas Railroad line had a terminal. Russell became president of the corporation; he insisted that the undertaking was a legitimate business enterprise of "honorable and reputable men, prominent in public and business life." Since there was no evidence that he had made any substantial monetary investment, the newspapers pointedly asked why he had been given such a large amount of stock.[14]

Prior to his father's election to the Presidency, the newspapers pointed out, none of Russell Harrison's endeavors had brought him large financial returns. But now the President's son was on the highroad to financial prosperity. His wife had acquired a wardrobe of fashionable gowns which aroused the envy of social Washington and widespread comment in the press. "Within two years or so," exclaimed the Brooklyn *Daily Eagle,* "her husband's income would not have been sufficient to provide for expenditures of such an amount as her costumes must have cost." Russell's friends had intimated that President Harrison himself had added to his son's income something every year for the purpose of enabling his daughter-in-law to make a good showing in society; but this explanation was spurned by the newspaper which, tracing the sources of Russell's income, commented: "Owing to fortunate investments of young Harrison made through the advice of Secretary of War Elkins, he is now in practically independent circumstances. . . . He is naturally thrifty and he has been able by the opportunities offered him through his father's official position to meet many men of wealth and prominence, who have let him in on the ground floor on several schemes which since have turned out profitably. It is only fair to say that none of them has had connection with Government work or has been dependent in any sense upon official favor." [15]

But these comparatively mild comments on Russell Harrison's activities turned later into much sharper criticism when it was discovered that the President's son continued to acquire stock in projects whose success did depend upon the attitude of Government officials in Washington. Russell always pleaded that the stock was put in his name without his prior knowledge. In one of these scandals, relating to development of land in the Yellowstone Park region, the Brooklyn *Daily Eagle* said: "Manager Waters of the Yellowstone Park Association, who put aside 5,000 shares of stock in trust for Russell Harrison, testifies that he did so without that young man's knowledge, but admits that he had asked him to see the Secretary of the Interior in Waters' behalf and felt he might want to call on him again. For the last three years young Mr. Harrison had a succession of these demoralizing surprises. His embarrassment must be like the setting hen that found so many nests full of eggs she didn't know which to cover." [16] It was revealed, too, that Russell's wife was on the Government payroll, drawing $5,000 a year salary on the "Utah Mission," a Western sinecure which in no way interfered with her social activities. Russell Harrison and his wife made the White House gay with brilliant parties.

Toward the end of Benjamin Harrison's term, Caroline Harrison died in the White House. Another election was approaching, and the President was hoping for re-election. He set out upon an extended speech-making trip on the Pacific Coast.[17] Russell and his wife were in the Presidential party; but also included was a niece of the late Mrs. Harrison, Mrs. Mary Scott Lord Dimmick, the widow of a lawyer. She had lived at the White House for several years; the Russell Harrisons, while their mother was living, were fond of this cousin. But now there were different prospects: Mrs. Dimmick rose in the affections of President Benjamin Harrison. Thereafter, the President and his son became estranged. Russell was not with his father as the outgoing President spent his last hours at the White House. Neither did he attend the inauguration of Grover Cleveland, the new Chief Executive. In no account of the inaugural ceremonies does the name of Russell Harrison appear; he was neither interested in the historical event which brought thousands to Washington, nor in comforting his father upon his passing from the high office for which another had been chosen by the American people. It was Russell's sister and her husband who remained at the White House on the day that Benjamin Harrison ceased to be President of the United States, and he was not among those who escorted the ex-President to the train when he departed from Washington.[18]

For a few years after his father ceased to be President, Russell Harrison was seldom in the public eye. He had become president of a street railway company in Terre Haute, Indiana; only when, in 1894, there was gossip that his wife was seeking a divorce did his name appear in the newspapers. The attractive Mrs. Harrison denied the rumors, saying that her purpose in making a trip to South Dakota was to take her little daughter to the Hot Springs there for treatment of a malady which the child had contracted during their stay at the White House.[19]

When the Spanish-American War broke out in 1898, Russell Harrison promptly enlisted and was commissioned a major. In December he was put in command of the suburbs of Havana to supervise the evacuation of the Spanish troops who had surrendered, and to protect them against the hatred of the native Cubans. A few days before Christmas, Major Russell B. Harrison raised the stars and stripes over Fort Atares, in full sight of the wreck of the U. S. battleship *Maine,* the sinking of which brought about our declaration of war against Spain. There had been an agreement that the American flag would not be raised in Havana or its suburbs until that New Year's Day, after the departure of the Spanish regiments. The commanding officer, Major General Lee, reprimanded Russell Harrison for raising the flag without orders, and he was instructed to lower the flag. This formal reprimand did not deter Major Harrison; for, although it was reported to headquarters that the flag had been lowered, newspaper reporters cabled to the United States that for several succeeding days the American flag was still flying on a tall staff over Fort Atares, plainly visible from the harbor and city.[20] Later, Russell B. Harrison was promoted to the rank of lieutenant colonel and made Inspector General for the territory surrounding Santiago. Among his responsibilities was the sanitation needed to safeguard the health of American troops. In inspecting hospitals, he contracted yellow fever in the summer of 1899. The Havana newspapers recalled that Harrison was a President's son; they printed bulletins of his progress, commenting that "his distinguished father will be glad to learn that the patient is on the high road to recovery." [21] He held the post of Inspector General until November 18, 1900, when the Secretary of War suddenly ordered that he be "honorably discharged as his services are no longer required." [22] He was then in Puerto Rico, and his wife was on a steamer, having sailed a few days earlier to join him. His friends charged that his dismissal was due to the apathy of ex-President Benjamin Harrison in the then current political campaign, but the War Department insisted that his dismissal was due only to the fact that there had been a rearrangement in territorial commands and, since Lieutenant Colonel Russell B. Harrison was only a volunteer, officers of the Regular Army had to be retained instead.

Ex-President Benjamin Harrison remarried in 1896, his second wife being Mrs. Dimmick. Both the daughter and the son of the ex-President bitterly resented this matrimonial event. When Benjamin Harrison died in March, 1901, his son was not at his bedside; and their mutual bereavement did not lessen the breach between the son and his stepmother. It was not upon Russell's arm that she leaned as they followed the coffin up the church aisle; Russell and his wife did not occupy the same pew as the stepmother.[23] When the will was read, the public learned that it was to his second wife that the ex-President had left the bulk of his fortune, and to the small daughter she bore him he made a specific bequest of $10,000. The residuary estate he divided into equal shares among this little girl and the two children from his first marriage, stipulating, however, that the share allotted to Russell should be kept in trust for the education of the latter's children. Apparently, Benjamin Harrison had loaned money to his son, and this indebtedness he canceled. When he drew his will two years before his death he had hopes of fathering another son and the document stipulated that "if a boy shall be born to me he shall bear my name, and my sword and sash shall be given to him instead of to my son Russell." [24]

The fortune which Benjamin Harrison left was ample, but the widow made application for a Government pension and there were rumors that Russell was opposing any such grant by Congress. He denied these reports; but in after years, when Russell himself was in his grave, efforts were still being made to obtain a pension for the second wife of the ex-President, and his half sister Elizabeth in her testimony before a Congressional committee had need to refer to the bitterness which had divided her father's children.[25]

We have seen Russell Harrison devoting his mechanical skill and administrative ability to the Mint of the United States, turning to journalism and the publication of newspapers and trade magazines, acting as Presidential secretary, and promoting industrial enterprises. We have traced his ventures in stock raising, and noted his career as an Army officer. But these did not comprise all his activities. This son of the twenty-third President added to engineering, journalism, politics, and business another profession—law. Admitted to practice in the Indiana courts, he acquired clients and also became counsel for the Mexican government—and consul of Mexico as well for the Indiana region! He remained the Mexican representative for twenty years. He became a member of the State Legislature—first, of the House of

Representatives and later, of the Senate—and his colleagues recognized his legal knowledge and made him chairman of the judiciary committees.

And in all these professional changes Russell Harrison continued his interest in military matters, remaining active in the affairs of the Spanish War Veterans which he had helped to organize; he rose to high place in the association, becoming the department commander for Indiana and national judge advocate. While in the Legislature he obtained appropriations for the establishment of hospitals, and financial aid enabling the veterans to hold reunions. From this arose another dramatic episode in the career of the President's son. In 1927 he sponsored and obtained from the Legislature an appropriation of a thousand dollars to help the Spanish War Veterans stage an encampment; later he discovered that a third of the amount had been spent in the purchase of jeweled medals for presentation to past commanders of the organization. Publicly charging that the State funds had been misspent, Harrison aroused the resentment and denials of the organization officials who had directed the purchase of the medals. They haled Harrison before a Veterans' court martial, charging him with having uttered false and malicious slander and libel against the officers; conviction would have meant expulsion from the association and degradation from his past high rank. Harrison pleaded not guilty, presented proof of his charges, and was exonerated. The judge advocate who prosecuted him intimated that Russell Harrison's accusation had been motivated by the failure to include him as a recipient of a medal; his attorneys denounced the innuendo, saying that he was actuated only by a sense of moral responsibility to the taxpayers of the State.[26] Certain it is that he had made enemies in high places; and, although no one in Indiana had ancestors of greater renown in American history, Russell Harrison was not regarded as sufficiently "prominent" to be included in the Mayor's list of two hundred Indianapolis citizens who were appointed to a reception committee to greet Charles Lindbergh.[27]

Russell B. Harrison died in December, 1936, at the age of eighty-two. It was at a time when newspaper readers were almost wholly intrigued with the romance of the British king who abdicated his throne to marry an American woman, and editors relegated to inside pages their brief accounts of the passing of this President's son. The reviews of his life were identical in the two leading journals of Indianapolis where he died, although their editorial comments were phrased differently. The Indianapolis *Star* remarked that "Mr. Harrison had a lively sense of humor and an endless fund of entertaining anecdotes . . . he was quick to resent any proposals which seemed to involve usurpation of power on the part of officeholders . . . his views on public questions were sound and he rendered able service to the voters of Marion County and the State." [28] The *News* editorialized on his distinguished lineage, recalling to its readers that Russell Harrison's great-great-grandfather was a signer of the Declaration of Independence, that his great-grandfather and father were Presidents of the United States. "His many interesting experiences in various parts of the country, and the unusual opportunities afforded to him for close association with national affairs," observed the editor, "enabled Russell Harrison to speak with authority on many matters of historical importance." [29] In Helena, Montana, where he was still remembered, the newspapers similarly recited the deeds and fame of his ancestors; one editor commented that "perpetuation of the name of Harrison in the civil and military annals of the United States devolved upon Colonel Russell Benjamin Harrison. His forebears had an active part in the affairs of the Nation from its inception, and pride in their service and achievements impelled him to emulate them." [30]

Russell B. Harrison was borne to his grave with military honors. Veterans of the Spanish-American War fired a salute, and taps were sounded as his body was lowered into its resting place.

16

Sons of the Rough Rider

THEODORE ROOSEVELT, PRESIDENT OF THE UNITED STATES, WAS ANGRY, and he wrote a letter to the editor of the New York *Sun* insisting that its reporter be removed from the environs of the Roosevelt home at Oyster Bay, where the President was spending the summer of 1902. The President's ire was not aroused by any criticism of his official acts, or of his political principles; reporter John O'Brien made no mention of these. The President's plaint was that O'Brien had written humorous pieces about the Roosevelt children—Theodore, Jr., Kermit, Archie, and Quentin. "Lese majesty," exclaimed the leading trade paper, devoting front-page columns to a discussion of this unusual episode in journalism. "In a letter to the managing editor the President complained that O'Brien was not upholding the ancient dignity of the paper. . . . O'Brien wrote things that were tinted with the radiant hues of his own imagination; he did not realize that he was talking about the President of the United States."[1] The newspaper had liked the sort of articles its reporter wrote, its readers liked them—but when the President wanted a reporter removed, the *Sun's* managing editor believed that was the best thing to do. So John O'Brien was replaced, and President Theodore Roosevelt had a long but pointed talk with his successor. The President's secretary also sent letters to other New York journals requesting the replacement of their reporters, but they refused to make any changes. So, the President "decided to be his own press agent."[2] He was tired, he said, of having his family photographed and written up. "My children are not freaks and therefore ought not to be photographed at every turn as if they were. When I go out to play tennis with my children, it is not a matter of public interest." Theodore Roosevelt was mistaken. That it is a matter of public interest what a President's sons are doing has been demonstrated again and again.

Long afterward, the eldest son of this twenty-sixth President, Theodore, Jr., wrote a book in which he said, "Our family is certainly no different in any material way from hundreds of thousands of others from Walla Walla to New York." [3] It is doubtful whether he himself held that belief: the family of Theodore Roosevelt *was* outstanding—in the White House and thereafter. "Teddy" Roosevelt, the "Rough Rider," was a dominant, vibrant personality—he became the symbol of virile American manhood, and the synonym of physical bravery and moral courage. As an individual and as Chief Executive, he left his imprint on his own generation and a tradition for those which followed. He did not resort to dueling pistols, as did Andrew Jackson, to avenge himself for aspersions on his character or veracity; but with devastating phrases or libel suits he abashed his critics and obtained vindication. He did not pen immortal documents, as did Thomas Jefferson, to proclaim equal opportunities for humans; but by his actions he taught tolerance and recognition of achievement regardless of birth, race, or color. He did not pilot a nation through the throes of civil war, as did Lincoln, to end "vested property rights"; but his attacks on "predatory wealth" and its enslavement of workers did much to emancipate his fellow Americans from the domination of powerful corporations. He did not marshal the spirit and material wealth of America, as did Wilson, to meet the threat of conquering autocracies abroad; but he forestalled attacks upon our rights by the policy, "tread lightly, and carry a big stick." Above all, he inspired in the youth of his time the ideal of fair dealing with their fellows, a love of adventure, and a hatred of sham and pretense.

As an infant, Teddy Roosevelt gave little promise of that vigor which characterized his mature years. "He was a fragile, patient sufferer in the early days of the nursery," his sister recalled, "struggling with the effort to breathe—for his enemy was that terrible trouble, asthma." [4] But this puny infant grew into a healthy, active boy, and became a robust, vigorous man. One of his biographers attributes this improvement in his physical condition to regular gymnastic exercises when he was young; [5] Theodore Roosevelt himself recounts that, after being worsted in an encounter with two mischievous boys, he resolved to develop strength and muscle for future self-defense, and took boxing lessons.[6] But it was also his love for outdoor life which inured him to physical exertion and developed the health and mental alertness that characterized him to the end of his days. His interest in natural history began, he tells us in his *Autobiography,* when he was still a small boy and, strolling on Broadway in New York, he saw a seal which had been killed in the harbor. Thereafter, the study of mammals and birds became an enduring passion. He was ten when his parents took him to Europe, Asia, and Africa, and he collected birds on the Nile, in Syria, in Palestine. On a subsequent journey, four years later, he continued his studies in fields and forests, writing detailed descriptions—and adding taxidermy to his activities.

Private tutors prepared him for Harvard; he entered that college in 1876, graduating four years later. The wealth and prestige of his family made this youth welcome in the homes of the foremost families in Cambridge and Boston.[7] His own appraisal of his Harvard education was that "there was very little in my actual studies which helped me in after life."[8] His chief interest was still the study of animal and bird life; with a friend he explored the Adirondack Mountains, and compiled a "catalogue of summer birds." He also began writing on another subject which intrigued him—naval warfare. Interest in ships was characteristic of the Roosevelt clan; we shall see that this Roosevelt was the first of several kinsmen who became assistant secretaries of the United States Navy, a post that has come to be regarded as a family inheritance![9]

Having completed his academic courses, Theodore Roosevelt studied law for a year. The legalistic concepts in the textbooks, as expounded in his classroom, were repellent to him, and he then regarded them as propagating injustice. He began to take an interest in politics with the realization that, since he possessed an independent fortune, he had no need to depend on public office for a livelihood and could crusade for his ideals without the hampering fear that he risked his means of support. Thus he accepted public office, and was indifferent to low salaries. This was an anomaly in politics; officeholders were practical politicians whose sole objective often was to enrich themselves, even if that involved succumbing to the temptations of bribery and graft.

But, regardless of his wealth, Theodore Roosevelt could seek political office only through the established medium of the organized party machinery. "At that day, in 1880, a young man of my bringing up and convictions could join only the Republican Party, and join it I accordingly did," he reflected thirty-three years after he embarked upon a political career. "The party was still treated as a private corporation, and in each district the organization formed a kind of social and political club. A man had to be regularly proposed and elected into the club." [10] Not that these district organizations were controlled by men of highest social standing or prominence in industries and the professions; on the contrary, they were dominated by the "lower class"—saloonkeepers, horsecar conductors, petty "ward heelers." These, the idealistic Roosevelt concluded, were the "governing class" in garnering votes and winning elections; and this scion of wealth and culture determined to gain their good will. He recognized that he himself at that time had neither the reputation nor the ability to win even a nomination for office, but his new-won friends knew how: they nominated him for the State Assembly, and he was elected. Theodore Roosevelt was then twenty-three. In the lower house of the New York Legislature he served three successive terms. In his sponsorship of progressive legislation he acquired the title of "Young Reformer." Fearlessly, he attacked dishonest politicians, and his reputation spread. Soon he was the recognized leader in the Republican Party of the younger element which was eager to oust corrupt political bosses.

On a trip to Europe in 1881 he married in London; during the following year, with his wife, he again traveled extensively in the Old World. In 1883 his wife died, leaving a little girl—the Alice Roosevelt who later intrigued the Nation with her independence, her wit, and her marriage. Within the same week of his wife's death, Roosevelt also lost his mother.[11] These bereavements led him to seek diverting activities in the West. He had bought a ranch in North Dakota, and there he went. In that "cowboy land," as he called it, the future President learned "the mind and soul of the average American." In 1886 Roosevelt remarried. Marriage to him was the goal of all that was noble in human society; his oft repeated credo was that "virtues are as dust in a windy street unless back of them lie the strong and tender virtues of a family life based on the love of one man for one woman." [12] This second wife bore him five children—four sons and a daughter. His love for her—whom after a quarter of a century of companionship he still called "darling, pretty Mother, my own sweetheart"—constantly finds expression in the letters he wrote to her or about her.[13]

In 1889 President Benjamin Harrison appointed Theodore Roosevelt a member of the Civil Service Commission. There is still preserved in the building of that agency in Washington the desk which he occupied. His was the firm conviction that positions in Government bureaus should be filled on the basis of experience and competence. It is a tribute to his "applied idealism" that, when the Democratic President Cleveland succeeded the Republican Harrison, Theodore Roosevelt continued as Commissioner. After six years, in 1895, the Mayor of New York City appointed him to the Board of Police Commissioners, and he became president of that Board during the following two years. Then, in 1897, President William McKinley made him Assistant Secretary of the Navy. It was not an appointment which came easily; there were other applicants. But Theodore Roosevelt had in Washington an influential champion—Henry Cabot Lodge of Massachusetts, then a member of the United States Senate. Between these two men there had begun a friendship which was severed only by death. Henry Cabot Lodge belonged to a family which was prominent in wealth, social prestige, and political power—he belonged to the "Cabots of Boston," with whom it was reputed only the Lowells would presume to converse and who themselves "talked only with God." [14] Being sponsored by Lodge, Roosevelt could not lose, even though his belligerent temperament inspired fears that, as Lodge wrote him, "you will want to fight someone." [15]

Theodore Roosevelt did not fight anyone in the Navy Department; he simply waited until his superior, the Secretary of the Navy, was absent and, as Acting Secretary, he took the initiative and on his own authority sent messages to the admirals of the United States fleet. It was February, 1898. In Cuba, which Spain had dominated and misgoverned for centuries, a revolution had grown to large proportions, and we sent the Battleship *Maine* to Havana harbor to look out for American interests. The *Maine* was sunk, with the loss of many lives, by an external explosion. The Spaniards claimed that this destruction of the ship was by the rebelling Cubans, and that it was calculated to involve the United States in a war with Spain. Sympathy for the oppressed Cubans and other motives aroused the American people against Spain, even though the Washington Administration was still undecided about going to war. Certain it is that the Spanish Government expressed a willingness to meet practically all demands of the United States, but the communications between the two governments were not disclosed to the American public until long after the war. At any rate, Theodore Roosevelt prepared for war: he cabled Admiral Dewey, commanding the American fleet in Asiatic waters, to be ready. War was soon declared; Dewey attacked and destroyed the Spanish fleet in Manila Bay. Theodore Roosevelt's foresight was justified.

Roosevelt was restless. Now that the decisive naval engagement was over, he wanted to play a more direct part in the war. He resigned his post in the Navy Department. Under a newly enacted law providing for volunteers, he aided in recruiting a cavalry division. He knew where to find horsemen with skill and daring. In his sojourn in "cowboy land" fifteen years previously, as he recounted in his *Autobiography*, "I made up my mind that the men were of just the kind whom it would be well to have if ever it became necessary to fight a war." To which he added, "When the Spanish War came, I gave this thought practical realization." In San Antonio, Texas, he gathered men reputed to be skillful and daring in the saddle. Thereafter they were known as "Roosevelt's Rough Riders"—although when they embarked for Cuba they left their steeds behind and, reaching the island, they charged the enemy on foot! [16] Theodore Roosevelt leading his men up San Juan hill became a story familiar to every schoolboy—for the rest of his life he was known as the "Rough Rider." [17]

Colonel Theodore Roosevelt—Teddy Roosevelt—returned to the United States a national hero. A few days later he was nominated for Governor of New York. Even the political bosses, hopeful that they could establish an *entente cordiale* with this reformer, foresaw his victory and joined in vocal approval. He did win, but he made no bargains with corrupt politicians. The Governorship was just a step to the Vice-Presidency. In 1900 Teddy was nominated for the second place on the Republican ticket, which was headed by William McKinley, then running for a second term. McKinley and Roosevelt won; on March 4, 1901, Theodore Roosevelt was inaugurated Vice-President of the United States. In the first week of the following September William McKinley, visiting an exposition in Buffalo, New York, was shot by an anarchist who had joined the line of men and women filing past the Chief Executive as he shook hands with them. In a few days McKinley died. Theodore Roosevelt, then tramping through Adirondack forests, was summoned and sworn in as President of the United States.

When Theodore Roosevelt at forty-two became President his oldest son, Teddy, Jr., was fourteen, Kermit twelve, Archie seven, and Quentin four. The two older boys were sent away to the exclusive preparatory school at Groton, but they returned to the White House for brief visits. Nevertheless, even without them, as the younger boys grew it was the unanimous verdict of all those who observed the juvenile segment of this Presidential family that they produced a maximum of uneasy commotion. Ike Hoover, whose forty-two years of White House service afforded him ample opportunity to make comparisons, depicts the irrepressible enterprises of the youngsters: "The life of the employees who took their responsibilities too seriously was made miserable. The children left no nook or corner unexplored. From the basement to the flagpole on the roof, every channel and cubbyhole was thoroughly investigated. Places that had not seen a human being for years were now made alive with the howls and laughter of the newcomers.[18] The house became one general playground for them and their associates. Nothing was too sacred to be used for their amusement, and no place too good for a playroom. The children seemed to be encouraged in these ideas by their elders, and it was a brave man indeed who would dare say no or suggest putting a stop to those escapades. . . ."[19] Colonel Crook, an onlooker on boys' pranks in the White House since the day of Lincoln, tells a similar story.[20] That neither erred in surmising that the President himself was often an abettor in the activities of his offspring was attested by the sons themselves when, grown to manhood, they wrote of their boyhood days. "Father always threw himself into our plays and romps when we were small as if he were no older than ourselves," recalled Kermit;[21] and Theodore, Jr., likewise recounts that even when the elder Teddy was President of the United States and overwhelmed with work, he always had time to devote to his children.[22]

The Roosevelt youngsters transformed several rooms of the White House into a menagerie. Their pets comprised a diverse collection of quadrupeds and a few birds—there were ponies, rabbits, guinea pigs, dogs, squirrels, raccoons, badgers. Ascribing to each some singular trait, they gave them descriptive names, such as "Bishop Doane," "The Prodigal Son," "Admiral Dewey," "Caesar," "Fighting Bob Evans."[23] The children and their pets were inseparable; it was the habit of Kermit to come to the breakfast table with a kangaroo rat in his pocket,[24] and Archie used the passenger elevator to transport his pony to an upper floor.[25] A multitude of stories regarding the Roosevelt pets were circulated, and found their way into the columns of even the most "dignified" newspapers which prided themselves upon publishing only important news. During the national-election campaign it was reported that Loretta, the President's parrot, was "imbibing lessons from a graphaphone, one of the phrases being 'Hurrah for Roosevelt.' "[26] The story was that the Roosevelt children had endeavored to teach the parrot also the name of the Vice-Presidential candidate, but the bird was interested only in the Chief Executive!

Although throughout their lives all of them had a deep interest in animals and all shared a liking for outdoor life, the four sons of the "Rough Rider" were decidedly different in their philosophies and their ambitions. The oldest boy—the President's namesake—most closely resembled his father in physical traits and mannerisms. A correspondent for a St. Louis paper described him as a diminutive replica of the elder Teddy; his smile was just as expansive and his gray-blue eyes were just as big and businesslike. The reporter remarked that "the only difference is that Teddy, Jr., is older in his ways than Teddy, Sr. There is a popular impression at Oyster Bay that little Teddy was close to forty years when he was born. He is the philosopher of the Roosevelt family—calm and dignified always."[27] The eminent social worker, Jacob Riis, an intimate friend of the Roosevelt family for a quarter of a century, similarly pronounced that "Ted is as like his father as two pins in his absolute fearlessness and occasional disregard of conventionalities when a direct point is to be gained."[28]

Teddy, Jr., attended Groton, the traditional school of the Roosevelt clans in the preparation for Harvard. In his first year he was stricken with double pneumonia, and the entire Nation read with deep anxiety the frequent bulletins which came from his sickroom. The President and Mrs. Roosevelt hurried from Washington to their son's bedside, and prominent newspapers devoted their front pages to reports regarding the suffering boy. At that time Prince Henry, brother of the Emperor of Germany, was about to embark upon a visit to the United States; but, sensing that the American people had neither time nor thought for royalty when the President's son was stricken, the Prince did not sail until the crisis was over.[29] Teddy's condition improved and he was removed to the White House. Regaining complete health, he went back to Groton. Having completed his studies there, he attended Harvard. But the Presidential father did not consider academic studies sufficient for his sons; after graduating from Harvard, Teddy, Jr., set out to acquire practical knowledge in the business world, learning all the phases of carpet manufacturing. Theodore Roosevelt himself described his son's preparation for earning a livelihood: "As soon as he had left Harvard he had gone into a mill, had worked with blouse and tin dinner pail, exactly like any other workman for a year; and when he graduated from the mill had gone out for the same firm to San Francisco, where he was selling carpets." [30] But being a President's son, it is likely that young Teddy's progress was more rapid than that of the other mill workers—he married the daughter of the corporation's President and principal stockowner.

It was a credo of Theodore Roosevelt that it would be an unspeakable disgrace if any of his sons should be delinquent in working hard in some honest occupation or should fail at the same time in "keeping himself in such trim that he would be able to perform a freeman's duty and fight efficiently as anyone if the need arose." [31] The need arose in 1917. In 1914 the German hordes invaded Belgium and all Europe was engulfed in the First World War. The conflict had raged for three years, with the majority of Americans content to remain aloof in fancied security on this side of the Atlantic; but there were men who foresaw that, sooner or later, this Nation too would be drawn into the conflict. A camp was organized at Plattsburg, New York, in 1917 to train officers, so that they would be ready when the call to arms came. All four sons of ex-President Theodore Roosevelt enrolled. Military formations and tactical problems were new to Teddy, Jr., but from his boyhood he had a knowledge of firearms, camping arrangements, and marches through varied terrain. He was a skilled rider and a marksman. This son of the ex-President possessed all the requisites of an army officer.

Theodore, Jr., completed his Plattsburg training and was commissioned a major in June, 1917, later being promoted to lieutenant colonel. He was always in the midst of carnage; proudly his father wrote, "Ted is seriously wounded; in his battalion all his four captains and two-thirds of his lieutenants have been killed or wounded; in his regiment the colonel and all three majors have been killed or wounded." The Rough Rider had instilled courage, and the son did not falter.[32] Wounded in the battle of Soissons, where he was also gassed, in 1918, he insisted upon returning to active duty and commanded his regiment in the important battles in the Argonne. His courage and ability won Teddy, Jr., the Distinguished Service Medal and Distinguished Service Cross; Belgium, France, and several other foreign nations also decorated him for gallantry.[33] Returning to the United States, he began his political career, as did his father, with membership in the New York Assembly. His election, in 1919, was not an easy victory, and his success was due in part to the prestige of the Roosevelt name; in the campaign his supporters constantly reminded the voters that this candidate was the son of the former President, Teddy Roosevelt, who had entered political campaigns with the challenge, "My hat's in the ring." The opponent of Teddy Roosevelt, Jr., was a tailor's son, and he said sarcastically, "My hat's in the ring too—and it isn't my father's."

Warren G. Harding, President from 1921 to 1923, appointed Teddy Roosevelt, Jr., Assistant Secretary of the Navy. In this important post he lacked his father's flair for revealing graft and lost the opportunity to become, like his sire, a "young Reformer"; instead, shrewd political manipulators used him as an unwitting medium to turn over Government oil properties to private exploiters—the notorious Teapot Dome scandal. There is no need here to retell the story of the collusion and bribery which astounded the Nation, sent a Cabinet member to prison, tarnished the reputation of prominent officials, and forced several wealthy conspirators to flee the United States to escape the penalties of their misdeeds. Here it is only necessary to note the role of Theodore Roosevelt, Jr.

Vast oil deposits in the West, the property of the Government, had been set aside as reserves for the American Navy. How vital is the supply of oil has been clearly demonstrated in World War II; without oil, our ships of war could not navigate the oceans; without oil, our mechanized armies could not maneuver on battlefields. Greedy men coveted these huge oil deposits then under the control of the Navy Department, in which Teddy, Jr., was second in command. The conspirators concluded that the Secretary of the Interior, Fall, would prove a more willing tool than the Secretary of the Navy, and they connived to effect the transfer of the control of the oil fields from the Navy Department to the Interior Department. Theodore

Roosevelt, Jr., neither knowing nor curious regarding these manipulations, assembled the documents essential for the conspirators' purposes and obtained President Harding's signature which gave Secretary of the Interior Fall full authority to lease the oil lands to operators on terms which gave them many millions, and would have exhausted the reserves upon which the Navy relied for future needs. Fall received $100,000 for his crookedness. Apart from his unknowing role in the machinations of his official chief, Theodore Roosevelt, Jr., performed creditably his task as Assistant Secretary of the Navy. Reviewing his work, the New York *Herald Tribune* said, "In that office he displayed great familiarity with naval affairs and much energy in promoting the efficiency of the service and the interests of its personnel." [34] That was the verdict of a friendly paper, years after the event. But while the Teapot Dome scandal was still fresh in the public mind, his political enemies made no mention of his good work as Assistant Secretary of the Navy; instead they stressed his failure to detect the conspiracy of the oil leases.

In September, 1924, a Republican convention in New York nominated him for the Governorship of that State, the Democrats selecting again as their candidate Alfred Smith, already serving as Governor by his election four years earlier. It was also the year for a national election, and astute observers predicted an easy Republican victory in most of the states. It was recognized that Alfred Smith was extremely popular, but there was an unmistakable trend away from his party. Theodore Roosevelt, Jr., resigned his post of Assistant Secretary of the Navy and returned to New York, traveling and speaking throughout the State. While no one claimed for him the magnetic individuality of his father, whose forcefulness, infectious enthusiasm, and inimitable phraseology were known throughout the world, still Theodore Roosevelt, Jr., possessed a personality which usually won the liking of even those who opposed him politically. In a merry vein a newspaper reporter friendly to Roosevelt's rival wrote of his first meeting with this candidate for Governor on election eve: "There's something likable about young Teddy Roosevelt. It's really too bad he's a Republican. I wouldn't want Al Smith to get hold of this, but I was prejudiced in Colonel Roosevelt's favor the moment I met him. I liked his sturdy handshake, which threw my thumb out of joint. I liked, too, his open smile." [35] Even newspapers which thought that normally he would have been a weak opponent for Smith, considered that this was a "Republican year." "With all due respect for the amiable qualities of Col. Roosevelt," observed the *Times,* "it has to be said that in an ordinary year the thought of singling him out as one fitted to defeat Governor Smith would have seemed not only audacious but just a little ludicrous. Neither in personality nor in grasp of the business of the State can the two men be compared. Yet we believe that the people are disposed to give the younger Roosevelt a fair hearing. They would be delighted to find in him the tradition of vigor associated with his honored name kept alive. But to assure anything like this the Colonel Roosevelt of today must stand on his own feet." [36] There were similar comments in other journals.

Theodore Roosevelt, Jr., protested that it was a handicap to be a President's son, that whatever he accomplished was attributed to the fame of his father.[37] There was no denying that his reputation among his fellow Americans was colored by the admiration and affection which they had had for his unforgettable sire. When he ran for public office his political sponsors seldom omitted mention of his filial kinship to that popular Teddy Roosevelt who had been Chief Executive of the Nation. Newspapers generally, like the New York *World,* referred to him as "a candidate who bears a great name," [38] and the independent *Times* said editorially that "as the son of his father he was brought forward mainly as a figurehead." [39] In fact, it was evident that his ambitions and his activities were patterned upon the career of his father—he sought the same public offices, both elective and appointive, and later endeavored to duplicate the elder Roosevelt's hunting adventures and authorship. More than that: deliberately or unconsciously this second Teddy Roosevelt was imitating the speech and mannerisms of the former President. The *Times* was not the only paper which believed such mimicry detrimental to the success of this President's son; it counseled, "He must leave off special efforts to look like his father and talk like him." [40] Newspapers of the period frequently caricatured this son of the former President in the Rough Rider's attire made familiar and famous by the father; a typical cartoon appeared in the influential New York *World,* picturing young Teddy with the cavalry sword with which his sire had led the charge up San Juan Hill, the "big stick" which he recommended should always be kept ready to defend American rights, and the spear symbolic of the African hunting trip upon which the ex-President embarked when he retired from the White House.

The contest for the Governorship was waged with unusual vigor and vehemence. Recognizing the importance of winning New York for the national ticket, the Republican campaign managers—fortified with many millions in cash—put forth every effort to win victory also for nominees for State offices, particularly for Theodore Roosevelt, Jr. His opponents were equally active; they did not underestimate the prestige of the Roosevelt name, and realized that their most effective weapon was to assail the recent record of Theodore Roosevelt while Assistant Secretary of the Navy.

Thus, the chief argument against Teddy Roosevelt was not his youth, as the party organ, the *Herald Tribune,* asserted.[41] When nominated for the Governorship he was thirty-seven; his father was only forty-two at the time he became President. The chief argument against this namesake of the Chief Executive who fought every attempted exploitation of the public domain was that the son either was neglectful or was incapable of protecting the Nation's property when oil leases valued at a hundred million dollars were turned over by bribed officials to a clique for several hundred thousand dollars. "Nobody has impugned the honesty of Theodore Roosevelt," said the *World* in a scathing editorial on "The Fitness of T. R., Jr.," charging that "he was too dull or too lazy to accept the responsibility of high office. He went about the routine of his work asking no questions that were impolite, 'getting people to bring the answers,' and signing when and where they told him the document still needed ink."[42] Opponents of Roosevelt did not let voters forget this role in the Teapot Dome scandal; and even those who took pains to admit his own integrity nevertheless repeatedly referred to the propensity of Theodore Roosevelt, Jr., to serve the interests of shrewd and corrupt politicians. Women took an active part in this campaign, and among them was Mrs. Franklin Delano Roosevelt, a cousin of the Republican nominee for Governor, and the opinion she voiced was typical of the attitude of those who were mildest in their attacks. "Of course, Mr. Roosevelt is a young man who is personally honest," she said at a public meeting a few days before the election, "he has a fine war record, but very little political experience, and his record in the public service shows him willing to listen to his friends and do as he is told."[43]

The voters made their decision in the first week of November: Theodore Roosevelt, Jr., was defeated in his ambition to become Governor of New York. He was the only one on the Republican ticket who failed to win; his opponent, Alfred Smith, was the sole Democratic victor. Whether it was the overwhelming popularity of Smith or the lack of public confidence in this son of a former President was debated extensively; the New York *Post*, commenting on the singular election of Smith, noted that his victory was not due to any approval by the voters of his party principles, because "if the voters had desired to express approval of the points which Smith had stressed in his campaign speeches, they would have given him a cabinet and a legislature. This they declined."[44] Whatever the reasons which prompted them, the majority of his fellow citizens did not wish Teddy Roosevelt, Jr., to occupy the Executive Mansion in Albany where his father had lived as Governor.

Still imitating his father, he embarked upon several explorations in India and Asia in 1925, 1926, and 1928–29. Upon his return, he wrote several books on his adventures, usually in collaboration with Kermit.

In 1929 Calvin Coolidge, then President, selected Teddy Roosevelt, Jr., as Governor of Puerto Rico. The Senate promptly confirmed the appointment. The assignment was no easy task. The masses on the island were desperately impoverished. Diseases—malaria, tuberculosis, hookworm—were prevalent. Malnutrition of children was conspicuous. Puerto Rico devoted most of its soil to the cultivation of sugar and coffee for export, neglecting to cultivate sufficient foodstuffs for the island's consumption. The economic and social problems would have been a formidable challenge to a Governor with even more administrative experience. The son of the unforgotten President Teddy Roosevelt set to work with zeal and perseverance. He stimulated a diversity of small manufactures and crafts, and revived the fine needlework which had been a tradition among the women of Puerto Rico. For these products he found markets on the island and in the United States. He encouraged the growing of food staples by rural families. He obtained from Congress appropriations for education and sanitary projects. There were some social leaders and political writers who asserted he neither accomplished nor attempted as much as was essential; they intimated that his political aspirations influenced his decisions and restricted his efforts. Teddy,

Jr., wanted, like his father, to be a candidate for the Vice-Presidency and a national election was at hand.

For two years the Governor managed to work without friction. The people liked him, recalling that he was the son of that picturesque Teddy Roosevelt who had helped to wrest the island from Spanish domination and ownership. His use of the Spanish language was pleasing to the inhabitants, even though his phraseology occasionally aroused much merriment. In one of his speeches, in referring to one-horse vehicles he used the literal equivalent for the words "drawn by single horses," telling his startled Spanish audience about "wagons pulled by *unmarried* horses." But as months went by his difficulties with the Spanish idiom were followed by more serious misunderstandings with local politicians. They resented his inroads on their long established prerogatives and powers when, as Governor, he undertook progressive measures which assumed supervision of the cities. "However badly reform may be needed municipal control is the backbone of political activity, and the parties and the politicians are in no mood to surrender their rice and beans," commented an astute San Juan editor.[45] Teddy Roosevelt, Jr., had failed to gain the support of any party, and his popularity waned.

Toward the end of his stay in Puerto Rico his administration was attacked violently by political critics who charged extravagance in the maintenance of his official residence and unjustified expenditures by him and his aides. When he heard these charges, Theodore Roosevelt, Jr., had already left the island; in New York he denounced the allegations as a "direct lie"; [46] he asserted emphatically that he had made no payments from the public treasury which were unauthorized by law. The leading paper of San Juan devoted many columns to auditors' reports, charges, and denials. It was evident that his continuance in the Governor's palace would merely increase the determined opposition and hamper, if not nullify, any further program of legislation sponsored by Theodore Roosevelt, Jr.

In January, 1932, President Herbert Hoover appointed Colonel Theodore Roosevelt, Jr., Governor General of the Philippines, and sent his name to the Senate for confirmation.[47] The nominee was then forty-four years old. There were some journals which, like the Chicago *Tribune,* saw in this appointment "a clever political move" on the part of President Hoover to associate the Theodore Roosevelt name with his Administration as an offset to a probable rival in the approaching Presidential election—Franklin Delano Roosevelt, then Governor of New York. The *Tribune* argued that the Roosevelt cognomen was endowed with potent allure among voters. "Without disparaging the ability or political strength of Gov. Franklin Roosevelt, it can hardly be denied that the Roosevelt name he bears has been a substantial factor in his popular appeal and has had much to do with making him the leading candidate for the Democratic nomination for President," editorialized the *Tribune*. The very name of Roosevelt, continued the Chicago paper, would bring prestige to the Administration.[48] Most newspapers, however, did not ascribe such political implications, even though few indulged in enthusiastic praise of the appointment. The sedate Boston *Transcript* believed that "none will question the fitness of Theodore Roosevelt to be governor-general of the Philippines. . . . Young Theodore has overcome the handicap of a great name by accomplishments in his own right." [49] The New York *Times* was less convinced of his qualifications, saying, "President Hoover's appointment of the Governor of Puerto Rico to be Governor-General of the Philippines is an instance of calling a man to be ruler over many things who has been faithful in ruling over a few"; [50] and the Los Angeles *Times*, similarly admitting that he started "with several years of experience as a colonial administrator, in which his record was good," contended that "administering the Philippines is an immeasurably more difficult task." [51]

In the capital of the Philippines the news of the choice was greeted with indifference; "perhaps due to the chilly weather, but more probably because of the lack of definite information about the appointee," explained the *Philippines Herald*.[52] The paper quoted one Filipino legislator as saying that "the only thing he knows is that the new appointee has the glamour of the Roosevelt name, but that he does not have the background of former Philippine governors-general"; another member of the Legislature expressed the hope that he would prove "the son of his father, and strive to do great things to keep the tradition of his family name"; and other local officials anticipated that Theodore Roosevelt, Jr., would prove "a chip off the old block." Leaders in business and professional circles withheld comment—they wanted to know more about his policies.

Within a week the Senate of the United States confirmed Theodore Roosevelt as Governor General of the Philippines. Thereupon the President of the Philippine Senate, Manuel Quezon, broke silence and expressed the opinion current among political leaders in the Philippines—they regarded the new administrator of the islands kindly because he was a President's son. "I do not know Governor Roosevelt intimately, though I met him once," said Quezon. "Coming as he does from one of the most prominent of New York families and the son of one of the greatest Presidents he is notwithstanding very democratic in his manners." [53] Whatever the attitude of those who discussed the appointment, in the United States or in the Philippines—whether there was praise, acquiescence, or criticism—there was always the allusion to Theodore Roosevelt, Jr., as a President's son.

If the new Governor General anticipated a rousing welcome by the Americans or an easy management of island affairs, he learned differently shortly after his arrival in the Philippines. Both the problems and the personalities would have taxed the capabilities, diplomacy, and resourcefulness of any administrator. As he himself wrote in his report of a year's progress, "It is easy to be an executive or a legislator when revenues are mounting, government activities expanding, salaries rising, and employment increasing." But in the Philippines, as in continental United States, that was a period of depression. He was faced with abnormal difficulties, but he made a sincere effort to improve conditions. American newspapers which, at the time of his appointment, expressed doubts about his capacity to administer the office, now gave him credit for his aims and exertions. Said the New York *Times* about his report, "The Governor General had firsthand knowledge of what he wrote. It is not what he had 'read of or heard of' but what he saw with his own eyes in his travels of more than ten thousand miles by boat, train, automobile, on horseback or afoot and in his ceaseless interest in the people." [54]

Probably, if he had had a longer time in which to carry on his work, he would have accomplished much more. But the President who had appointed him was defeated in the election of November, 1932, and the party of Theodore Roosevelt, Jr., was voted out of power. A new Administration in Washington had taken office in March, 1933, and it was tactful for the incumbent Governor General of the Philippines to resign. The resignation was promptly accepted. "In relinquishing his post in the Philippines, Governor General Roosevelt left behind him many friends among the natives," reported the New York *Times,* "but the American colony was not demonstrative in bidding him goodby. This attitude is not unusual. No recent Governor General has been popular with the Americans in Manila. If he endeavored to understand the Filipinos and cooperated with them, he can hardly have failed to displease the others." [55] The *Philippines Herald* printed many columns in corroboration of these observations. Although the Americans on the islands were wrathful because this President's son was "too easy" in his dealings with the native population, the Filipino leaders lauded his work and his objectives. Manuel Quezon, whose opinion on the appointment of Roosevelt had been unenthusiastic, now bade him farewell with the praise that he was the island's best friend and that "his achievements were unparalleled." [56] Following his withdrawal from public office, this eldest son of the twenty-sixth President made several successive, but not successful, business connections. Finally, he became an official of a book-publishing company. He had long wanted to have a part in the making of books.

In 1941 we were again at war with Germany, and again Teddy Roosevelt, Jr., left an office desk to serve in the Army of his country. At the end of the First World War he was a colonel, and now he was elevated to the rank of brigadier general. He was placed in command of the 26th Infantry which he had commanded on the battlefields during the First World War. This President's son spurned the safety of an office job; he wanted to train and lead his troops in actual combat, to share their dangers. "Through the training period soldiers of his Division soon recognized that General Roosevelt was not an armchair officer," commented the New York *Herald Tribune.* "He went through all the rigors of a private half his age and taxed his endurance to the utmost." [57] At first he was sent to Africa; then he was in battles in Italy; finally, he was on the battlefields of Normandy. Everywhere he was in the vanguard of the assault on enemy positions and everywhere he was in the midst of danger. Press reports recounted that he had a jeep shot from under him.

Theodore Roosevelt, Jr., died in his sleep in July, 1944. To his widow, several months later, there was awarded the Congressional Medal of Honor in recognition of his bravery and incessant toil.[58] Had this President's son succumbed to battle wounds, he could not have given more to his country. The citation of the War Department reflected his courage and his devotion:

For gallantry and intrepidity at the risk of his life above and beyond the call of duty on June 6, 1944, in France. After two verbal requests to accompany the leading assault elements in the Normandy invasion had been denied, Brig. Gen. Roosevelt's written request for his mission was approved and he landed with the first wave of the forces assaulting the enemy-held beaches.

Although the enemy had the beach under constant direct fire, Brig. Gen. Roosevelt moved from one locality to another, rallying men around him, directed and personally led them against the enemy. Under his seasoned, precise, calm and unfaltering leadership, assault troops reduced beach strong points and rapidly moved inland with minimum casualties. He thus contributed substantially to the successful establishment of the beachhead in France.

Much more than Teddy, Jr., however, Kermit—the second son of the Rough-Rider President—typified the dominant traits of his father. Without affectation and without any effort either "to follow in his father's footsteps" or to imitate any of his mannerisms, Kermit still reflected the same love of adventure, the same hunter's prowess in jungle and forest, the same warm-hearted attachments.

In their childhood all the children of Theodore Roosevelt were taught to ride and shoot, to swim and row, to fell trees, and to engage in all the other activities of outdoor life; [59] but Kermit became more adept than the others.[60] Like his older brother, he went to Groton and later to Harvard. But his textbook studies were interrupted by periods of travel in foreign lands. He was only twenty when Theodore Roosevelt, at the end of his Presidential term, embarked upon his explorations in Africa, and took Kermit with him. Kermit soon proved his knowledge of wild life and his marksmanship; and the proud father wrote to his daughter: "Kermit killed a leopard yesterday. He has really done so very well! It is rare for a boy with his refined tastes and his genuine appreciation of literature—and of so much else—to be also an exceptionally bold and hardy sportsman. He is still altogether too reckless; but by my hen-with-one-chicken attitude, I think I shall get him out of Africa uninjured; and his keenness, cool nerve, horsemanship, hardihood, endurance, and good eyesight make him a really good wilderness hunter." [61] With a copy of Kipling's poems always in his pocket and a gun constantly in hand or within reach, Kermit trekked through the African jungle; he and his father shot five hundred and twelve beasts and birds which, with the exception of a dozen retained as trophies, were given to the Smithsonian Institution in Washington where some were mounted and put on display.[62] Four years later father and son again went on a journey of exploration, this time into the wilderness of Brazil. "My son and I killed seventeen lions between us," reported Theodore Roosevelt in his thrilling *Through the Brazilian Wilderness;* they also shot elephants, buffaloes, leopards, rhinoceroses, and other beasts; Kermit was one of the three men who had ever killed the great forest animal called the bungo—he shot two of them.[63]

Kermit had graduated from Harvard in 1912, and turned to banking and engineering enterprises in South America. He had married in 1914 and was settling down to a tranquil life in New York when Germany made her first attempt to conquer the neighboring nations. England and France, prompted both by love of human freedom and the knowledge that a victorious Germany would next suppress them, entered the bloody struggle. The United States remained neutral.

With his brothers and hundreds of other young Americans who foresaw that their country would ultimately become engulfed in the conflict raging across the Atlantic, Kermit Roosevelt in 1917 enrolled at the Plattsburg camp for training as an officer; it was a citizen camp, without official status in our Army. He did not wait until the United States declared war against Germany; impatient to get into the actual warfare, he enlisted in the British forces in Mesopotamia and Palestine. His military preparation was meager; perhaps because of his reputation as a hunter but more likely because he was a President's son he was commissioned a captain on the staff of the commanding officer, General Sir Frederick Maude; his efficiency and cool courage won him the British Military Cross.[64] When American armies were put into the field, he resigned his British commission and put on the uniform of his own country. He was given command of a battery of field artillery.

While one brother was killed and two others suffered serious wounds in battles, Kermit emerged from the First World War unscathed. Nor did he suffer any injuries in any of his encounters with the ferocious beasts in the jungles of Africa and Asia. He did lose a thumb, and the loss was due to the very medium which medical science was using to cure human ills! When he was still a boy, radium was used to remove a wart, and he received "an overdose" of that treatment, necessitating the removal of his left thumb twenty years later, in 1927.[65]

Back in civilian life, Kermit began a career as an executive of various steamship corporations. "Kermit Roosevelt Gets Job," the New York *Times* headlined a short column in September, 1919, reporting that this second son of the former President was appointed secretary of the American Ship and Commerce Corporation, a holding company for two consolidated ship-construction firms. Thereafter his activities were on five continents. We read of him in Brazil, negotiating for interned German ships; [66] seeking concessions in Turkey; [67] discussing ships in Assam; and conferring with shippers and shipbuilders in England. These frequent business trips he alternated with hunting and exploring excursions; he was usually accompanied by Teddy, Jr. The older brother was aware, as the elder Theodore Roosevelt had been, that Kermit was expert in all that made these trips successful. Said Teddy, Jr., "In the early days Kermit did not care for natural history. Now he is a much better taxidermist than I am. I have seen him skin a mouse while riding on a pad elephant, and do a very good job of it." [68]

Kermit shunned politics, and cared little for public notice. But, because he was a President's son, some of his actions gained publicity. He typified his father's courage in defending those in whom he had faith, despite the criticism of prominent men or adverse public opinion. An incident occurred in 1922 which aroused against this President's son the questioning comment of editors and the condemnation of the clergy. A well-known sports promoter, Tex Rickard, was on trial for assault. Kermit Roosevelt, who since a meeting with Rickard in South America ten years previously had met him frequently in New York, was a character witness for the defendant. The prosecuting attorney asked Kermit whether he knew that Rickard had operated a gambling house in Alaska and another in Nevada where he took in over a hundred thousand dollars the first night. Yes, he knew that Rickard was a gambler, but he still regarded him an honest man, said Kermit, persisting, "I shouldn't say that he had a bad character because he ran a gambling house. A man who runs a gambling house isn't necessarily a bad character any more than a man who runs a church is necessarily a good character." [69] "The first half of this contention it would be difficult to maintain against a determined antagonist," editorialized the New

York *Times*.[70] But religious leaders were sharper in their censure. A prominent pastor, Dr. Christian Reisner, delivered a sermon denouncing Kermit's thesis.[71] Kermit made no apologies; he merely reiterated his favorable appraisal of Rickard.

Kermit was the only son of Theodore Roosevelt who was friendly to or had personal associations with the second President bearing the Roosevelt name—Franklin Delano Roosevelt—and he was occasionally a guest on that President's fishing cruises. Political enemies attempted to link Kermit's shipping interests with White House influence; at one Senatorial hearing a Republican member hinted that when Kermit was aboard the President's yacht, radio messages came to him from the International Mercantile Marine Corporation "giving him instructions what to say to the Chief Executive." This groundless charge amused the editors of non-partisan journals, among them the New York *Times,* which said humorously, "If Kermit Roosevelt told President Franklin Roosevelt anything, it was to cast his hook further out or else try a different bait."[72]

When, in 1939, Germany plunged the world into a second war Kermit Roosevelt again refused to wait until his countrymen assumed their part in the struggle. Once again he joined the British Army and was commissioned a major. He served in Norway and in Egypt until the autumn of 1940, when illness compelled his return to England. When the United States declared war, Kermit became an officer in the American Army. He was sent on a mission to Alaska and there, in June, 1943, died from natural causes.[73]

Like those of his father, the friendships of Kermit Roosevelt were enduring, and even after he had been laid in his grave he lingered in the thoughts of those with whom he had associated. A year after his death, more than five hundred men and women crowded a New York church to attend memorial services.[74] To perpetuate his deep interest in Anglo-American cooperation, his widow transferred to the Government from his estate property and money for a Fund to be used for "fostering a better understanding and a closer relationship between the military forces of the United States and those of the United Kingdom by sponsoring lectures or courses of instruction to be delivered by officers of the British Army at the United States Military Academy and elsewhere in the United States and by officers of the United States Army at Sandhurst Royal Military College and elsewhere in the United Kingdom." A joint resolution passed by the Congress of the United States accepted the funds.[75]

Although the two older brothers—Theodore, Jr., and Kermit—were more frequently in the glare of newspaper publicity, the third son of ex-President Roosevelt—Archibald—was no less successful in civilian pursuits, no less patriotic, no less courageous in a soldier's role.[76] Graduating from Harvard at twenty-three in 1917, he immediately joined his brothers in military studies at Plattsburg; soon thereafter he was an officer in the American Army battling the German invaders in France. With the indifference to danger which characterized his entire life, Archibald Roosevelt fought in areas deluged with shells, poison gas, and shrapnel. He was wounded during the violent German attacks in the spring of 1918. Wrote the father, proud of his son's valor: "Archie's arm was badly fractured and a shell splinter went into his knee; he continued in command for some time, until the loss of blood overcame him; it was fourteen hours before he reached a hospital; a French general gave him the *Croix de guerre* while he was on the operating table." [77] Leaving the hospital, Captain Archibald Roosevelt was sent back to the United States and underwent a slow convalescence at Oyster Bay; partially recovered, he accompanied his father when the latter delivered his impassioned appeals for an overwhelming victory which would end German aggression for all time.[78]

Archie's arm remained paralyzed beyond the war's end. When he believed that he had recovered fully from his wounds he made plans to resume his civilian activities. It was announced that he would join the Sinclair Oil Company in Chicago; [79] but when he arrived in that city he was stricken with an attack of the trench fever which he had contracted on the battlefields of France, and the recurrent effects of poison gas further complicated his illness.[80] When he finally did recover completely, he continued quietly his business pursuits. Returning to New York, he became a partner in an investment house. Seldom did his name appear in public print.

The Rough Rider had said that he wanted his sons to pursue diligently their chosen occupations in time of peace and to become soldiers when there was war. Archibald was successful in the banking and brokerage business until war came again in 1941.[81] Then again he became an officer in the Army of the United States. He was raised to the rank of lieutenant colonel; the dispatches from the Pacific told of his nonchalance where battles raged most fiercely. Particularly, in New Guinea his courage astonished and inspired the men under his command. "Roosevelt is a good officer," commented his men, "but he's got too damn much guts." [82] Typical of the reports describing his valor, was a dispatch in the New York *Times* which told of the capture of Salamaua:

The daring observational tactics of Lieut. Col. Archibald B. Roosevelt, son of the late President Theodore Roosevelt, contributed directly to the fall of Salamaua, an enlisted man from an amphibious engineering unit disclosed today. Colonel Roosevelt had been with the Forty-first Division's 162d Regiment throughout its record-breaking 76-day period of combat.

Our troops occupied Salamaua Saturday. On the previous Wednesday, Colonel Roosevelt, with two officers and three enlisted men, made a reconnaissance tour of Salamaua harbor. Under his orders we went close to the isthmus until Jap guns started firing at us, then turned west across the harbor. Colonel Roosevelt stood up with a map in his hand and every time a gun fired jotted down its position. They fired at us for half an hour, barely missing us several times. The Colonel noticed I was scared and said: "You're safe with me. I was wounded three times in the last war and that's a lucky charm." The next day our artillery landed squarely on those guns and the Japs never fired them again. That was when their resistance ended—and Colonel Roosevelt should get most of the credit for the final blow.[83]

We have reviewed the careers of three sons of the Rough-Rider President. The life of the youngest—Quentin—is equally worthy of his illustrious father. Quentin remained in Washington throughout his father's term. He attended a public school not far distant from the White House, and his first day in the classroom made an indelible impression on its students. Nearly thirty years later one of his classmates, a journalist in his mature years, recorded the excitement: "The arrival of the son of the President of the United States in our dingy, red-brick school occasioned an undeniable flurry among a class of fifty-odd youngsters who watched with hopeful scrutiny for signs of his being snobbish and stuck-up." [84] But Quentin was democratic, and won the affection of his young schoolmates. As impetuous as his older brothers, bent on pranks, he had also a deep regard for the maxims stressed in Ben Franklin's *Almanack*—especially for the ones about the virtue of thrift. The Presidential father himself was startled by Quentin's concept of economy, and he recounted an amusing story in one of his letters. "The other day," wrote Theodore Roosevelt to his older son Kermit, "we were discussing a really dreadful accident which had happened: a Georgetown young man, having taken a young girl in a canoe on the river, the canoe upset and the girl was drowned; whereupon the young man, when he got home, took what seemed a cold-blooded method of a special delivery letter to notify the parents, and Quentin solemnly chimed in with, 'Yes, he wasted ten cents.' There was a moment's eloquent silence, and then we strove to explain to Quentin that what we were objecting to was not in the least the young man's spendthrift attitude." [85] This youngest son of the President, as rated by his teacher, made a good record both in studies and behavior. Completing the primary grades, he began more advanced courses in the high school of Alexandria, in Virginia, seven miles distant from the Capital. At the age of twelve he spent a summer in Europe; at Rheims for the first time he saw airplanes, and these early ships "like birds in the air" kindled his interest in flying.[86]

He was nearing twenty when his brothers were studying military tactics at Plattsburg, and he joined them. None of the Roosevelt sons was more eager to take part in the battles across the ocean than was the youngest son, Quentin; it was his intention, if the United States continued to remain out of the war, to enlist in the Canadian Army. He felt that we had already waited too long to join the nations in mortal combat with Germany in her first attempt to conquer the world. Even before his father spoke out against pacifism, twenty-year-old Quentin burst into indignation that Americans were holding back. "We are a pretty sordid lot, aren't we, to want to sit looking on while England and France fight our battles and pan gold into our pockets? I wondered, as I sat by my fire, whether there are any dreams in our land any more." [87] Shortly after, in April, 1917, the Congress of the United States did declare war on the Imperial German Government, and Quentin Roosevelt, like his three older brothers, enlisted in the Army. As was his impatient wish, he was assigned to the Air Corps.

After the required training, Quentin was placed in charge of a large flying field to superintend the training of other aviators. Later he was sent to France. Like many of our young aviators, he lacked the experience of the enemy flyers who had had long preparation for their planned war; but his eagerness, intelligence, and a natural flying instinct compensated for the absence of longer practice. Soon he was piloting planes over the battle area; in the decisive struggle at Cha-

s'abonne aux Bureaux du Journal, 5, RUE DES ITALIENS, A PARIS (9e), et dans tous les Bureaux de Poste

TEL PÈRE, TELS FILS

La mort héroïque du capitaine aviateur Quentin Roosevelt, fils de l'ancien président des Etats-Unis, ajoute une nouvelle page de gloire et de deuil à l'histoire de l'amitié plus que séculaire qui unit l'Amérique et la France, dans une magnifique confraternité d'armes, pour la défense du droit éternel et des libertés du monde.

Le président Roosevelt, dont la vie publique et privée fut toujours un admirable exemple de courage libéralement prodigué au service des plus nobles causes, est un des hommes d'Etat qui ont le plus efficacement contribué au rapprochement de toutes les forces morales de l'humanité sur le champ de bataille où va se décider l'avenir de la conscience humaine. Tout de suite il a protesté contre l'agression qui a déchaîné la guerre et qui, par la violation de la neutralité de la Belgique, a donné, de prime abord, la mesure de l'immoralité de l'agresseur.

Si l'ancien combattant de Cuba n'est pas venu lui-même, comme il le désirait, prendre sa place au milieu du combat et, selon sa coutume, au plus fort du péril, c'est que des obstacles plus puissants que sa volonté l'ont retenu aux Etats-Unis où d'ailleurs il ne cesse de servir, par tous les moyens en son pouvoir, la cause à laquelle il a sacrifié de tout cœur ses plus chères affections. Il nous a donné ses quatre fils, tous engagés volontaires, tous animés de la plus belle émulation d'héroïsme et inspirés des hautes pensées dont la tradition paternelle a illustré leur foyer natal. L'un d'eux, le plus jeune, déjà cité à l'ordre pour une série d'incomparables prouesses, vient de tomber au champ d'honneur. Un autre est blessé.

Puisse la grande âme du président Roosevelt trouver dans cette épreuve la consolation et le réconfort que voudrait lui apporter notre amitié fraternelle! Il sait, il a souvent dit, mieux que personne combien la beauté du sacrifice librement consenti est féconde en bienfaits pour les générations qui viendront, après nous, recueillir les fruits de nos efforts et de nos souffrances. Ceux qui furent les héros d'une juste cause et les martyrs d'un idéal ne cessent pas d'être présents à la mémoire des siècles et d'agir par une incessante résurrection qui multiplie à l'infini la vertu de leurs actes. Ainsi vivra parmi nous le capitaine Quentin Roosevelt, aimé des frères d'armes qui furent les témoins de ses exploits, honoré des hommages doux et tendres de sa patrie qui le pleure avec fierté, entouré de l'amour de la France qui a recueilli ses reliques sacrées et qui veillera pieusement sur sa tombe glorieuse. — *G. D.*

AN EX-PRESIDENT'S SON DIES FOR HIS COUNTRY

Quentin Roosevelt, youngest son of the "Rough Rider," was shot down in France in aerial combat during the first World War. Like all French journals, the Paris *Le Temps* paid tribute to the young aviator—and to his illustrious sire. "Like Father, Like Son" is the caption. (*Le Temps,* July 18, 1918)

teau Thierry he was frequently out patrolling the skies. It was here that his career was ended in death. The Paris edition of the New York *Herald,* on July 17, 1918, was the first to mention the rumor that Quentin's plane had been shot from the skies; in a short column on the front page it told the American colony in the French capital, "Lieut. Quentin Roosevelt, youngest son of Theodore Roosevelt, has been brought down in an aerial battle with a German in the present fighting, according to word which was brought to Paris last night. The report, which lacks official confirmation, stated that the young aviator's machine was seen to burst into flames." [88]

The following day the report had official confirmation, and very few American newspapers failed to print the news. The leading French paper paid tribute to this soldier's death of the son of the ex-President of the United States. *Le Journal* commented, "His heroic end adds a new and glorious page to the history of more than secular friendship which unites America and France in a magnificent confraternity of arms for the defense of eternal right and the world's liberty." [89] And *Le Temps,* under the caption, "Like Father, Like Son," said: "Lieutenant-Aviator Quentin Roosevelt has just met with a glorious end on our front. . . . Lieutenant Quentin Roosevelt had already distinguished himself as a fighting aviator of a high order, and had brought down his first enemy plane"; [90] but most of the article was a tribute to the father of the dead flier, the ex-President of the United States, Theodore Roosevelt. Thus it was in nearly all the eulogies of Quentin Roosevelt. From high officials of foreign governments and from thousands of Americans in all stations of life came messages of sympathy to the Roosevelt home at Oyster Bay.[91] Other young Americans met death on the ground and in the air; and the War Department in terse official notes notified the bereaved parents. But Quentin Roosevelt was a President's son; to his father went a personal message from General Pershing, commander of all the American armies in France, and the Secretary of War sent a transcript of Quentin's record.

Thus lived the sons of the Rough Rider—the strenuous and inspiring Theodore Roosevelt, twenty-sixth President of the United States. Their lives reflected the credo of their illustrious sire: "Only those are fit to live who do not fear to die; and none are fit to die who have shrunk from the joy of life and the duty of life." [92]

17

Sons of William Howard Taft

ABOARD AN ARMY TRANSPORT PLYING THE PACIFIC IN APRIL, 1900, TWO boys were playing on deck. The watchful mother called the elder, about ten, Robert; the younger, nearing three, was named Charles. They were the sons of William Howard Taft, recently appointed head of a Commission to govern the Philippines, now en route with his family to assume his post at Manila. Nine years later these boys were to become President's sons; in the meantime they were to be schooled far from the land of their birth, in the islands where for centuries Spanish had been the native tongue. It was a hundred years since the sons of a future Chief Executive had spent their childhood in foreign lands; the Adams sons in the eighteen-hundreds learned their elementary lessons in Europe; the sons of other Presidents were educated in countries other than their own, but their academic pursuits there were in the more advanced stages. The sons of Taft, like the sons of John Adams and John Quincy Adams, were to hear around them as the mother tongue of their playmates a language other than English.[1]

William Howard Taft, educated for a lawyer's career, alternated his activities in the legal profession with periods of public service. Two years after he graduated from the Cincinnati College of Law in 1880, he was appointed to the Government post of Collector of Internal Revenue. Thus he combined with the wealth and prestige of his family the opportunity, in an official capacity, to mingle with the prominent and influential men in his State. After a year as Collector, he resumed the practice of law in which he had had a year's experience; in four years he became the judge of the Superior Court of Ohio. Three years later he received a second appointment at the hands of the President of the United States—as Solicitor General of the United States. After two years in that important post, he again mounted the judicial bench—as United States Circuit Judge. William Howard Taft achieved his successes without the apprenticeship of toil and hardships. The Tafts of Cincinnati were a prominent and powerful clan—the owners of banks, the publishers of newspapers, the mentors of dominant political personalities; members of the family had no need to rely solely on experience or proven capabilities to reach high place. William Howard Taft spent two more years expounding legal theory as dean of the law school at the University of Cincinnati; then, without practical knowledge of statecraft or previous service in governmental administration, he was appointed a member of the Philippine Commission and later became the Governor General of the Philippines. Withal he made a creditable record in governing the islands; then, in 1904, although he was entirely unacquainted with military affairs, he was recalled to the United States to become Secretary of War. Mrs. Taft relates how, en route to America, the Taft family stopped off in Japan, where the generals concluded that like themselves a secretary of war was a master of military science. Military maneuvers were staged for William Howard Taft, and the Japanese war minister asked Taft's opinions about some military problems. In her reminiscences of the journey, the wife of William Howard Taft relates the amusing story: "The Japanese Minister of War was a soldier . . . and he assumed at once, in common with all the other army officers whom he encountered, that Mr. Taft was a soldier, too. . . . These Japanese warriors proceeded to credit him with all manner of special knowledge which he had never had an opportunity to acquire and to speak to him in technical terms which, it must be admitted, strained his ability for concealing his ignorance."[2]

The man who made William H. Taft Governor General of the Philippines and Secretary of War was the then President of the United States—Theodore Roosevelt. Between these two men there was a deep friendship, reminiscent of the attachment which Andrew Jackson had for Martin Van Buren. To Andrew Jackson, Van Buren owed the Presidency; to Theodore Roosevelt, Taft no less was indebted for his election as Chief Executive. But there the parallel ended. Van Buren always remained a staunch supporter of Jackson, risking his own political fortunes. William Howard Taft made no sacrifices for his champion; he was invariably the one to profit. Martin Van Buren continued the policies of his predecessor; Taft strayed from Roosevelt's objectives. Van Buren and Jackson remained friends till death ended their association; Taft and Roosevelt drifted apart, and became rival candidates. As to why and how, the historians differ.[3] Here we have need only to record that, while serving as Secretary of War, William Howard Taft was nominated by the Republican Party as its candidate for President. That nomination was dictated by the incumbent President, Theodore Roosevelt.[4] Taft was elected, and inaugurated on March 4, 1909. With him to the White House went the two boys—Robert and Charles.

Robert was nearing fifteen when, after four years in the Philippines, he returned to the United States with his father, who had just been appointed Secretary of War. He had been born in Cincinnati in 1889, half a year before his father became Solicitor General of the United States. The family moved to Washington, back to Ohio, and then to the Orient. En route to Manila, Mrs. Taft and the children spent a summer in Japan; there Robert contracted diphtheria. In the Philippine capital he was thrown from a carriage. But these childhood episodes left no permanent injuries; and, once again in his native land, Robert Taft pursued the activities of the average American boy. When his parents returned to the national Capital, Robert was sent off to the Taft School at Watertown, Connecticut, of which his uncle was the head. In the year his father became President, this elder Taft son was at Yale—the traditional college of the Taft clan.[5] There Robert made a brilliant record; he graduated in 1910, and the Class Book recited his numerous honors: "He took a Philosophical Oration appointment and is president of Phi Beta Kappa. He won the Woolsey Scholarship, the Barge Mathematical Prize, a Berkley Premium and the second Ten Eyck Prize. He was president of the University Debating Association and debated on the Academic interdepartment team in 1908 and 1909." [6] But it was not only in scholarship that this President's son excelled; he rowed on the sophomore crew, was active in college fraternities, and served as treasurer of the Y.M.C.A.[7]

After obtaining his degree at Yale, Robert spent three years at Harvard studying law. Again he ranked highest in his class. During the First World War, his weak eyes preventing Army service, Robert was appointed Assistant General Counsel of the Food Administration.[8]

However, the elder son of the twenty-seventh President was eager for a career in politics. In 1920 he entered the race for a seat in the Ohio Legislature. Elected to the lower house, he served six years—as Speaker during the last year. During the succeeding five years he devoted himself to his law practice and his business interests, but the urge for the political arena was strong. In 1931 he was again elected to the Legislature, this time to the Senate; there he devoted his efforts to a revision of the Ohio tax laws. Robert Taft's concern about taxation was not prompted by mere academic interest; during the two decades since his college career he had acquired a fair share of worldly goods, and had become both stockholder and director in numerous corporations.[9] The scope of his financial activities was reflected in the record of his Yale class, published twenty-five years after his graduation; none of his classmates had fared so well: "Robert Alphonso Taft is a director of the Cincinnati Street Railway Company, the Cincinnati Union Terminal Company, the Central Trust Company, the Covington & Cincinnati Bridge Company, the Cincinnati Terminal Warehouses, the American Book Company, the S. A. Gerrard Company, the Cincinnati Realty Company, and the Dixie Terminal Company."[10]

Living on a forty-acre estate near Cincinnati, this President's son had all the advantages which, very often in our history, have raised ambitious men to the highest office: he had independent means, influential family connections, the prestige of a Presidential father, residence in a State which only in rare instances failed to support his party's nominees. In 1936 Robert A. Taft was Ohio's "favorite son" at the national convention which nominated the Republican candidate for President. No informed political observers regarded him seriously as the probable nominee. But, two years later, he did obtain high office—becoming a United States Senator.

In 1938 Robert Taft won the Republican nomination in Ohio as a candidate for the United States Senate; in the fall he toured the State, addressing many political rallies. It cannot be said that his campaign speeches reflected a grasp of the world events which men with greater vision then foresaw. During the weeks which preceded the election press reports from Tokyo told of Japan's purpose to force China into a solid bloc with Manchukuo and the Japanese Empire for the political and economic domination of East Asia—Nippon hurling its defiance at the Western democracies.[11] Newspapers were relating the detailed confessions of German spies in New York, divulging the Nazi plans against the security of the United States.[12] From Paris came long messages describing Hitler's maneuvers to destroy the League of Nations, his determination to rearm Germany. Our own Secretary of State,

Cordell Hull, was crying out against the machinations of the totalitarian States and their latent threats to our safety. But we seek in vain for some realization of these sinister trends in Taft's appeals for votes; we find him solely denouncing the incumbent Administration.[13] In short, he was a politician seeking votes, not a statesman bent on warning against impending dangers. But it must be noted that his opponent likewise was oblivious of the imminent world crisis, and with similar blindness appealed for ballots by merely defending the national Administration which Taft decried.

In November, 1938, Robert A. Taft was victorious. He was then forty-nine years old, described as "long-legged and slender, open-faced and of serious mind." [14] Aware that he was a President's son, columnists and feature writers made him the subject of long articles. "Once again a Taft will be in Washington," exclaimed the artist-journalist S. J. Woolf. "When Congress convenes in January Robert A. Taft, son of a former President, will take his seat as United States Senator from Ohio. Already the word has gone around that the new Senator will bear watching, that he will carry on the family tradition and that he is Presidential timber." [15] Ohio papers which, prior to the election day, were noticeably meager in their editorial praise of Robert Taft, now exulted in his victory. Said the Cleveland *Plain Dealer:* "To the nation this morning the Republicans of Ohio present Robert A. Taft, son of a former President of the United States: the man who captured the Senatorial nomination in a primary no one thought he could win, who later challenged a White House favorite son and now bowls him over to climax his own achievement. Mr. Taft is this morning the most potent Republican on the national stage. Ohio's independent electorate makes him so." [16] Other Ohio journals interpreted Taft's victory not as a personal triumph but as the result of a voters' rebellion against the policies of the Administration at Washington; the Columbus *Dispatch* commented that "by electing Robert A. Taft to the United States Senate, the people of Ohio have administered a smashing blow to the New Deal." [17] "It will be admitted," observed the *State Journal,* "that the Ohio results are a part of the general pattern." [18] "The result of these elections," concluded the Toledo *Blade,* "must be interpreted as a rebuke to the policies of the New Deal." [19]

An objective appraisal of Robert Taft's Senatorial activities leaves the impression that, either through an innate dislike for change or belief that it was politically astute, this President's son adopted a credo of opposing everything proposed by leaders of the rival party—and even by some prominent members of his own. His speeches were filled with the monotonous phrase, "objection to." [20] It cannot be denied that there were times when he crusaded against proposed legislation which the majority of his fellow citizens also disapproved; but his habitual opposition to many proposals proved right and expedient by subsequent events eclipsed his efforts for desirable laws.[21] Yet he did perform a service in promoting discussions regarding waste in Government expenditures. Said Arthur Krock, the able political commentator of the New York *Times* who was in sympathy with Robert's budgetary objectives: "Senator Taft has pounded steadily at spending and the deficit. On the floor and in many public speeches he has demanded a start toward the eventual balancing of the budget, and in answer to the President he set forth a specific plan. Mr. Taft has done much to clarify what will be the major campaign issue, especially if he is the Republican nominee." [22] But many other unbiased political writers did not agree that Taft had presented any constructive plan as a remedy for the procedure he denounced. At any rate, as Krock implied, the ambition to be the Presidential nominee set the tempo for Robert Taft's activities as a Senator; therein lay his weakness and his failure to become a real leader who could inspire a nationwide following.

Robert Taft's aspiration to be the candidate of the Republican Party for the Nation's highest office came near fulfillment in 1940. For a year preceding the nominating convention in June his friends had used every method to gain for him publicity and popularity; he made numerous speeches which were given prominent space in leading newspapers, and was photographed in the performance of humble tasks which reflected his interest in his fellow Americans; the number of the telephone in his private office was changed to ME 1940.[23] When the convention met in Chicago the hotels swarmed with Taft supporters, and on the day of the balloting the auditorium echoed with cheers for the son of the twenty-seventh President. Thomas Dewey had been placed in nomination first, and then followed the speech of an Ohio editor naming Robert Taft as the candidate.[24] Said the speaker: "Ohio, Mother of Presidents, brings to this convention a great American. He has a constructive program. He has knowledge and experience in international affairs. He has imagination and courage. He is an amazing vote getter. . . . Ohio's candidate comes to us from one of America's most distinguished families. . . . He is an amazing vote getter."[25]

In accordance with the routine in political conventions, the nominating speech was followed by a parade of the delegates pledged to vote for Taft, and adherents in the visitors' galleries added their approval with shouts, handclapping, and horn blowing. "The Taft people made so much noise and had so much pep," reported the Chicago *Tribune,* "that at the end of ten minutes it looked as tho no more business would be accomplished during the evening."[26] Exclaimed an Ohio Congressman: "We can keep it up all night if we want to, but let's give three cheers for the next President, Bob Taft."[27] But the prediction was not realized: Bob Taft did not become President, neither did he become his party's candidate for that office.

On the first three ballots Thomas Dewey of New York polled the highest number of votes, reaching 315; Robert Taft, starting with 129, acquired 212 on the third ballot. In the fourth poll, Dewey dropped to 250, and Taft increased his strength to 254. But a third candidate had emerged to challenge both: Wendell Willkie. Beginning with 105 votes and scorned by his two leading rivals, Willkie accumulated 306 on the fourth ballot, reached 429 on the fifth while Taft mustered 377, and soared to 659 in the final, sixth, canvass with Taft dropping to 312. Thus Wendell Willkie, and not the President's son, became the Presidential candidate of the Republican Party.[28] Robert A. Taft still remained United States Senator.

Nevertheless, despite his defeat, Robert Taft had become firmly convinced that in coming years public opinion would again veer to the credo to which his party had clung for half a century, and that he could later achieve the Presidency by an unswerving opposition to newer, progressive policies currently approved by a vast majority of his fellow Americans. No other explanation could account for his uncompromising championship of concepts which even prominent members of his own party repudiated. The diminishing group of "conservatives" were very willing that this President's son should assume the leadership in opposing liberal legislation; Robert Taft did not disappoint them in his zeal or in the extent of his efforts. That his principles and his methods were advantageous to his party was questioned by seasoned students of American politics. Said Walter Lippmann: "Though Mr. Taft is an intelligent man, who would always get a high mark in school, he has never acquired sufficient wisdom and understanding to be a good and sound conservative in times like these. He is probably more responsible than any other single man for leading the Republican Party into blind alleys of dumb obstruction on the vital issue of our time." [29]

Meanwhile his younger brother came to public notice. Although Robert A. Taft had obtained more conspicuous public office, it was Charles whom the nonpartisan press regarded with greater admiration. As we have seen, he was not yet three years old when his parents took him to the Philippines—he was by seven years Robert's junior. Even as a youngster he asserted himself, and a Manila newspaper was prompted to editorialize, "Charles, a baby of three, is king of the household." [30] This yielding to his whims whetted his desire to dominate, and he extended his juvenile tyranny to other children; Mrs. Taft recorded that "Charlie used to order about the gardener's two little boys, a few years older than himself, but about his size. He used to order them around in a strange mixture of Spanish, Tagalog, and English which made me wonder at my wholly American child, but it was an effective combination since he seemed to have them completely under his thumb and, as he reveled in his sense of power, he never tired of playing with them." [31] His proud mother described him: "Charles was an attractive child, . . . people stopped to watch him. . . . He had big, dark eyes, soft brown curls, very deep dimples, and a charming smile that was always in evidence." [32] He later lost his curls, but he always retained his physical attractiveness and captivating personality.

Named after an uncle whose prominence and activities were often mentioned in the newspapers, this younger son of William Howard Taft was referred to as Charles Phelps, 2nd. Charles was about seven when he returned from his four years' stay in the tropics. He attended the public schools in Washington. Later, like his brother, he went to the Taft School at Watertown, Connecticut; but he spent more time in Washington than did Robert. It was Charlie who, in the summer of 1908, hurried through the corridors of the War Department, carrying to his father—then Secretary of War—the bulletins which came in from the Republican convention engaged in nominating a candidate for the Presidency.[33] Finally this youthful messenger brought to his impatient father the awaited news: William Howard Taft was the nominee. In the following November Taft was victorious; in March, 1909, Charles Taft became a President's son.

Charles followed the Taft tradition and attended Yale. His classmates called him "Charlie" or "Tafty," and the Class Book noted that he was a President's son.[34] More athletic than his older brother, he was a member of the university track and football teams, and for two years captain of the basketball team.[35] While he did not lead his class in scholarship as had Robert, Charles did win academic distinction: in the freshman year he received honors of the first grade and the Galpin Latin Prize; in the sophomore year, a first-grade Premium in Latin composition; and in the junior year a Philosophical Oration appointment and a second Ten Eyck Prize. He was president of the Freshman Debating Union, and a member of the Student Council; and he took part in the college dramatic presentations.[36]

War against Germany having been declared in 1917, Charles Phelps Taft enrolled in the student military courses, and was appointed a corporal. After a month's drilling, he left the college campus and enlisted in the regular Army; training at Fort Myer, Virginia, he went overseas as a battalion sergeant major in the field artillery. Soon he acquired officer's rank as first lieutenant. In the meantime he had married the daughter of the president of America's largest clock company. After the war had ended, Charles P. Taft returned to Yale, and received his bachelor's degree with the Class of 1918.

Continuing at Yale, he graduated from its Law School in 1921. After four years of private practice in Cincinnati, Charles P. Taft, 2nd, was elected prosecuting attorney of Hamilton County, and he held that post for a year. His fearless attacks on corrupt officials won him public confidence and approval; his prosecution of a prominent wife murderer obtained for him headlines in a nationwide press.

He developed oratorical talent, and his reputation spread beyond his own State; we find quotations from his speeches printed not only in Ohio journals, but also in prominent newspapers of the large cities of other states. Strangely, his own parents had not heard him in this role until his father, then an ex-President and Chief Justice of the United States, attended the anniversary ceremonies of the Y.M.C.A. at Washington toward the close of 1927: the principal orator was Charles P. Taft, 2nd.[37] His public addresses were characterized by a clarity and sincerity which evoked the admiration of newspaper editors particularly qualified to appraise orators and orations. On Memorial Day, 1928, Charles Taft was one of the speakers at Lincoln University in the Tennessee mountains; his theme was the citizen and politics. The subject, as the New York *Times* pointed out, was discussed often; but his presentation was singled out for comment. He analyzed the political sentiment in Cincinnati, and the public uprising there against corrupt politicians. The *Times* regarded him as the type of official who could assure good government: "He is by all accounts a worthy and able young man, but he was born in the political atmosphere and the flavor is on his tongue. Given a leader like him, many communities rouse themselves to the labor of throwing out the machine politicians and putting government on a higher level." [38] Within a decade the youngest son of ex-President Taft became nationally known. During the year 1937 Charles Taft was often in the news, as a speaker on social and political themes. He voiced his denunciation of communism before a D. A. R. convention; [39] discussed democracy at a college commencement; [40] analyzed the relationship between religion and business.[41] Whether he spoke before a political organization or addressed a conference of social workers, important journals accorded him notice and editorial comment.

With the passing years it became evident that there was a deep cleavage between the economic and social philosophies of the two sons of the twenty-seventh President. The astute commentator, Thomas L. Stokes, summed up the widespread opinion of nonpartisan editors: "It seems there are two brothers, surname Taft. Robert A. and Charles P. —'Bob' and 'Charlie.' Their father was President. . . . Both are Republicans—but what a difference! . . . To this onlooker, it appears that the younger brother, Charles P., is taking on the tariff—as on other issues—a broad national and international viewpoint, while the Senator is taking the narrow, backward glance of the standpat G. O. P., based on localism and economic isolation." [42] Publicly, in radio talks and in addresses before varied audiences, Charles enunciated viewpoints in sharp contrast to the doctrines voiced by his older brother in the Senate, in press interviews, and in public speeches. Charles epitomized his credo on international relationship in a State Department publication: "We must stand for justice and honor as well as for enlightened self-interest in those economic relations with the world abroad." [43] The dramatic moment in the conflict between the views of the two Taft brothers came when Charles Taft, in May, 1945, came before the Ways and Means Committee of the House of Representatives, and vigorously supported the reciprocal-tariff program which Robert had vehemently denounced.

Not alone in editorial eulogies did Charles P. Taft reap rewards for his support of the policies of the incumbent Administration. While his brother Robert, constantly attacking the principles and governmental activities of the party in power, was deliberately kept from councils which played important roles in the conduct of the global war or had a voice in executive agencies, Charles was repeatedly appointed to public posts; while Robert A. Taft was relegated to the Senatorial office to which the citizens of Ohio had elected him, Charles came to high places in Government boards without contesting for votes—he received his offices from the President of the United States. He was made a member of the Federal Mediation Board,[44] held various commissions in agencies dealing with social problems,[45] became a member of the State Department staff. As Chairman of the Area Committee for Coordination of the Planning of United States Agencies, he outlined plans for providing assistance in the economic rehabilitation of the East Indies.[46] Later he became the director of the Office of Transport and Communications Policy, and in this capacity Charles P. Taft voiced his strongest opposition to the views held by his older brother.

As was often intimated by the friends of Robert, the prominence of Charles in public affairs stemmed entirely from the wartime Government posts to which he was appointed by his brother's political adversary, President Franklin D. Roosevelt. In the summer of 1945 momentous changes occurred: Roosevelt died suddenly in April, and the war ended several months later. For more than a year thereafter, the activities of Charles P. Taft received little mention in the press. In contrast, his brother's name continued to make headlines. The death of the wartime President made no change in the views and utterances of this older Taft brother. The constant criticism which Robert Taft had voiced against the Roosevelt Administration was now directed against the new President, Harry Truman; Robert Taft continued to be the opponent of all that was proposed or favored by the Democratic regime and the incumbent Chief Executive. Other members of his party remained silent or were cautious in their censure, particularly when there was danger of antagonizing organized labor; but the eldest son of the twenty-seventh President lost no opportunity to express publicly his antagonistic views. When Truman urged the adoption of the monetary plan formulated at the Bretton Woods Conference, winning the support of prominent Republicans, Robert Taft was among the very few Senators who were in vehement opposition. "Senator Taft has been playing Horatius at the Senate bridge," observed a prominent political commentator. "He has been holding back the Bretton Woods world financial peace agreements, but soon he will have to swim for it."[47] Similarly, when the President advocated higher wages and controlled prices, Robert Taft denounced the policy as "ridiculous, dangerous, and ultimately impossible";[48] when the drivers of Washington busses struck for higher pay, Taft declared that the strike was due to the President's proposal of increased salaries for Government employees.[49]

In the closing weeks of November, 1945, the Senate considered the appointment of an American representative on the Security Council of the United Nations.[50] Once again Robert Taft became spokesman for the irreconcilable isolationists bent on keeping the United States out of such international organizations. Months earlier the Senate, by a vote of 89 to 2, had ratified the San Francisco Charter, which had envisaged our full participation in a world council to curb future aggressors. Taft had then voted for the Charter, but it was no secret that this was part of a strategy which anticipated later nullification of the almost unanimous ratification by means of strangling curbs on the power of the American members on the United Nations boards. Now he was making a desperate effort to circumvent the declared objectives of the San Francisco conference, which had been publicly approved by the President, by Congress, and by the overwhelming majority of his countrymen. By argument, by parliamentary maneuvering, he tried to prevent the passage of a bill giving reality to our membership in the world council. The pages of the *Congressional Record* are filled with the shrewd arguments and astute motions of this elder Taft son.[51] Robert Taft's contention was that, without the restrictions and conditions he proposed, the American delegate alone would hold in his hands the power to bind the American Government and determine when and where our armed troops should be used. This power to declare war, he argued, was vested by the Constitution in Congress, and the decisions which were to be made by the American representative on the United Nations Council would be tantamount to treaty making which, under the Constitution, required ratification by the Senate. However debatable may have been his premises and conclusions, one of his repeated assertions could not be disputed: that few of his fellow Senators remained in the chamber to hear his arguments on this subject so vital to the welfare of their country; Robert

Taft was justified in his rebuking reference to "the Senate of the United States, practically all of its members being absent throughout the entire debate on the bill." [52] Certainly there was no debater on either side more persistent in presenting his views, more zealous in defending his position, or more alert in contesting the facts advanced by his adversaries.

A few papers, still in bitter opposition to American participation in a world league, lauded Robert Taft and supported his arguments. The Chicago *Tribune,* the leader of the "isolationist press," quoted long extracts from Robert's Senate speeches,[53] but the large majority of newspapers endorsed an active role in the United Nations for the United States. In the Senate there was a predominant sentiment for granting to the American member full powers. Finally realizing that only a few of his Senate colleagues would support his strategies, he "deleted three provisions of his amendment and asked a test on the remainder." [54] The Senate rejected his proposal.[55] Outstanding Republicans—among them Austin of Vermont, Saltonstall of Massachusetts, and Vandenberg of Michigan—voted against him. Robert Taft was the undisputed leader of the "irreconcilables," and his name was mentioned as a possible candidate of the conservative Republican Party in the forthcoming Presidential campaign of 1948; typical of the high praise was a speech made in the House of Representatives by a Congressman [56] denouncing the policies of the Democratic Administrations and suggesting candidates for his own party. For President he named Robert Taft of Ohio, "to carry out a program to establish fundamental Republican principles as our basic national policy." [57]

The numerous and extended speeches which Robert Taft made in opposition to American participation in a world organization did not exhaust his entire antagonism to Administration policies. With equal vehemence he voiced censure of Government spending, and his views on this subject won approval in journals which disliked his attitude on international relations. During the first week of December, 1945, he was the principal speaker at several dinners of trade associations. "Senator Taft Comes to New Jersey!" proclaimed a circular of the New Jersey Taxpayers' Association, on which was printed a photograph of Robert. "Senator Robert A. Taft is the son of the late President William H. Taft . . . an outstanding advocate of Constitutional government and governmental economy in the taxpayers' interest." [58]

THE REVERIE OF A PRESIDENT'S SON

The distinguished cartoonist Marcus deftly depicted the ambition of Robert A. Taft, elder son of the twenty-seventh President, to match the career of his father. (New York *Times,* Aug. 3, 1947)

The Washington *Post,* editorially commending his speech, called it "an attack on spending." [59] A few days later Robert spoke again at the convention of another trade association, repeating his criticism of Government expenditures.[60] The anti-Administration journals printed his remarks on their front pages, and even newspapers friendly to the Democratic regime gave space to excerpts of the address. The year ended with Robert's outspoken opposition to the Administration's employment program and the President's advocacy of national health insurance.

The year 1946 brought still more publicity for Robert A. Taft. It was obvious that the incumbent Democratic Administration was losing popular support, and there was increasing probability that the elections during the forthcoming fall would veer in favor of the Republicans. That implied, in the opinion of most observers, that Robert would gain in political power as an outstanding spokesman for the Republican conservatives in the Senate. Some members of his party in that body, however, would not follow his leadership. In fact, during the first week of the year several Republican Senators disputed his enunciation of "Republican policy" and called Robert "a reactionary." [61] It was to be expected, therefore, that he would also clash with Democratic members. The press devoted much space to these feuds between Robert and his Senatorial colleagues.[62]

Nevertheless, Robert persisted in asserting his leadership. He wrote articles for magazines, assuming the role of program-maker for the Republican Party.[63] He delivered numerous radio talks,[64] continuing to denounce the Administration policies,[65] especially the labor legislation proposed by the President. With remarkable energy Robert Taft delivered long speeches on the Senate floor, argued before Congressional Committees, addressed gatherings of professional men and business leaders. There was no doubt that he meant to be constantly in the public eye; anticipating a Republican victory in the November elections, he intended that success to be associated with his personal activities. "One of the most interesting political developments recently is the obvious rebirth of ambition in Senator Robert A. Taft to be President," commented one shrewd political writer; [66] and this opinion was echoed by other Washington correspondents.

The elections having resulted in an overwhelming Republican triumph, Robert Taft did become the recognized leader of the conservative wing of the Republican Party.[67] "Taft of Ohio is the biggest political figure in Washington," concluded *Time,* calling him "the boss of probably the most efficiently organized G. O. P. Senate the nation has ever seen." [68] This widely read magazine devoted two full pages to a review of Robert's mannerisms and ambitions, illustrating the lengthy article with a photograph of his Presidential father, and picturing Robert himself on the cover. Friend and foe alike, at the end of 1946, acknowledged that Robert A. Taft was a dominant, influential figure in American politics. The New York *Times* named him as the first "key man" in the new Congress, saying that he had dictated the successful Republican strategy. "His candidacy in 1948 is now regarded by many as a certainty," remarked the *Times* on New Year's day of 1947.[69] "Taft shows early that he is Senate boss," said another well-qualified observer.[70] Certain it was that politicians and the public were intensely interested in his views, and the newspapers printed his remarks on their front pages.[71]

But Robert Taft's triumph was short-lived. By mid-March it became evident that he could not have undisputed sway over all the Senatorial members of his party. He could not impose upon them all his own opinions, nor control their votes to obtain all his objectives. More than that: columnists dramatized the revolt against his leadership, and an avalanche of editorial criticism followed several of his pronouncements on public issues.[72]

Robert Taft was censured most for his violent opposition to the confirmation of the nomination of David Lilienthal as head of the Atomic Energy Commission. Lilienthal's selection by President Truman was praised by a vast majority of the Nation's newspapers; public opinion was decidedly in favor of the appointment, and it was urged by the country's leading churchmen, scientists, industrialists, and statesmen. "Mr. Taft has compromised his own position of leadership in the Senate," was the verdict of the New York *Herald Tribune,*[73] heading its editorial "Mr. Taft's Boner." Robert was unrelenting in his insistence that Republican Senators should continue to oppose Lilienthal's appointment, which prompted the independent Washington *Post* to say, "If Mr. Taft persists in this line, which can never be sustained under any reasonable analysis, he will be doing a grave disservice, not only to his own reputation and that of the party he represents, but to the influence and prestige of the United States." [74] Although two-thirds of his Republican colleagues joined Robert Taft in voting against Lilienthal's confirmation, half as many refused to accept his dictum. Well-informed commentators agreed that his futile opposition lessened his reputation among his countrymen.

Similarly, Robert aroused much unfavorable criticism because of his utterances regarding the trials of the Nazis who plotted the war. He called the Nuremberg trials "an outrage against justice," [75] and asserted that the hanging of the eleven Hitler co-conspirators "will be a blot on the American record." [76] Unquestionably, few Americans agreed with these opinions. Some hinted that Robert Taft, thinking of future Presidential campaigns, had an eye on the "German vote" in crucial states. But there were others who maintained that "few men in public life allow political expediency to figure so little in their calculations as does Senator Taft." [77]

If Robert Taft lost in public esteem because of views which were repudiated by an overwhelming majority of his fellow Americans, it was also true that this loss of popularity was offset by his stand on other issues—particularly on labor legislation and on taxation.[78] Nevertheless, during the spring of 1947 there was an unmistakable drop in Robert's popularity; and, as the months passed, polls of public opinion reflected a reversal of his former status among Republican voters as the most favored candidate for the Presidency.[79]

While Robert's name appeared very frequently in newspaper headlines, his younger brother Charles obtained comparatively little publicity. No longer a government official, Charles P. Taft resumed his law practice as head of a prominent legal firm in Cincinnati, Ohio. Occasionally, he made public addresses.[80] One of his talks bore an unusual resemblance to Robert's speeches: Charles criticized the President and the Secretary of State as inefficient administrators, and warned against "soaking the rich." [81] Later he was afforded an opportunity to display his own executive ability by his election to the board of directors of a publishing house.[82]

In December, 1946, Charles was chosen to head the Federal Council of Churches, being the first layman ever to hold that post.[83] The opening line of the press association reports mentioned that he was "the son of the former President of the United States." [84] Thus recognized as a leading figure in fostering religion, this second son of the twenty-seventh President was a welcome speaker wherever churchmen gathered. In the spring of 1947 Charles P. Taft enunciated his social credo before four thousand attentive listeners at the Northern Baptist Convention. Said he: "I believe in our economic system with all its faults. But mistakes of the system need to be pointed out, and especially those which shock the Christian conscience."[85]

Such were the divergent paths of the two sons of William Howard Taft. Their temperaments were unlike in their childhood years and in their college careers; their political philosophies differed when they grew to manhood. What will be the respective roles of these President's sons in the "atomic era" now unfolding? That will be determined as postwar readjustments continue, and as a shattered world presses for the solution of unforeseen social and economic problems. Only then will there be an answer to the query propounded by one political commentator: "Is it to be the Bob Taft or Charlie Taft Way?"[86]

18

Sons of Calvin Coolidge

IN THE EARLY MORNING DARKNESS OF AUGUST 4, 1923, AN AGED VERmont farmer trudged down the steps from his second-story bedroom—a kerosene lamp in one hand, a Bible in the other. He was John Coolidge, who had spent his years tilling the soil, reading the Scriptures, and serving as justice of the peace. In the plain parlor of his frame farmhouse he had often notarized mortgages and deeds for his neighbors, had occasionally married a rural couple. Under the State law he could administer oaths. But it was no transaction in land and no wedding ceremony that he legalized that night; his mission was far more unusual and far more exalted. He had been aroused from his sleep to swear in a new President of the United States—his own son, Calvin Coolidge.[1]

Calvin Coolidge had not been elected President. In the campaign of 1920 he was merely the Republican nominee for Vice-President; the party had selected Warren G. Harding as its candidate for President. Harding and Coolidge were elected, and were inaugurated respectively as President and Vice-President on March 4, 1921. As was the wont of the American people, it was the Chief Executive whose actions were of interest to them, and after they had cast their ballots millions of voters could not even recall whom they had chosen as Vice-President. But now Warren G. Harding had died suddenly[2] and, as provided in the Constitution, Vice-President Calvin Coolidge became the thirtieth President of the United States.[3]

Thus, unexpectedly and without the intention of the American electorate, Calvin Coolidge achieved the highest office in the land.[4] His fellow citizens who had been uninterested while he held the inconspicuous post of Vice-President now wanted to know about this farmer's son; writers who previously had made no mention of him in biographical volumes, now began to print long reviews of his career.[5] The story was that of a serious and determined man who, without wealth or family prestige, prepared for the legal profession but made public service his career. Admitted to the Massachusetts bar, he had opened a law office in the small town of Northampton; there for two decades he was an unimportant attorney, while he became prominent in politics. Three years out of Amherst, in 1898 he had become a member of the City Council; a year later, City Solicitor. In 1906 he was elected to the State Legislature; four years later the people of Northampton chose him Mayor. From this post he was elected, in 1911, State Senator, and became President of the State Senate in 1913. Fostering friendships among the powerful of his State, he was nominated and elected Lieutenant Governor in 1915, and re-elected for the two succeeding terms. In 1918 Calvin Coolidge became Governor of Massachusetts. It was while Governor that he became a national figure. In 1919 the police of Boston went on strike. Governor Calvin Coolidge publicly proclaimed that there "could be no strike against public order"; citizens of Boston volunteered to replace the striking policemen, and the strike was soon ended. Although impartial observers asserted that the Governor had failed to act when the strike was imminent, the public acclaimed his final action. His popularity among those who regarded him as the "bulwark of law and order" spread beyond the boundaries of Massachusetts, and the leaders of the Republican Party appraised his increasing popularity.[6]

There were some newspapers which began to voice the opinion that Calvin Coolidge was well qualified to become the Republican candidate for President. The party convention met in Chicago; but there were aspirants who were more prominent than the Governor of Massachusetts. In fact, there were too many determined contenders; and, while the supporters of the rival contestants indulged in oratory on the convention floor, the party bosses gathered in a hotel room and decided who should be the candidate: Warren G. Harding, then United States Senator from Ohio. When the balloting was resumed, a few votes were cast for Coolidge, but the dictate of the party leaders was carried out, and Harding became the nominee. The delegates were now ready to depart for home, and there were many empty seats when the time arrived to nominate a candidate for Vice-President. What occurred was described by Chauncey M. Depew, whose presence at many nominating conventions made him a qualified observer: "Very few conventions have a dramatic surprise, but the nomination of Governor Coolidge of Massachusetts for Vice-President came about in a very picturesque way. He had been placed in nomination for President, but not for Vice-President. . . . When the balloting was about to start, a delegate from Oregon who was in the rear of the hall . . . shouted: 'Mr. Chairman, I nominate for Vice-President Calvin Coolidge, a one-hundred-per-cent American.' The convention went off its feet with a whoop and Coolidge was nominated hands down." [7]

It was not his political progress, however, that made the thirtieth President "good copy" for the newspaper writers who were assigned to describe the new occupant of the White House. It was the personal characteristics of Calvin Coolidge that intrigued these reporters and became legends among their readers. Coolidge's boyhood had been spent on a farm, where work and thrift were the essentials of survival, and the maxim, "silence is golden," the rule for getting along with neighbors. His parents were imbued with the tenets of an austere religious faith; and Calvin, as an able writer summed it up, "grew up with their traits and those of a pinched community: frugality, taciturnity, industry, conservation, piety, and puritanical honesty." [8] Particularly, Calvin Coolidge became known for his laconic utterances; both in admiration and derision he was frequently referred to as "Silent Cal." This reluctance to speak filled those about him with uncertainty regarding his views and intentions; how his silence affected those within the White House walls has been recorded by Irwin Hoover, who had served under a dozen Presidents: "For over four years I never had a conversation with President Coolidge. Other Presidents were apparently eager to hear about what had been done by former administrations. Coolidge answered all questions with just 'yes' or 'no,' or made inquiries which could be answered in a similar manner. The whole atmosphere among the employees was one of fear and trembling, lest they lose their jobs just on a notion of the President. He never appeared to appreciate any efforts they put forth to serve him and left them in a state of constant anxiety." [9] This taciturnity was a Coolidge trait long before he had become President. There was a story that while he was Governor his wife attended an afternoon tea and Coolidge phoned to her, asking that she return to the Governor's mansion. The conversation comprised eight words: "Is this Grace? This is Cal. Hop home." [10]

Coupled with this sparsity of spoken words was Calvin Coolidge's strict economy in his monetary affairs; and from Washington there came numerous tales of his frugality. "Coolidge thrift is a byword in Capital circles," exclaimed the New York *World* within a few weeks after he had succeeded the open-handed Warren Harding.[11] But it was not alone of his own finances that the thirtieth President was mindful; with equal zeal he saved public funds, shunning the customary distinctions which surround the Presidency. "I can ride like any other American," he asserted, rejecting a special train offered by railroad officials.[12]

While the taciturnity and austerity of Calvin Coolidge were still more pronounced when contrasted with the lavishness and urbanity of the preceding President, Warren G. Harding, the public found more interest in the Coolidge occupancy of the White House: Harding had been childless, but now again there were juvenile antics in the Presidential family. Calvin Coolidge, at thirty-two, had married Grace Goodhue, and she had borne him two sons. Happily, it was not the father's severe traits but their mother's genial disposition that these boys inherited. Grace Goodhue Coolidge possessed a gracious temperament; while mistress of the White House she won the affectionate regard of the public, the press, and Washington officialdom. Said one biographer of the thirtieth President: "Grace Coolidge was at least six years younger in age and sixty years younger in manner; vivacious, cheerful, friendly. In most features she was Calvin's antithesis."[13] Prominent metropolitan newspapers, like the New York *World,* sensed the widespread interest of their readers and published large photographs of "The White House Children."[14]

At the time their father became Chief Executive the elder of the Coolidge sons, named John, was just seventeen; his brother, Calvin, Jr., was two years younger. Both boys had attended the public schools at Northampton, Massachusetts, and then entered Mercersburg Academy at Mercersburg, Pennsylvania. During their summer vacations they worked on farms, earning money to supplement the limited allowances they received from their father.

The fateful August in which Harding's death raised his father to the Presidency found John Coolidge at a citizens' military camp at Fort Devens, Massachusetts. He had arrived on August first in an Army truck with forty other youths; inconspicuously, he performed the tasks assigned him, taking part in the military drills as an equal member of his company. Probably some of those about him knew that his father was then Vice-President, but young America was never impressed with that station in officialdom. Within a few days John Coolidge became the center of interest at the camp: he had become a President's son. The press associations sent reporters to interview and describe this seventeen-year-old lad whose father had suddenly risen to the Nation's highest office. A special correspondent wired to the New York *Times:* "Since his father was elevated to the Presidency, however, he has been besieged by photographers and interviewers. An inevitable question has been, 'How does it feel to be the son of a President?' and young Coolidge confesses that he doesn't feel a bit different from when he was the son of a Massachusetts Governor. His principal fear seems to be that because he is a President's son he may be held in awe rather than as a good pal."[15] The report continues, "John Coolidge is a 'regular fellow' was the unanimous verdict of the buddies of the President's eldest son at the Citizens' Military Training Camp. A bit reticent and retiring, but withal a good mixer, young Coolidge, who inherits his father's blondness . . . has entered enthusiastically in camp activities."

While his elder brother was mastering the rudiments of military tactics, the younger son of President Calvin Coolidge was earning three and a half dollars a day piling up bundles of tobacco on a farm at Hatfield, Massachusetts.[16] He was described as "a slender, blue-eyed youth."[17] "Calvin Coolidge, Jr., was a typical American boy," commented the Washington *Star,* "mischievous and full of vigor, but in public almost quiet and demure. He was always the first with a hearty laugh, however, at the slightest provocation."[18]

Calvin, Jr., was of a very athletic disposition and fond of sports. It was this love of manly physical contests that cut short his career. During his vacation, in July, 1924, he played tennis on the White House grounds and stubbed his toe. Infection set in; but the Presidential father had been accustomed to many such bruises during his own boyhood on a farm. The wound did not heal, and within a week Calvin, Jr., was stricken with blood poisoning. Removed to an Army hospital, he rallied slightly and then it became evident that he was dying. Blood transfusions failed to check the ebb of his strength, and the six eminent specialists could not avert the end. At his bedside was his father, the President of the United States, recalling a similar scene in Washington when Abraham Lincoln watched the passing of his favorite little son Willie.

The news that the President's son had died was printed on the first pages of numerous newspapers, with large photographs of the attractive boy whose youthfulness and unostentatiousness had pleased the public. The New York *Times* expressed the prevailing sentiment: "Calvin Coolidge, Jr., second son of the President of the United States, lived exactly the same kind of life as millions of other American boys, notwithstanding the fact that . . . for almost a year his home was the White House." [19] The American flag was at half-staff over the White House [20] and a guard of Marines watched the coffin; [21] the dead youth was a President's son.[22] Although it was on the eve of a national election and at that very moment a convention in New York was selecting a candidate to oppose Calvin Coolidge, partisan feeling gave way to sympathy for the bereaved father in the White House. Editorials in leading journals voiced public regret that the President's son had died so young. "In such a grief as has befallen the President and Mrs. Coolidge the sympathy of the whole country flows out to them," said one of the Nation's foremost papers. "Party differences are stilled when a great sorrow enters the White House. This was shown when Abraham Lincoln lost his son and will be shown even more conclusively now that Mr. Coolidge has lost his. The President may be sure in his sore affliction of the sincere condolence of all the people." [23]

After the death of his younger brother, the surviving son of President Calvin Coolidge became a still more interesting topic for newspaper writers. John Coolidge graduated from Mercersburg Academy in June, 1924, and in the autumn of that year he entered Amherst. Contemporary reports indicate that he wanted neither favoritism nor deference because of his father's exalted position. He participated in diverse college activities, and was content with playing inconspicuous roles. He engaged in boxing bouts, and his prowess in such fisticuffs won him the nickname "Butch." [24] He took part in the college theatricals; as a junior, he sang in the chorus of the Gilbert and Sullivan comic opera, *Iolanthe*.[25] But these activities in the pugilistic ring and on the dramatic stage did not interfere with John's progress in scholastic studies. He knew that his Presidential father would not permit absences from classrooms; the elder Coolidge was uncompromising in the requirement that his sons apply themselves diligently to their textbooks; not even during the Inauguration ceremonies in Washington was John permitted to miss classes for more than a single day. This stern discipline was novel in the

White House; Ike Hoover, who since Lincoln's day had observed how frequent and how prolonged were the visits of other Presidents' sons, recorded in his memoirs: "John Coolidge, the President's son, came for the day only; arriving at eight in the morning and leaving at seven in the evening. John wanted to stay on, but it was felt he could not spare the time from college." [26] Somehow, young Coolidge found ample time for his textbooks and for other interests—including girls. Among co-eds he was exceedingly popular. There were rumors aplenty that John was the choice of Florence Trumbull, the daughter of Connecticut's Governor; but often other girls gave utterance to their admiration of the President's son, and these opinions made headlines. Thus, a short column in the conservative New York *Times* was captioned, "John Coolidge a Peach," quoting a sophomore of Mount Holyoke College. Said this young lady, "John is a perfect peach. He is so very polished and smooth and he dances divinely. They talk about his being shy and reserved—well, he certainly is a peach." [27]

Of course John was aware that his father in the White House was duly apprised of the son's activities; a secret-service agent [28] watched over the President's son at Amherst. On the college campus there was occasional speculation whether John would elope, eluding the scrutiny of the guard. All these episodes in John's collegiate career were reviewed by the editors of the junior class book—it was even noted that, with Coolidge thrift, the President's son had purchased a second-hand leather jacket for winter wear:

> Coolidge came to college with a second-hand pea jacket, a perfect complexion, and an air of perfect boredom. These possessions he has guarded jealously and has augmented them in his three years here with a very slight knowledge of the saxophone, a slighter acquaintance with the art of pugilism, some seven thousand scented letters from admiring school girls, and a scrap-book bulging with newspaper clippings arranged alphabetically from "Elopement" to "Secret Service." "John is really a darn good gent but so reserved it's hard to get acquainted with him." So saying, the entire college bodies of Amherst, Smith, and Mt. Holyoke excuse themselves to their friends for not spending their vacations in the White House.[29]

The newspapers reprinted this campus appraisal, referring to John as "Butch Coolidge." [30] None of the papers noted John's uncollegiate dislike of color: of the one hundred and thirty-eight members of his class, he was one of only three who shunned striped or colored ties—he wore austere black.[31]

In June, 1928, John Coolidge was one of the hundred and twenty-seven who graduated from Amherst with the degree of Bachelor of Arts. He did not win the highest honors, but was among the sixty-seven given the grade "rite." Nevertheless, he was a President's son, and a photograph of him in cap and gown was the only one that graced the page of the New York *Times* on which were described the graduation ceremonies not only at Amherst, but also at Princeton and Yale.[32] Under a two-column caption, "John Coolidge Will Ask Dad What to Do after Graduation," a prominent Indianapolis newspaper discussed his future after graduation from Amherst. "With much of his father's reserve and tactfulness of speech, combined with Mrs. Coolidge's graciousness, John frankly admitted his plans were vague. He said he did not think he would continue his studies at Harvard law school or any other college. He intimated he would seek some business connection."[33] Just completing his twenty-first year, this President's son planned to talk with his father at the White House regarding his career.

There being no more campus news to report, the American press kept the reading public interested in John's romance. Newspapers reported his visits to the Connecticut Governor's mansion. In September, 1929, the President's son married the Governor's daughter. It was a gala day for the inhabitants of Plainville, Connecticut, where the wedding took place. The Hartford *Daily Times* noted that "housewives dropped their work and joined the throng of sightseers. Factory workers abandoned their machines to mingle with the crowd. Business men closed their shops. Families came from all directions."[34] A leading New York tabloid, wanting "a feminine angle," sent a girl reporter who reported that "John, scion of famous taciturnity, spared one smile during the whole proceedings—a sidelong glance and boyish grin at his mother as he started down the aisle out of the church with his bride."[35] The wedding took place in the presence of eighty-two guests, in a little church where the bell was rung by an eighty-four-year-old sexton who had performed that task for seventy years.[36] Other papers described the wedding as "brilliant." "Notable Guests Join in Tribute to Florence and John," headlined one journal, and it described how John had kissed his bride—"He puckered his lips before he reached her."[37] There was speculation regarding the gift which ex-President Coolidge gave the bridal couple, and the Governor's wife was quoted as saying, "It was a substantial check."

After his marriage to the daughter of Connecticut's Governor, young Coolidge made his home in his wife's State. He became a traveling passenger agent for the New York, New Haven & Hartford Railroad, and he continued in that capacity for a decade. His name seldom appeared in public print, and it was news when his fellow townsmen, in the 1938 pre-election campaign named him a delegate to a political convention; both newspapers and periodicals noted the occurrence. *Time,* chronicling the unexpected, commented: "John Coolidge, 32, son of the 30th President, traveling passenger agent for the New York, New Haven and Hartford R.R. returned to his home in Orange, Conn. to find that his colleagues on the Orange Town Committee had delegated him to attend the Republican State Convention. Said John Coolidge, 'I'll be glad to do whatever I can—locally—to keep the Republican Party alive.' "[38] In the fall of 1940 he became ill, and upon his recovery took a six-months leave of absence.[39] In the following summer the press associations reported that John Coolidge was resigning his post with the railroad; all the newspapers which carried the dispatch noted that he was an ex-President's son, and they quoted the praise of an unnamed "railroad spokesman" who said, "We are sorry to see him go. Mr. Coolidge has made a lot of friends here."[40]

After his resignation, John Coolidge announced that he "was looking around for some small manufacturing concern."[41] In a few months he found a business to his taste. As President of the United States, Calvin Coolidge had impressed upon the American people the vital need of analyzing and controlling the financial operations of their Government; his name became a symbol of system and thrift. It was not surprising that the interest of his son should turn to systematizing methods. We hear of John Coolidge in Hartford in the fall of 1941; he had been elected president and treasurer of a company manufacturing manifold forms.[42] The New York *Times* printed a photograph, three years old, on its financial page; John, like his Presidential father, shunned cameras and seldom posed for pictures willingly.

19

Sons of Herbert Hoover

IN THE AUTUMN OF 1912 A MINING MAGAZINE IN LONDON ANNOUNCED the publication of Agricola's *De Re Metallica* in English. It is extremely doubtful whether, at that time, a thousand Americans knew or cared that the original text had been written in Latin in the sixteenth century; and it is equally doubtful whether many more in the United States were impressed by the fact that the translators were Herbert Clark Hoover and his wife, Lou Henry Hoover.[1] Seventeen years later, in March, 1929, copies of this edition of Agricola were eagerly sought by book collectors, and the couple who had put into English the work of the forgotten Roman author were of great interest to Americans: Herbert Clark Hoover had become President of the United States, and his wife mistress of the White House.

The interest in Herbert Hoover had been aroused during the preceding November when the Republican national convention nominated him as its candidate for the Nation's highest office, but even the most resourceful commentators found difficulty in delineating his personality. "Long sketches of Herbert Hoover fill the newspapers as a result of his nomination for President, and millions of people are familiar with his career, but not one in a thousand knows anything about the real man," observed a leading paper.[2] If the public was unacquainted with his personal characteristics it was because never before had he been a candidate for public office, and for many years had lived abroad beyond the observation of his countrymen.[3]

Born on an Iowa farm, of Quaker parents, Herbert Clark Hoover[4] was orphaned before he was ten.[5] Sent to Oregon, he was reared by an uncle who combined the practice of medicine with farming and an interest in mining. There the future President became intrigued with the earth's internal treasures, and resolved to become a geologist and mining engineer. At seventeen, he entered Stanford.[6]

On the college campus, during his last year, Herbert Hoover met Lou Henry, the daughter of a bank cashier.[7] Like young Hoover, she had studied geology and metallurgy; their mutual interests led to friendship and love.[8]

Receiving an A.B. in geology, Herbert Hoover turned to gold mining in New Mexico and Colorado. He had already acquired knowledge of exploratory surveying with geological expeditions as an assistant in surveys conducted by the State of Arkansas and the United States Government.[9] Then he went to Australia, becoming inspecting engineer and engineer in chief for British mining companies. In 1898 he returned to California, married his college sweetheart, Lou Henry, and the bridal couple sailed for China. There he increased his fame and his wealth, organizing syndicates in which he was a substantial stockholder and directing genius.

Finally the Hoovers settled in London. It was here that they undertook their literary task of translating Roman treatises on mining; both of them were conversant with Latin, and together they converted Agricola into English.

While the Hoovers were in England, the German hordes made their first attempt to conquer Europe. The year was 1914. With Teutonic disregard of their treaties and international law, the Germans invaded Belgium, leaving devastation and starvation in their path. Later the United States entered the war, and Germany was defeated. To Herbert Hoover, already in Europe, had been assigned the task of relieving hunger and want on the Continent, and he accomplished his task brilliantly; in the words of the Liverpool *Post,* "He became during the war and in the years immediately following the war an almost legendary figure of impersonal efficiency. His name became a household word as the man who filled Europe's empty pantry."[10]

It was not true, as was later surmised by the London *Times,* that "at the end of the war Herbert Hoover was soon marked down as a likely man for the Presidency."[11] On the contrary, political leaders who dictated Republican nominations had found their men first in Warren G. Harding and later in Calvin Coolidge. These were traditional party members; Herbert Hoover had no party status. In fact, at one time he was regarded as an adherent of the Democratic Party. But the Republican President, Calvin Coolidge, made him Secretary of Commerce, and here he continued what a British paper called "a romance in efficiency."[12] Then unexpected events made Herbert Hoover the Republican nominee for the highest office: Calvin Coolidge did not "choose to run" for another term; the Democratic Party named as its candidate Alfred Smith, an outspoken opponent of liquor prohibition which Hoover considered "a noble experiment." And, religion became an issue in the campaign.[13]

In November, 1928, Herbert Clark Hoover was elected President of the United States; the Los Angeles *Times* epitomized the event: "Hoover's rise was a political epic. No stranger story has been unfolded by political fates than that of the rise of Herbert Hoover to the Presidency."[14] This was something new in our political history: Herbert Hoover, unlike his predecessors, had achieved no military glory, had never enthralled the public with oratorical eloquence, had won no previous political contests. The New York *Times* was justified in saying, "Mr. Hoover takes the highest office in the gift of his countrymen. . . . They have seen him climb to the height of his ambition not by the ordinary political route, but by paths which have been blazed by his energy, versatile ability, and sterling character."[15] Similarly, other journals emphasized that this President had not been a professional officeholder. "The first spokesman of a new dynasty took the Presidential oath yesterday," commented the New York *World,* stressing the analogy between engineering and governmental administration—both requiring analytical judgment and due deliberation.[16]

Two sons accompanied Herbert Hoover to the White House: Herbert, Jr., nearing twenty-six; and Alan, four years younger. The President's namesake was one of the only three Presidential sons who were born in a foreign land;[17] Herbert, Jr., came into the world in London, England, in August, 1903. Nevertheless, Herbert Hoover, Jr., was a typical American boy. Newspapers had not waited until Herbert Hoover, Jr., had actually become a President's son; prognosticating that his father would be the victor in the forthcoming election of a Chief Executive, they began five months in advance to chronicle the activities of the "son of the Republican Presidential nominee"; and, when he acted as usher at the wedding of a former classmate, the New York *Times* devoted half a column to the event.[18]

Up to the time of his father's nomination and elevation to the Presidency, the life of Herbert, Jr., paralleled the unpublicized careers of other American youths whose parents possessed education, wealth, and wide friendship. But now he was a President's son, and there were pressed upon him opportunities and responsibilities not usually accorded to men of his years or experience. A week after Inauguration Day this oldest son of the Chief Executive was inspecting airplane factories as the representative of a prominent air line. Workmen in the plants were surprised that so important a task was entrusted to one so young, and they were told who his father was. "H. Hoover, Jr., Shows Skeptics He Is Really President's Son," was the caption of a special dispatch from Hackensack, New Jersey, to the New York *Times;* the article related that "Herbert Jr. was chaffed by some men he met, who insisted that he was not the son of the new occupant of the White House." [19] This visit to Hackensack and those to factories elsewhere were reported on the front pages of the principal New Jersey newspapers. "Hoover Jr. Visits Teterboro, President's Son Makes Flight After Inspecting Hackensack Plant," headlined an article in the Newark *Star-Eagle,*[20] and blackface type in the *Evening News* announced, "Teterboro Airport Viewed by Herbert Hoover, Jr." [21]

When, in August, 1929, the airship *Graf Zeppelin* made its round-the-world cruise, Herbert Hoover, Jr., as "radio expert" for a Western air line spoke over a coast-to-coast network on the "Roads of the Sky." [22] He predicted that commercial planes would be equipped with two-way telephones by which pilots could be in constant communication with landing fields.[23] The President, in Washington, attending a baseball game, did not hear his son's broadcast. A week later, young Hoover was engaged to describe the *Graf Zeppelin*'s visit to Los Angeles.[24] The press associations commented that "nearly all of the United States was linked yesterday morning by radio when a word-picture of the arrival of the *Graf Zeppelin* at the Pacific Coast was told by Herbert Hoover, Jr." [25]

His interest and activities in radio engineering received wide publicity, and few weeks passed without some mention in newspaper columns regarding the President's first-born. He was sought after to write for trade journals,[26] to give his views on radio in airplanes; [27] he was appointed on committees to study radio in aviation.[28] Finally, barely twenty-seven, he was elected president of Aeronautical Radio, Inc.[29] During the autumn there was an interruption in his numerous activities; he contracted a lung ailment which forced him to leave the air line where he was technical adviser on radio.[30] At first he went to his father's fishing camp on the Rapidan River in Virginia; later the White House physician ordered him to the North Carolina mountains at Asheville.[31] There he rented a cabin, and was joined by his wife.

Press dispatches had predicted that the President's son would have his parents and his own family around him to cheer his Thanksgiving dinner, but his wife returned to California to bring the children, and his father remained at the White House where Alan was a guest. The local paper, in a boxed article on the front page, sympathized with the ailing Herbert, Jr., because he would not have the Chief Executive with him. "Hoover to Spend Holiday Alone at Cottage Here," was the blackface caption in the Asheville *Times*.[32]

In the succeeding months Herbert, Jr., slowly regained his health. At Asheville he planned a broadcasting station; [33] but in the early summer he returned to his California home.[34] His interest in aeronautics was still intense, and it was reported that he would teach radio engineering at the California Institute of Technology.[35]

Meanwhile, the name of the younger brother also made headlines. When his father became Chief Executive, Alan Hoover was a senior at Stanford University; coming to the Capital on Inauguration Day, Alan was bewildered by the excitement in Washington for, despite a downpour, this was the most enthusiastic March 4 in many years.[36] At first the President's younger son had no liking for the splendor of his father's official residence; it is recorded that one day he exclaimed "that if he did not get away from the White House pretty soon, it would give him the 'willies.' " [37] Alan did get away, returning to his college studies at Palo Alto, California. In June Alan was among the thousand and seventy graduates at Stanford University, one of the two hundred to receive a degree in economics.[38]

Being a President's son, Alan's movements were watched by the press associations; in mid-July a dispatch from Stanford University reported that "the younger son of the President is en route to Washington to join his parents. He will spend most of the summer at the White House, after which he plans to enter Harvard for postgraduate work"; [39] on the following day a dispatch from Washington recorded that at the White House "there was a family dinner to mark the arrival of Alan who recently completed his studies at Leland Stanford University." [40] Herbert, Jr., was also present. Alan's stay at the White House was marred by a stomach ailment, and the

President's physician ordered him to bed. Within a few days he appeared to have recovered,[41] and during the first week in August he accompanied his parents on a fishing trip on the Rapidan River, in the Blue Ridge Mountains of Virginia, where the President was accustomed to relax from official cares.[42] In the party were several Cabinet officers. Alan continued to improve, being attended by his mother.[43] News of Alan's illness was followed by rumors that he was engaged to the daughter of the Governor General of the Philippines,[44] the conjecture being occasioned by a photograph in which the President's son and the Governor's daughter were standing near each other. The engagement was denied.

In September, 1929, Alan enrolled at the Harvard Business School; in one of the college dormitories he engaged a small suite of study, bedroom, and bath; [45] he had no roommate, as was the usual custom. Reporters flocked to the college campus to interview him, to photograph him, and to record his voice. But the President forbade his young son to talk when posing before motion picture cameras.[46] This injunction was revealed when Alan, eager to convince skeptical photographers that he was really the President's son, "to dispel doubts . . . showed them a telegram from his father. This message stated that Alan might pose for photographers but that he must not speak."

The first Christmas week spent by the Hoovers in the White House was enlivened by a party given to the children of President-elect Rubio of Mexico and of the Mexican Ambassador. Alan acted as host. "Mexicans Fêted by Alan Hoover," headed a column in the leading Washington paper, describing the children's party.[47] "Sitting at the head of the table, Alan Hoover kept the youngsters chattering with delight," the wife of the President-elect explained. Señora Rubio's word for Mrs. Hoover's son as a host was the Spanish equivalent of the American "swell"—the untranslatable *simpatico*.[48] More to his liking, probably, was a dance given for Alan at the White House by his parents. More than a hundred young people danced to the music of a leading Washington band.[49] On New Year's night Alan left the Capital to resume his studies at Harvard; [50] there he continued for two years in the Harvard Graduate School of Business Administration, obtaining a Master's degree in 1931.[51]

In March, 1933, having been defeated for a second term in the election of the preceding November, Herbert Hoover ended his

Presidential career. He returned to California, where his sons had already established residence. Herbert, Jr., served as communications engineer for one air line,[52] and later became consultant for a transcontinental system.[53] For a year he held a teaching fellowship in the California Institute of Technology, meanwhile practicing his profession as a construction engineer.

With the genius for solving engineering and mining problems which had made his father famous and wealthy, Herbert Hoover, Jr., repeatedly startled the oil industry with inventions which made easier and more accurate the discovery and location of oil deposits. In February, 1940, he made public the construction of a "divining rod" which measured even infinitesimal atoms of gases which seep to the surface, separating and identifying them, thus determining hidden oil deep in the earth.[54] During the momentous months of 1941 the ex-President's son assumed another role: he devoted his inventive mind to the construction of testing mechanisms which later made American war planes supreme in combat. His efforts and his achievements brought him both greater reputation and added wealth; what he was accomplishing was too technical for the layman's mind, but it was certain that he had become an important part of America's wartime industry. *Time,* like numerous other periodicals, noted that he was a President's son and attempted to explain to its readers his scientific endeavors, commenting: "Last week Herbert Jr. was an able young geophysicist. This week he is becoming an important defense manufacturer. To his Consolidated Engineering Corp., big Sperry Gyroscope Co. turned over one whole branch of its business: instruments to measure vibration and strain in airplanes, ships, etc. Consolidated has been interested chiefly in seismographic oil prospecting, which involves much the same technique of studying sound waves and reflections as Sperry's vibration strain instruments. Now at its plant in Pasadena, Calif., Consolidated will use Sperry's patents, machinery and tools on a royalty basis, fill Sperry orders with Sperry products, do research work." [55]

In March, 1942, the press reports again related that the ex-President's son was "the inventor of a new way to 'map' the subterranean structure of the earth's crust," and a patent was issued to him and an associate; the patent rights were assigned to a California engineering corporation.[56] Herbert Hoover, Jr., perfected other inventions nine months later. The New York *Times,* in language bewildering to the layman, reprinted the scientific description of these mechanical innovations: "Two patents were issued to Herbert Hoover, Jr., son of the former President, for improvements in the seismic exploration of oil. A dynamite explosion sends artificial earthquake waves down into the earth and these waves are reflected up from different depths. As they come up from greater and greater depths, they become more and more feeble, and require more and more amplification to affect the recorders. Customarily the amplification is increased automatically. But the single control device used produces distortion. By adding another control with opposite distortion, Mr. Hoover removes this defect, and also extends the range of amplification over which the instrument can be used." [57] That the invention was an aid to the industry was soon attested by the adoption and use of the device by the largest oil-producing company. At forty Herbert Hoover, Jr., was president of a prominent engineering corporation [58] and directing head of several other companies.

While his older brother delved for the earth's riches below the surface, Alan's interest was above ground—as a rancher, a farmer, an orchardist. He called himself a "California rancher"; [59] press dispatches referred to him as a "California farmer." [60] Not that he himself guided a plow, threshed a field of grain, or pruned a tree; on the contrary, this younger son of the thirty-first President reaped rewards for not farming! Alan's agricultural career began at a time when the Government was paying farmers to curtail their crops; [61] being part owner of a ranch at Bakersfield, California, he received from the Federal treasury $4,800 as his share for not growing cotton.[62]

In March, 1937, four years after his father had left the White House, Alan, then thirty, married in California. He had become engaged during the preceding month, and brief dispatches had been wired by the press association to its member newspapers, noting that the bride-to-be had been graduated from the University of California and that Alan was "interested in the Greenfield Delta Farms Company which operates a large ranch near Bakersfield, California." [63] The Los Angeles *Times* predicted that "marked simplicity would prevail at the wedding of Alan Henry Hoover, younger son of ex-President and Mrs. Herbert Hoover"; [64] when, on the following day, this paper reported the ceremony the account was relegated to an inside page of a second section.[65] No list of guests was printed;

the article stated that Alan was married at the home of his bride's parents, and described the room decorations: "The bridal party stood before a peach-blossom-wreathed plate-glass window in the drawing room. A peach tree in full bloom growing outside the window added more beauty to the picture. . . . The bridegroom's parents, Herbert Hoover, only living ex-President of the United States, and Mrs. Hoover, came from Palo Alto to attend the ceremonies." [66] Similarly, metropolitan papers in the East relegated to their inside pages the meager account of the wedding, although the New York *Times* devoted a few more lines to the bridal costume, reporting that "the bride wore an ice-white brocaded satin gown with train. Her veil was held by a wreath of orange blossoms. She carried a bouquet of gardenias and bouvardia. . . . Herbert Hoover, Jr. was best man." [67]

Alan continued his interest and investments in California farm land; during the years following his marriage he increased his acreage; in the spring of 1944 the Associated Press reported that he had sold part of his holdings for $452,000,[68] still retaining substantial agricultural properties.

Thus the earth yielded its riches to the two sons of the thirty-first President.[69] Of course, their father's occupancy of the Nation's highest office brought them the acquaintance of the influential in industry, in public affairs, in social circles. But there is no indication that they ever sought to capitalize their sire's Presidential prestige for personal advancement; certain it is that Herbert Clark Hoover, leaving the White House in the midst of a depression, had little popularity to share with his sons. However, their own futures were secure. The father had come to the Presidency with a record of achievements in private enterprise and a large fortune. His sons would have had economic independence and prominent friends irrespective of the father's official position. More than that: from their father the sons had acquired inventive genius and financial astuteness. The majority of American voters refused Herbert Hoover a second term, and millions of his fellow Americans disagreed with his policies; nevertheless, in appraising Presidents' sons and parental influence, the objective historian may agree with the mother's last will and testament—that the sons of Herbert Hoover were "lucky boys to have such a father." [70] And the father had reason to be proud of his sons.

20

Sons of Franklin D. Roosevelt

FRANKLIN DELANO ROOSEVELT, FOR TWELVE YEARS PRESIDENT OF THE United States, is still too near the lens of the present to be delineated without the high lights of world acclaim or the shadows of bitter political animosity; posterity will view him in better focus without the dazzling devotion or clouded dislike of contemporary adherents or antagonists. But his sons, like other Presidents' sons, may be viewed with dispassionate appraisal. Possibly because their father occupied the Presidential office longer than any other Chief Executive, perhaps because they themselves followed their individual inclinations more than did the offspring of previous Presidents, and certainly because in the past there were lacking the film, the radio, and the extraordinary press to give publicity on so vast a scale, the sons of Franklin D. Roosevelt have been in public view as were no Presidents' sons before them. No other sons whose fathers occupied the White House have aroused so much curiosity, comment, or criticism; every episode in their careers has kindled nationwide interest—their marriages, their money-making, their medals, their dividends, their divorces, their dogs.

The sons of no other President have been so often the targets of political attacks whose real aim was to embarrass the Presidential father; no other Presidents' sons afforded opportunities for attack so frequently, or so conspicuously. Others, such as the sons of Grant and Theodore Roosevelt, were themselves aspirants for public office, and against them rival candidates hurled the charge that they were trading on the fame of their Presidential fathers. William Henry Harrison, even before his month's occupancy of the White House, was censured for obtaining for a son a position in the Government land office; and President Benjamin Harrison suffered somewhat from innuendoes that his son, a private secretary, had become rich as a result of his relationship to the President. But not since Martin Van Buren, the eighth President, a hundred years before, had political enemies of a Chief Executive indulged in censure of his sons to detract from public confidence in the father. Even then, the President's son himself was engaged in political activities—John Van Buren had acquired a reputation of his own which was also the object of attack. But the sons of Franklin D. Roosevelt held no elective public office, and were candidates for none.

That Franklin Delano Roosevelt was a devoted father, there can be no question; but between him and his sons there did not exist that comradeship and constant intimacy which characterized the relationship between earlier Presidents and their sons—particularly, the Adamses, Martin Van Buren, Rutherford Hayes, and Theodore Roosevelt.[1] This can be explained only in part by the fact that the thirty-second President for a long period was unable physically to engage in the activities of his sons; the cause lay also in the individualistic personalities of the sons themselves who, undeterred by the father and with seeming indifference regarding the effect of their activities upon his political fortunes, pursued their several, independent ways. Thus, when the friends of Franklin Roosevelt were risking their own political futures in seeking a third term for the President, one of his sons actually was advocating the candidacy of a rival; when a prominent industrialist and an influential publisher were using all their resources to end the career of the Presidential father, a son married the daughter of one, and a second obtained employment from the other. Nor did they hesitate publicly to oppose the reforms which Franklin Delano Roosevelt proudly proclaimed as his ideals; while the President and his wife were pleading for the adoption of a Constitutional amendment prohibiting the employment of child labor, the eldest son was using his efforts and influence against the ratification of the proposed amendment by the Massachusetts Legislature.[2]

Mrs. Franklin Roosevelt said that the demands of official duties kept the father and sons apart. "There is a certain sacrifice made by the family of those who serve their country in any capacity," remarked the President's wife when they moved into the White House. "We laugh about it a great deal when I formally make an appointment for the children to see their father at given hours when something comes up which really must be discussed and decided." [3] The Roosevelt sons usually made their own decisions; their independence, their aggressiveness, and their defiance of public criticism were unmatched in all the chronicles of Presidents' sons. "They are a thrifty tribe, these Roosevelts," commented a writer in the Boston *Globe*, "they marry young, get a job, and carve a niche for themselves in the business or professional world. . . . No drones in F.D.R.'s family, . . . some day they may become economic royalists despite their father's teaching." [4]

Four sons—James, Elliott, Franklin, Jr., and John Aspinal—became the objects of nationwide interest on that epochal fourth of March, 1933, when their Presidential father, Franklin Delano Roosevelt, rode through cheering crowds from the Capitol to the White House. James was then nearing twenty-six, Elliott was three years younger, the President's namesake was eighteen and a half, and John had just passed his seventeenth birthday. The newspapers were aware of their readers' curiosity regarding the personalities and activities of these Presidential sons, and reporters were watchful for stories about them. They had not long to wait.

Half a year after his father's inauguration newspapers were insisting that the President's eldest son was meddling in Massachusetts politics; the conservative Boston *Transcript* printed columns to show that "James Roosevelt had virtually stepped into the role of patronage dictator, personally selecting officials for Federal posts." [5] James' endeavors were first publicized when he obtained for his friends appointments as receivers of closed banks, from which posts experienced banking men were ousted; one of his appointees was a drug clerk who was described by the New York *Times* as being "elevated from the prosaic job of mixing prescriptions." [6] Soon young James extended his activities to include approval of all job seekers. This was not to the liking of the ranking Senator, whose followers looked to him for jobs made possible by the recent party success. "Who is the official almoner of Federal Democratic patronage in Massachusetts, the son of the President or the senior Senator?" asked the New York *Times;* the paper's astute editorial correspondent in Boston telegraphed the answer: "Were it not for the remarkable statement of young Mr. Roosevelt at a dinner a fortnight ago the situation would not be so perplexing. He then all but asserted outright that candidates for appointive offices would be wise to obtain his endorsement." [7] The dispatch discussed the rumor that the President's son is building his own political machine with the Governor's office as his objective; the

Times' observer contrasts the experience of James with that of the leader he seeks to displace: "The qualifications of the young crusader are that he is the son of the national leader who won an overwhelming victory last November; the qualifications of the veteran Senator are inherent in the position he holds and the battles he has won."

The storm of resentment subsided only when it was learned that James was planning a trip to Europe; his sailing date, it was believed, would mark the end of his interference in matters which the Democratic leaders in the State regarded as their own established prerogative. This hope was described by a political commentator well versed in Massachusetts politics: "There is a conviction . . . that relief for the weary hopeful will not appear until along Sept. 27. That is the date on which James Roosevelt, son of the President, around whom much of the fury over patronage splutters, is scheduled to embark for a trip abroad. . . . The turbulent murky waters of patronage possibly will have become placid and crystal clear by the time of his return." [8]

James Roosevelt did leave the United States for a sojourn in Europe. Abroad, as a President's son, he was entertained by the British Prime Minister; was received by the Pope and the President of France; and was invited to the palace of the Italian dictator, Mussolini.[9] The Paris edition of the New York *Herald* devoted a column to his arrival in the French Capital, saying that he was "as genuinely modest as his younger brother, Franklin D. Roosevelt, Jr.," who had visited there during the summer.[10]

Upon his return to the United States the President's eldest son forsook politics and embarked upon a career of business affiliations which often made headlines and afforded his father's adversaries much opportunity for innuendo, criticism, and startling allegations. In the summer of 1935 James Roosevelt became president of the National Grain Yeast Corporation, a New Jersey company which planned to manufacture industrial alcohol. Had he not been a President's son it is not likely that the press would have delved into the history of the corporation; but soon there were allegations—and denials—that the backers of the enterprise had underworld connections.[11] Political opponents of his father intimated that James was employed by the corporation solely because his influence could be used to obtain the Government permits necessary in operating the plants. James resigned his post in November of the same year, officials of the company saying that the directors were dissatisfied because James divided his time with other interests.[12]

In 1936 the President embarked on an extended journey to South American countries, and his eldest son went along as his military aide, having been commissioned a lieutenant colonel in the Marine Corps. James was then twenty-nine. In a subsequent political campaign, unfriendly newspapers discovered that, while on the cruise, James Roosevelt was drawing the active-duty pay of an officer of the rank to which his father had appointed him.[13]

During the early part of 1937 James took up residence at the White House and became his father's secretarial aide. In July of that year the President made James his full-fledged secretary, but with all of his vast powers as the Chief Executive of the Nation he himself could not administer the oath of office to his son because he held no notary public commission! [14]

For a long time there had crept into the newspapers veiled intimations that the eldest son of the President, having abandoned his law studies, was reaping large sums in selling insurance to corporations; brokers who had spent their lives in the insurance business regarded this youthful newcomer with astonishment and resentment. Said the magazine, *Time:* "For six years insurance circles have gossiped about the selling exploits of James Roosevelt, how, after his father's nomination in 1932, the fortunes of his lanky eldest flowered like the lilies in paradise. . . . Jimmy is a specialist in everything—life, fire, marine, air and group insurance. . . . The insurance fraternity is as startled . . . as the medical fraternity would be if a youngster who had never attended a medical school suddenly turned out to be America's greatest specialist in the eye, ear, nose, and throat, in abdominal and pulmonary surgery, in obstetrics, pediatrics, and chiropody." [15] Now the lucrative exploits of the President's son ceased to be merely "talk in the trade," and the stories gained wider currency.

An abundance of evidence came to public notice in the summer of 1938. In Boston, Jimmy's name loomed conspicuously in a hearing before a court auditor. An action had been brought by an insurance broker against a prominent bank for thirty thousand dollars, representing the amount of commission on $800,000 insurance which the broker alleged had been contracted with his agency but was switched by the bank to James Roosevelt.[16] The bank, as reported by the Associated Press, countered that it was free to give its business to Jimmy, and that there was no evidence of political gain to itself.[17]

It was, however, a magazine article which made Jimmy's insurance business the topic of nationwide discussion—the subject of Congressional debate and of editorials, and the theme of conversation in clubs, restaurants, and in homes. In the first week of July, 1938, millions of readers, opening the current issue of the *Saturday Evening Post,* saw an intriguing caption on the first page: "Jimmy's Got It." The article was by a well-known writer, Alva Johnston. The opening paragraph related that a prominent insurance agent named Riehle had worked out a plan for a ten-million-dollar policy on the life of George Washington Hill, president of the foremost cigarette manufacturing company, to compensate the corporation's stockholders in the event that death should deprive them of his exceptional abilities. The agent had negotiated for nearly two years, and was confident of obtaining the issuance of the policy with his resultant commission. However, this agent was not to reap the reward of his labors; the *Post* article told why: "He had the impression that he had the deal set. But one day, shortly after the Democratic Convention of 1932 had placed Franklin Delano Roosevelt in nomination for President, another insurance agent telephoned to Riehle and said, "I understand you have Hill sewed up." "I think I have," said Riehle. "Well, think again," said the other agent, "Jimmy's got it." "Jimmy who?" "Jimmy Roosevelt." [18] And the writer delineated how James Roosevelt had learned that the head of the tobacco corporation was considering the life-insurance plan, how he had phoned his father's secretary to "tell father to be nice to Mr. Hill, I want to get his insurance," and that James Roosevelt had finally obtained the policy, though the amount had been reduced. The magazine recited other instances in which James Roosevelt managed to obtain business which formerly had been given to other agencies. And these successes, Alva Johnston said, brought an income of from $250,000 to $1,000,000 annually to Jimmy.

The eldest son of the President was not long in denouncing the charges and hints in the *Post* article. At that time in the Mayo brothers' famed hospital, he issued a statement denying that his earnings were as large as intimated or that his success in the insurance business was due to the fact that his father was President of the United States; it was stated that James "naturally is indignant over certain outright misrepresentations. . . . He has requested his attorneys to consider the matter for future consideration."[19] At first prominent newspapers, generally, refrained from editorial comment; they merely reprinted portions of the magazine article. Some journals which did discuss the allegations that the President's eldest son had established a flourishing insurance agency set out to disprove that his income was in the million-dollar bracket, but raised no question regarding the motives which prompted dominant corporations to shift their business from other agents to the President's eldest son. The Boston *Evening American,* for instance, announced that it had reliable data "to refute the *Post* story"—its "refutation" being that Jimmy's total taxable income for the five preceding years had been only $170,000.

Six weeks after the *Post* article was published Jimmy's own detailed answer appeared in *Collier's,* a magazine with very extensive circulation. His rejoinder, under the title "I'm Glad You Asked Me," was in the form of an interview written by an experienced and well-known reporter, Walter Davenport. The opening paragraphs described the President's son in his hospital room, his diet, his prolific mail. Surely, he deserved public sympathy in this need to defend himself from his sickbed against unjust attacks. What was the defense? Author Davenport acknowledged that the public mind was startled and disturbed by "the unusual situation of a socially active young Roosevelt who, tiring of trying to crawl through college on an allowance of $250 a year, went to work while still a student and suddenly found himself wallowing in an income of from $200,000 to $2,000,000 a year."[20] This, the writer said, prompted him to ask the President's son, face to face, about his insurance business. Yes, admitted James readily, it was true he was in the insurance business—as a member of Roosevelt & Sargent. He had chosen the insurance business for his career because his father, prior to his election as Governor of New York, had been an official of an insurance company. James' first association with an agency was with a Boston firm which paid him twenty-five dollars a week—for work in his spare time. He wrote a jewelry policy for his grandmother, insured his father-in-law's automobile. But some financial promoters, appraising the prestige of the Roosevelt name, reorganized the company and made James vice-president—raising his salary from one hundred dollars a month to fifteen thousand dollars a year. James surmised that the salary was not occasioned by his experience or ability; "I wasn't being kidded," he admitted to his interviewer,

"I knew perfectly well that they were paying me for the name and any value the name might have. I had no illusions that as an insurance solicitor I was worth $15,000 a year on my ability alone. But they did things in a grand manner—opened beautiful offices in Boston and a branch in New York." [21] He did not know exactly what he was supposed to do, but he did consider that the salary justified his quitting law school. He took stock of himself and his future: he had put in four years at Harvard, but did not get a degree because he had flunked in languages. "And I didn't have enough on the ball to get into Harvard Law School, so I entered the law school of Boston University just after returning from my honeymoon."

The promoters, James' story continued, had overestimated the pulling power of Jimmy's family name—his father had not yet reached the Presidency—and the organization was dissolved. James then became associated with another agency, on the basis of commissions—a tremendous drop from his recent salary. In the meantime his father's political fortunes soared. James severed his connection, and formed a partnership with an insurance broker named Sargent; but it was James' name which took first place in the firm's designation—Roosevelt & Sargent. The success of the new organization was phenomenal; Roosevelt & Sargent wrote policies for the largest corporations in the land. "Sure I got into places I never would have if I wasn't the son of the President," James Roosevelt said, "but son or no son, I got tossed out a lot too. Listen, fellows, prospects don't wilt because you're the son of a President." Then, in denial of the assertion that his annual earnings aggregated a quarter of a million to a million dollars, the article in *Collier's* reproduced photostats of James' income-tax reports, from the files of the Collector of Internal Revenue, indicating that his yearly income had ranged from only twenty-one to fifty thousand dollars.

Jimmy's indignant denials were not restricted to articles in magazines. An enterprising radio director—the veteran Abel Schecter of the National Broadcasting Company—rightly concluded that millions of Americans would eagerly listen to Jimmy's side of the story; and, even before his rejoinder appeared in *Collier's,* Schecter induced the President's son to broadcast an answer to the *Post* article and the newspaper comments which had followed it. Reviewing the broadcast three years later, Schecter remarked that "it is hard to believe that as recently as 1938 the income of James Roosevelt, son of the President, was virtually a national issue." [22] Certain it was that "no man had ever before given his side of an income squabble on the radio." James was interviewed by Walter Davenport, the author of the forthcoming *Collier's* article; the questions and answers, in the main, were the same as in the printed version. This radio conversation, like all such interviews, was prearranged and rehearsed; but it was skillfully performed, and left an impression of spontaneous indignation on the part of James Roosevelt, who burst out, "Tell me if I seem crazy for having the idea, but I have the feeling that being the President's son, some people would be calling me a crook no matter what business I entered." [23] He asserted that his firm had made it "a rule not to handle any business known as political insurance. These are insurance contracts required by Federal, State, and city or local governmental bodies—and second, all our clients have understood that our services were strictly confined to insurance. Apropos of the indirect tie-up with politics, I challenge anyone to show that, because of doing business with me, anyone at any time has ever been placed in a preferred position, or because of failure to use my services anyone has ever been prosecuted, persecuted, threatened, or in any way harmed by a Government agency." [24]

All these retorts by the President's son, in print and on the air, came at a time of Congressional elections, with his Presidential father touring the country and delivering speeches to defeat nominees who opposed his legislative program. It was to be expected that some of the President's political enemies would impute to his son the selling of Administration favors in return for insurance business. Some political-minded newspapers did not hesitate to indulge in direct charges. But the greater number of journals censured Jimmy's activities in milder terms. The Philadelphia *Public Ledger,* under the caption, "Son Jimmy Brands Income Story Lie—Admits Father's Prestige Helped Him, but Denies Receiving Direct Aid," printed the United Press report of the Alva Johnston story, and Alva Johnston's retort that "the statement of James Roosevelt is a plea in practically every respect except as to the size of his income. In that respect he is not doing badly. . . . His own statement shows that his business boomed when he went into the White House as Secretary to the President." [25] A few papers did devote a paragraph or two to the incident. The crusading St. Louis *Post-Dispatch,* on its editorial page, summed up its opinion in four lines, captioned "Advice to Young Men": "To make a sure-fire success in the insurance business, and thereby gain a competence on which to enter public life and serve your fellow men, get your father elected President of the United States." [26] The Los Angeles *Times* was more critical, editorializing that "so far the defense appears to be that, while the substance of the charges is true, the amount gained has been exaggerated," and the paper considered that the defense submitted by the President's eldest son merely "shows that a young man just out of Harvard, where his scholastic record was unbrilliant" received income ranging from twenty to fifty thousand dollars, and that this was in fact only part of his income as he had assigned to his wife a half interest in his firm in order to reduce surtaxes.[27]

As criticism of James grew sharper, his friends and political associates of his father stressed the fact that none of the corporations which had given business to the President's son had in any way asked Government favors. In answer to this protest, even journals friendly to the Administration contended that nevertheless some of Jimmy's clients might have been animated by expectations. Typical of this viewpoint was the comment of the Boston *Herald,* which, quoting from the writings of Franklin D. Roosevelt that "passive acquiescence by unthinking people in the actions of those who shrewdly turn to personal advantage the opportunity offered by public office is out of step with modern ideals of government and with political morality," now criticized the President's son for obtaining insurance from corporations: "Although it may be true that James never so much as intimated that the purchaser of a policy from him would also purchase favors from his father's administration at Washington, it is inconceivable that some of his customers did not consider that possibility when signing on the dotted line." [28] Perhaps the severest rebuke came from the pulpit. In Detroit the pastor of the Temple Baptist Church in a Sunday sermon referred to the alleged revelations as "the greatest earthquake in America's political history," declaring that "what the Stavisky scandal of Paris was to France, overthrowing the French government, and what the Teapot Dome scandal was that sent Albert Fall, the Cabinet member, to the penitentiary, Colonel Jimmy's using the name of his distinguished father to make a couple of millions may prove to be the greatest earthquake in American political history." [29]

Unquestionably, interest in the business ventures of the President's son was kept alive by astute politicians who calculated that public censure of James' dealings with corporations would prejudice voters against his father's party. The campaign and election over, other themes displaced Jimmy in public discussion. It was not until eighteen months later that newspapers again editorialized on Jimmy's insurance business. During the spring of 1940 it was revealed that Roosevelt & Sargent had obtained the insurance of the American President Steamship Line, headed by William G. McAdoo who had been appointed to that post by President Franklin D. Roosevelt. Some journals questioned the propriety of giving to the President's son the insurance business of a corporation which was financed with Government funds and whose director owed his post to James' father. The Washington *News* exclaimed, "Again—Jimmy Got It," and continued, "Jimmy Roosevelt's papa had William G. McAdoo appointed to the $25,000 job as head of the American President Steamship Line. And Mr. McAdoo had the line give its insurance business to Jimmy's firm, Roosevelt & Sargent, Inc. If you ask Jimmy's papa why he selected Mr. McAdoo, he might say that he considered 'Mac' the best of all possible shipping operators. Maybe he is. . . . If you ask Mr. McAdoo why he gave the insurance account to Jimmy's firm, he might say that Jimmy's firm writes the best of all possible insurance policies. It must be a good policy to make Mr. McAdoo, whose headquarters are in Chicago, go all the way to Boston, headquarters of Roosevelt & Sargent, Inc. Of course this is none of our business, except for some slight indirect interest deriving from the fact that we are citizens and taxpayers and the U. S. Government owns 90 per cent of the common stock of this shipping company and the R.F.C. lent it $4,500,000 and the U. S. Maritime Commission gave it a subsidy of $3,000,000. And of course, there is nothing illegal about it. It's only a question of taste —and smell." [30]

A critical press kept alert for any preference or privilege accorded to the President's eldest son. In the closing days of January, 1945, he made headlines again; from Chicago there came a report that the Union Pacific's crack streamliner had been delayed more than an hour after its scheduled starting time to permit James Roosevelt and his wife to make connections. It was stated that James had sent a telegram asking that the train be held, but railroad officials denied that the belated start was due to his request, and each in turn denied responsibility for the incident. Said the headline in the Detroit *News*, "Train Held for a Roosevelt? Whodunit? 'Not I,' Say All." [31] About twelve years had passed since the name of James Roosevelt first made headlines—writers and editors alike found him exceedingly "good news copy." But he was not the only son of President Franklin D. Roosevelt who intrigued the American people.

Among the four sons of Franklin D. Roosevelt the second, Elliott, was most often in the public eye. Not only because he had been divorced twice and had three wives before he was thirty-five, but also because of his meteoric progress in business ventures and in military service. Young Elliott, unlike his brothers, had no time for academic studies at Harvard: his agile mind dwelt on opportunities in the workaday world. We hear of him, then only twenty-three, at the very beginning of his father's Presidential term. At that time there had been a rupture in the diplomatic relations between Russia and the United States, and it had been the policy of the American Government to discourage commercial relations with the existing Soviet regime; in fact, every difficulty had been put in the way of making shipments to Russian ports.

In October, 1936, the chairman of a Senate committee disclosed an affidavit by an airplane manufacturer, made a year earlier, that he at one time held a contract with Elliott Roosevelt for the expected sale to Russia of fifty military airplanes which would have yielded a commission of half a million dollars to the President's son. The airplane designer and builder, Anthony Fokker, was questioned about why he had made this agreement, involving such a large commission, with young Roosevelt, and he testified that his company considered Elliott's influence very important in negotiations with the Russian purchasing agency and the bank which was to finance the transaction, and anticipated also sales to other European nations, "counting on the willingness of high foreign officials to receive Mr. Roosevelt as the son of the American President." The deal was not consummated, but Fokker asserted that a settlement was made by paying $5,000 in cash to Elliott and a check for a slightly larger amount which was never cashed.[32] Elliott denied these allegations, insisting that his arrangements with Fokker did not contemplate the sale of military planes or dealings with foreign governments, and that the $5,000 he received was not for him personally but for a salesman associated with him.[33] Later, Fokker likewise asserted that only commercial planes were to be sold.[34]

In the meantime, Elliott's matrimonial affairs intrigued newspaper readers. He had married the daughter of a wealthy Philadelphia manufacturer, and had become the father of a son; in July, 1933, this union was ended by a Nevada divorce and five days later Elliott married a Texas heiress. Thereafter we read much of Elliott's financial transactions. He became director of a radio network in Texas, owned by his father's political enemy, the publisher William Randolph Hearst.[35] Press dispatches made mention of his activities on behalf of candidates for public office. It was hinted that his influence had made certain the appointment of a former Texas Governor to the Federal bench, that he was making political deals and paving the way for his own political ambitions. This he denied. *Time,* delving into these rumors, reported, "He obtained a judgeship for his friend, the Governor, and it was gossip among politicians that the latter would help the President's son in election to some office—possibly the lieutenant governorship. Elliott asserted emphatically: 'I do not plan to run for any political office now, in two years from now, or four years hence.'" He did, however, increase his importance in Texas politics by organizing a new State radio-broadcasting network of twenty-three stations, acquiring a substantial monetary interest and becoming directing head of the enterprise.[36] Once again he associated himself with those who were most active and bitter against his father —Elliott affiliated his radio station with the broadcasting system whose stock was fifty per cent owned by the anti-Roosevelt Chicago *Tribune* station.[37] To what extent this second son of Franklin Roosevelt profited by his ventures in radio we do not know; unlike James, he was not incited to publicize his income-tax returns. It was said, however, that it was his wife who supplied most of the funds to purchase the radio stations, and some of the transactions were in her own name. Neither the press nor the public was surprised, or was impelled to be critical because the reputed wealth of his wife, the prestige of his father, and his own aggressiveness enabled him to rise in the radio field to a place usually beyond youthful executives with his limited experience—that he had obtained financial aid from other sources was not revealed to the public until six years later.[38] What did stir up the censure of editors, politicians, and the man-on-the-street was Elliott's commission as captain in the Air Corps.

"Elliott's Got It," headlined the Buffalo *Evening News,* using the phrase which had become familiar in referring to his brother James' insurance business; the cause of its outburst was explained in the editorial: "The appointment of Elliott Roosevelt to a captaincy in the Army Air Corps has aroused a lively controversy. A few days ago Elliott announced that one of his father's sons ought to be in the military service as an example to the 16,500,000 young men between 21 and 35 who are subject to conscription for a year's military training. He applied, not to a recruiting sergeant, but to the Chief of Staff, who promptly gave him a captaincy in the Air Corps procurement division." [39] It was true: the President's son took his oath in the office of General Arnold, Chief of the Air Corps. If Elliott's friends had grounds to regard as the President's political critic the journal which complained of the preferential treatment accorded the President's son, they could not charge partisan bias to many other newspapers which, in much harsher terms, censured Elliott's commission. Chief among these was the Emporia *Gazette,* whose famed editor, William Allen White, wrote a scathing editorial. "Last week Elliott Roosevelt enlisted in the Army and got a captain's commission," wrote White, "watch carefully during the enlistment period and see if the son of any other citizen of this United States, without military training, goes in as a captain." [40] The editor of the *Gazette* did not merely censure "the special privilege conferred upon the President's son," but also the fact "that the American people take it. They take it lying down . . . with a cynical shrug." White was mistaken: neither the people nor the press "took it lying down"; they protested in the only way they could—in denunciatory editorials and indignant letters to the newspapers.

Elliott Roosevelt did not long remain a captain. He rose to major's rank, to lieutenant colonel, to colonel. There was widespread comment that, had he not been a President's son, his rise would not have been so rapid. Critical "letters to the editor" became more numerous in the newspapers of large cities and in the less widely circulated journals of smaller towns. Another election was approaching, and some of these protests were from political-minded citizens. Some voters sent their censures to members of Congress; one Representative read the letter received from a constituent who alleged that the President's sons were "receiving preferential treatment in the armed services." [41] Elliott Roosevelt, in Egypt, read the criticism; from the battle zone he answered the attack upon him and his brothers, writing to the Representative from his Texas district; he attributed the criticism to political adversaries of his father. "Such criticism aimed at men who are fighting for their country strikes me as sort of unfair," protested Elliott. "They can't answer back. We feel we are fighting for all America. We are not in politics. . . . We, as soldiers, don't care whether or how much [a Congressman] disagrees with the President, but for God's sake let us fight without being stabbed in the back for the sake of politics. . . . If I ever get home and am out of the Army I'll be glad to stand up for my own honor, but in the meantime see if he won't lay off. . . . I have been in every lousy spot the Air Corps can think of to send its men." [42] Elliott Roosevelt was not without champions in the halls of Congress. Many members rose to defend him, to recount his services, and to praise his ability and courage.

Nor was the press always critical. Very often magazines and newspapers gave prominent space to his activities and to episodes which revealed his ability or courage; his pilot was quoted as saying that at times Elliott crowded into a small plane which did not permit his wearing a parachute.[43] Commented one prominent magazine, when Elliott was discovered in December, 1942, in Africa a lieutenant colonel and head of a photographic unit, "Up from captain since he joined the Air Forces in 1940, the President's second oldest son (32) is a veteran of photographic flying in the Arctic, Britain, and Iceland. In Africa he has one of the Air Force's most dangerous jobs, including what pilots and photographers call 'dicing'—flying as low as 100 feet over enemy targets for close-up pictures. Roosevelt has 'diced' Tunisia, Sicily, and Sardinia, and he is still trying to pile up more combat-flying time than any other man in his unit. One reason for his zeal: he knows that many men in the Army look with suspicion on 'the President's son.' " [44] Even newspapers unfriendly to his Presidential father, like the Washington *Times-Herald,* published favorable reports about Elliott's work in the Italy-based Air Force which, one of its correspondents cabled, was "a vital branch of the United States armed forces in the Mediterranean theater. He is commanding officer of all this camera reconnaissance. But that doesn't mean sitting at a desk." [45] For this work Elliott received the Distinguished Service Cross, the citation noting "heroism and extraordinary achievement while participating in aerial flights." [46]

Reports of Elliott's military progress were displaced, in March, 1944, by news more intriguing to the reading public: the President's son was being sued for divorce by his second wife. They had been married nearly eleven years, and she had borne three children.[47] The petition filed revealed that Elliott and his wife had separated during the preceding October, and noted that she possessed separate and ample financial resources to take care of the children. Speculation immediately arose whether Elliott had fallen in love with another woman, and within a few months rumors were cabled from London that he "was engaged to a captain in the Women's Army Corps." [48] The story, first printed in a leading weekly magazine, was widely published, and included a corroborating interview with the mother of the reported bride-to-be; in a later interview the mother said the report was entirely in error.[49] A few days later Elliott himself issued a statement denying his engagement.[50] However, although the London romance did not blossom into marriage, Cupid was more successful a few months later—in Hollywood, California. Elliott Roosevelt became engaged to a film actress who was a young divorcee and mother of a five-year-old son. They were married in December, on a mountaintop near the rim of the Grand Canyon in Arizona; Elliott's ten-year-old daughter—the offspring of his second wife—was the maid of honor.[51]

Newspaper writers, on the alert for "good copy," watched with eagerness the activities of Elliott Roosevelt, and reported his movements in the United States and abroad. This second son of the President had a way of being present where epochal events occurred or where the mighty of the earth gathered. He was among the first who flew to the airfield which the American Army had constructed in Russia; he was aboard ship at the secret Atlantic rendezvous when his Presidential father and Winston Churchill drew up the famed "Charter"; he was at his father's side at Casablanca where the global military movements were determined; he was in Africa where the President stopped off with the high military leaders en route to Teheran. His personal affairs, too, had supplied material for many columns of reporting—Elliott's career was colorful, unpredictable, startling. But, while editors had recognized the widespread public interest in his Army career, his business associations with his father's political enemies, and his three marriages, they were yet to discover that interest in these themes was to be eclipsed by the nationwide outcry about Elliott's "flying dog."

The incident, as is still remembered, occurred at a time when the United States Senate had under consideration the promotion of Elliott from the rank of colonel to that of brigadier general. Few readers gave much attention to that news item—public interest had already exhausted itself in the discussion of his advancement from captain to colonel. But, in the third week of January, 1945, another report was flashed across the continent: to make room on an Army plane for Elliott Roosevelt's dog, three American service men were ejected from their seats! That *was* news; it became the dominant theme in newspapers, on the radio, in Government offices, on street corners, in the halls of Congress, on trains, in homes and restaurants—everywhere. "We would not go so far as to say that the story of Elliott Roosevelt's dog has blanketed the news of the great Russian offensive," said the New York *Herald Tribune,* "but we venture to guess that as a subject of discussion from coast to coast it is a strong rival." [52]

The facts were undisputed: an eighteen-year-old Navy gunner, Leon Le Roy, after thirty months' service in the Pacific was on an Army transport en route to his home in Antioch, California, where his father had died recently. At Memphis, Tennessee, Le Roy and two other Navy men were ordered to leave the plane because the space of the three seats occupied by them was required for a large crate containing a mastiff. The men in uniform protested—they had been in the service of their country and felt that they were entitled to more consideration than the canine freight. They were told curtly that they were rated only "C," but that the crated dog had "A" priority. They examined the label on the crate: the dog was from the President's son; it was consigned from Washington to his actress wife in Hollywood, California. And, as was revealed later, upon his arrival at the airport there, an Army major personally delivered the dog to the Roosevelt home.[53]

It was undeniable, as the incisive Washington *Post* declared, that "the episode had, of course, unleashed a lot of petty political sniping at the President that was misdirected and unfair"; [54] but it was equally true, as expressed by a less friendly journal, that the public was aroused "for the very simple reason that . . . it represents the type of scandal to which a democratic society is most sensitive." [55] The War Department explained that the service men had been taken on the plane as a favor, "since cargo planes were not ordinarily used for passengers," and that, therefore, the displaced service men had no grounds for complaint.[56] But this was a very lame attempt to justify an inexcusable blunder; the press, the people, and Congress demanded to know who had authorized this privileged treatment of Elliott's

THE CHILDREN'S HOUR!
THE FRONT PAGE
ELLIOTT AND HIS POOCH
STREAMLINER HELD UP OVER AN HOUR WAITING FOR JIMMY
CONGRESS TO INVESTIGATE ELLIOTT'S PROMOTION TO BRIG. GEN
TALBURT

THE PROBLEMS OF A PRESIDENTIAL FATHER

In jocular vein the famed cartoonist Talburt pictured Franklin D. Roosevelt, then President, perusing news items regarding his sons—episodes which incited wide public discussion and editorial comment. (Scripps-Howard newspapers) dog. From London, the President's son gave the Associated Press his version: he had never asked the Army Air Transport Command to fly his dog across the continent, but had merely suggested that it be taken along "if an empty bomber happens to be going that way on an operational flight." He added that he himself had brought the dog from England to America when he made a flight to Washington.[57] His statement, far from quieting adverse comment, kindled still further censure because valuable space on an ocean-crossing plane in a crucial period of the war was used to transport a dog—the private property of a President's son. Nor was the national sentiment softened when it was further revealed that this was not the only dog transported by Elliott from continent to continent.

The clamor for an official inquiry was speedily heeded by the Senate Military Affairs Committee, which appointed a subcommittee to make an investigation of this transportation of Colonel Roosevelt's dog on a military aircraft with high priority rating. The subcommittee called upon the ranking officer of the Air Transport Command, Major General George, for a report, and he submitted a lengthy account of the incident. In the preceding November, Elliott had departed from a European air field in a bomber, under his command, for the United States by way of Iceland. Why the trip was undertaken was not explained. In addition to Colonel Roosevelt, the bomber carried four officers and five enlisted men and, other than personal baggage, the only cargo was Elliott's dog Blaze weighing 110 pounds, and a female pup about twenty pounds in weight. The dogs were put aground at a Maine airport, given veterinarian care, and later taken by another plane to New York. Thence, a third plane carried the two dogs to Washington—the pilot having been informed that they belonged to the President's son. After the dogs had arrived in the Capital, a White House station wagon picked them up at the airport. Several weeks later Elliott's sister phoned the assistant chief of staff for priorities, headquarters Air Transport Command, requesting that the dog Blaze be flown to Elliott's wife in Hollywood; and, while the report asserted that no request was made for the high priority, the assistant chief accorded the dog an "A" and the canine cargo left on a military cargo aircraft. From Dayton, Ohio, besides cargo and dog, were Le Roy and the two other Navy men, all three being on emergency leave. At Memphis, Tennessee, additional cargo was put aboard displacing the three service men, but Elliott's dog remained in a space equivalent to the three seats needed for the service men had they been permitted to continue their journey. The particulars related in the Army report were slightly at variance with the version first transmitted by the press agencies, but it confirmed the aggravating fact that Elliott Roosevelt's dog, and not the men in the uniform of their country, was permitted to occupy space on an Army plane. Blaze became a symbol of privilege and preference for a President's son.

The stage was set for acrimonious debate when the Senate came to consider the promotion of Elliott Roosevelt to the rank of brigadier general; the nomination had been brought up several weeks earlier, and consideration of it had been postponed. There were other names on the list of colonels whom the President had asked the Senate to elevate, but Majority Leader Alben Barkley realized that solely in Elliott's case would confirmation be contested. The clerk having "read sundry nominations in the Army," Senator Barkley said, "Inasmuch as there is only one of them which I think will occasion any comment, that being the nomination of Colonel Elliott Roosevelt, I ask unanimous consent that his nomination be taken up first and disposed of." [58]

Thereupon began the spirited discussion which fills ten pages of the *Congressional Record*. Demanded one Senator: "Will the Military Affairs Committee furnish the Senate with information as to the number, names, and character of instances in which men entering the service with the rank of captain, without previous military experience or qualifications as specialists, have risen in a period of four years to the rank of brigadier general?" The question was not unexpected; another Senator, objecting to Elliott's promotion, had data at hand. He asserted that there were then in the Army 9,600 active colonels, "any one of whom is ready for promotion when it comes his way, if it ever does. Of those 9,600 colonels, 2,351 were graduates of the Military Academy at West Point. They are men who have spent four years in study and preparation for their chosen profession, the Army of the United States. Those men naturally have the ordinary human reaction of protest against the advancement of youngsters who are wholly and completely amateurs in the military game, except for recent activity in the present war." [59] And he cited distinguished military leaders who did not achieve the rank of brigadier general until they had served many years in the Army, in contrast to Elliott's four years of military experience. Argued the Senator: "General Robert E. Lee had thirty-six years of service in the Army before he became a brigadier general. General George Marshall was in the Army for thirty-five years before he became a brigadier general. General Arnold had thirty-two years to his credit, General Eisenhower thirty years, General Pershing twenty-four years, and General MacArthur twenty-one years before reaching the rank of brigadier general." [60]

Elliott's Senatorial friends did not remain silent; they contended that, even though it usually takes a long time to achieve the rank of brigadier general, there have been instances of more rapid promotion. "Throughout the entire history of our Army there have been glorious exceptions of men who won high rank in less time than has Elliott Roosevelt, and for acts which were probably not equal to or greater in importance than his," declared one member. "I am not in the least sorry that in the Civil War, in 1861, General Forrest rose from the rank of lieutenant to that of lieutenant general within two years, I am not sorry that Custer rose from the rank of second lieutenant to that of major general in two years. I am especially not sorry that General Sheridan was able to rise from a second lieutenancy to a lieutenant generalcy within the period of three years." [61]

The spirited arguments continued, but it was noticeable that a large number of Senators refrained from voicing their opinions. In the ballot which followed the debate, fifty-three members voted to confirm Elliott's nomination, eleven to block the promotion. But thirty-one members abstained from voting. It was evident that political considerations influenced some of those who voted on either side, and also those who did not vote. But the net result was that Elliott Roosevelt became a brigadier general.

While the two older sons of Franklin Delano Roosevelt—James and Elliott—made headlines and were the subjects of public discussions and Congressional debates, the two younger of the four sons—Franklin, Jr., and John—were also participants in events which newspaper reporters and editors considered interesting to their readers.

Franklin Delano Roosevelt, Jr., born in August, 1914, was not the only son to whom the future President gave his own name; another son, born five years earlier, had been christened Franklin Delano Roosevelt, Jr., but lived only nine months to bear his father's name—he was born in March, 1909, and died in November of the same year. Had he lived he would have been his brother Elliott's senior, but the surviving Franklin Delano, Jr., came into the world four years after

Elliott's birth.[62] Thus, this living namesake was nearing nineteen when his father was inaugurated President in 1933.

Franklin, Jr., was prepared for college at the famed Groton School. He graduated in June, 1933, and was awarded the first prize for debating and the prize for having "combined to the greatest degree scholarship and ability in athletics." [63] Like his father, Franklin, Jr., later attended Harvard; like his father, too, in his teens he began to travel in Europe. He went to France, to England, to Spain; he was a President's son and American ambassadors abroad entertained this youngster with much enthusiasm. Returning to the United States he resumed his Harvard studies and became prominent in college athletics. Press reports about his activities were not, however, restricted to the Harvard campus; Franklin, Jr., liked to drive automobiles at a faster pace than city ordinances allowed, and his car was involved in a number of collisions. We read of suits against him in Boston and in New York, of arrests for speeding in New Jersey, Connecticut, Rhode Island, and New Hampshire.[64] The press recognized the widespread curiosity concerning this namesake of the President, and prominent newspapers such as the Philadelphia *Public Ledger* kept their readers informed of his movements, giving space even to unimportant items such as, "F.D.R., Jr., in Pittsburgh for Friend's Bridal." [65] At a wrestling match in Philadelphia, Franklin, Jr., became indignant when a newspaper photographer attempted to take his picture at the ringside; the President's son seized the camera and smashed it on the concrete floor; the conservative New York *Times* considered the episode newsworthy and devoted a column to details of the tussle.[66]

Like his older brother Elliott, Franklin, Jr., was indifferent to the censure which his Presidential father hurled at financiers and wealthy industrialists whom he called "economic royalists," dangerous to the welfare and ideals of the American people; the son liked these "economic royalists"—and fell in love with the daughter of one of them, Ethel Du Pont! That the Du Ponts were outspoken opponents of the President, that they were in the forefront in the election campaigns to defeat him, that their wealth and influence supported his political enemies were matters of no concern to Franklin Delano Roosevelt, Jr.; he became engaged to Ethel Du Pont and in July, 1937, married her. The wedding excited the entire Nation, not only because the bride was heiress to one of America's largest fortunes but also because the parents of the bride and groom were considered irreconcilable political foes. Scores of writers and photographers were sent to the Du Pont estate to report the events on the wedding day and to picture in print and film the personages who attended the ceremonies. Three companies of troops guarded the President and his family, and Army engineers set up a field kitchen on the Du Pont grounds.[67] Wedding presents filled two large rooms and an adjoining hall, and the President's wife discussed the wedding plans both in her newspaper column and on the radio.

Here was an event to arouse interest and speculation: how would the Chief Executive, the leading exponent of democratic equality, mingle with the princes of the industrial empire? The writer for the New York *Post* said that Romance had dissolved political animosities and that harmony prevailed. "The wedding, solemnized in the candle-lit Christ Church while a thunderstorm gathered and broke outside brought together the Nation's first political family, flanked by scores of relatives and New Deal chieftains, and its ranking industrial clan, anti-New Deal to the core. . . . All political differences, however, were forgotten during the austerely beautiful Protestant Episcopal single-ring ceremony in the flower-banked little church which has been the scene of Du Pont weddings and christenings for seventy-eight years." [68] Some likened the political feud between the Du Ponts and the President to that between the irreconcilable Montagues and Capulets who had made impossible for Romeo and Juliet what was achieved by the President's son and Ethel Du Pont; but the President's journalistic foes derided the analogy, exclaiming, "If this was a wedding of Romeo and Juliet, as the Nation's press has heralded it, the only outward indication was in the lustrous Juliet cap of synthetic orange blossoms enframing the smiling young bride's blonde hair . . . , for Montagues and Capulets both attended and merrily. . . . Political differences dividing the two powerful dynasties were checked at the church door." [69] But, despite its outspoken dislike of the President and his family, the Chicago newspaper devoted ten columns to descriptions of the bridal couple and the guests; in all the excitement Franklin, Jr., was reported the least disturbed—while the important personages were arriving he went for a swim in the Du Pont private pool, saying, "I can't stand sticking around waiting like this."

After his graduation from Harvard, Franklin, Jr., studied law at the University of Virginia; then, having obtained his degree, he began a clerkship in a Wall Street law office. He was now twenty-six; his salary was reported as two thousand dollars a year.[70] The legal profession, however, did not engross all his time or talents; in the following months he wrote a song, "I'll Spend the Rest of My Life with You," and it was sung over the radio.

Thus the activities of the three older sons of the thirty-second President continued to be "good copy": alternately, James, Elliott, and Franklin, Jr., became absorbing subjects for editorials and popular discussions. What of their younger brother, John Aspinal? His name, too, was blazoned in headlines—both in Europe and in his native land. During the first four years of his father's Presidency, John was outside the dazzling publicity which surrounded the older Roosevelt sons. But, during the summer of 1937, he went abroad; his escapades there made the front pages of many American newspapers—particularly, an episode in France. It was in August, and the locale was Cannes, where the city officials charged that the youngest son of the American President had squirted champagne in the face of the Mayor, and roughed him with a bouquet of flowers. There was a flower fête, and the leading hotel placed at the disposal of John and a Harvard classmate a carriage from which they could review the parade; the Mayor came to the side of the vehicle to greet John Roosevelt and the latter took a bottle of champagne from a bucket on the carriage floor and squirted the contents into the face of the city dignitary. The Mayor, the Associated Press quoted his aides as saying, "retired as gracefully as possible." [71] John denied the report, and his mother maintained her faith in his veracity, saying, "I am sure John told the truth when he said he didn't do it, because I have never known him to tell anything but the truth. He is one of the most dignified of my children; he never did anything like that at home and I can't imagine him doing any such thing abroad." [72] When he returned in the following month, the reading public had lost interest in the French escapade, curiosity having been aroused by a reported romance between John and a Boston debutante, Anne Lindsay Clark, who was visiting the White House.[73]

John was married in June, 1938, in the little Massachusetts town of Nahant; [74] in anticipation of the presence of the President of the United States, the press associations and leading newspapers sent their ablest writers to report the wedding. But, according to the Associated Press correspondent, "there was no invasion of curious onlookers to the number of 200,000 as early estimates had indicated. Instead, townsfolk to the number of about 2,500 gathered about the canopied entrance to the Old Boston Church and scattered groups along the road from Nahant to Salem, the route of the Presidential motorcade, totaled at the highest mentioned figure only 30,000." [75] After his honeymoon, John found himself a job in a Boston department store. His initial salary was $18.50 weekly, and many editorial writers were impelled to discourse upon the theme of a President's son starting at the "bottom of the ladder" as stock clerk in a store; the meditative columnist of the New York *Times* remarked, "That is why it sounds just a bit different when a young man named Roosevelt starts at the bottom of the ladder than if his name is Smith or Jones." [76] In Boston, where young men married to heiresses usually began their careers behind impressive desks, there was unstinted praise for the son of Franklin Delano Roosevelt who spurned the use of White House prestige to pave the road to success for him; typical of the journalistic approval was the comment of the *Globe's* columnist: "John Roosevelt, youngest son of the famous family, now happily married, is on his own, got himself a job, and is going to learn the art of merchandising. That's better than joining the colony of rich men's sons, idling away his time in a cocktail lounge and sponging on his parents, as so many of them do." [77]

In the midst of their peacetime activities, there came into the lives of the Roosevelt sons the interlude of soldiering. We have seen how Elliott, when the Nation conscripted its youth, obtained a captaincy, advanced to colonel, and finally acquired the star of a brigadier general. James, who long before the war had been made a colonel of Marines, rejoined the armed forces as a captain; soon he regained the rank of colonel, and was sent by his Presidential father on confidential missions to China, Burma, and Egypt.[78] Later he was stationed in Washington, acting as coordinator of military reports. Franklin, Jr., and John chose the Navy.[79]

As the war progressed the Roosevelt sons were reported from varied parts of the globe and, either by design or coincidence, one or more of them always happened to be present when their Presidential father met the great of the world. Thus when the Chief Executive flew to the epochal conference at Teheran in November, 1943, Lieutenant Franklin D. Roosevelt, Jr., was in the plane beside him,[80] and when the head of the American Nation dined at the headquarters of the

British Commander at Cairo, both Franklin, Jr., and Elliott Roosevelt were among the dozen guests. Even while he had the lowest rank of ensign, the President's namesake accompanied the Prime Minister of Great Britain on a trip to Iceland. In London, Franklin, Jr., a mere lieutenant, was invited to a dinner which the American Chief of Operations in European waters tendered to a South American naval delegation.[81] Since they were the President's sons, the press allotted to their activities prominent space usually accorded to ranking officers or deeds of exceptional valor.[82]

Elliott's name appeared often in press reports; frequently he returned to the United States and gave interviews to the newspapers on military operations,[83] or was photographed at New York night clubs with his sister or society leaders.[84]

On the twelfth of April, 1945, all the Presidential sons were in foreign lands or on distant seas. In the late afternoon of that day there was flashed to all parts of the world a tragic message: "President Franklin Delano Roosevelt died suddenly." Then the teletype spelled out another message:

> April 12, 5:56 P.M.—The four Roosevelt sons, all of whom are in service, were notified of the President's death by messages from Mrs. Roosevelt. She told them that the President had done his job to the end and that she knew he would want them to do so too.

With the defeat of both Germany and Japan, it was announced that three of the Roosevelt brothers were returning to civil pursuits. The eldest son of the late President finally took up residence in California, purchasing a large home in Beverly Hills. Public interest in Jimmy had subsided, and the leading papers no longer gave prominent space to his activities. However, his friends foresaw a political future for him, and the local paper intimated that James Roosevelt might become a candidate for the Governorship of California. "There is still much vote-getting power in the magic of the Roosevelt name," editorialized the Beverly Hills *Citizen.*[85]

Elliott left the Army in mid-August,[86] but it was not his military career that now made headlines. In the early summer of 1945 his name had again appeared on the front pages of many newspapers, and for months remained the subject of nationwide discussion. A well-known columnist, Westbrook Pegler, had charged that during his father's Presidency, Elliott had obtained a loan of $200,000 from

John Hartford,[87] the head of America's largest grocery chain; and that, instead of repaying the borrowed money, the President's son settled his debt for $4,000—Hartford later charging off the loss of $196,000 from his income and thus reducing his tax liability to the Federal Treasury. So startling and so grave was this accusation that the leading papers in sixty large cities made no mention of it, fearing libel suits if the charges were proved to be without foundation. But bolder editors did publish the story—particularly those who had previously intimated that the Roosevelt sons were capitalizing on their father's prestige and official power. At first the public refused to believe that even a President's son could borrow two hundred thousand dollars from an astute business man and later satisfy his creditor with a repayment of two per cent of the principal. Many newspaper readers were aware that for years Pegler had written scathing denunciations of the activities of the Roosevelt family. But soon his charges were corroborated. From Danville, Illinois, where the Government was then prosecuting a suit against the largest retail grocery chain, which was accused of monopoly, the attorney for the president of the company issued a statement admitting the fact that the loan of $200,000 had been made in 1939 to the President's son and that, three years later, four thousand dollars was accepted in full settlement of the loan.[88] The chain's attorney resented the inference that the loan had been made and a fraction of the amount accepted in full payment in expectation of Government favors. "A pretty picture," retorted the Chicago *Tribune*. "It seems pretty clear that John Hartford didn't go about with $200,000 in his pocket in the hope that he would run into Elliott Roosevelt and could persuade Elliott Roosevelt to borrow it. That incident took place in 1939. In 1942 Elliott bought back his notes and the collateral for $4,000. Meanwhile, Mr. Hartford and his company were indicted for violation of the antitrust laws. Perhaps as long ago as 1939 . . . Elliott had reason to believe that a prosecution was under consideration. . . . In these circumstances Elliott sought out Mr. Hartford and put the bite on him."[89] The journal quoted was, of course, always critical of the Roosevelt sons. But even less antagonistic papers questioned the propriety and motives of the loan.

"Let's have the facts," demanded the Detroit *News*, "a public airing of the circumstance of Elliott Roosevelt's loan would seem advisable and, in spite of his own reluctance to discuss the matter, the move for it should come from his dead father's own best friends. . . . What is of consequence is only the implication that those who allegedly interceded with the lender in the late President's behalf promised Governmental favors in exchange for the loan or for its ultimate settlement at a small fraction of face value." [90]

Typical of the viewpoint of the nonpartisan newspapers was the editorial in the independent Washington *Post*. Captioned "Scandal or Slander?" it reviewed the acknowledged facts and asserted, "It is of the highest importance that all the circumstances surrounding the loan of $200,000 from the head of a huge business corporation to a son of the late President of the United States be investigated and disclosed. . . . About six years ago Elliott Roosevelt wanted money for the purchase of a radio station in Texas. . . . The first thing to observe is that this story cast great suspicion on the actions and motives of all concerned. The utter impropriety of the whole transaction is emphasized by the fact that at the time the loan was settled for one fiftieth of the original amount, at least two and possibly three suits by the United States Government against the A & P chain for violation of the antitrust laws were in litigation. Thus the precise nature of Mr. Hartford's interest in making the loan is open to serious question. He is reported to have explained . . . that he considered it unjust that a young man should be handicapped in business merely because he was the son of a President. It might be observed that the sons of shoemakers, day laborers, clergymen, poor widows, and others are also handicapped in business, since they too are often lacking in funds. . . . Moreover, it would appear from the influence exerted in Elliott Roosevelt's behalf that he was anything but handicapped by his status as a President's son." [91]

Newspapers throughout the country now blazoned headlines predicting an official report by the Congressional investigating committees; photographs of Elliott Roosevelt and the group of committee members were spread over many columns of prominent dailies.[92] But, as the weeks passed, it became evident that Elliott's loan and its settlement were not to be appraised solely on the basis of law and ethics, but had taken on political aspects as well—Republican leaders saw in the episode an opportunity to embarrass and impugn the integrity of the recent Democratic regime. In contrast, ardent supporters of the late President were fearful that publicity of Elliott's financial transactions [93] might cast a shadow on the memory of the Presidential father. The House Ways and Means Committee sat behind closed doors, and the voluminous testimony was transcribed in secret. If the public expected an early and unequivocal report from official sources, it was doomed to disappointment.

From June to October there was a deluge of rumors concerning the progress of the investigation. The Republican members pressed the inquiry and called upon the Treasury Department for data on the income-tax returns of Elliott and John Hartford, who had deducted the loss from his income.[94] A month later it was reported that the Treasury had completed its study,[95] but the Department's press releases merely reiterated known facts and claimed that the "inquiry is continuing." Late in August, after two months of study, the committee again went through the motions of reaching some conclusion. "Elliott Roosevelt's Loans are Scanned by House Group for 3 Hours and Put Aside," was the headline in the New York *Times* summarizing a two-column dispatch from its Washington correspondent.[96] Astute commentators, accustomed to the way of political Washington, predicted that the Congressional committee would "deliberate" until the public either forgot the incident or lost interest. Their prognostications were accurate: the Congressional inquiries degenerated into a political squabble, and partisan committeemen signed separate reports in defense or condemnation of the loan to Elliott.

Meanwhile, Franklin Roosevelt, Jr., bought a country estate at Woodbury, Long Island; in nearby New York City he joined a law firm headed by Charles A. Poletti who, for a few months, had been Governor of New York and was later military governor of various Italian cities occupied by American troops. "Mr. Roosevelt is a sensible man," commented Poletti, "he is planning to get a good grounding in the law." [97] The firm was handling a variety of cases, and Franklin, Jr., would acquire general legal experience. Having married the heiress to the Du Pont fortune, whose father and family dominated huge corporations, it was not likely that young Roosevelt would need to seek clients as would other law graduates with equally limited experience.

But it was evident that the late President's namesake was not content merely to lead an inactive career, secure in a substantial income from his own inheritance and his wife's wealth. Out of uniform, he interested himself in the problems of demobilized servicemen who were unable to find homes in the metropolis. Franklin, Jr., believed that the Mayor, Fiorello La Guardia, could aid in providing adequate shelter for the men, many of whom had lived in foxholes overseas, and he headed a delegation to the City Hall. Politically, La Guardia owed much to the Roosevelt family; in his campaigns for Mayor he profited by the support of the White House occupants, who were outspoken in their praise of him—both Franklin D. Roosevelt and his wife. But it was now apparent that, his Presidential father having died, politicians were not concerned about pleasing Franklin, Jr. "Nobody Home," was the caption in the periodical, *Newsweek,* for a photograph of the late President's son vainly waiting to see the Mayor.[98] "F. D. R., Jr., not pleased with City Hall," continued the report. "Six servicemen and veterans led by Franklin D. Roosevelt, Jr., were given the brush-off by Mayor Fiorello H. La Guardia when they tried to see him about temporary housing for thousands of homeless veterans. After a week of vain telephoning for an appointment, Roosevelt took the delegation to City Hall. The Mayor was not in. After a 45-minute wait, Roosevelt left." One columnist described Franklin, Jr., as "roaring mad at Mayor La Guardia." [99] Other commentators saw in his renewed interest in the legal profession and his espousal of social causes an ambition to achieve political success. "Franklin D. Roosevelt, Jr., is on his way in politics," speculated another writer, "the late President's third son who inherited not only his father's name but all that went toward making up his father's political IT—vitality, good looks, sanguine temperament—has established a residence in New York and joined a politically tinged firm." [100]

If Franklin Roosevelt, Jr., discovered that, since the death of his Presidential father, he was subjected to unexpected rebuffs by politicians who had been accustomed to treat him with deference, his brother Elliott was experiencing a still greater change in his own status.[101] As the year 1945 was drawing to a close press reports told of "social setbacks" which the most imaginative columnists would never have predicted: newspapers headlined an Associated Press report that the New York *Social Register* had "dropped the name of Brig. Gen. Elliott Roosevelt, son of the late President." [102] Society commentators asked why, but "a spokesman for the Social Register Association, publisher of the *Register,* said no information ever was given as to why names were dropped or added." [103] Probably, Elliott was little concerned whether or not his name was listed by the self-appointed arbiters of Society's elite; but there quickly followed another slight which must have aroused his resentment.

For generations some member of the Roosevelt family had been a vestryman or warden of the St. James Episcopal Church at Hyde Park; Elliott's father had served in that capacity for forty years; [104] James had been a vestryman for fifteen years. The President's death and James' resignation created vacancies, and Elliott was elected by the church authorities to fill one of the posts. But he was not permitted to assume the duties of vestryman; his selection was banned by higher authority, the Bishop of New York, Right Reverend William T. Manning. Said the Bishop: "I have notified the vestry of St. James Church at Hyde Park that Gen. Elliott Roosevelt is not in good standing in the church and therefore is not eligible for the office of vestryman and cannot serve in that office." [105] The Bishop's decision was publicized in the newspapers before it was received by the Hyde Park vestry,[106] by whom it was announced that "Mr. Roosevelt had planned to decline the nomination anyway." [107] The Nation's press speculated about why Elliott had been banned from the church office, and the explanation was advanced that his divorces had barred him. "The marriage canons of the Protestant Episcopal Church are explicit on the subject of divorce," observed *Newsweek* in a full-page article on the episode. But, as other periodicals pointed out, while their father was President, Elliott's brother James had served as vestryman despite his divorce and remarriage.[108] Although they considered it their duty to bow to the dictum of Bishop Manning, the members of the Hyde Park church regarded the ban as unfair to Elliott.[109] In fact, the monthly magazine of the Protestant Episcopal Church questioned Bishop Manning's authority to overrule the deliberate choice of the vestrymen at Hyde Park.[110]

The year 1946 began with the Roosevelt sons scattered across the continent: James was in California, his younger brothers in the East. It was a time when the thoughts of most Americans were of their own sons and brothers who had been soldiering across the seas, and millions of readers were most eagerly scanning the papers for news of their homecoming. Nevertheless, editors considered that the public was still interested in the sons of the late President, and prominent space was allotted to their activities. Thus, in January, press dispatches told of Elliott's sojourn at Hyde Park for the year-end holiday; [111] and the press associations reported plans for a radio broadcast by Franklin, Jr., from the White House, the occasion being the annual appeal for funds for the victims of infantile paralysis.[112]

At the end of February, 1946, James Roosevelt announced that he was going into politics, as the director of the newly organized Political Action Committee. It was reported that he was being paid $25,000 a year for his work.[113] James disclaimed any plans to run for public office.[114] He immediately embarked upon a speech-making tour to publicize the objectives of his organization. At a meeting before the new political group in Philadelphia he asserted that "it takes courage and persistence to be independent." The press associations, reporting the speech, referred to him as the "son of the late President."[115] Commentators, too, reminded their readers that this was "the eldest son of the late President Franklin Roosevelt."[116]

James continued his talks in other cities, criticizing the President who had succeeded his father.[117] His speeches were praised by those who shared his views but they also aroused opposition, particularly from those who had been unfriendly to his Presidential father. Several members of Congress charged that his opinions were un-American;[118] one Congressman asserted, "Poor Jimmy, he may not know it, but he is no longer in a position to speak for the Democratic Party. He has now joined the Communists."[119]

After his speech-making tour, James returned to California; and, in July, was appointed State Chairman of the Democratic Central Committee. Again, the opening sentences of the press reports noted that he was the "son of the late President."[120] About the same time James became a radio commentator, discussing current events over two small stations in Los Angeles and San Francisco. His selection, said a leading magazine, was prompted by the belief that he had inherited the magic of his Presidential father, but it was acknowledged that James was an able speaker and had a good voice.[121]

It soon became evident that, in assuming the role of State Chairman, the eldest son of the thirty-second President had undertaken a very difficult task which would have taxed the astuteness of more experienced politicians. As was summed up by one press association, "James Roosevelt, eldest son of the late President Franklin Delano Roosevelt, found himself in a tempest of criticism while essaying his first big political venture."[122] California newspapers were filled with charges and counter-charges.[123] Many issues were involved in the ensuing campaign; when the votes were counted, it was discovered that even the prestige of James Roosevelt's name could not bring victory to the candidates he sponsored.

James did not restrict his political activities to platform speeches and the radio; leading magazines gladly purchased his written articles. Always, in printing them, the journals reminded their readers that this author was a President's son. Thus, the opening phrase on the title page of one publication was "F. D. R.'s eldest son urges"; [124] and in another "James Roosevelt, the eldest son of the late President." [125]

The success of James Roosevelt as an author, in arousing widespread discussion and in monetary reward, was eclipsed by his brother Elliott. In the early summer of 1946 there were rumors that this second son of Franklin Roosevelt was writing a book, and that one of the foremost magazines had contracted to pay him thirty thousand dollars for the serial rights.[126] While columnists speculated regarding his theme, Elliott's name appeared in the news because of a fine imposed upon him in a New York village for speeding at sixty-five miles an hour.[127] In August, parts of his unpublished book appeared in *Look,* a magazine whose circulation was among the highest in the United States. Elliott's narrative revealed unknown incidents at the meetings of his Presidential father with the world's great. Entitled *"As He Saw It,"* the articles described the personal traits of Britain's wartime Prime Minister, Winston Churchill, and of the Russian dictator, Stalin. It also purported to give *verbatim* conversations between the late President and the leaders of the Allies who were directing the war against Hitler. Elliott's delineations were resented in England, and his understanding of the conferences derided,[128] one prominent Briton asserting that Elliott was merely a boy who overheard what adult men had said but could not comprehend what they were talking about. Elliott's mother, writing in her own column, denied that her son had intended to criticize Churchill; his object, she explained, was only to accentuate the contrasting personalities of the two wartime leaders, Churchill and Roosevelt.[129]

The appearance of the complete book increased the controversy. In England, it was resented bitterly, a typical comment being that "the book proves nothing except that great men often have silly sons." [130] American newspapers differed in their appraisal of Elliott's account of the historic conferences at which he was present, and his grasp of the epochal events which occurred there. *Time* judged that

Elliott's views on international affairs were not likely to impress many readers.[131] "Much of what Elliott sets down in print is on its face piffle," editorialized the Los Angeles *Times*.[132] Nevertheless, numerous papers regarded the volume as an accurate account of men and events. At any rate, the book became a "best seller." [133]

Apart from criticisms of Elliott's qualifications as an observer and his ability to appraise great leaders, the editors of some journals questioned the propriety of his revelations. A number of editors were scathing in their denunciation of his publicizing the remarks which his Presidential father had uttered in secrecy.[134]

These adverse comments did not seem to trouble the second son of Franklin D. Roosevelt. Even unfavorable criticism increased the demand for his book, and chapters were reprinted in widely circulated periodicals.[135] There was no question that Elliott's writings attracted public attention. Publishers besieged him with lucrative offers to enlarge his literary activities. In the closing months of 1946 it was announced that Elliott Roosevelt, accompanied by his attractive wife, was going to Russia. *Look* had commissioned him to write another book. Elliott's name appeared frequently in newspaper columns as the press associations reported the progress of his journey to and within the Soviet Union.[136]

Toward the end of November, 1946, Elliott was again in the headlines. He was quoted as saying, at a reception in Moscow, that the United States had violated its pledges to Russia, while the Soviets had observed their promises faithfully. Elliott had also pronounced, it was said, that the United States had embarked upon imperialism. The account of Elliott's statements was cabled by an experienced correspondent of an outstanding American magazine,[137] and was immediately printed on the front pages of newspapers throughout the United States.[138]

The American public was aroused. The State Department in Washington called upon its Ambassador in Moscow to investigate the incident. Across the Atlantic came additional reports from the press associations. Elliott was quoted as blaming the embassy for misquoting him; Elliott denied that he had blamed the embassy; [139] Elliott denied the denial; [140] Elliott refused to be interviewed.[141]

Elliott and his wife returned to the United States on Christmas Eve. Reporters and photographers swarmed about them as they emerged from the plane at New York.[142] He was asked whether he had made the remarks attributed to him, and he replied that he "heard accounts of it, but I was unable to read these accounts and therefore I have nothing to comment about it at the present time."[143] But he was more outspoken in criticizing the incumbent President. Remarked the New York *News:* "Elliott Roosevelt, the late Franklin D. Roosevelt's most vocal son, obviously regards himself as the sole heir to the mantle of his father's political philosophy."[144]

Hardly had the furor regarding Elliott's remarks in Moscow ebbed when another startling announcement was made: Elliott Roosevelt had interviewed the secluded and taciturn Stalin! Here, indeed, was surprising news. The Russian dictator had never granted an interview to an American reporter for ten years. Under the caption "Elliott's Scoop," the Washington *Post* expressed the belief of many newspapers that this feat was not merely the result of Elliott's experience, ability, or reputation as a reporter. "Many a big shot, whose by-line has been known for years to millions of readers, has made the attempt to interview Stalin," editorialized the *Post,* "the best any had been able to do was to leave a list of questions with somebody in the generalissimo's outer office. . . . Ace Roosevelt's meteoric career in journalism had begun."[145]

The controversy regarding Elliott's literary productions increased. Publishers became more eager to print whatever bore his name. Elliott wrote several articles for various magazines,[146] and there were rumors that his royalties were very large. The radio networks recognized public interest in this Roosevelt son, and he made several broadcasts. But an incident at one of them made more headlines than his remarks: it was reported that Elliott's press agent resented remarks addressed to Elliott's wife, and struck the reporter who uttered them.[147]

While his two older brothers were making headlines in politics and in book-writing, the third son and namesake of the dead President Franklin D. Roosevelt was also engaged in activities which won mention in the newspapers. Franklin D. Roosevelt, Jr., like James, had embarked upon a political career; but, unlike the eldest Roosevelt son, Franklin, Jr., continued to reside in New York State where his father had first won prominence. Like his sire, Franklin, Jr., likes people—a valuable trait in winning popular good will. Political commentators, especially those who had admired his father, began to suggest that this was the son who most fully embodied the personality of the elder Roosevelt.[148] Headlines referred to him as "F.D.R., Jr." As early as March, 1946, the so-called "liberal" periodicals considered him worthy of lengthy articles—notice which they did not accord to James or Elliott.[149] Even the conservative New York *Times*, in September of the same year, devoted a page of its Sunday magazine to a description of his personality and his views, illustrating the article with a large drawing by a distinguished artist.[150] Some columnists asserted that Franklin, Jr., was offered an assistant secretaryship in the Cabinet, and that he refused it.[151] With the astuteness which characterized the political success of his famous father, Franklin, Jr., assumed the championship of veterans, urging adequate housing for them.[152] He took a prominent part in the organization of the American Veterans' Committee,[153] and soon became the recognized spokesman in a much publicized attempt to combat Communist influences.[154] He crusaded, too, for the end of racial discrimination; in December, 1946, President Truman appointed him a member of the President's Committee on Civil Rights.[155] During the spring of 1947, as national housing chairman of his veterans' group, he boldly assailed the older American Legion, accusing that organization of neglecting the needs of homeless veterans.[156]

As months passed, editors began to recognize increasing public interest in this President's son, and allotted more space to his opinions and his pictures.[157] Franklin, Jr., was photographed in New York when a Legion of Merit medal was pinned on his breast pocket,[158] and in Washington where he appeared at a "black-tie reception" attired in a gray business suit.[159] Astute politicians also realized his mounting publicity and the prestige of his name, and welcomed him as vice-chairman of the Washington chapter of a newly organized political group.[160] They considered that there was magic in the familiar initials by which his famous father was known. In a photograph of himself, the Mayor of Minneapolis and the Chairman of the American Veterans' Committee, the other two were identified by their full names, but the title referred to the President's son merely as "F.D.R., Jr."[161] During the spring and summer of 1947, the letters "F.D.R., Jr." captioned numerous press reports. Franklin, Jr., was gaining in experience and in self-confidence.

The fourth and youngest Roosevelt son displayed neither a flair for politics nor a talent for writing. Quietly, John Roosevelt settled in the California town of Pasadena and resumed the business career which had been interrupted by the war. Since he was a President's son, the press associations reported the unspectacular event that he had become an executive in a chain of clothing stores.[162] Until the spring of 1947 his name seldom appeared in the news columns. But in May of that year a strike by clerks in the stores of his chain revived public interest in John.[163] *Life* published a full-page photograph of this Roosevelt businessman going through the picket line which surrounded the building in which his company's offices were located.[164]

Such is the chronicle of the sons of Franklin Delano Roosevelt, thirty-second President of the United States. Their father had been the Chief Executive longer than any other President in the Nation's history; they themselves were thus longer in public view as scions of the White House occupant. Their father's political power and renown spread to every portion of America and to the four corners of the earth; similarly, their own personalities became the theme of world-wide interest. What will be the roles of these Presidential sons in this atomic era? Will the fame of their father or their own abilities advance their careers? Certain it is that their names will often appear in public print—they are a President's sons.

Presidents' Sons—by Legend or Adoption

21

"Son" of George Washington

COLONEL GEORGE WASHINGTON, ACCOMPANIED BY HIS ORDERLY, WAS riding toward Williamsburg, the gay Capital of his native Virginia. The year was 1757, and his military fame had already spread throughout the American colonies for he had been an officer both in the militia of the Virginia colony and in the British army, fighting against the French and Indians. He had served under General Braddock, who had been defeated; now the militia was being reorganized and there were plans to reduce Washington's rank, although he alone had managed to save his regiments from annihilation.[1] He was hastening to Williamsburg to submit his resignation to the Governor of Virginia. He found himself on the banks of the Pamunkey River, along which stretched the vast acres of Colonel Daniel Parke Custis, who had died two years previously. Just beyond the riders was the mansion, named the White House. The overseer of the estate greeted Washington, and urged him to rest, and to meet the mistress, Lady Martha Dandridge Custis, the young widow of Colonel Custis. Washington reluctantly complied and met Martha; her cordiality made him forget his former eagerness to proceed on his journey.

There was a tradition that Daniel Parke Custis had courted other girls but that his father, a very wealthy landowner, would not give his consent to his union with any of them because the girls' dowries were not sufficient; but Martha Dandridge, a girl of seventeen, won the father's favor, and the son married her quickly in fear that his parent might change his mind. The forebears of Martha's young husband were outstanding not only in their wealth but also in their strong determination and intense emotions. One of them left his entire fortune to an illegitimate daughter; another made a will, which he later destroyed, making a favorite Negro slave boy his sole heir. Even after they were in their graves, their resentments were kept fresh: one of them wanted to make it known that he had been unhappy with his wife, and his will imposed upon his son the duty of inscribing upon his tombstone the fact that he had been joyous only during the years of his bachelorhood.[2] There is no record that Daniel Parke Custis acquired any of these ancestral traits, but he did inherit great wealth; he left not only extensive lands but also a multitude of slaves, real estate in Virginia towns, and large amounts of English pounds deposited both in London and in America. Martha had borne him four children, two of whom survived him, a boy and a girl. How great was the fortune which their father had left them is evidenced by the appraisal which George Washington later made of the son's share: "fifteen thousand acres of land, three hundred Negroes, lots in Williamsburg, and ten thousand pounds in the banks."[3] The share of the widow, Martha Custis, was also very substantial.

George Washington married Martha Custis in the first week of January, 1759. When she became his wife, he obtained control of her fortune. Within the next nine months he wrote four letters to the London commission merchants, formerly representing the Custis estate, explaining "how necessary it would be to address, for the future, all your letters which relate to the estate of the deceased Colonel Custis, to me."[4] Washington was very meticulous in keeping detailed accounts of the finances of himself, and of his wife's two children who became his wards. The girl died suddenly at thirteen. The son, John Parke Custis, had reached manhood when the Revolutionary War broke out; he became Washington's aide-de-camp and accompanied his stepfather in all the campaigns from Massachusetts to Yorktown, where he was present at the surrender of Lord Cornwallis. Then he contracted a fever and died. George Washington reached his bedside just as he was breathing his last, and this episode has been the subject of many fanciful descriptions. This dead son of Martha Custis Washington left four children, three girls and a boy. The two eldest girls went to their mother's home; the younger children remained with their grandmother Martha—Eleanor Custis, aged three, and George Washington Parke Custis, a few months old. It is this boy whom many biographers of George Washington called the latter's "adopted son."

The allusions to this grandson of Martha Washington as the adopted son of the first President are not warranted.[5] That Wash-

RECOLLECTIONS

AND

PRIVATE MEMOIRS

OF

WASHINGTON,

BY HIS ADOPTED SON,

GEORGE WASHINGTON PARKE CUSTIS,

WITH

A MEMOIR OF THE AUTHOR,

BY HIS DAUGHTER;

AND

ILLUSTRATIVE AND EXPLANATORY NOTES.

BY

BENSON J. LOSSING.

"First in War, First in Peace, and First in the Hearts of his Countrymen."
Gen. Henry Lee's Oration.

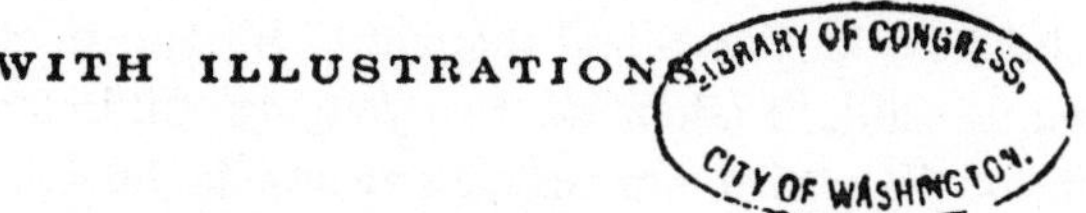

NEW YORK:
PUBLISHED BY DERBY & JACKSON.

1860.

THE ORIGIN OF A LEGEND

Title page of a work by Martha Washington's grandson, G. W. P. Custis, printed after his death. His daughter called him the "adopted son" of George Washington—thus circulating a myth which has no historical basis.

ington himself intended to assume the role of father, there is certainly no documentary proof; nevertheless, the descendants of George Washington Parke Custis always referred to him as the adopted son of George Washington. We shall see that the first President never applied to him the term "son," either in the letters which he addressed to him, or in communications regarding him. In his will, Washington refers to him as "my wife's grandson and my ward," even though in that testament he also states that, when he despaired of progeny of his own, he regarded Martha's relatives as his. Custis was seventy-seven years old at his death, and while he was fond of designating himself "the child of Mount Vernon" [6] he never called himself the child of George Washington. "Few men were better known," said the Washington *Evening Star* when he passed away,[7] but no newspaper in the Capital called him the son or adopted son of George Washington.

How, then, came biographers to call George Washington Parke Custis the adopted son of George Washington? It may be that they derived that impression from the famous Savage painting—*The Washington Family at Mount Vernon*—which depicted the Father of his Country with Martha Washington and her two little grandchildren. It is more probable that they had in mind the title page of a book which the daughter of Custis edited after his death. It comprised a series of articles which her father had written, entitled, "Recollections and Private Memoirs of George Washington." When she published these memoirs, she herself called them *Private Memoirs of Washington by his Adopted Son.* In a foreword to the book it was related that, when George Washington stood at the deathbed of John Parke Custis and thought of his two smallest orphaned children, he said, "I adopt the two younger children as my own." [8] This allusion in varied phraseology recurs in many subsequent biographies. With the passing years, the version increased in definiteness, until writers began to assert that George Washington "legally adopted" this boy and his sister.[9] In contrast to these statements it should be noted that, in the Preface which was written by George Washington Parke Custis himself, he made no direct claim of any similar relationship—merely stressing his knowledge of Washington because "taken from my orphaned cradle to his paternal arms, nourished at his board, cherished in his bosom, from boyhood to manhood, I ought to know something of the first President of the United

States." [10] In fact, in a letter to an Alexandria newspaper, relating to the placing of a memorial stone at the site where George Washington was born, he refers to himself only as "George W. P. Custis, the son of John Parke Custis." [11]

It is obvious that Custis' daughter who wrote with such definiteness about George Washington's "adoption" of her father had no personal knowledge of the deathbed scene which she described; the tale was probably conjured up in the imagination of the historian, Benson J. Lossing, who aided her in the composition of the foreword to her father's reminiscences. Lossing had a flair for the dramatic, and later recounted a similar story in a book of his own; he tells how Washington reached the house where John Parke Custis had just died: "The great man bowed his head in deep sorrow, while his tears flowed free. Then he spoke soothing words to the widowed mother and said, 'Your two younger children I adopt as my own.' " [12] Lossing, well acquainted with the writings of the first President, embellished the letter which Washington wrote to Lafayette, telling about his presence at the death of John Parke Custis, and expressing his own sadness at the death of his wife's only son. But neither in that letter nor in any other letter did George Washington say that he was adopting as a son the orphaned infant, George Washington Parke Custis.[13]

If, however, the historian is not warranted in regarding George Washington Parke Custis as having been formally adopted as a son of George Washington, there is still reason to include him in this review of Presidents' sons because, even as a ward, the public attributed to him a filial status and he received that notice and acclaim which stems from such a relationship to the President of the United States.

The infant George Washington Parke Custis was first taken to Mount Vernon and there, with his little sister, he spent a happy childhood under the watchful eye of his adoring grandmother Martha. George Washington called his wife's little grandson "Washington," and provided private tutors for him and his older sister. As the boy grew older he was sent in rapid succession to several colleges, but his progress was slow and his interest in academic pursuits decreased with the passing months. George Washington had become President in April, 1789; the Capital of the United States, at first in New York, was removed to Philadelphia and young Washington

Custis preferred the activities in the Pennsylvania metropolis to college classrooms. He had matriculated at St. John's College in Annapolis, where it had been hoped he would take some interest in his studies. When the disinterested Custis, at the end of Washington's term, came home for a vacation and expressed his unwillingness to continue at St. John's, George Washington let his ward return to the college to collect his belongings.[14] Custis was then induced to attend Princeton. Here he made greater efforts to acquire academic knowledge, and George Washington wrote him that the assurances that Custis was

applying diligently to your studies, and fulfilling those obligations which are enjoined by your Creator and due to his creatures, are highly pleasing and satisfactory to me. I rejoice in it on two accounts: first, as it is the sure means of laying the foundation of your own happiness, and rendering you, if it should please God to spare your life, a useful member of society hereafter; and secondly, that I may, if I live to enjoy the pleasure, reflect that I have been, in some degree, instrumental in effecting these purposes.[15]

When, in 1797, his term of office was ended, the first President returned to Mount Vernon and his wards again made their home in that mansion overlooking the Potomac. At the end of 1798, there arose the prospect of a war with France, and George Washington was commissioned to organize and command an army. One of the generals whom he selected chose George Washington Parke Custis as an officer of his cavalry regiment; Custis, not yet eighteen, was duly nominated by President John Adams, and confirmed by the Senate. There were men who possessed wider experience and more administrative ability, but the prestige of being a member of the ex-President's ménage was sufficient to obtain preference. Unquestionably, the Father of his Country had intimated his desire to have Custis thus commissioned; Washington himself told his reasons in a letter to David Stuart, who had married Custis' widowed mother. Said George Washington:

A thorough conviction that it was a vain attempt to keep Washington Custis to any literary pursuits, either in a public Seminary, or at home under the direction of any one, gave me the first idea of bringing him forward as a Cornet of Horse. To this measure too I was induced by a conviction paramount in my breast, that if real danger threatened the Country, no young man ought to be an idle Spectator of its defence.[16]

George Washington Parke Custis wanted all the regalia of his rank, and George Washington wrote lengthy letters to Government officials and friends to obtain for his ward the customary sword, bridle, and other trappings of a cavalry officer.

My ward, Mr. Custis, having entered into the Service of his Country, as a officer of Dragoons, I wish to equip him with everything suitable thereto; in a handsome, but not expensive style.[17]

He ordered a pair of pistols and horseman's sword, all of them silver mounted, the best kind of saddle (but not a bridle, as Custis already had a handsome one), and an elegant uniform. The ex-President was eager also to obtain promotion for his wife's grandson; three months later we find him writing to the Secretary of War, suggesting that Custis be given higher rank; [18] in his letter Washington appraises much more highly than he had previously the qualifications of Custis:

As vacancies have happened in the Cavalry by non-acceptances, etc., and promotions have begun; may I ask if there would be any impropriety in letting Mr. Custis step from a Cornetcy, into the Rank of Lieutenant? If I mistake not, in the arrangement given, he stands the first for promotion; that is, he was made senior Cornet. The Major Generals were desirous of placing him as Lieutenant in the first instance; but, his age considered, I thought it more eligible that he should enter into the lowest grade of Commissioned officers. If ample fortune, good Education, more than common abilities, and good disposition, free from Vice of any kind, give him a title, in the 19th year of his age, his pretensions thereto (though not to the injury of another) are good. But it is not my desire to ask this as a favour. I never have, and never shall, solicit any thing for myself, or connexions. I mean nothing more than the statement of a fact, in order to bring his situation to view.[19]

George Washington Parke Custis was not destined to acquire military fame. The threat of war disappeared, and he was never called upon to lead troops; he spent his time around Mount Vernon and on the surrounding Virginia estates. In December, 1799, George Washington unexpectedly died; young Custis was absent and did not return until after the funeral. Washington's will left Mount Vernon to his oldest nephew, Judge Bushrod Washington, to whom he also bequeathed his books; to Custis, he left a large tract of land elsewhere and also some real estate in Washington. The will itself, both in phraseology and bequests, dispels the thesis that George Washington regarded Custis as his "adopted son"; the Father of his Country would not have divided his property in that manner had he considered himself the foster father. Three paragraphs in the will refer to his wife's grandson:

THIRD—And whereas it has always been my intention, since my expectation of having issue has ceased, to consider the grandchildren of my wife in the same light as I do my own relations and to act a friendly part by them, more especially by the two whom we have reared from their earliest infancy, namely, Eleanor Parke Custis and George Washington Parke Custis. . . .

FOURTH—Actuated by the principle already mentioned, I give and bequeath to George Washington Parke Custis the Grandson of my wife and my ward, and to his heirs, the tract I hold on four-mile Run in the vicinity of Alexandria containing one thousand two hundred acres more or less;—& my entire Square, number twenty-one, in the City of Washington. . . .

LASTLY—I constitute and appoint . . . & my ward, George Washington Parke Custis (when he shall have arrived at the age of twenty years) . . . Executor of this Will & Testament. . . .

Young Custis continued to live at Mount Vernon until the death of Martha Washington in 1802. At twenty-three he married Mary Lee Fitzhugh and the couple made their home in a mansion which he had built on the west side of the Potomac, and named "Arlington." From this union came the daughter who married Robert E. Lee, the Commanding General of the Southern armies during the Civil War. This was the daughter who edited her father's reminiscences and called him "the adopted son of George Washington." Washington Custis lived the life of a Virginia gentleman. His wealth permitted him to indulge his taste for private yachts, fox hunting, and travel. Even though the illustrious Washington himself had never regarded him thus, there was about George Washington Parke Custis the aura of a President's son; and distinguished visitors came to the Arlington mansion. Even the President of the United States, Andrew Jackson, rode out from the Capital to call on Custis and his beautiful wife.[20]

Custis prided himself on his oratorical prowess; and he acquired a fair reputation as a public speaker, being called upon to deliver addresses on a wide variety of subjects and before a diversity of audiences. He delivered an oration at the funeral of a general killed by a mob,[21] at a celebration of Russian victory over Napoleon, at a meeting to protest against restrictions on citizens, and before agricultural societies. He also wrote newspaper articles on events in the career of George Washington, and he dramatized events in American history.[22] He tried to write plays, and was proud that one of them, *Pocohantas or the Settlers of Virginia, a National Drama in 3 Acts,* was performed twelve times in a Philadelphia theater.

Occasionally, he engaged in some business enterprise; he built a grist mill, which operated successfully. The magic name of Washington was not overlooked by the manipulators of various projects; George Washington Parke Custis was accorded the honors of public acclaim while they reaped the monetary profits. In 1836, some New York promoters conceived the scheme of establishing a commercial city on land adjoining the Capital. The President, Andrew Jackson, laid the cornerstone of the first building, and George Washington Parke Custis delivered the dedication speech "when the high wind and roar of the waves on the shore nearly drowned out the voice of the orator." [23]

Apart from these excursions into commercial fields, Custis preferred the less strenuous role of a "country gentleman"; his mansion being in the environs of the nation's Capital, he mingled in Washington society and became widely known to the thousands who lived in the city or came to visit it and included the nearby Custis mansion in their tours. His genial personality, in his elderly years, won him friendly notice. Some writers [24] have indulged in very extravagant eulogies of Custis, whom they regarded with admiration and awe as the descendant of the great George Washington. Other writers, less impressed, recognized his social graces and "vivacity of manners." [25] Eugene E. Prussing, tracing the inheritance of the estate of George Washington, observes that "Custis lived the life of a very wealthy country gentleman and a dilettante in art, literature, and science. He posed a bit on political occasions. He attended, for example, every presidential inauguration from Washington's second to Buchanan's. He entertained Lafayette and other foreigners lavishly." [26]

The outstanding trait of Custis' personality was his enduring pride in his association with George Washington. He became obsessed with the desire to have his name perpetuated, despite the fact that his only child was his daughter. He therefore left his estate to her only in trust, stipulating that it should descend to her eldest son who should take "my name and arms," and should be renamed George Washington Custis Lee.[27] George Washington Parke Custis died in 1857. The Washington *Evening Star,* in a single paragraph devoted to his death, said, "He was the last survivor of the family of George Washington . . . having been the grandson of Mrs. Washington"; [28] the Washington *Union* remarked that "for several years he had stood alone in his relations to the Father of his Country, ever anxious, with filial reverence and affection, to illustrate his character." [29] Other periodicals praised his geniality and courtesy, and noted that he left great wealth which he had acquired through inheritance and marriage. A few fraternal organizations passed resolutions, and several of them followed the funeral cortege to the final resting place.

Thus ended the career of George Washington Parke Custis, whom legend regarded as "the adopted son" of the first President of the United States.

22

Son of Andrew Jackson

THE FACT THAT ANDREW JACKSON WAS NEVER MODERATE IN HIS emotions made him a national idol as well as the object of intense animosities; and it also proved to be for his country both a boon and a danger. Andrew Jackson was as unreasoning in his hates as he was unrestrained in his affections. He never forgot friends, and never forgave enemies—or those he believed to be his friends or enemies. His unswerving loyalties rejected conditions; his pride tolerated no hint that he, himself, lacked a single attribute which characterized "a gentleman."[1] We have seen him, as President of the United States, the champion of Peggy O'Neal's questioned chastity, disrupting his Cabinet in her behalf, chiefly because her husband, Major Eaton, "is my friend and I would go down to my grave with dishonor if I were to desert him."[2] Wc have seen him sending troops to end the threat of nullification in South Carolina, mostly because the proponent of State rights was John C. Calhoun who, Jackson learned, had censured the latter's unauthorized acts in Florida.

There still remain his letters denouncing each and every one to whom he ascribed a single uncomplimentary remark about himself, his family, his friends, or his political supporters. And, when his pen or his voice could not still such attacks upon his private or political actions, he turned to the dueling grounds—inflicting wounds and death upon all who impugned his honor. All through his life Andrew Jackson regarded himself and those he loved as beyond the pale of doubt, criticism, or censure. There must be no questioning of what Andrew Jackson did or directed to be done—whether as military commander, as public official, or as private citizen.[3] His concept of his own unfailing sense of propriety was epitomized in his communication to an Army paymaster who could find no legal sanction for

Jackson's requisitions for payment to Indian and Negro troops who had fought in the battle of New Orleans against the British in the War of 1812; Jackson tersely told him, "It is enough for you to receive my order without inquiring. You are not to know whether I have received authority from the War Department." [4]

The American people were content: they did not ask whether Jackson had authority to invade Florida, to exact unconditional surrender from the Creek Indian tribes, to keep men in the militia even though their terms of enlistment had expired, to fight at New Orleans while American envoys were in Europe to negotiate peace—the American people did not ask whether Jackson had authority, knowing he did *not*—but they approved what he did. In rapid succession they made him Prosecuting Attorney, Judge, Commanding General, Congressman, Senator, President of the United States.

Who was this man who, despite his violent actions and arrogant bearing, became the hope of the "common people" of his generation? Andrew Jackson was born in South Carolina and was a boy when war raged between the American colonists and the British army sent across the Atlantic to crush the efforts of George Washington and his compatriots to establish an independent sovereign Republic. Both his parents died before Andrew was of school age; his two older brothers, soldiers in the Revolutionary forces, succumbed to fever in military prisons. Thus Andrew, still in his teens, was left without a living relative. He himself had fought with the American troops; captured by the British and mistreated, he never forgot the brutal treatment and his hatred of the English soldiery inspired his victories over the English army in our second war with Britain. Without kin to guide or aid him, the orphaned Andrew resolved to build his own future and make the world recognize him.

Early in life Andrew Jackson assumed the bearing of a man above the fellows about him. "It is hard to find anything in Jackson's inheritance which accounts for this pretension," said the historian John Spencer Bassett after delving into all the records.[5] Nevertheless, no one ever questioned those pretensions; in fact, he was accepted as a "top-class man" wherever he moved. Probably, it was because he began his career among the sport-loving citizens of Charleston, South Carolina—and gambling is always a leveler of social disparities. Jackson, with love and knowledge of horses, frequented the race tracks in the

Carolinas; when a mere youth in Charleston and in Salisbury, North Carolina, he "swaggered among the elite, carrying himself with the air of a man of fortune." And, even if they did not invite him into their homes, he acquired the traits and demeanor which marked them as "men of quality"—and he probably acquired also some of their money in betting. At any rate, his foremost biographer, Parton, tells us that when Andrew Jackson migrated to Tennessee his material possessions were far above those of a young man who had not yet undertaken any trade or profession.

Andrew Jackson did not make horse racing the dominant interest in his career. He probably regarded it as a means to an end—the mark of social prestige. He studied law; and, when he arrived in Nashville—then a new town—he was a professional man. Here, as a frequenter of the race track and the cock-fighting arena he came into contact with men who were regarded as of the "upper strata," and he enlarged his friendships. He continued to amass worldly goods, and soon became a rich and prominent citizen.

Then Andrew Jackson married. The circumstances reflect the America of the sparse settlements, the involved legal proceedings, and the slow communications in the closing days of the eighteenth century. In the infancy of our Republic there were no city hotels, no apartment houses, no restaurants, no cafeterias. If unmarried men had no paternal roofs to shelter them, or if they were absent from their family homes, they obtained shelter and nourishment at boarding houses—private homes usually owned by widows, who, suddenly left without other income, rented their rooms and served meals. In capacious dining rooms the boarders would gather around long tables, and here daily they would augment their acquaintances and cement friendships. After leisurely consuming abundant "home-cooked victuals," the fellow boarders would gather in the "sitting room"—and there another guest, invisible but not unknown to the assembled roomers, would work his art: Cupid. It was thus in Philadelphia that the future President, James Madison, met the Quakeress Dolly Payne, and married her; and many other prominent statesmen similarly felt the first throbs of love within the walls of a boarding house. It was thus that Andrew Jackson met Rachel, the daughter of the widow Donelson who operated the boarding house where Jackson made his home. Rachel had been married to a man named Robards who had deserted her and who had instituted divorce proceedings. At the time of Rachel's meeting with Jackson she believed that her husband had obtained the decree and she regarded herself divorced.

Andrew Jackson married Rachel Donelson in 1791; later, learning that at that time her divorce decree had not been final, he formalized the union with another ceremony in 1794.[6] These events were discovered and publicized by his political opponents when Jackson was a candidate for the Presidency in 1828. Some, like the austere moralist John Quincy Adams, held the opinion that "Jackson lived some time in adultery with his wife"; [7] but generally this infringement of a legal technicality was attributed to faulty court procedure. The attack upon his wife's honor intensified his devotion to her. Parton says that Jackson loved his Rachel "with the entireness which belongs to the love of men, and to them only, whose lives are pure from puberty to gray hairs," [8] despite her lack of physical attractiveness, and her inferiority to him in mentality and social graces. "It was remarkable," observes Parton, "that General Jackson, though himself an adept in drawing-room arts, and at home in elegant society, was blind to the homely bearing and country manners of his wife. . . . He was tall and slender. She was a short and stout woman. The spectacle is said to have been extremely curious when they danced a reel together." [9] Her education was very limited, but allegations of her complete illiteracy have been disproved by Jackson's biographer, who discovered a few letters written by her, one of them eight pages long. "The spelling of these epistles is bad, of course, and the grammar not faultless; but their existence is at least sufficient to refute a common opinion . . . that Mrs. Jackson could not write. Unlearned, however, she was in the lore of the schools, though not so in that of the woods, the dairy, the kitchen, and the cabin. . . . He had a happy home. Mrs. Jackson, besides being an excellent manager and mistress, was also a kind and jovial soul. She had a wonderful memory, which contained a great store of anecdotes and tales." [10] To Andrew Jackson, despite her lack of charm in the eyes of others, Rachel was an ideal woman; after forty years of life together he engraved her virtues on three sides of her tombstone, with the closing lines, "A being so gentle, and yet so virtuous, slander might wound, but could not dishonor. Even death when he tore her from the arms of her husband, could but transport her to the bosom of her God." [11]

Jackson had remodeled the Hermitage, and its halls resounded with the chatter of Rachel's nieces and nephews, the offspring of her six brothers, most of whom lived not far distant from the Jackson plantation. But Rachel herself bore no children; and in 1809, after years of married life, the owners of the Hermitage gave up all hope of heirs. Then, one of Rachel's sisters-in-law brought twins into the world—boys. This ailing wife of Rachel's brother Savern Donelson had other small children, and both ill health and her husband's meager finances made these new infants a burden. Andrew Jackson and his wife adopted one of them, naming him Andrew, Junior. Parton relates that it was Rachel who brought him home and presented him to her husband,[12] but there was a legend in Nashville that Jackson himself tied the squalling infant in a large handkerchief and took him to Rachel.[13]

That the little tot received from his foster parents an abundance of affection, there is no doubt. Rachel must have shared the anticipation of future years which Jackson depicted in one of his letters to her when little Andrew, reaching maturity, "will take care of us both in our declining years. From our fondness toward him, his return of affection to us, I have every hope, if he should be spared to manhood, that he will with careful education, realize all our wishes." [14]

During the first few years of his existence this adopted son was separated from Jackson who, first as commander of the Tennessee militia and later as general in the United States Army, was at various times campaigning against the Indians, the British, and the Spaniards. In her labored phrases, Rachel tells her husband about little Andrew; in one of her letters when the child was five she writes, "Our Dear Little Son is well he sayes maney things to sweet papa which I have no time to mention." [15] And a month later she informs Jackson, "Your Dear Little Andrew is well never did I see a Stroger mark of affection than in that Child your Letter he Claspt it to his bosome and went to bed with it. Some time in the Night he Calld oute where is my paper Letter I hunted and put it in his hand he then put it in his bosome." [16] And Andrew Jackson, after cataloguing the number of Indians slain, replies, "I hope shortly to put an end to the war and return to your arms; kiss my little Andrew for me, tell him I have a warrior's bow and quiver for him." [17] "Say to my son, I expect to see him shortly on his cosee filly," he writes again from Mobile in October, 1814, "that he must learn to ride, be a good boy and never cry, that he must do everything his sweet mama tells him, and he must learn to be a soldier." [18] That expectation was never realized; the adopted son of Andrew Jackson shunned the soldier's role, though he fathered two sons who, as officers in the Civil War, fought for the South.[19]

The boyhood of Andrew, Jr., was uneventful. He received a fair education. Andrew Jackson instilled in the mind of the growing boy the code of ethics which was his own guide in his personal and political career. When absent from home, he included in his letters to Rachel brief messages for his adopted son. "Say to my son I have not recd his promised letters," he entreated his wife. "Say to my son, to remember my advice, that was, never to make a promise but what he complies with; always to reflect before the promise is made, but when made, to be sure to comply with it." [20] And three weeks later, "Say to my son I have recd his letter, and forgive his mistake; tell him I noted it that he might hereafter be more carefull, least by carlessness he might be lead into a habit of mistakes injurious to him in his passage through life. Say to him he must attend to his writing and spelling." [21] Andrew, Jr., was then about fifteen years old. From Washington Jackson sent a book to his adopted son "to read, but not to deface—it is the one presented to me by Genl Rogers, sketches and charecters of the sages of the Revolution."

In December, 1828, after Jackson's election to the Presidency, Rachel died at the Hermitage; Fate had let her share all the attacks in the campaign, but denied her the glory of being a President's wife.

Early in 1829, after Jackson's inauguration as President, his adopted son fell in love with the daughter of a Major Smith. Young Andrew, anticipating the directness of a later century, courted the girl and expressed to her his ardent affection and desire to marry her—without first informing her parents of his emotions and intentions. This, in the eighteen-twenties, was a great "social error" unworthy of gentlemen; and Andrew Jackson hastened to explain and apologize to the girl's father, sending a note by the erring Andrew, Jr. "I am fearful he has committed an error; if he has, I trust you will ascribe it to his youth, diffidence and inexperience," wrote the President of the United States, "and allow him to make atonement for it for which purpose I send him to you. . . . He has made known to me, since his return, the attachment he has formed for your amiable daughter, which he informs me has been expressed to her and if not reciprocated, has at least won her favorable opinion. He has erred in attempting to address your daughter without first making known to you and your lady his honorable intentions and obtaining your approbation, but he has been admonished of this impropriety and he now awaits upon you to confess it." [22] He tells the father of the courted girl about Andrew's splendid character and his prospects of worldly goods, "He has been reared in the paths of virtue and morality by his pious and amiable Mother, and I believe has walked steadily in them; the only hope by which I look to the continuation of my name; and has a fortune ample enough with prudence and economy, and more than enough without them."

Either Major Smith or the girl herself was not receptive to Andrew's suit. In July he returned to the plantation near Nashville, and there Cupid again enmeshed him. This time he became infatuated with a spirited, flirtatious girl named Flora. Andrew Jackson, concerned about young Andrew's activities, writes him from Washington, "On the other parts and objects of your visit home, I pray you to act with circumspection. You are young, and now for the first time distant from me, but I have confidence that you will steer clear of evil company, and all kinds of disapation." [23] The President counsels him: "I have but one word to add on the subject you communicated to me. As you have fixed your affections on Miss———— say to her, you have known each other from your childhood, and it is useless to delay. An answer you expect and a candid one, to which you will submit without murmuring, if it be adverse to your wishes. You have too good an opinion of her to believe she would wish to coquett you, put it now in her power—have a final answer." [24]

It is apparent from the correspondence between Andrew Jackson and his adopted son that he fears Andrew, Jr., may become involved in an affair with Flora; he is eager either to have them married without delay or to bring about a breach between them. But Flora is not to be stampeded into matrimony. Within a week the uneasy father writes again to Andrew, Jr., marking the letter "confidential":

My Son, Having your happiness at heart more than my own, for since I have been deprived of your dear mother, there is no happiness or contentment for me this side of the grave, none but what your society, and your welfare and prosperity, and that of your family, should you have one, can afford, . . . you can Judge of the anxiety I have that you should marry a lady that will make you happy, which would add to mine, seeing you so. You are very young, but having placed your affections upon Miss Flora, I have no desire to controle your affections, or interfere with your choice, early attachments are the most durable, and having been raised together in the same neighbourhood, I have only to remark that no good can flow from long courtship. Therefore I would recommend to you to be frank with her, say to her at once the object of your visit and receive her answer at once. Under your situation this I think will be right, and you have a claim upon her to meet you with Frankness, and should her reply be adverse to your wishes, you ought not to be offended, but continue to treat her as a friend. So soon as you see and converse with her write me with candor the truth on this important subject to yourself and no less to me as your father and friend. Should Miss Flora not favour your wishes, then my son, I have one request to make of you, that is that you will give out all idea of Marriage for the present, until you see and advise with me. Yr affectionate father.[25]

In the White House, Andrew Jackson was impatiently awaiting word about the outcome of Andrew, Jr.'s, affair with Flora. After three weeks he writes a long letter to the youth, inquiring whether Flora is still residing with her guardian and, in the midst of detailed instructions about activities on the plantation, the worried foster father injects his meditations on Andrew's amour:

I would like to hear how you have settled your matter with Miss F. she is a fine girl, but you being young she may try to keep you within her toils, without giving you a definitive answer. Permit this not to be the case—have a final and positive answer, and let it be as it may, close the matter finally with her. if favorable, Marry, and bring her on with you, if unfavorable, wish her happy, cherish her as a friend, but have it understood that hereafter you remain her friend without any other views. and I beg you my son, that you enter into no more love affairs, until you see me. You have many years yet for the improvement of your mind, and to make a Selection of a companion. Remember my son, that you are now the only solace of my mind, and prospects of my happiness here below, and were you to make an unhappy choice, it would bring me to the grave in sorrow.[26]

That Jackson himself was eager to see an end of the affair without marriage between Andrew and Flora is evidenced by the letter he wrote to Andrew a month later, when he heard that relations between the two were at an end. "I expected the result you name with Flora," he wrote Andrew, Jr., "she is a fine little girl, the daughter of my deceased friend and I esteem her much, but as I told you she has give herself up to coquettry and I warned you of the fact—treat her with

I expected the result you name with
Flora. she is a fine little girl. the daughter of
my deceased friend & I esteem her much. but as
I told you she has given herself up to coquetry
& I warned you of the fact. I feel her with all
kindness, but I assure you I am happy at the
result, as I seldom ever saw a coquett make
a good wife, & when you marry, I sincerely wish
you to marry a lady who will make a good
wife, & I a good daughter, as my happiness
depends much upon the prudence
of your choice. Therefore I am happy
you are clear of your little engagement
with Flora. and all I have to request is, that
you will engage in no other without
first obtaining my advice. I had no wish
to interfere with your choice, & particularly
when you stated, there had been some
little engagement. you know I have
counselled you from your childhood
to make no promises, or engagements,
but what you punctually perform, therefore before engagements are formed, or
promises made, it ought to be on mature
reflection, and when made religiously performed. I will only add I am happy you
are now free from all engagements

PRESIDENT ANDREW JACKSON WARNS ADOPTED SON AGAINST WILES OF COQUETTE

Jackson's adopted son became enamored of a girl named Flora. Jackson urged either an immediate marriage or a termination of the affair. Learning that the two lovers had parted, Jackson wrote: "I am happy of the result, as I seldom ever saw a coquett make a good wife." (*Papers of Andrew Jackson,* Library of Congress)

Kindness, but I assure you I am happy at the result, as I seldom ever saw a coquett make a good wife, and when you marry, if ever, I wish you to marry a lady who will make a good wife, and I, a good daughter, as my happiness depends much upon the prudence of your choice. Therefore I am happy you are clear of your little engagement with Flora, and all I have to request is, that you will engage in no other without first obtaining my advice."[27]

Several years went by before this President's son by adoption became involved in affairs of the heart regarding which any record remains. He spent part of the time at the Hermitage plantation, superintending the overseers and at other times he lived in Washington or in Philadelphia. In the latter city was his twin brother, Tom Donelson, who was later appointed a Collector of Revenue.[28] Both young men were, at birth, merely nephews of Andrew Jackson—the sons of his wife's brother—but one becoming a President's son, even though by adoption, had a career of security and ease; the other twin, by contrast, contented himself with the government post obtained for him by an indulgent uncle.

It was on one of his visits to his brother, in 1831, that Andrew met Sarah Yorke. He did not heed his foster father's injunction to consult with him before offering his affections and future to a woman; Andrew, Jr., fell in love with Sarah and told his father that she possessed every attribute of feminine worthiness. Andrew Jackson accepted his son's appraisal. Again he counseled a speedy marriage. The girl herself wrote to the President, and appears to have captivated him from the first. This time Andrew, Jr., had chosen well, and during all the remaining years of his life Andrew Jackson had reason to rejoice that, unlike the daughter of Major Smith or Flora, Sarah Yorke had definiteness of purpose and stability.

My son, I have perused with interest the letter of Sarah's which you have submitted to me. Since my heavy and irreparable bereavement in the death of my dear and ever to be lamented wife, the only object that makes life desirable to me is to see you happy and prosperous, and permanently settled in life; united to an amiable wife of respectability, one whose disposition and amiable qualities are calculated to make you happy. Your happiness will insure mine, for the few years which I can expect to live. You say that Sarah possesses every quality necessary to make you happy. The amiability of her temper and her other good qualities which you represent is a sure pledge to me that she will unite with you in adding to my comfort during my life. You will please communicate to her that you have my full and free consent that you be united in the holy bonds of matrimony; that I shall receive her as a daughter, and cherish her as my child. I find that you are engaged to each other; the sooner this engagement is Consummated the better.[29]

Andrew, Jr., did not wait. A few weeks after receiving Jackson's warm approval, he married Sarah Yorke. There were no "society reporters" in those days, and none of the Philadelphia journals described the wedding ceremony or listed the guests present. The *United States Gazette,* two days after the event, printed in the customary "Married" column a brief announcement: "Married, on Thursday evening, by the Rev. Mr. Barnes, Andrew Jackson, Esq., Son of the President of the United States, to Miss Sarah, the daughter of the late Peter Yorke, Esq. of this city." [30] Several days later an almost identical paragraph appeared in another newspaper, but Andrew was referred to as the "adopted" son of the President.[31]

It was not in keeping with Jackson's temperament to manifest his affection for his daughter-in-law merely in words. He gave her the treasured jewelry which had belonged to his beloved Rachel; he directed Andrew to remodel the Hermitage, to redecorate and recarpet any room Sarah might want for herself; he later bought for the couple a plantation near his own.[32] He hoped Sarah "in due season may present you with a fine daughter—if so, I will claim to name it Rachel." [33]

Andrew Jackson, even though deluged with Presidential tasks, found time to write letters to Sarah; they were sincere and affectionate missives. To Andrew, Jr., he wrote minute instructions about every phase of plantation activities. It was evident that Jackson had misgivings about the ability of his adopted son to manage the large estate; it was not by accident that his close friends, on trips to Tennessee, always visited the Hermitage; they sent Jackson detailed reports of talks with the overseers—the men in charge of cotton growing and farming, the women in charge of poultry, and those who looked after the cattle. And they added their own observations and opinions about the appearance and industry of the slaves, the conditions of the fences, and the crops. Andrew, Jr., then twenty-five, had begun to make purchases of land and materials on credit—and Jackson in Washington was confronted with unpaid bills and maturing promissory notes. Again and again he counseled Andrew, Jr., to delay new commitments until cash was available. "My dear Andrew, attend to my advice, it is that of a father," the harassed President pleaded, "let us economise until we are again clear of debt, then by laying up your cash from your productions, you can always purchase land or other things at a fair price." [34] Letter followed letter stressing the same theme—the avoidance of debt; despite the entreaties and the warnings, Andrew, Jr., became involved in repeated transactions, and Andrew Jackson invariably freed him from the debts.

And as his debts accumulated, the family of Andrew, Jr., continued to increase, as Sarah added to the number of her children. Throughout the years 1833 to 1835 the correspondence between Andrew Jackson and his son referred to the debts of Andrew, Jr., and the confinements of his wife. And, amid all these problems and difficulties, at the end of October, 1834, the Hermitage burned down. Andrew Jackson thought only of Sarah's distress. "Tell Sarah to cease to mourn its loss, I will have it rebuilt," he wrote the son, and he arranged to have Sarah and the children at the White House while the Hermitage was reconstructed.

The events clouded the thoughts of Andrew Jackson; he was fearful that he would soon die and that his adopted son, bearing his name, might tarnish the fame he had achieved. In April, 1835, Andrew Jackson again penned a long letter: "My dear Andrew, I have been quite unwell. . . . My son, as my life is uncertain, and we know not at what moment we may be called hence, I now address you with the fondness of a father's heart. I wish to bring to your view the situation you now, and will hereafter, occupy, that it may be a stimulant to your proper conduct in all time hereafter. It is well known that I have adopted you as my own son and you are to represent me when I am called hence. . . . Your conduct standing as my representative, the son of a President, draw upon you the eyes of the world, and the least deviation from the rules of strict decorum and propriety are observed and commented on by all our enemies, and those who envy you your situation . . . this my son, ought allways to be before your eyes." [35] The Presidential father makes reference to the dissipation and death of Andrew's cousin; he comments on the dangers of debt, and on the dishonor of broken promises.

Andrew Jackson did not die then; he lived ten years longer. And Andrew, Jr., did not end his indebtedness then; he continued to involve himself in debt throughout the remainder of his father's life—and for years thereafter. Jackson continued as President of the United

States until March, 1837; during the last half year of his term Andrew, Jr., acted as his private secretary.[36]

In the spring of 1837, after eight years in the White House, Andrew Jackson returned to Tennessee and the Hermitage. He was then seventy. For the next few years he lived at the Hermitage, resuming the role of a planter. Letters which he wrote throughout the years of his absences are proof that, no matter how deeply involved in military operations or political activities, Jackson always kept himself informed about his plantations; and the detailed instructions which he sent to Andrew, Jr., or others whom he held responsible for operations leave no doubt of his intimate knowledge of farming, cotton cultivation, stock raising, and horse breeding. Now the ex-President gave these matters his personal attention. He was happy in the midst of the family circle composed of his adopted son, and the latter's wife and children.[37] But this contentment was marred by the speculations of Andrew, Jr., whose mounting debts forced the aged Jackson to sell parts of his land and to borrow the additional funds needed to pay Andrew's notes which Jackson had endorsed, and others which Andrew himself had endorsed to accommodate a man named Ward who had become bankrupt.

The crisis came in December, 1839, less than two years after Jackson left the White House. "My son, A. Jackson, Junr, by security for Albert Ward has got himself involved, and Ward's creditors is tareing his property to pieces, by executions, principally Bank debts kept secrete from the world now made known by Judgts," he wrote to a friend.[38] To meet these obligations, forced upon him by the stupidity and speculations of his adopted son, Jackson sold cotton, and arranged also to borrow three thousand dollars. But that was not enough. Old and ailing, Andrew Jackson set out in December storms to seek loans from friends in New Orleans. Aboard a steamship on the Mississippi, "struggling in floating ice, in mists of falling snow," his only goal was to save his adopted son from debt and he wrote Andrew, "I hope for the better, and when the worst comes we must try somehow to meet, and I hope all these things will result to your benefit in the end, and be a shield to prevent you hereafter from running in debt for things useless to your comfort or prosperity or that of your family." [39] And then he pleads with his adopted son: "Recollect my son that I have taken this trip to endeavour to relieve you from present embarrassments, and if I live to realize it, I will die contented in the hope that you will never again encumber yourself with debt, that may result in the poverty of yourself and little family of so much promise and whom I so much love." [40]

From old Army comrades in New Orleans, Andrew Jackson did obtain substantial amounts; they neither asked nor needed written receipts, because they knew this ex-President never forgot his obligations. But he needed still more, and during the following spring he asked a Reverend Hardy Cryer, a clergyman who often negotiated for him, to find a buyer for a valuable tract which Jackson was willing to sell at almost half its value. He explained to Reverend Mr. Cryer why he was in need of cash: "A little imprudence has caused this necessity, and I would always sacrifice property, than the credit of my adopted son or myself. . . . I will live within my means, and my son from his paid for experience, I am sure, will never be indebted again when clear of his present difficulties. therefore my dear Sir it is that I am so solicitous to make the sacrifice and sale of the land to get him clear of debt and myself from his liabilities." [41]

Thus the years went by, alternating periods of paying off old debts and still newer obligations incurred by Andrew's desire to enlarge his own plantation. Andrew Jackson died in 1845. He left a will made two years before his death, explaining that it was necessary to change an earlier will because "since executing my will of the 30th of September 1833, my Estate has become greatly involved by my liabilities for the debts of my well beloved and adopted Son Andrew Jackson Jnr. which makes it necessary to alter the same." Parton relates that when Jackson told his life-long friend Major Lewis that he was leaving his entire estate to Andrew, Major Lewis ventured to remonstrate, and advised that a part of the property should be settled upon Sarah and her children—enough to secure them against want in case his son's speculations should continue to be unsuccessful. "No," said the General after a long pause, "that would show a want of confidence. If *she,*" pointing to the tomb of Rachel in the garden, "were alive, she would wish him to have it all, and to me her wish is law." [42] The will provided for payment of sixteen thousand dollars to friends from whom he had borrowed the funds to repay Andrew's debts, and a few minor bequests were made. The rest of his wealth he left to Andrew; and, to make his intention clear, his will stipulated:

The true intent and meaning of this my last will and testament is, that all my estate, real, personal, and mixed, is hereby first pledged for the payment of the above recited debts and interest; and when they are fully paid, the residue of all my estate, real, personal, and mixed, is hereby bequeathed to my adopted son A. Jackson, Jr., with the exceptions hereafter named, to him and his heirs forever.

. . . .

Lastly, I appoint my adopted son, Andrew Jackson, Jr., my whole and sole executor to this my last will and testament, and direct that no security be required of him for the faithful execution and discharge of the trusts hereby reposed in him.

The estate which Andrew Jackson, Jr., inherited was very large; it was variously estimated by the press as comprising between five hundred and a thousand acres in Tennessee,[43] and a fine cotton plantation on the Mississippi River.[44] But Andrew could not repress his habits of speculating; in the words of the Nashville *Dispatch*, "shortly after the death of Jackson, young Andrew launched his bark on the troubled waters of the world, and gradually exhausted his fortune." [45] At one time he opened up an iron works near the mouth of the Cumberland River; he risked and lost a substantial sum in working lead mines in Tennessee. "Through some cause or other, he failed in every business in which he engaged," concluded the Nashville newspaper which reviewed his career. Andrew Jackson, Jr., lacked the agricultural knowledge of his foster father as well as the business acumen which had enabled the unlettered President to acquire the large plantations and to produce the profitable crops. After the fertile lands were willed to Andrew, Jr., "the worms ate his cotton, the river flooded his plantations." [46] He became desperate for money, first mortgaged his slaves and then drove them off in the dead of night to sell them down South. Finally he sold the plantation in Mississippi, possibly in fulfilling a promise made to his foster father a few months before the latter's death, when Andrew Jackson wrote of Andrew, "I have his positive pledge, if I am taken away, he will do it." [47] And he also disposed of the Tennessee land to a farmer; finally, he sold the Hermitage and the surrounding ground to the State of Tennessee, but he retained the right to live in the mansion. What Andrew Jackson two decades previously had anticipated and feared became a reality: "The industry, economy and energy of Mr. A. Jackson Jnr. may fail to succeed." [48]

Andrew survived the ex-President for twenty years, residing quietly at the place where he spent almost all his years. In the Civil War he remained "neutral," although one of his sons, fighting for the Southern cause,[49] died upon the battlefield, and another—also named Andrew Jackson—rose to the rank of brigadier general in the Confederate army. In April, 1865, Andrew returned from hunting near the Hermitage; as he was climbing over a fence, his gun was accidentally discharged, and his hand was filled with shot. Lockjaw set in, and he died within a week. A correspondent of the New York *Times,* visiting the Hermitage a few months after his death, reported that the adopted son of President Andrew Jackson had been regarded favorably by his neighbors.[50] But only one newspaper in adjoining Nashville noticed the death of this "President's son."

References and Explanatory Notes

Notes on Foreword

1. Thus, in defining what should constitute Lincoln bibliography, there are included "all printed books and pamphlets dealing principally with Abraham Lincoln, his ancestry, his wife, children, stepmother, and sister" (Paul M. Angle: "Lincoln Bibliography," *Lincoln Quarterly,* June, 1941), but deliberately and specifically excluding material relating to the individual career of Robert T. Lincoln—the only son of Abraham Lincoln who lived long enough to provide a basis for appraising the influence of the exalted place of his father. Another example may be cited: Truslow Adams in nearly five hundred pages of his admirable *The Adams Family,* although including John Quincy Adams and Charles Francis Adams, devotes but a hundred words to all the other sons of the second and sixth Presidents.

2. Franklin Pierce had fathered three sons, but all of them died in childhood before the father became President of the United States. James Buchanan was a bachelor. The other Presidents without sons were: Thomas Jefferson, James Madison, James Monroe, James K. Polk, William McKinley, Woodrow Wilson, and Warren G. Harding. Some of these were childless. Andrew Jackson, as noted in the final chapter of this volume, adopted a son; an unfounded myth also ascribed to George Washington the adoption of a son.

3. Particularly, the sons of the twenty-seventh President and of the thirty-second President—the Tafts and the Roosevelts—continued to be in the public eye.

Sons of John Adams

(Pages 1 to 29)

1. *Writings of John Adams.*

2. John Quincy Adams: *Life of John Adams,* Vol. 1, pp. 84-85.

3. *Lives of Celebrated Women,* by Author of *Peter Parley's Tales,* 1844, p. 53.

4. *Familiar Letters of John Adams and His Wife,* 7 July, 1774.

5. Rev. T. Sharp: *The Heavenly Sisters,* 1822.

6. Thomas Jefferson, even after Abigail Adams had told him of her lingering resentment because of the mistaken belief that he had deprived her son of a Federal appointment wrote her: "Neither my estimate of your character, nor the esteem founded in that, has ever been lessened for a single moment." (*Writings of Thomas Jefferson,* Vol. XI, p. 50. Letter of Sept. 17, 1804.)

7. John Quincy Adams: *supra,* Vol. I, p. 42.

8. *Ibid.,* Vol. I, pp. 84-85. After he had retired from the Presidency, John Adams reflected that family prestige and not merely ability was the factor in political successes. "In theory, all governments profess to regard merit alone," he wrote to a friend, "but in practice, democratical government certainly regards it as little as any." (*Correspondence between Hon. John Adams and William Cunningham, Esq.,* 1821. Letter of Feb. 24, 1804.)

9. *Letters of John Adams Addressed to His Wife,* 15 April, 1776.

10. *Ibid.,* 3 December, 1775.

11. *Ibid.,* Philadelphia, 8 October, 1776.

12. *Ibid.,* Yorktown, 25 October, 1777.

13. *Ibid.,* 17 February, 1778.

14. *Letters of Abigail Adams.*

15. *Ibid.,* Letter clxxxiii, 1780, and others.

16. *Ibid.,* Letter clxviii, L'Orient, 14 May, 1779.

17. John Quincy Adams to George Bancroft, March 31, 1838. The original letter, now in the New York Public Library, was printed in the *Bulletin of the New York Public Library,* X, pp. 249-50.

18. John Quincy Adams to Abigail Adams, Sept., 1787. Massachusetts Historical Society, Vol. XVI, 2nd series, p. 358.

19. John Quincy Adams: *Diary,* Massachusetts Historical Society, Vol. XVI, 2nd series, pp. 363-64.

20. *Ibid.,* p. 37. If we are to believe reports published after the death of Adams, he came to love Miss Frazier. A writer for the Newburyport *Herald,* in 1864, told of an interview he had with the aged John Quincy Adams while the latter lingered at his Congressional desk at the close of a session; Adams was quoted as confiding to the writer from the town

where he lived as a law student, "What I have never before uttered within the sound of human ears, that in all which constitutes genuine beauty, loveliness, personal accomplishments, intellectual endowments, and perfect purity in life and heart, Miss Mary Frazier excelled them all. I loved her then . . . I love her memory now." (Newburyport, Mass., *Daily Herald,* June 30, 1864.)

21. *Ibid.,* p. 365.

22. *Ibid.,* p. 382.

23. *Ibid.,* p. 352.

24. *Ibid.,* p. 421.

25. *Ibid.,* p. 338.

26. John Adams to John Quincy Adams, Jan. 23, 1788. Massachusetts Historical Society, Vol. XVI, 2nd series, p. 410.

27. *Writings of John Quincy Adams,* ed. by Ford, Vol. VII, p. 299.

28. John Quincy Adams to Thomas B. Adams, Feb. 1, 1792. Massachusetts Historical Society, Vol. IV, 2nd series, pp. 61-65.

29. John Adams to Wm. Cunningham, Jr., Oct. 15, 1805. *Correspondence between Hon. John Adams and William Cunningham, Esq.,* 1823, p. 35.

30. Abigail Adams, anticipating her husband's election to the Presidency, had written to her son not to expect any appointment under his father. His pride stung that his mother should deem him capable of wanting favors from his father, John Quincy replied: "I hope, my dear and honoured mother, that you are fully convinced from my letters . . . that upon the contingency of my father's being placed in the first magistry, I shall never give him any trouble by solicitation for office of any kind." (John Quincy Adams: *Memoirs,* Vol. I, p. 194.) John Quincy Adams asserted that his success was due to his own ability and efforts. (*Bulletin of the New York Public Library,* X, p. 249.)

31. Washington to John Adams, Library of Congress, Feb. 20, 1797. The letter was made known by John Adams in 1808, to prove that George Washington held a high opinion of John Quincy and also felt indebted to him for his aid in the Genêt episode. Wrote John Adams to Cunningham: "The letter of General Washington would have remained in obscurity forever . . . had not a mean vengeance been hurled on the subject of it [J. Q. Adams], for no other offence than his sterling integrity." (*Correspondence, supra,* p. 42, Nov. 7, 1808.) Washington also wrote a letter direct to John Quincy commending his ability. (*Writings of Washington,* Vol. 35, p. 394. Letter of June 25, 1797.)

32. *London Marriage Licenses, 1521–1869,* compiled by Joseph Foster, London, 1887.

33. *Memoirs* of John Quincy Adams, Vol. I, p. 199.

34. An example is Adams' attachment to the theater. While in Washington he went so frequently to see plays that Louisa asked him why. He replied to his wife: "You ask me why I frequent the theater . . . because I have all my life had a very extravagant fondness for that species of entertainment. . . . Perhaps this is news to you, after more than twenty-

five years of marriage. It is nevertheless true." (*Writings of John Quincy Adams,* ed. by Ford, Vol. VII, p. 298. Letter to Louisa Adams, Aug. 28, 1822.)

35. It has been said that John Quincy was recalled as Minister to Prussia for the sole reason that the retiring President did not want his son to continue under the Administration of the incoming President, Thomas Jefferson. This is not borne out by the note which John Adams wrote to his Secretary of State, John Marshall, directing him to prepare the recall documents. John Adams told Marshall, "It is my opinion this minister ought to be recalled from Prussia. Justice would require that he should be sent to France or England, if he should be continued in Europe." Since these two posts were already filled, John Adams ends with, "Besides, it is my opinion that it is my duty to call him home." (John Adams to John Marshall, Jan. 31, 1801. *Writings, supra,* Vol. II, p. 498.)

36. *Writings of Thomas Jefferson,* Vol. XI, p. 50.

37. Josiah Quincy: *History of Harvard University,* Vol. II, p. 291.

38. The leading historians have described the political ferment of this epoch. An interesting description may be read in John B. McMaster: *History of the People of the United States,* Vol. V, pp. 55-81. Of course, Henry Clay and his adherents played the decisive role in the final choice of Adams; intriguing sidelights of the political manipulations are detailed in William Ernest Smith: *The Francis Preston Blair Family in Politics,* Vol. I.

39. The Twelfth Amendment to the Constitution, proposed by Congress on December 9, 1803; ratification by three-fourths of the states was announced by Secretary of State Madison on September 25, 1804. Until the adoption of Amendment XII, the method of choosing a President by the House of Representatives was provided for in the original Article II, Section I, of the Constitution. Both under the original Article and under the Amendment, the choice was by states, each state having one vote—the majority of each delegation deciding for whom the state vote was cast; however, until the Constitution was amended, the choice by the House was from the five highest instead of the three highest.

40. James G. Blaine, in his *Twenty Years of Congress,* commented that "no other man in the country has held so many great places as Martin Van Buren." (Blaine: *Twenty Years of Congress,* Vol. I, p. 85.) It is surprising that Blaine overlooked the career of John Quincy Adams, who held a greater number of important posts—and was even appointed to the Supreme Court of the United States, an honor which he declined.

41. John Quincy Adams asserted that the opposition to himself had its origin in the animosities which had been held against his father. Writing to the historian George Bancroft, he asserted, "In considering the causes of hostility which has pursued *me* throughout my political life, you will find much of it hereditary hatred of a tory progeny against my father." (John Quincy Adams to George Bancroft, 25 Oct., 1835. (*Bulletin of the New York Public Library,* X, p. 248.)

42. Boston *Independent Chronicle and Patriot,* April 8, 1829.

43. Boston *Journal,* Feb. 25, 1848. But there were other journals which did not share the opinion that succeeding generations would view John Quincy Adams more favorably than did his own. Typical of these was the Boston *Statesman,* always antagonistic to the Adams Administration, which said at the end of his Presidential term: "Mr. Adams affects to believe that posterity will acquit him. It must be the posterity of a very distant age, so distant as to be wholly unacquainted with his conduct, that shall pass a favorable judgment upon him. But posterity will be more severe upon him than his contemporaries." (Boston *Statesman,* April 9, 1829.)

44. Bryce: *The American Commonwealth,* Vol. II, Ch. LXXIV.

45. *Memoirs* of John Quincy Adams, Vol. VIII, p. 105.

46. *Ibid.,* Vol. VIII, p. 450.

47. Bryce: *supra,* Vol. I, Ch. VIII.

48. Julia Gardiner Tyler: *Reminiscences.* His bald head was the theme of many newspaper reporters. "Our attention is now attracted to a ray of light that glistens on the apex of a bald and noble head," wrote the correspondent of the Washington *Democratic Review,* "it proceeds from the wonderful man who in his person combines agitator, poet, philosopher, statesman, critic, and orator—John Quincy Adams." (October, 1837.)

49. McMaster: *History of the People of the United States,* Vol. VII, pp. 52-53. The tricky efforts of his opponents, luring him into the presentation of a petition from slaves, may be found in the report of the Massachusetts Anti-Slavery Society, 1838.

50. J. Q. Adams to Edmund Quincy, 28 July, 1838, Washington *Chronicle,* Aug. 7, 1838.

51. A typical example may be read in the *National Intelligencer* of Washington, Feb. 20, 1847.

52. New York *Journal of Commerce,* Jan. 23, 1848.

53. Bloodletting was prevalent for centuries in America as in Europe, recognized as a "cure" by physicians almost up to the twentieth century. It was assumed that ailments were caused by "bad blood"; *ergo,* the remedy was to drain off the cause of the malady. Barbers or "surgeons" made incisions in the veins, covered the opening with a glass cup, pressed down to obtain a vacuum. Leeches were also used as blood-suckers; Swedish leeches, particularly, were advertised for sale "wholesale and retail" to the end of the Civil War. (Medical advertisements in New Orleans *Times,* May 7, 1865.) Similar advertisements appeared much earlier in many American newspapers, praising leeches imported from other European countries; in 1828 one Samuels Clark in Washington informed "friends and the public" not only that he was recommended by prominent physicians as efficient in "cupping and bloodletting" but that he also had for sale "a good supply of Portuguese leeches." (*United States Telegraph,* Feb. 7, 1828.) A rival Dr. Gurand had "several hundred foreign leeches, which he offers for sale, by the dozen or more." John Quincy Adams was not the only ex-President whose life was shortened by "cupping" or bloodletting; George Washington's end was hastened in the same manner. Marshall records that "believing bloodletting to be necessary, he procured a

bleeder who took from his arm twelve or fourteen ounces of blood." (Marshall: *Life of Washington,* Vol. V, p. 361.) The effect of this procedure, as viewed by modern medical science, has been discussed in the *Virginia Medical Monthly,* January, 1927. (Dr. Walter A. Wells: "Last Illness and Death of George Washington.") The public was so accustomed to bloodletting as the salvation of ailing humans that the eminent physicians who attended President William Henry Harrison when he was stricken in March, 1841, issued a bulletin explaining why they did not apply this accepted remedy; said the five Washington doctors who signed the report of the President's death, "The age and debility of the patient, with the immediate prostration, forbade a resort to general bloodletting." (Richmond *Enquirer,* April 9, 1841.)

54. New York *Tribune,* March 8, 1848.

55. Lossing: *Field Book of the Revolution,* Vol. II, p. 66.

56. Boston *Advertiser,* Feb. 29, 1848.

57. London *Times,* March 28, 1848.

58. Outstanding works on John Adams and John Quincy Adams (such as *The Adams Family,* by James Truslow Adams) devote two or three sentences to the two younger sons. No encyclopedia makes mention of them; and, as will be seen, obituaries in newspapers were limited to a phrase or a sentence.

59. *Familiar Letters of John Adams and His Wife,* 10 Dec., 1779.

60. *Ibid.,* John Adams to Abigail Adams, 11 Dec., 1779.

61. *Works of John Adams,* Vol. III, p. 269.

62. Abigail Adams to John Adams, 7 Dec., 1781.

63. Massachusetts Historical Society, Vol. XVI, p. 377.

64. Alma M. Bevis: *Diets and Riots, An Interpretation of the History of Harvard College,* p. 85. In her intriguing little volume Miss Bevis describes the frequent gatherings of the protesting students under the "Rebellion Tree" on the college campus. In 1805 the student body took an oath not to continue with classes unless better bread and butter was served; two years later there was a rebellion against spoiled soup. Various classes had grievances of their own, and staged what in our day would be called "strikes"; in 1792 the Freshmen declared all men equal and refused to doff their hats to Seniors as had been the long-established custom. (Alfred K. Moe: *History of Harvard,* p. 62.)

65. Josiah Quincy: *History of Harvard,* pp. 279-83.

66. *Diary,* Sept. 6, 1787.

67. In editing the diary of John Quincy Adams (published as *Memoirs*) the son Charles Francis Adams omitted numerous entries which referred to family affairs. Some of the omitted portions were later published by the Massachusetts Historical Society, but still the references to Charles have remained deleted.

68. In contrast, at other times, the newspapers did record the travels of John Adams and of his wife. For example, three months after the death of Charles, the Philadelphia *Gazette* and other journals noted that "Mrs. Adams, the Lady of the President of the United States, arrived in this city yesterday evening, on her way to Massachusetts." (Philadelphia *Gazette of the United States,* Feb. 18, 1801.)

69. *Works of John Adams,* Vol. IX, p. 577.

70. *Ibid.,* Vol. IX, p. 578, John Adams to Elbridge Gerry, 30 Dec., 1800.

71. *Ibid.,* p. 581, John Adams to Thomas Jefferson, 24 March, 1801.

72. *Letters of Abigail Adams,* 11 Feb., 1795.

73. "Berlin and the Prussian Court of 1798." *Journal of Thomas Boylston Adams.*

74. *Bulletin of the New York Public Library,* XIX, pp. 833-35.

75. John Adams to Abigail Adams, 4 Feb., 1799. *Letters of John Adams Addressed to His Wife.*

76. "Letters of Thomas Boylston Adams," American Antiquarian Society, 21 May, 1799.

77. *Ibid.,* Letter of 16 June, 1799, p. 92.

78. Thomas B. Adams to William Smith Shaw, 29 July, 1799. Edited by Charles G. Washburn, American Antiquarian Society, Vol. N.S. 27, pp. 101-02.

79. *Ibid.,* 20 Sept. 1801, pp. 158-59.

80. *Ibid.,* Dec. 2, 1800.

81. *Ibid.,* April 5, 1801, p. 149.

82. Boston *Columbian Centinel,* Aug. 30, 1806.

83. Notes of Rev. John Pierce of Phi Beta Kappa Meetings, Massachusetts Historical Society, Vol. IX, 2nd Series, pp. 112-13.

84. Prominent historical treatises and less serious works have asserted that Thomas Boylston Adams was Chief Justice of the highest court of Massachusetts. Thus, in the *Bulletin of the New York Public Library,* prefacing his diary, it is stated, "From 1809 to 1811 he was Chief Justice of the Supreme Court of Massachusetts." (*Bulletin of the New York Public Library,* XIX, p. 804.) Similarly, in a typical biography of Abigail Adams, it is said, "And Thomas . . . became a judge and was to rise to the highest bench in his State." (Dorothea Bobbé: *Abigail Adams,* p. 312.) Such statements are erroneous. As demonstrated by Charles G. Washburn in a study of Massachusetts courts, Thomas B. Adams served in an inferior court. (Worcester American Antiquarian Society.)

85. Boston *Evening Gazette,* March 17, 1832; similarly, although the *Daily Advertiser and Patriot* of March 14, 1832, devotes a paragraph to the drowning of an intoxicated man and an equal amount of space to a lost child found dead, the reference to the youngest son of the ex-President was noted in a single line: "Died, in Quincy, 12th inst. Hon. Thomas B. Adams."

86. John Adams to Samuel Adams, May 4, 1784.

Sons of John Quincy Adams

(Pages 30 to 49)

1. John Quincy Adams: *Memoirs,* May 11, 1807.

2. *Ibid.,* Vol. V, p. 219.

3. George completed his classical studies at Harvard in February, 1818. At that epoch in our colleges several citizens were required to sign a bond for prospective graduates before they were permitted to take the final examination. Thomas Boylston Adams, the brother of John Quincy Adams, was one of George's bondsmen. (T. B. Adams to William Shaw, Feb. 10, 1818. American Antiquarian Society, Vol. N.S. 27, p. 176.)

4. *Memoirs, supra,* Vol. VII, pp. 128-32.

5. Newspapers referred to the *Benjamin Franklin* variously as a "steamboat," "steamship," "steam packet," or "packet boat." Only twelve years had elapsed since Robert Fulton proved the practicability of utilizing steam in water navigation; sailing ships were still crossing the ocean. On its return trip to Providence, after the drowning of George W. Adams, the *Benjamin Franklin* accomplished the shortest passage from New York—15¼ hours, shorter by 17 minutes than any previous record. (New York *Evening Courier,* May 5, 1829.)

6. New York *Journal of Commerce,* May 1, 1829.

7. New York *Evening Courier,* May 1, 1829; Washington *Intelligencer,* May 4, 1829; Nantucket (Mass.) *Enquirer,* May 9, 1829; Washington *National Journal,* May 4, 1829. It is difficult to determine what portions of these reports were the result of original investigation or interviews, and what part merely reprints from the New York journals. That many of the out-of-town papers, as was prevalent at that period, copied the first account is evidenced by the recurrent misspelling of the word "berth" as "birth."

8. New York *Commercial,* April 30, 1829.

9. Baltimore *Republican and Commercial Advertiser,* May 4, 1829.

10. *Ibid.,* June 15, 1829.

11. *Memoirs, supra,* Vol. VII, pp. 159-60.

12. Letter of J. Q. Adams to Charles F. Adams, Sept. 3, 1876. See George F. Hoar: *Autobiography of Seventy Years,* II, p. 147.

13. *Memoirs, supra,* July 30, 1825.

14. *Ibid.,* Vol. VII, pp. 508-9.

15. Russell Jarvis was the most conspicuous and outspoken foe of the Adams Administration in the Capital. He had his fingers in many political pies. The virulent attacks of his own pen he supplemented with cullings from other antagonistic editors who vied with each other in the vocabulary of abuse. As co-owner of a Washington newspaper—the *United States Telegraph* —he had an effective medium for his polemics. To his editorial functions he

added the lucrative role of printing Congressional documents. He also "solicited and prosecuted claims and accounts against the United States Government" (*United States Telegraph,* Feb. 4, 1838), and his advertisement catalogued many services he could render in obtaining speedy settlements for his clients. In this venture he had as a partner one Joseph Watson who, under his own name, also operated a separate agency, with a branch in Columbus, Ohio, representing claimants for Western lands. It appears that, despite the antagonism of the Administration, which he attacked so vigorously, Jarvis had close contacts in some Federal bureaus, and he functioned in the same manner as the professional lobbyists of our own day.

16. Boston *Statesman,* April 22, 1828.

17. New York *Enquirer,* April 29, 1828.

18. Rutland (Vt.) *Herald,* April 22, 1828. Newspapers friendly to the President invariably charged that his private secretary was assaulted because he was a member of the President's family. Typical of this contention was the comment of a Cincinnati paper that "the person assaulted was *the President's son,* and it is most probable that this relationship was the principal inducement to perpetrate the outrage." (*Daily Gazette,* April 29, 1828.)

19. Boston *Statesman,* April 22, 1828.

20. The politically-wise Salem *Observer* called the affair a "disgraceful transaction," but anticipated that the majority of the committee would oppose punishment of Jarvis. (Salem, Mass., *Observer,* May 26, 1828.)

21. In his written statement to the Committee John admitted that he had said, "There is a man who, if he held my idea of propriety in the conduct of a gentleman, ought not to show his face in this house." (Baltimore *Patriot,* June 13, 1828.)

22. House of Representatives, May 16, 1828.

23. *National Intelligencer,* June 17, 1829. John engaged in some business enterprises which proved unsuccessful.

24. *Memoirs, supra,* Vol. II, p. 327.

25. Brooks Adams: *Charles Francis Adams.*

26. *Ibid.*

27. *Memoirs, supra,* Vol. V, p. 219.

28. *Ibid.,* p. 220.

29. Brooks Adams: *Charles Francis Adams,* p. 224. Some newspapers criticised Charles Francis Adams for his publication of his father's memoirs, asserting that it was unfilial to divulge the lack of complete happiness in his father's marital life. Said the New York *World,* in its two-column editorial, "This may be very honest, but it is not agreeable, and we do not exactly see how the son should care to put it in print." (New York *World,* Aug. 17, 1874.)

30. C. F. Adams: *Reflections upon the Present State of the Currency.*

31. "In theory, all governments profess to regard merit alone, but in practice, democratical governments certainly regard it as little as any." (John Adams to Wm. Cunningham, Jr., Feb. 24, 1804. *Correspondence between Hon. John Adams and Wm. Cunningham, Esq.,* 1823.)

32. Probably he observed that the deaths in 1830 and 1832 of his father's brothers were scarcely noted in the press. Political animosities were intense, and extended to the families of those who held public office. Thus, when the wife of President Andrew Jackson died some papers would not even print the news. When the brother of Charles Francis Adams fell overboard, a leading Baltimore paper editorially referred to the ungenerous attitude of the partisan press at the passing of Mrs. Jackson, and expressed the hope that the journals would not yield to similar bitterness in withholding sympathy from the father, John Quincy Adams. (Baltimore *Republican,* April 2, 1829.)

33. *Charles F. Adams,* by his son, p. 44.

34. McMaster: *History of the People of the United States,* Vol. VII, pp. 548-49.

35. *Diary of James K. Polk,* Chicago Historical Society's Collection, Vol. VI, p. 67.

36. New York *Evening Post,* July 21, 1851.

37. "What Makes Slavery a Question of National Concern?" Lecture delivered at New York, Jan. 30, 1855, pp. 44-48.

38. Said the ex-slave, Frederick Douglass: "Such men as . . . Charles Francis Adams . . . men whose courage had been equal to all other emergencies—bent before this Southern storm, and were ready to purchase peace at any price." (*Life and Times of Frederick Douglass,* p. 365.)

39. *Harper's Weekly,* April 20, 1861.

40. London *Daily News,* Nov. 23, 1886.

41. James Ford Rhodes: *History of the Civil War,* p. 77.

42. George F. Hoar: *Autobiography of Seventy Years,* Vol. II, p. 131.

43. London *Daily News,* Nov. 23, 1886.

44. London *Morning Post,* Dec. 5, 1861.

45. *Ibid.*

46. London *Globe,* Nov. 27, 1861.

47. London *Times,* Nov. 29, 1861.

48. *Ibid.*

49. London *Globe,* Nov. 28, 1861.

50. *Ibid.,* Nov. 29, 1861.

51. Willis Fletcher Johnson: *America's Foreign Relations,* Vol. II, p. 23.

52. The New York *Times,* in an impartial appraisal after a lapse of two decades, attributed his success both to his own ability and to his prestige as a son and grandson of Presidents; its verdict was that "it is doubtful if any other American in that post at that time could have done as much and as well. . . . Nor did his lineage and his quiet pride count for nothing. His grandfather and his father had not only been Presidents of the Union, but the one had signed the treaty that closed the Revolution, the other the treaty that ended the war of 1812. It was a title of nobility no English minister could ignore." (New York *Times,* Nov. 22, 1886.)

53. *The Crisis,* May 6, 1863.

54. Willis F. Johnson: *America's Foreign Relations,* Vol. II, p. 77.

55. Adam Badeau: *Grant in Peace.*

56. Boston *Transcript,* May 24, 1886.
57. London *Mail,* May 24, 1886.
58. New York *World,* April 20, 1872.
59. Brooklyn *Daily Eagle,* April 25, 1872.
60. Springfield (Mass.) *Republican,* Nov. 23, 1886.
61. Charles Francis Adams to David A. Wells, April 18, 1872. Cincinnati *Enquirer,* April 25, 1872.
62. Brooklyn *Daily Eagle,* April 25, 1872.
63. Cincinnati *Enquirer,* April 25, 1872.
64. *Ibid.,* May 4, 1872.
65. *Ibid.*
66. After his installation as vice-president of the Massachusetts Historical Society, Charles Francis Adams invited the members to his home, and the official report of the meeting recorded that the occasion was enjoyable.
67. Springfield (Mass.) *Republican,* Nov. 23, 1886.
68. Boston *Transcript,* Nov. 22, 1886.
69. Boston *Post,* Nov. 22, 1886.
70. London *Mail,* Nov. 24, 1886.
71. London *Times,* Nov. 24, 1886.
72. Boston *Transcript,* May 24, 1886.

Sons of the Little Magician

(Pages 50 to 72)

1. Said the astute, matter-of-fact Scotchman, Colonel McKenzie, who became acquainted with all the American politicians: "If Martin Van Buren is the magician they call him, he is a singular one, for he makes no flourishes with strange sounds; draws no magic circles on the floor; nor does he open any wizard's book to read his own fate or that of others. He casts his horoscope from the returns of votes, and makes his calculations from probable changes. Such a man is a politician, hard to be met, for he is wary and ready for any emergency." (Nashville *Republican,* Feb. 28, 1835.) That Van Buren was "wary" in expressing unconsidered opinions on political themes was noted by all those who met him, otherwise he talked with animation and interest. We have an earlier description of him in a Washington paper: "He entered into conversation with a great deal of freedom and ease. He was small in stature. There was great neatness in his person. *His remarks were made with caution.*" (Washington *Chronicle,* April 4, 1829.)
2. Title page of David Crockett's *The Life of Martin Van Buren,* 1835.
3. John Quincy Adams: *Memoirs,* April 4, 1829.
4. *Americana,* Vol. 25, pp. 411-20.

5. *Childe Martin: An Epic Poem.*

6. Martin Van Buren himself was very proud of his phenomenal success in politics. Looking back upon his career at the age of 71, he asserted in his *Autobiography* that no other man "without the aid of powerful family connexions . . . had been elevated by his countrymen to a succession of official trusts, not exceeded perhaps, either in number, in dignity, or in responsibility by any that have been committed to the hands of one man—consisting of the respective offices of Surrogate of his County, State Senator, Attorney General of the State of New York, Regent of the University, Member of a Convention to revise the Constitution of the State, Governor of the State, Senator in Congress for two terms, Secretary of State of the United States, Minister to England, Vice-President, and President of the United States." (*Autobiography,* Chapter I.) It is to be noted that, although President Jackson nominated Martin Van Buren Minister to England, the Senate refused to confirm and, consequently, Van Buren was never legally our Minister. James G. Blaine, in his *Twenty Years of Congress,* forgetting the career of John Quincy Adams, comments that "no other man in the country has held so many great places" as Martin Van Buren. (Blaine: *Twenty Years of Congress,* Vol. I, p. 85.)

7. Parton, in his exhaustive biography of Jackson, described Peggy as "a witty, pretty, saucy, active tavern-keeper's daughter who makes free with the inmates of her father's house and is made free with by them." (Parton: *Life of Jackson,* Ch. 17.)

8. John Quincy Adams: *Memoirs,* Vol. VIII, pp. 356-57. The observations of Adams, a stern moralist and a bitter political opponent of Jackson, cannot be accepted as a conclusive unbiased verdict on Peggy O'Neal. However, the student may find abundant material in contemporary records to justify even a harsher opinion than was expressed by the historian Parton.

9. Both having entered political life in Tennessee, Jackson regarded Eaton as the most loyal among all his friends. In 1824, Jackson wrote to his nephew: "My friend Eaton has acted like a friend; he is worthy of, and shall receive my warmest gratitude so long as I live." (*Correspondence of Andrew Jackson.* Jackson to Andrew Donelson, Feb. 2, 1824.) Eaton, too, wrote the first biography of General Jackson, and the booklet was published widely as a campaign document. The newspapers which supported Jackson in his several campaigns for the Presidency invariably devoted space to the activities of John Eaton; and his marriage to Peggy O'Neal was noted in journals which seldom made mention of such events. For instance, the Boston *Columbian Centinel,* as did numerous other papers, printed, "Married, in Washington City, on the evening of New Year's day, the Hon. John H. Eaton, Senator from Tennessee, and biographer of Genl. Jackson, to Mrs. Margaret Timberlake, widow of the late Purser T. of the navy." (Boston *Columbian Centinel,* Jan. 10, 1829.)

10. Adams: *supra,* Vol. VIII, p. 184. The correspondence between Jackson and Martin Van Buren makes references to these slights. (Martin Van Buren: *Autobiography,* Chapter XXVI.)

11. John C. Calhoun: *Works,* Vol. VI, Appendix, p. 438.

12. *Ibid.,* p. 439. John C. Calhoun explained that he set down his opinions because he foresaw that the affair would remain a much discussed theme in after years.

13. William M. Meigs: *Life of John C. Calhoun,* Vol. I, p. 383. In retrospect, Martin Van Buren, who played such an important role in the episode, referred to it as the "Eaton imbroglio," commenting that it was "an affair . . . which . . . exerted perhaps a more injurious influence upon the management of public affairs than could be ascribed to any of the disturbing questions of the period of which I write." (*Autobiography,* Chapter XXVI, p. 339.)

14. *Correspondence of Andrew Jackson.* Endorsement of letter from Gen. Call, April 28, 1829. (Vol. IV, p. 29.)

15. Andrew Jackson had married Rachel Donelson Robards in the mistaken belief that she had been legally divorced. A detailed account of the involved divorce proceedings, and Jackson's second marriage to Rachel, will be found in *General Jackson's Lady,* by Mary French Caldwell, pp. 156-57.

16. *Correspondence, supra.* Letter to Mary Eastin, Vol. IV, p. 186.

17. Peggy also outlived her second husband; and, in the 23 years of this last widowhood, she continued to retain her beauty and to remain an interesting subject for newspaper writers. (New York *World,* Sept. 20, 1868; and other papers.) She returned to Washington and, in 1873, dictated an autobiography, asserting that she had been a model of chastity, that her mother had been a sister of a New Jersey governor, that her father had been educated and wealthy. The penned manuscript remained unpublished for sixty years; in 1932 it was printed in book form by Charles Scribner's Sons (*The Autobiography of Peggy Eaton.*) The original manuscript is in the Library of Congress at Washington.

18. Both Peggy and her husband later turned against Andrew Jackson, and he bitterly reflected that "never did I so much regret the ingratitude and depravity of man, more than I have the course of Major Eaton." (*Correspondence of Andrew Jackson.* Jackson to Amos Kendall, May 15, 1841.) Martin Van Buren recorded that Jackson turned to the wall the portrait of Eaton which had hung in the drawing room at the Hermitage. (Martin Van Buren: *Autobiography,* Chapter XXVI, p. 365.)

19. Martin Van Buren to Andrew Jackson, Jan. 13, 1832. Bassett: *Correspondence of Andrew Jackson,* Vol. IV, p. 397.

20. "My family," Martin Van Buren noted in his *Autobiography,* "was from Holland, without a single intermarriage with one of different extraction from the time of the arrival of the first emigrant to that of the marriage of my eldest son, embracing a period of over two centuries and including six generations."

21. Powell: *List of Officers of Army of the United States.*

22. General Order No. 59, Adjutant General's Office, Aug. 29, 1837.

23. *Autobiography,* p. 402. Martin Van Buren was in error. At that time Abraham held a captain's commission in the First Dragoons. (Powell: *List of Officers of Army of the United States.*)

24. *Ibid.*

25. Lynch: *An Epoch and A Man,* p. 400.

26. On the same day, and for gallantry in the same engagements, another West Point graduate was raised to similar rank—Robert E. Lee. (Powell: *List of Officers, supra.*)

27. New York *Herald,* March 18, 1873.

28. *History of the State of New York,* edited by Alexander C. Flick, New York State Historical Association, Vol. VII, Chapters VI and VII.

29. The derelictions of John Van Buren were by no means the worst among Yale's students during that period; that intemperance and riotous activities were rampant is attested in the University report, *Two Centuries of Christian Activities at Yale.* (Ed. by James B. Reynolds and others, 1901.) For example, encounters between "college bullies" and sailors were so frequent that a Committee on Seamen was organized to end the altercations. During John's last two years at Yale a religious movement was vigorously pressed by the students of the Yale Theological School, resulting in "the conversion of very wicked young men." (*Two Centuries of Christian Activities at Yale,* pp. 80-82.) John Van Buren graduated with the class of 1828, being one of the 82 who received the degree of Bachelor of Arts. (*Catalog of Officers and Graduates of Yale University, 1701–1915,* pp. 110-11.)

30. *Autobiography,* p. 445.

31. Speech of Charles Ogle, House of Representatives, April 14, 1840.

32. David McAdam: *History of Bench and Bar of New York.*

33. Lynch: *An Epoch and A Man,* p. 339.

34. *Van Buren Papers,* Library of Congress, April 29, 1838.

35. "Court Circular," which appeared in the London *Chronicle,* July 26, 1838; with slight variations in the description, an account of the brilliant function was published also in the London *Times* of the same date.

36. *Congressional Record,* April 14, 1840.

37. David McAdam, in his *History of Bench and Bar of New York,* attributes the nickname to an episode during an earlier sojourn in London, explaining that "at a court ball he danced with Princess Victoria," a circumstance which fastened upon him the popular title "Prince John." While the sobriquet "Prince John" is particularly identified with John Van Buren and during his lifetime was applied solely to him, he was not the first President's son to whom the title was appended. The enemies of John Quincy Adams used the term in newspaper attacks on the latter's son and secretary, young John Adams. We find this appellation very frequently in prominent journals of that period which devoted most of their columns to political discussions, such as the New York *Enquirer* and Boston *Statesman* (May 1, 1828).

38. *Diary of James K. Polk,* Chicago Historical Society's Collection, Vol. IV, pp. 245-46, 19 December, 1848.

39. John Bigelow: *Retrospections of An Active Life.*

40. *Congressional Globe,* 27th Congress, 1st Session, Vol. 10, p. 1.

41. *Ibid.,* p. 180.

42. *Ibid.,* Appendix, pp. 145-46.

43. *Congressional Globe,* 27th Congress, 2nd Session, Vol. 10, pp. 658, 693, 262, 279.

44. Thus we find that, after listening to John's discussion of the tariff question, John Quincy Adams merely noted in his diary: "June 20—On the Tariff bill, Hiram P. Hunt made an hour speech for a protective tariff; John Van Buren, anti-tariff." (*Memoirs of John Quincy Adams,* Vol. XI, p. 182.)

45. David Crockett filled his *Life of Martin Van Buren* with sarcasm and innuendo, but he did not relish a similar life written about himself by those whom he regarded as unfriendly. Whereupon, he published a notice in several papers repudiating the biography "purporting to present a history of his life, adventures and eccentricities," announcing that he himself would write a more accurate account of his career. (Nashville *Republican,* Jan. 16, 1834.)

46. An example of "Lives" of candidates published in newspapers is the "Extra Globe," printed as a special supplement by the Washington *Globe,* May 18, 1859. Van Buren regarded it as an important factor in his political career, and preserved it in his papers. The leaflet dealt particularly with Martin Van Buren's attitude toward the War of 1812—a subject of very lively discussion in his campaign. The "Extra Globe" is now in the library of Congress. (*Van Buren Papers,* No. 8541, Vol. 36.)

47. Letters addressed to Martin Van Buren, Esq. by "Corrector." The writer was James Cochrane; under the pseudonym he attacked every trait and activity of Martin Van Buren.

48. William C. MacKenzie: *Life and Times of Martin Van Buren,* 1846, p. 148.

49. *History of the State of New York,* edited by Alexander C. Flick, New York State Historical Association, Vol. VII, p. 66. Chapters VI and VII give in detail John Van Buren's activities in state and national politics.

50. The New York *Evening Post,* April 9, 1851.

51. *Ibid.,* May 31, 1851.

52. Columbus (Ohio) *Crisis,* Dec. 10, 1862.

53. G. Ticknor Curtis: *Life of Buchanan,* Vol. II, p. 603. John Bigelow, editor of the New York *Evening Post,* considered that John Van Buren's speeches "attracted far more attention because of offensive gibes and jokes at the expense of others in which he indulged than for anything he showed an inclination to applaud" (John Bigelow: *Retrospections of An Active Life*), but that opinion was expressed after the two had quarreled; earlier, Bigelow's professional appraisal of John's eloquence must have been high, since that editor printed John Van Buren's speeches in full length upon the front pages of his influential paper. Probably a more objective appraisal of his oratorical talent is that by the historian Alexander, who has made a careful study of New York politics: "He was not an impassioned orator. He spoke deliberately, and rarely with animation or with gestures. . . . But he was marvelously pleasing. His perennial wit kept his audience expectant, and his compact, forceful utterances seemed to break the argument of an opponent as a hammer shatters a pane of glass." (Alexander: *A Political History of the State of New York,* Vol. II, pp. 128-30.)

54. As early as 1828 we find him the subject of lengthy editorials in a number of prominent papers. The Boston *Statesman* referred to him as a great actor who "justly earned a brilliant histrionic reputation." He had come to Boston at the age of twenty "unheralded and almost unknown, and was now, after a period of but a little more than two years . . . acknowledged on all hands to be the greatest actor of the country, and without a superior on the stage." (Boston *Statesman,* Oct. 14, 1828.) With the passing years the reputation of Edwin Forrest went even beyond his ability as an actor. He won fame also as an orator, both on account of superb delivery and eloquence in composition. It was he who was chosen to deliver the Fourth of July oration in New York in 1838, and the address was accorded first-page space in prominent newspapers. (Washington *Chronicle,* Aug. 10, 1838.) So great was his popularity and so extensive his personal following that shrewd politicians nominated Forrest for a seat in Congress, but the actor declined, saying that his art would not permit the practice of politics. (Washington *Globe,* Nov. 7, 1838.)

55. Odell: *Annals of the New York Stage,* Vol. VI.

56. New York *Herald,* May 11, 1849.

57. William Macready retired from the stage in 1851; Edwin Forrest continued in Shakespearean roles for twenty years longer.

58. Some papers denounced the actor for bringing the suit. Said the New York *Sunday Dispatch,* "There seems to be something unspeakably strange in a man's uttering to the public gaze such charges; and yet they are what Mr. Forrest now sends before the Court of Common Pleas of Philadelphia." (*Sunday Dispatch,* Aug. 18, 1850.) The legal phraseology to which the New York paper objected was the affidavit filed in the divorce suit in which Forrest asserted that he "demeaned himself as a kind and affectionate husband, and although by the laws of God, as well as by their marital vows, they were bound to that chastity which should be inseparable from the marriage state, yet the said Catherine Forrest, in violation of her marriage vows, hath for a considerable time past, given herself to adulterous practices, and has been guilty of adultery with a certain George Jamieson."

59. New York *Herald,* Dec. 17, 1851.

60. *Ibid.,* Dec. 18, 1851.

61. New York *Evening Mirror,* Jan. 26, 1852.

62. New York *Herald,* Jan. 27, 1852.

63. Immediately after the trial, thirty prominent women of New York presented Charles O'Conor with a beautiful silver vase, in token of his chivalrous defense of a woman in distress. A group of lawyers, elated that his rival, John Van Buren, had met legal defeat, gave O'Conor a massive silver pitcher engraved with the motto: "From God cometh the succoring champion." On all occasions, lawyer O'Conor responded, it had been his cardinal principle to defend right without thought of material reward—Mrs. Forrest was just one of many. A quarter of a century later the myth was exploded: Attorney O'Conor, instead of having given his service gratuitously, had re-

tained nearly all of the alimony in fees, about $60,000. (New York *Times,* March 26, 1876.)

64. Chauncey M. Depew, himself famed for oratorical eloquence, said that John Van Buren "was an eloquent speaker and had a faculty of entrancing a crowd with his wit and of characterization of his opponent which was fatal. . . . I have seen crowds, when he was elaborately explaining details necessary for the vindication of his position, . . . remain with close attention, hoping for what was certain to come, namely, one of those sallies of wit, which made a speech of Van Buren a memorable thing to have listened to." (Chauncey M. Depew: *My Memories of Eighty Years,* pp. 41-43.) Contemporary press reports corroborate this appraisal. When John spoke at a Democratic rally, "a shout from twenty thousand throats greeted this distinguished son of the Empire State, . . . his speech was listened to with great attention." (*Ohio Patriot,* September 5, 1856.) Even when he merely proposed a toast, he was accorded "tremendous applause." (New York *Weekly Herald,* March 23, 1844.)

65. Francis P. Blair to Martin Van Buren, Sept. 27, 1839. *Van Buren Papers,* Library of Congress.

66. *Van Buren Papers.*

67. Typical are the letters of John C. Rives, *Van Buren Papers,* May, 1844.

68. Francis P. Blair to Martin Van Buren, Jr., Oct. 16, 1849. *Van Buren Papers.*

69. Similarly, Martin, Jr., on his visits to the Blair home near Washington, wrote to his father lengthy reports on political affairs in the Capital. (*Van Buren Papers,* letters of May 7 and May 25, 1850.)

70. Martin Van Buren to Gouverneur Kemble, June 13, 1854; to Martin, Jr., Sept. 19, 1854; to Thomas Benton, Oct. 3, 1854; to Martin, Jr., Nov. 12, 1854. *Van Buren Papers.*

71. Martin Van Buren: *Autobiography,* Chapter XIX, p. 220.

72. William L. MacKenzie: *Life and Times of Martin Van Buren,* 1846, p. 200.

73. *Van Buren Papers.*

74. *Annual Report* of American Historical Society, 1918, Vol. II, p. 3.

75. John died in 1866, aboard a steamer returning from England. When his death became known the courts in New York adjourned their sessions, and the bar associations passed resolutions of regret. (New York *Times,* October 17, and October 18, 1866.) Numerous eulogies were delivered at his funeral, which was attended by many men prominent in politics, in finance, and in the professions. (*Ibid.,* Oct. 20, 1866.)

76. *Inquiry into Origins and Course of Political Parties of the United States,* by the Late ex-President Martin Van Buren, 1867.

Son and Father of Presidents

(Pages 73 to 85)

1. Sanderson: *Signers of the Declaration of Independence.*
2. Bonney: *Historical Gleanings.*
3. William E. Peters: *Ohio Lands and Their History.*
4. Lossing: *Field Book of the War of 1812.*
5. *Ibid.*
6. *Papers of William Henry Harrison,* Library of Congress, Vol. 6, No. 1081.
7. *Ibid.,* No. 1088.
8. *Ibid.,* No. 1091.
9. *Ibid.,* No. 1102.
10. Letter of Harrison to Gen. Van Rensselaer, May 8, 1828. Bonney: *Historical Gleanings,* p. 437.
11. Ohio Historical Society Publication, Vol. III, p. 70: General Harrison to Findlay, Dec. 2, 1832.
12. *Ibid.,* p. 72: W. H. Harrison to J. Findlay, Dec. 7, 1832.
13. *Ibid.,* p. 77: W. H. Harrison to J. Findlay, July 4, 1832.
14. *Ibid.,* W. H. Harrison to J. Findlay, Dec. 2, 1832.
15. J. S. Harrison: *Pioneer Life at North Bend.*
16. *Cyclopedia of American Biography,* Vol. 3, 1915.
17. J. S. Harrison: *Pioneer Life at North Bend.*
18. *Congressional Globe,* Appendix, May 10, 1854.
19. *Ibid.*
20. Letters to John J. Crittenden, March, 1858. *Papers of Crittenden,* Library of Congress.
21. Lossing: *Field Book of the War of 1812,* pp. 573-74.
22. Cincinnati *Daily Enquirer,* May 28, 1878.
23. Cincinnati *Daily Times,* May 30, 1878. Cincinnati *Daily Enquirer,* May 30, 1878.
24. New York *Tribune,* May 31, 1878.
25. Cincinnati *Daily Enquirer,* May 31, 1878.

Sons of John Tyler

(Pages 86 to 107)

1. Henry A. Wise: *Seven Decades of the Union,* pp. 58-59.

2. Not only editors of unfriendly papers, but also writers of letters to the newspapers, invariably made allusion to the fact that Tyler had not intentionally been chosen President of the United States; a typical letter appeared in the Richmond (Va.) *Shield* of November 13, 1841: "John Tyler . . . although by accident the Chief Magistrate of a free and mighty people." Adherents of John Tyler resented the appellation "accidental President," and some party editors gave vent to their condemnation of the term. "Many of the papers hostile to Mr. Tyler, after exhausting the vocabulary of vilification and epithets, in terms of derision, have styled him the *accidental* President," the Washington *Madisonian* retorted angrily. "For the heathen or the Mohammedan thus to attempt to cast ridicule on one of the acts of an all-wise Providence and profane the name of the Almighty, would not be a matter of serious surprise; but when we see those who claim to be professors of the Christian religion, and worshippers in the holy temple, guilty of this flagrant conduct and committing such unpardonable sin, it should raise a blush on the cheek of every one who lays claim to being a Christian, and believes in the existence of a supreme being." (The *Madisonian,* July 5, 1844.)

3. Texas, originally a part of Mexico, had declared its independence as a separate Republic in 1835; after a decisive victory over the Mexican army, a constitution was adopted in 1836, and a president was elected. Ten years later, Texas desiring to join the American Union, an effort was made to effect that purpose by a treaty between the Republic of Texas and the United States; but the Senate refused to ratify the treaty. John Tyler managed to bring about the annexation of Texas through a Joint Resolution of Congress which did not require a two-thirds vote as did treaties. . . . The gold pen with which the annexation bill was signed was given by Tyler to his second wife, and she wore it around her neck as a momento of her husband's greatest achievement. (Bryan: *History of the National Capital,* II, p. 448.)

4. John Tyler to Letitia Christian, Dec. 5, 1812. Published in New York *Times,* March 30, 1912.

5. L. G. Tyler: *Letters and Times of the Tylers,* Vol. I, p. 11. In contrast to his shyness during his youth, Robert later became an impressive public speaker. Comment in the newspapers varied with their own political bias. Thus, an anti-Tyler paper criticised Robert's remark before an Irish gathering that he "thanked God he was not an Englishman," and suggested that "Mr. Robert Tyler should invent some other language to utter his fooleries in."

(New York *Sunday Mercury,* Oct. 15, 1843.) But other papers praised his speeches and reprinted them either in part or in full. (*Madisonian,* Nov. 21, 1844; Richmond *Enquirer,* Oct. 14, 1853.) Robert's reputation as an orator spread to Europe, one of his speeches appearing in the London *Times* and in the Paris *Journal des Debats.* (Georgetown *Advocate,* Dec. 23, 1843.)

6. *Ibid.,* p. 530.

7. *Ibid.,* p. 531.

8. *Ibid.,* p. 534.

9. *Ahasuerus* (1842); *Death, or Medorus' Dream* (1843).

10. *Papers of John Tyler,* Library of Congress: John Tyler to General Thompson, May 12, 1838. Some newspapers mocked Robert's poetic ambitions. Said the New York *Sunday Mercury,* "Bobby Tyler really intends to publish a volume of poems! Another aspirant for 'poetical horrors'!" (Jan. 2, 1842.)

11. John Bernard: *Retrospections of America,* p. 164. Priscilla's father had been born in England, but it was in America that he made his reputation as a tragedian. When John Tyler became President, Cooper left the stage and obtained an unimportant post at the New York Custom House.

12. Particularly, during the Presidential term of James Buchanan, politicians recognized Robert's leadership. Indicative of his power at the Pennsylvania State Convention in March, 1860, is the notation in a letter of a prominent politician, Benjamin Brewster, to R. M. T. Hunter that "Mr. Robert Tyler (and two others) . . . are the triumvirate that rule us here by the permission of the Power they hold from the President." (American Historical Association: *Correspondence of Robert M. T. Hunter,* Vol. II, p. 298. Letter of March 5, 1860.)

13. *History of the State of New York,* ed. Flick, Vol. VII, p. 83.

14. Philip G. Auchampaugh: *Robert Tyler, Southern Rights Champion.*

15. *Ibid.* Robert Tyler summed up his own concept of integrity in a single sentence: writing to a leading Philadelphia citizen, he said, "In one thing you certainly do not err, and that is in supposing me incapable of the meanness of stating an untruth for a political or any other object." (Robert Tyler to Francis Cooper, Sept. 28, 1852; published in Bedford, Penn., *Gazette,* Oct. 8, 1852.)

16. L. G. Tyler: *supra,* Vol. II.

17. New York *Herald,* July 7, 1844. John, Jr., had succeeded Robert as his father's secretary, and was proud of his official status, although he received no compensation. John Quincy Adams, always scornful of the Tyler progeny, recorded in his diary that this second son of John Tyler had his visiting cards engraved "John Tyler, Jr. Private and Confidential Secretary of his Excellency John Tyler, President of the United States." (*Diary of John Quincy Adams,* ed. Nevins, p. 543.)

18. Norfolk (Va.) *Herald,* July 4, 1844.

19. Washington *Globe,* July 8, 1844. John's combats did not always take place upon the "field of honor." On one occasion, he was floored by a Lieutenant Avery, at a Washington party. (Baltimore *Sun,* Feb. 9, 1845.) The

journal captioned its account of the fistic affair, "A Duel on the Tapis."

20. Philip G. Auchampaugh: *supra.*

21. *Ibid.* John, Jr., resented any implication that he was seeking political appointments. Once he wrote indignantly to all the Washington papers: "I have not been, am not, and do not mean to be an applicant for office." (*Madisonian,* April 12, 1845.)

22. Historical Society of Pennsylvania: John Tyler, Jr. to Henry A. Wise, November 2, 1859. This episode is discussed also in McMaster: *A History of the People of the United States,* Vol. VIII, pp. 420-421. At the outbreak of the Civil War, John, Jr., hurried to Montgomery, then the capital of the seceded states, and, unknown to his father, obtained a clerical post in the Confederate war office. It was he who wired his father at Richmond that Fort Sumter had been bombarded. (Richmond *Enquirer,* April 13, 1861.) Thereafter, he acquired military rank, becoming a major and, for a few weeks, acting chief of the bureau. (J. B. Jones: *A Rebel War Clerk's Diary,* Vol. I, p. 36.) Later, despite considerable opposition, he was transferred to the field. (*Ibid.,* Vol. I, p. 78.) Toward the end of the war, he delivered speeches to inspire continued resistance. (Richmond *Sentinel,* Feb. 25, 1865.) In the spring of 1886 he petitioned Congress for compensation for his work as Presidential secretary forty-two years earlier. He asserted that "at the close of the administration of President Tyler, your petitioner was so impoverished that he was compelled to sell a gold watch to enable him to leave Washington for his home in Virginia." (*Senate Report No. 1833, 49th Congress, 2nd Session.* Feb. 10, 1887.) This was at variance with his letters to the newspapers in 1845 when he had declared that he "had been detained in Washington by a severe attack of illness." (*Madisonian,* April 12, 1845.) The Senate committee debated John's petition and, a year later, decided that he had no claim against the Government. In the last years of his life, nearing seventy, John Tyler, Jr., regaled Washington with his reminiscences which were tinged both by a fading memory and an abundant egotism. He ascribed to himself some of the achievements which had marked the career of his older brother, Robert. (Brooklyn *Daily Eagle,* April 15, 1895.)

23. American Historical Association: *Correspondence of Robert M. T. Hunter,* Vol. II, p. 298. "Robert Tyler has become the special counselor and confidant of President Buchanan," declared a Trenton newspaper, "for several days in succession he has been closeted, hour after hour with the President, and it is anticipated that the Executive message will be slightly Tylerized." (*Gazette and Republican,* Nov. 24, 1858.)

24. Even Abraham Lincoln had repeatedly acknowledged that Congress could not constitutionally interfere with slavery; he definitely enunciated that concept when he was a member of the Illinois Legislature, and he consistently voiced that conviction during all of his debates with Douglas when the two were seeking election to the United States Senate in 1858. Abraham Lincoln summed up his belief when he was about to become President of the United States: "I have no purpose, directly or indirectly, to interfere with the institution of slavery in the States where it exists. I believe I have

no lawful right to do so, and I have no inclination to do so." (McMaster: *supra,* Vol. VIII, p. 327.)

25. Richmond (Va.) *Enquirer,* May 10, 1861; Richmond *Express,* May 14, 1861. Robert counseled that the Southern states be permitted to secede peacefully. (Richmond *Enquirer,* Jan. 15, 1861.) This enraged Union sympathizers in Philadelphia, and self-appointed "vigilance committees" stormed his home. (*Ibid.,* April 18, 1861.) Robert sent his family to Virginia, and himself was forced to flee. (Philadelphia *Inquirer,* Sept. 15, 1861.) His property was confiscated. (*Rebellion Records,* Vol. III, p. 28.)

26. L. G. Tyler: *supra.* Robert Tyler's acquiescence in the final outcome of the armed struggle was typical of the attitude of the Southern leaders who had been most loyal to the Southern cause and had most ardently defended the right of secession. Similarly, General Robert E. Lee and other military commanders devoted themselves to rebuilding their beloved Southland, and bent their energies to persuade their compatriots to do their share in building a greater United States. For example, General Joseph E. Johnston, asked for his views on the outcome of the war, replied: "We of the South referred the question at issue, between us and the United States, to the arbitrament of the sword. The decision has been made, and is against us. We must acquiesce in that decision, accept it as final, and recognize the fact that Virginia is again one of the United States—our duties and interests coincide." (Quoted in *The New Era,* Greeneville, Tennessee, Sept. 2, 1865.)

27. Mobile (Ala.) *Daily Register,* Dec. 6, 1877; Montgomery *Advertiser,* Dec. 3, 1877. Said the Mobile *Register:* "In the death of Col. Robert Tyler, of Montgomery, the State of Alabama loses one of her best and ablest citizens. It was not only his distinguished descent that gave him prominence among the people of his adopted State. He was a man of very decided ability, of great purity of character, and of unflinching patriotism."

28. *Americana,* Vol. 14, 1920, p. 205. "The ancestor, Lyon Gardiner, is said to have purchased the entire island from the Indians for 'ten crates of trading cloth.' Later the title was confirmed by the English earl who had been given earlier proprietary rights by the King. One of the subsequent Gardiners entertained the pirate Captain Kidd who buried some of his stolen treasures there." (*Dictionary of American History,* Vol. II, p. 372.)

29. Julia Gardiner Tyler: *Reminiscences.* Cincinnati *Graphic News,* June 25, 1887.

30. *Memoirs of John Quincy Adams,* Vol. XXI, p. 67.

31. Henry A. Wise: *Seven Decades of the Union,* pp. 233-34. Long after his retirement from the Presidency, John Tyler indulged in sentiments usually characteristic of much younger men. He wrote on serious political problems, but he also penned verses; one of these was published in a Virginia newspaper, "Lines addressed to a Long Island lady, urging her to migrate to Virginia." (Alexandria *Gazette,* Feb. 23, 1857.)

32. G. Ticknor Curtis: *Life of James Buchanan,* Vol. I, p. 529. Except where political adversaries derided the union to belittle John Tyler, or de-

fending journals voiced their approval, newspapers generally took little notice of the marriage. For example, an Illinois paper devoted four paragraphs to a discussion of political affairs, and in the same issue used four lines in reference to the Presidential matrimonial adventure, saying: "John Tyler, a few weeks since, married a daughter of Mr. Gardiner of New York. He traveled from Washington to New York incog accompanied by his son, and one or two members of his cabinet." (*Tazewell County Whig* (Tremont, Ill.), July 12, 1844.)

33. The Washington *Madisonian,* July 1, 1844.

34. *Ibid.*

35. New York *Herald,* July 3, 1844.

36. L. G. Tyler: *supra,* Vol. II.

37. New York *Times,* May 26, 1865.

38. New York *World,* April 26, 1874.

39. *Papers of John Tyler,* Library of Congress, Vol. III, No. 654.

40. L. G. Tyler: *supra,* Vol. II, p. 652.

41. *Papers of John Tyler,* Vol. VII, No. 414.

42. Lyon Gardiner Tyler: *John Tyler and Abraham Lincoln.*

43. Brooklyn *Daily Eagle,* April 14, 1895.

44. *Americana,* Vol. 14, p. 205.

45. Some of the papers came to light nearly half a century later; it was then that the circumstances of their removal from John Tyler's home during the Civil War were recounted in the *Journal of American History:* "About June 15, 1864, the Ninth Army Corps, while on march from Cold Harbor to the James River, passed along a road that led by the rear of the residence of ex-President John Tyler at 'Sherwood Forest,' Charles City, Virginia." (*Journal of American History,* 1911, p. 613.)

46. Lyon Gardiner Tyler, in the introduction to Auchampaugh's *Robert Tyler, Southern Rights Champion.* Said Lyon Gardiner Tyler: "Robert Tyler was a half-brother who, as I was always informed by those who knew him—especially by my mother—was a man of excellent ability and character. I never knew him personally because of a great difference in age and distance of residence between us."

47. *Papers of John Tyler,* Vol. V, No. 29.

48. *Ibid.,* Vol. VII, No. 416.

49. L. G. Tyler: *A Criticism of the "History of the American People" by David Muzzey.*

50. L. G. Tyler: *John Tyler and Abraham Lincoln.* Lyon's younger brother, Robert Fitzwalter, had died earlier. About this youngest son of John Tyler there is very meager information in contemporary records. He became a farmer in Virginia, and his last days were spent in a home for the aged.

51. *Ibid.*

52. John Tyler's first wife, the mother of Robert and John, Jr., was a Protestant and of Southern ancestry; his second wife, the mother of Lyon and the other sons, was born in the North and, after the death of her Presidential husband, became a Catholic. Said the Richmond *News Leader:* "The

overwhelming tragedy of those dreadful times is reflected in the fate of the Tyler family. Maritally, it was a 'house divided.'" (Richmond *News Leader*, Feb. 13, 1935.)

53. Richmond *Times-Dispatch*, Feb. 13, 1935.

54. *Ibid.*

55. Richmond *News Leader*, Feb. 13, 1935. This obituary was pronounced by the editor of *Americana* as "the beginning and end of editorial comment upon the life of Lyon Gardiner Tyler." (*Americana*, Vol. 29, pp. 455-59.) However, the eulogy omits characteristics evidenced in the Tyler papers which came to light later.

56. Richmond *Times-Dispatch*, Feb. 13, 1935; *ibid.*, Feb. 14, 1935.

Son of Old Rough and Ready

(Pages 108 to 123)

1. L. G. Tyler: *John Tyler and Abraham Lincoln*, p. 26.

2. Similarly, Sherman's march through the Carolinas was deliberately calculated to spread destruction, the military objective being to deprive the Southern armies of supplies and subsistence. Sherman's own report to the Chief of Staff, in a concluding paragraph, tells of this ruin: "I cannot even with any degree of precision recapitulate the vast amount of injury done to the enemy. . . . In general terms, we have traversed the country from Savannah to Goldsboro, with an average breadth of forty miles, consuming all the forage, cattle, hogs, sheep, poultry, cured meats, corn meal, &c. . . ." (Sherman to Major General Halleck, April 4, 1865. Savannah *Republican*, May 8, 1865.)

3. U. S. Grant: *Personal Memoirs*, Vol. II, p. 521.

4. New York *Times*, May 9, 1865.

5. Taylor: *Destruction and Reconstruction.*

6. Grant: *Personal Memoirs*, Vol. I, pp. 101-2.

7. McMaster: *History of the People of the United States*, Vol. VII, p. 547.

8. Washington *Star*, July 11, 1850.

9. Lamb's *Biographical Index.*

10. Mrs. John Logan: *Thirty Years in Washington*, pp. 628-29.

11. Much has been written about this romance between the second daughter of Zachary Taylor, who was known as "Knox," and Jefferson Davis. At the time they fell in love Taylor, then a colonel, was commanding officer at Fort Crawford where Davis was a lieutenant. Taylor objected emphatically to the marriage of Knox, and there have been numerous versions regarding both the cause of the father's dislike of Davis and the elopement of the girl. (New York *Herald*, Sept. 6, 1942.) In his exhaustive biography of Jefferson Davis, Robert McElroy explodes many of these legends, asserting

that Zachary Taylor had no personal objection to Davis but, his older daughter being already married to an army officer, Taylor did not want this other daughter to endure army life also. (Robert McElroy: *Jefferson Davis,* Vol. I, p. 33.) Knox Taylor's married life was short; moving to Davis' Mississippi home, she died within a few months. At the time of his rise to the Presidency of the Confederacy, Davis had a second wife, Varena Howell. (Eron Rowland: *Wife of Jefferson Davis.*) It is also an interesting sidelight that, while the only son of "Old Rough and Ready" fought so zealously for the Southern cause, his sister—the older daughter of Zachary Taylor—was married to an officer in the Union Army, Robert Wood, Assistant Surgeon. When she was widowed and in financial need, Congress unanimously voted her a pension. (New York *World,* Feb. 15, 1873.)

12. Taylor: *Destruction and Reconstruction,* p. 229. Obituary in New York *Times,* April 13, 1889, refers to him as "the only son of Zachary Taylor, born near Louisville, Ky."; Lamb's *Biographical Index* states, "Son Richard, born at Baton Rouge, La."; The Yale University *Obituary Record of Graduates* indicates that he was born in New Orleans; similarly, *General Officers of the Confederate Army,* compiled by Gen. Marcus J. Wright, lists New Orleans as the birthplace.

13. *Southern Illustrated News,* Sept. 13, 1862.

14. Taylor: *Destruction and Reconstruction,* p. 160.

15. New York *Times:* April 13, 1879.

16. Taylor: *Destruction and Reconstruction,* pp. 18-19.

17. Beveridge: *Abraham Lincoln.*

18. New York *Times,* May 3, 1861. Sentiment favoring the dissolution of the Union was not restricted to the South. There were prominent men in the North who advocated the separation of the slaveholding states from the free. General Scott was willing that the Southern States withdraw peaceably. "Let the erring sisters go," he argued. Andrew Johnson, perhaps closer to Lincoln than any other prominent Southern statesman, was quoted in an Illinois paper as saying that the Abolitionists in the North equally with the slaveowners in the South were eager to dissolve the Union. "Hear what Andrew Johnson says," said the *Weekly Argus* in 1863, continuing, "there are two parties in existence who want dissolution. Slavery and a Southern Confederacy is the hobby. Sumner wants to break up the government, and so do the abolitionists generally. They hold that if slavery survives, the Union cannot endure. Secessionists argue that if the Union continues, slavery is lost." (Rock Island, Ill., *Weekly Argus,* Nov. 4, 1863.)

19. Speech of Charles Francis Adams, *Congressional Record,* 1861.

20. Appleton's *Annual Cyclopedia,* 1861.

21. Richmond *Enquirer,* May 10, 1861.

22. Richmond *Express,* May 14, 1861.

23. *Official Journal of the Convention of the State of Louisiana,* 1861.

24. *Ibid.*

25. *Messages and Papers of the Confederacy,* compiled by Richardson, Vol. II, p. 265. Secretary of State Benjamin to John Slidell, 19 July, 1862.

26. Vicksburg (Miss.) *Daily Herald,* May 11, 1865.

27. Natchez (Miss.) *Courier,* May 8, 1865.

28. The Meridian (Miss.) *Clarion,* May 3, 1865, quoted in the New Orleans *Times,* May 7, 1865.

29. New York *Times,* April 13, 1879.

30. Taylor: *Destruction and Reconstruction,* p. 206.

31. Gideon Welles: *Diary,* Vol. 3, p. 172, March 25, 1867. Not only was Richard Taylor regarded with respect by the military leaders who had lately fought against the Southern armies, but he was welcomed into the social circles of distinguished Northerners who had vehemently opposed the Confederacy. His personal charm quickly won the confidence of former "enemies." Thus, Henry Adams describes him at a Washington dinner party: "General Dick Taylor, himself one of the best of rebel Major Generals . . . a first-rate raconteur and whist player," adding "a son of a former President of the United States." (*Letters of Henry Adams,* ed. Ford, p. 309. Adams to Charles Milner Gaskell, 28 Nov., 1878.)

32. *Obituary Record of Graduates of Yale College,* p. 357.

33. New York *Times,* April 13, 1879.

Son of Millard Fillmore

(Pages 124 to 129)

1. Buffalo Historical Society, Vol. X.

2. James Grant Wilson: *Presidents of the United States,* pp. 259-60.

3. John Quincy Adams: *Memoirs,* Vol. VIII, p. 388.

4. Lyon G. Tyler: *Letters and Times of the Tylers.*

5. U. S. Grant: *Personal Memoirs,* Vol. I, p. 9.

6. Brooks Adams: *Charles Francis Adams,* p. 224. Massachusetts Historical Society.

7. Martin Van Buren: *Autobiography.*

8. Robert Johnson to Andrew Johnson, March 18, 1865. *Papers of Andrew Johnson,* Library of Congress.

9. Hayes Memorial Library: *Index and List of Letters and Papers of Rutherford B. Hayes.*

10. Library of Congress: *Handbook of Manuscripts,* p. 180.

11. J. Scott Harrison: *Pioneer Life at North Bend.*

12. At any rate, Robert Lincoln was persuaded to leave unharmed the bulk of his father's letters and papers. (Hertz: *The Hidden Lincoln,* p. 17.) They remained sealed in the Library of Congress and, under the terms of Robert Lincoln's will, were opened to public inspection on July 26, 1947.

13. Buffalo *Commercial Advertiser,* March 12, 1874.

14. Fillmore's influence with his party adherents in Congress was decisive;

they had confidence in his judgment and political astuteness. "When Fillmore says a thing is right, we always vote for it," was a typical remark of Democratic members. (New York *World,* March 9, 1874.) For the "common man" of his own generation as well as for Americans since was his crusade for the abolition of imprisonment for debt; his was the dominant share in enacting legislation which was vigorously opposed.

15. Julia G. Tyler: *Reminiscences.* Discovering that the admired Fillmore was a married man, the enthusiastic Julia gives us no further description.

16. "Hiram C. Day's Reminiscences." Buffalo Historical Society, Vol. XI, p. 500.

17. Buffalo Historical Society, Vol. XI.

18. Barre: *Life of Fillmore,* p. 82.

19. Buffalo *Commercial Advertiser,* March 9, 1874.

20. Buffalo Historical Society, Vol. XI.

21. For a while Powers Fillmore had an apartment on the third floor of a brick business building where Grover Cleveland, later President of the United States, also had bachelor's quarters. The son of the ex-President and Cleveland became warm friends. (Allan Nevins: *Grover Cleveland,* p. 66.)

22. Buffalo Historical Society, Vol. XI. The original marriage contract is now in the Fillmore Collection of the Society.

23. Buffalo *Express,* Nov. 18, 1902.

24. Nearly a century has passed since Commodore Matthew C. Perry forced upon the Japanese unwelcome contact with Western civilization. (*Senate Documents,* 33rd Congress, 2nd Session, Vol. 6, No. 34.) He found them in 1854 as we found them a hundred years later—hating the white men and their customs, evasive, clever, yielding only to superior material force.

25. It was Fillmore's first wife, Abigail Powers, who first aroused in the future President an interest in books. It is said that to her is due the credit for establishing a library in the White House. When Fillmore became President there were no books in the President's residence, and she prompted the Chief Executive to ask Congress for an appropriation. (Buffalo *Express,* Nov. 18, 1902.) The President's wife selected for the library a large oval room on the second floor. (Roy Franklin Nichols: *Franklin Pierce,* p. 239.) Of course, earlier Presidents, notably Thomas Jefferson and John Quincy Adams, were avid readers and took to the White House very large book collections of their own.

26. Nevins: *Grover Cleveland—A Study in Courage,* p. 74.

27. Buffalo *Express,* Nov. 16, 1889.

28. *Ibid.,* Nov 17, 1889.

29. *Ibid.*

Sons of Abraham Lincoln

(Pages 130 to 149)

1. Nicolay and Hay: *Lincoln,* Vol. III, p. 290.
2. Herndon: *Life of Abraham Lincoln,* p. 136.
3. Beveridge: *Abraham Lincoln,* Vol. I, p. 506.
4. F. B. Carpenter: *Six Months at the White House.*
5. John Hay: *Life in the White House,* p. 320.
6. Julia Taft Bayne: *Tad Lincoln's Father.*
7. John Hay: *supra,* p. 330.
8. Washington *National Republican,* Nov. 4, 1861.
9. W. H. Crook: *Memories of the White House.*
10. William E. Barton: *President Lincoln,* p. 222.
11. Mrs. John A. Logan: *Thirty Years in Washington.*
12. F. B. Carpenter: *supra.*
13. Nashville *Dispatch,* April 28, 1865.
14. New York *Times,* April 22, 1865; May 5, 1865.
15. Archives of the United States. Bill of Sands & Harvey, April 19, 1865.
16. Chicago *Daily Journal,* July 2, 1860.
17. W. H. Crook: *supra.*
18. John Hay: *supra,* pp. 330-31.
19. Angle: *New Letters of Lincoln,* p. 373.
20. F. B. Carpenter: *supra.*
21. Sandburg: *Abraham Lincoln,* Vol. III, p. 417.
22. Julia Taft Bayne: *supra.*
23. Katherine Helm: *Mary, Wife of Lincoln.*
24. *Ibid.*
25. Barton: *supra,* p. 65.
26. In the Tyler papers now in the Library of Congress will be found the opinion of Jesse W. Weik, who collaborated with Abraham Lincoln's law partner, Herndon, on the *Life of Abraham Lincoln.* Writing to Lyon Gardiner the historian, Weik said, "After 1859, when Robert Lincoln was sent to college, he knew but little about his father and political affairs. Prior to 1859, he was too much of a boy to be interested in such matters." (Jesse W. Weik to Lyon Gardiner, March 20, 1917. *Papers of John Tyler,* Vol. VII, No. 479.) In the nearly 19,000 Lincoln papers which Robert gave to the Library of Congress, there is but one communication between the President's son and his father.
27. *Illinois State Journal,* Jan. 30, 1936.
28. Beveridge: *supra,* Vol. I, p. 386, "Lincoln to Speed."
29. *Illinois State Register,* July 26, 1926.
30. Beveridge: *supra,* Vol. I, p. 506.

31. Barton: *supra,* p. 66.

32. F. Lauriston Bullard: "Abraham Lincoln and Henry Adams." *The Abraham Lincoln Quarterly,* Vol. I, March, 1941, p. 271.

33. Sandburg: *supra,* Vol. III, p. 416.

34. Barton: *supra,* p. 174.

35. Rhodes: *History of the Civil War,* p. 16.

36. New York *Times,* July 25, 1865.

37. *"The War and Harvard College Boys,"* Boston *Herald,* May 18, 1861.

38. Harvard College: *Roll of Students Who Served in the Army or Navy,* July, 1865.

39. Herndon: *supra,* p. 34, note.

40. Richmond *Enquirer,* May 10, 1861.

41. Sandburg: *supra,* Vol. III, p. 416.

42. Katherine Helm: *supra,* p. 227.

43. Nicolay and Hay: *supra,* Vol. X, p. 213.

44. Jesse Grant: *In the Days of My Father.*

45. Library of Congress: Lincoln MSS.

46. *Illinois State Register,* June 28, 1926.

47. Nicolay and Hay: *supra,* Vol. X, pp. 213-14.

48. Many newspapers, in reviewing Robert Lincoln's career, stated erroneously that he witnessed his father's assassination. For instance, the Chicago *Tribune* (July 27, 1926) remarked, "That evening he was in the theater when John Wilkes Booth shot and fatally wounded his father." This inaccurate account was spread by a prominent press association, and widely circulated. Robert Lincoln himself asserted that he was at the White House when the tragic event occurred at Ford's Theater. (Letter of Edward Breck, New York *Times,* Aug. 22, 1926.)

49. *Illinois State Journal,* June 30, 1936.

50. Washington *Evening Star,* Sept. 25, 1868.

51. *Ibid.,* Sept. 25-26, 1868.

52. *Illinois State Register,* July 26, 1926.

53. Chicago *Daily News,* July 26, 1926. This limited experience in public service was emphasized by the newspapers which disapproved his appointment as Secretary of War. Said the Boston *Transcript:* "The personal history of the new Secretary of War is a brief one, except in so far as it falls within that of his father, the martyr President. He owes his appointment to the two Senators from Illinois who, doubtless, reflect the sentiments of a vast public which ardently desires that the *son of such a father* may achieve the highest political success." (Boston *Transcript,* March 7, 1881.)

54. New York *World,* May 10, 1884.

55. In fact, the political leaders believed they could double their chances by nominating *two* Presidents' sons! The two being the son of Abraham Lincoln and the son of Ulysses S. Grant. Long after, the newspaper publisher, Henry Stoddard, enthused about the glamor of such a ticket, observing that it would have been irresistible had the politicos effected it in an earlier campaign; in his autobiography, Stoddard wrote about the proposed nominations:

"One ticket they considered had great possibilities if it should hit the people right . . . that was a 'father's son' ticket—made up of Robert T. Lincoln and Frederick D. Grant. Lincoln and Grant! What names to conjure with! In 1880 such a ticket might have been an ideal, victory-winning outcome of that convention struggle; but eight years later it would have been an experiment. While the national leaders were debating it, Fred Grant was defeated for election as Secretary of State of New York. That sealed the fate of the Lincoln and Grant ticket." (Henry L. Stoddard: *As I Knew Them,* p. 157.)

56. Omaha *Republican,* Feb. 13, 1887.

57. Rutland (Vt.) *Herald,* Feb. 4, 1887.

58. Atlanta *Defiance,* Oct. 23, 1886.

59. Atlanta *National,* Feb. 6, 1887. In the memorable National Convention of 1912, in which the irreconcilable followers of Taft and Teddy Roosevelt were struggling to make their favorite the Presidential nominee, a secret plan was evolved to obtain the nomination for Robert T. Lincoln by swinging the Negro delegates en masse to his support and thus making the President's son the compromise candidate. The originator of the scheme was General James Clarkson, who was considered "a friend of the Negro race" because in pre-Civil War days his father in Iowa had aided five hundred Negro slaves to escape to Canada, and General Clarkson himself had appointed many Negroes to office. As was revealed by his son in 1924, General Clarkson had addressed a ten-page letter to a prominent Negro delegate-at-large, Henry Lincoln Johnson, whose influence among his fellow-Negro delegates was very great. The letter itself is an extremely interesting document: it called upon the Negroes to use their "balance of power," to take advantage of the opportunity and play the historic role of deciding who should be the Presidential nominee, and thus obtain recognition of their rights. However, the Taft supporters barred the entrances to the convention hall, and thereby prevented the letter from reaching Johnson before Taft was nominated. (New York *Times,* June 1, 1924.)

60. *Illinois State Journal,* Aug. 31, 1887.

61. George F. Hoar: *Autobiography of Seventy Years,* Vol. II, p. 216. There were other political leaders who recommended Robert Lincoln for high office, even though they did not know him personally. When President Chester Arthur asked the influential Senator Fred Frelinghuysen (later his Secretary of State) to suggest members for his Cabinet, Frelinghuysen urged the appointment of Robert Lincoln as Attorney General, writing, "Lincoln is *said to be* a good lawyer." (Letter of Frelinghuysen to Arthur, Dec. 2, 1881. Library of Congress.) Henry Adams, who recorded that he had "known him slightly for some years," was equally reserved in his appraisal of Robert Lincoln; writing to a friend he remarked that Robert "is a good fellow, rather heavy, but pleasant and sufficiently intelligent." (*Letters of Henry Adams,* ed. Ford, p. 398. Adams to Charles M. Gaskell, 21 April, 1889.)

62. Katherine Helm: *Mary, Wife of Lincoln,* pp. 296-97.

63. Louisville *Courier Journal,* June 1, 1909.

64. Bingham Collection, Library of Congress.

65. New York *Tribune,* March 5, 1902.

66. *Illinois State Register,* July 26, 1926.

67. Emanuel Hertz: *The Hidden Lincoln.*

68. Robert T. Lincoln attempted to arrogate to himself the right to determine what might be done in all matters pertaining to his father. He insisted that the former secretaries of Abraham Lincoln, Nicolay and Hay, should submit to him before publication every page they wrote for their *Life of Abraham Lincoln.* He attempted first to prevent the publication of Herndon's biography of Lincoln, later attempted to buy up all the copies on sale in England. When the City of London was about to erect a Lincoln statue, sculptured by Barnard, Robert Lincoln through the American Ambassador in London insisted that a statue by St. Gaudens should be substituted. (New York *Times,* July 27, 1926.)

69. Gideon Welles: *Diary,* Vol. III, p. 444.

70. Indicative of the indifference with which important newspapers viewed the passing of Robert Lincoln, the San Francisco *Examiner* devoted three full pages to sports, mentioned that a prominent actor was appearing on the stage in a characterization of Abraham Lincoln—but did not print the news that the President's son had died! The Chicago *Tribune* carried several paragraphs on its 6th page; the Jacksonville *Times Union* printed a half-inch on the 15th page; the New Orleans *Times-Picayune* used a half-inch on the 10th page. Similarly, other papers printed merely a short paragraph or two far removed from the front page; some newspapers made no mention at all that the son of Abraham Lincoln was dead.

71. Chicago *Tribune,* July 27, 1926.

72. St. Louis *Post Dispatch,* July 27, 1926.

73. San Antonio *Express,* July 27, 1926.

Sons of Andrew Johnson

(Pages 150 to 161)

1. The respect and admiration which, prior to the Civil War, both the public and the press, alike in Tennessee and outside that State, had for Andrew Johnson were much greater than many modern historians mention. Contemporary newspapers hailed his political successes and acclaimed his ability in glowing terms. Typical of these eulogies was the editorial comment in the Nashville *Union* when the Legislature of Tennessee (as was the mode of electing Senators at that time) chose him to represent that State in the United States Senate: "Andrew Johnson was yesterday, in convention of the two houses of the general assembly of Tennessee, elected a Senator in Congress for six years. . . . In this action the people of Tennessee place in the Senate

of the United States the first intellect of the day." (Nashville *Union,* quoted in Washington *Union,* Oct. 13, 1857.)

2. Salmon Chase to Andrew Johnson.

3. New York *Post,* March 6, 1861.

4. Abraham Lincoln and Andrew Johnson served at the same time in the House of Representatives: Lincoln, as a member from Illinois; Johnson, representing Tennessee. Thus they became acquainted fifteen years before the outbreak of the Civil War.

5. Nashville *Banner,* June 19, 1861.

6. *Ibid.,* June 27, 1861.

7. Jefferson Davis, the President of the Southern Confederacy, denounced this reversal of the secession movement which had received approval at the previous election; he exclaimed, "Thus the government of the state of Tennessee was subverted and overthrown, and the people subjugated." (Jefferson Davis: *A Short History of the Confederate States,* p. 359.) The opposite view was expressed by ex-President Millard Fillmore who, in later years, publicly acclaimed Johnson because "when . . . your own State swung from her moorings under the Constitution and drifted into the turbid stream of secession, you stood like a rock in the midst of the ocean, against which the waves of rebellion dashed in vain." (Sept. 3, 1866. Buffalo Historical Society, Vol. XI, p. 109.)

8. New York *Times,* April 17, 1865.

9. *Ibid.,* Sept. 2, 1865.

10. *Ibid.,* May 5, 1865.

11. *Ibid.,* May 25, 1865.

12. 39th Congress, 1st Session.

13. Nashville *Dispatch,* April 29, 1865.

14. At the beginning of the Civil War, when Andrew Johnson maintained Union supremacy in Tennessee, the Southern press expressed their venomous hate of him; but when, after the close of the conflict, Johnson deprecated the harsh treatment advocated by rabid Northerners, the papers of the South voiced their opinion of Johnson, and praised him. An example was the Memphis *Argus;* in 1861 it editorialized, "We should like to see Andrew Johnson's lying tongue torn from his foul mouth, and his miserable carcass thrown out to poison mad dogs, or hung on a gibbet as high as Haman, to feed the carrion buzzards." But, in 1866 we find the same paper expressing the opinion that "the iron firmness, the undismayed soul of a single man (Andrew Johnson) is all that stands between us and the fateful vortex of anarchy and resultant despotism which has engulfed the lives and fortunes of so many millions before us. Let us rally to the side of that man, determined to save or perish with the Republic." (Quoted in St. Louis *Evening News,* July 21, 1866.)

15. Frank Cowan: *Andrew Johnson, His Private Life.*

16. After his death there was found a pencilled note which he had written when he was stricken with cholera. In it he proclaimed his credo to battle for his ideals, no matter what the cost. (Nashville *Union and American,* Aug. 31, 1875.)

17. Nashville *Dispatch*, April 5, 1865.
18. Nashville *Union*, April 6, 1865.
19. *Johnson Papers*, Library of Congress. Col. Robert Johnson to Maj. N. H. McLean, Oct. 12, 1862.
20. *Ibid.*: Robert Johnson to Andrew Johnson, Oct. 16, 1862.
21. "Petition of Officers to Colonel Robert Johnson," July 26, 1862. *Johnson Papers*, Library of Congress.
22. *Johnson Papers*, Vol. 83.
23. *Johnson Papers*, Vol. 115.
24. Gideon Welles: *Diary*, Vol. II, March 31, 1866.
25. *Johnson Papers*, Vol. 114.
26. Washington *Star*, Dec. 15, 1866.
27. *Ibid.*
28. Nashville *Daily Press and Times*, April 24, 1869; Cincinnati *Commercial*, April 26, 1869.
29. Nashville *Republican Banner*, April 24, 1869.
30. New York *Times*, April 28, 1869.
31. *Johnson Papers*. Andrew Johnson, Jr., to Andrew Johnson, Vol. 158, No. 25,660.
32. *Ibid.*, Vol. 159, No. 25,849.
33. *Ibid.*, Vol. 159, No. 25,881.
34. *Ibid.*
35. Greeneville *Intelligencer*, Oct. 2, 1874.
36. *Ibid.*
37. Gregory: *List of American Newspapers.*
38. Cincinnati *Daily Enquirer*, June 6, 1878.
39. Nashville *Union and American*, Aug. 31, 1875.

Sons of Ulysses S. Grant

(Pages 162 to 186)

1. Like Grant, Woodrow Wilson made several changes before he adopted a first name that satisfied him. We are told by the White House attaché, Ike Hoover, that when he "went to Princeton to arrange for the removal of President Wilson's effects to Washington, I noticed his books were autographed in various forms:

Thomas W. Wilson
Thomas Woodrow Wilson
T. W. Wilson
T. Woodrow Wilson
Woodrow Wilson."

(Irwin H. Hoover: *Forty-two Years in the White House*, p. 111.)

2. Jesse R. Grant: *In The Days of My Father; Dictionary of American Biography,* Vol. VII.

3. U. S. Grant: *Personal Memoirs,* Vol. 1.

4. New York *Times,* May 7, 1895. Thus, Franklin Roosevelt was not the first to address a request to some future President when he wrote a note asking an appointment for the infant son of Colin Kelly when the boy reached the age required for admission to West Point. The letter is in the Archives of the United States.

5. U. S. Grant: *supra,* Vol. I, pp. 46-47.

6. Jesse R. Grant: *In the Days of My Father,* p. 157. Compare with courtship of John Tyler.

7. Richard Taylor: *Destruction and Reconstruction,* p. 242.

8. "Diary of Capt. Richard L. Ogden." New York *Tribune,* Jan. 31, 1897.

9. U. S. Grant: *supra,* Vol. I, p. 239.

10. *Americana,* Vol. 7, July, 1912, p. 1028.

11. *Ibid.* p. 1025. It is interesting to note that when Grant was freed from Army commands and public office he did express opinions very readily not only on military matters and historical events, but also on current political and economic problems. John Russell Young, who accompanied Grant on his world journey, recorded quite a number of interviews with Grant and also his conversations with rulers of various countries. (John Russell Young: *Around the World with General Grant.*)

12. Southern generals, among them Richard Taylor, have argued that Vicksburg was surrendered to Grant much sooner than there was need. The fact that the commander had been born in the North gave rise to the charge that he was not loyal to the Confederacy. Grant asserted that to have continued resistance would have meant the useless slaughter of the Confederate troops. An interesting account of his views may be found in the interview he had with John Russell Young, recorded in the latter's *Around the World with General Grant.*

13. Neither the scandals during his Administration nor a later excursion into Wall Street which brought ruin to many banks and losses to individuals could mar the faith of the American people in the integrity of this military idol. As was expressed by one paper, "People were prepared to forgive almost anything to a man to whom the country owes so much as to him." (Boston *Post,* May 17, 1884.)

14. W. H. Crook: *Memories of the White House.*

15. U. S. Grant: *supra,* Vol. I, p. 248.

16. *Ibid.:* Vol. II, p. 110.

17. Jesse R. Grant: *supra,* p. 86.

18. *Dictionary of American Biography,* Vol. VII, p. 487.

19. New York *World,* Oct. 21, 1874. While Fred was courting, the son of a Navy Yard paymaster was impersonating him at Boston hotels, and forging his name to checks. (Washington *Star,* April 29, 1874; Boston *Advertiser,* April 28, 1874.)

20. New York *Times,* Oct. 22, 1874.

21. Chicago *Daily Tribune,* Oct. 24, 1874.

22. *Ibid.*

23. Chicago *Inter Ocean,* Oct. 21, 1874.

24. President Grant was enraptured with his son's wife. Writing a few days after the wedding to his old military secretary, General Badeau, Grant said: "Fred's wife is beautiful and is spoken of by all her acquaintances, male and female, young & old, as being quite as charming for her manners, amiability, good sense & education, as she is for her beauty. Mrs. Grant and I were charmed with the young lady and her family." (Badeau: *Grant in Peace,* p. 474. Letter dated Oct. 25, 1874.)

25. New York *Daily Graphic,* Oct. 23, 1874.

26. Chicago *Daily Tribune,* Oct. 21, 1874.

27. *Ibid.,* Oct. 24, 1874.

28. *Ibid.,* Oct. 21, 1874. Historians chronicling the trends in fashions and economists analyzing changes in fabric yardage requisite to clothe the feminine figure will find much for reflection in the trousseau of Ida Marie Honoré in the year 1874. The Chicago papers described the gowns, the suits, and the lingerie with which the wife of the President's son was beginning her married life. "Particular mention should be made of a delicate blue silk," observed one journal, "the train was trimmed with four rows of knife plaitings three inches in width, while above all this was a ruffle about four inches wide, made of silk, the center being gathered in seven shirrs, and the top finished by a standing ruffle. The side widths were finished in semi-circle trimmings, same as that worn upon the skirt, starting at the waist and terminating at the hem; an apron deep and pointed covered the front, which was trimmed with a broad band of blue ostrich feathers, while beneath it was a deep, heavy silk fringe completing the whole. Bows of silk were placed on every breadth." (Chicago *Inter Ocean,* Oct. 21, 1874.)

29. Washington *Evening Star,* Oct. 28, 1874.

30. Jesse R. Grant: *supra,* p. 199.

31. New York *Times,* Jan. 6, 1876, and March 10, 1876.

32. Jesse R. Grant: *supra,* p. 12.

33. W. H. Crook: *Memories of the White House.*

34. San Francisco *Call,* Jan. 2, 1899.

35. Badeau: *Grant in Peace.*

36. Cornell University *Register,* 1874–75.

37. Badeau: *supra,* p. 475. Letter dated Oct. 25, 1874.

38. Jesse R. Grant: *supra,* p. 223.

39. Badeau: *supra.*

40. John Russell Young: *Around the World with General Grant,* Vol. I, p. 32. Jesse's criticisms were so frequent that occasional praise by him was reported to America with ironic comment. Thus, the European correspondent of a leading New York newspaper devoted a paragraph to Jesse's praise of a banquet tendered his father in Paris: "Nothing could give more pleasure to the people of France and America than to know that Mr. Jesse Grant expressed his satisfaction with his dinner and general treatment. That young

man, we know, has had the reputation of being a little *difficile*." (New York *Tribune*, Nov. 19, 1877.)

41. New York *World*, May 9, 1884.

42. New York *Daily Tribune*, April 25, 1882.

43. Badeau (*Grant in Peace*, pp. 416-20) and others have endeavored to prove that ex-President Grant was not aware that Grant & Ward were manipulating Government contracts, or active in other questionable practices. However, contemporary newspapers published documents which indicated that Grant did know. It was said that the letters had been written by others and he merely signed them. This, however, was not compatible with Grant's temperament; when Badeau later claimed the authorship of part of the *Memoirs*, Grant proclaimed that during his entire Army career and also as President of the United States he had personally written all his orders and documents "bearing my name." (U. S. Grant to Gen. Adam Badeau.)

44. New York *World*, May 15, 1884.

45. Badeau: *supra*, p. 421. Some official audits differ from these appraisals. The transactions of Fred Grant particularly, involving loans, deposits, and debts, are typical of the "high finance" of that period. Readers with a bent for complicated finance will find data in the New York *World* and the Court records.

46. New York *Journal of Commerce*, May 7, 1884.

47. Boston *Post*, May 6, 1884.

48. New York *World*, May 1, 1884.

49. *Ibid.*, May 6, 1884.

50. New York *Times*, May 10, 1884.

51. New York *World*, May 8, 1884.

52. Savannah (Georgia) *Morning News*, May 10, 1884.

53. Boston *Transcript*, May 8, 1884.

54. San Francisco *Morning Call*, May 9, 1884.

55. Boston *Post*, May 17, 1884. The debate regarding Grant's knowledge of the transactions of the bankrupt firm invaded the churches. From the pulpit the famed Henry Ward Beecher eloquently absolved U. S. Grant from any knowledge or responsibility. But other ministers, among them the Rev. Pullman, pastor of the Church of Our Savior, were equally vehement in pronouncing that Grant was aware of Grant & Ward's misdeeds. (New York *World*, May 17, 1884.)

56. New York *World*, May 14, 1884. After the failure of Grant & Ward, the ex-President began writing his *Personal Memoirs*. He had anticipated that this work would bring him $30,000; but, two years after his death, the trade paper *Bookman* estimated that Mrs. Grant had received $494,600 from the sale of the *Memoirs*, the gross receipts being $3,000,000. By the summer of 1887, 312,000 sets were sold. (*Public Opinion*, July 23, 1887.) In subsequent years the sales mounted still higher.

57. New York *Post*, May 23, 1884. New York *Times*, May 9, 1884.

58. New York *World*, May 26, 1884.

59. Boston *Transcript*, May 8, 1884.

60. New York *World,* May 10, 1884. The father had a far more exalted opinion of them. Badeau tells us that "he admired the talents of his sons as if it had been extraordinary; he declared Ulysses had a marvelous business capacity; that Colonel Grant was fit to command armies; that Jesse was a mathematical genius." (Badeau; *supra,* p. 414.)

61. Washington *Sunday Herald,* Sept. 18, 1887.

62. Boston *Globe,* Sept. 16, 1887.

63. St. Louis *Anzeiger des Westerns,* Sept. 16, 1887. The German vote was then extremely important in "close states" and, in anticipation of the national election the following year, politicians were much impressed by the comment in papers printed in the German language.

64. Atlanta *Constitution,* Sept. 16, 1887.

65. Chicago *News,* Sept. 15, 1887.

66. Albany (N. Y.) *Journal,* Sept. 15, 1887.

67. Philadelphia *Journal,* Sept. 19, 1887.

68. "The nomination is said to be indicative of a strong sentiment looking toward Robert Lincoln for the Presidency next year. If Colonel Grant is elected this fall . . . that sentiment may become very positive." (Indianapolis *Journal,* Sept. 15, 1887.) Henry Stoddard, in his review of Presidential nominations, describes the plan to nominate a "father-son" ticket which was to have included as the Presidential and Vice-Presidential candidates the sons of Abraham Lincoln and U. S. Grant. (Stoddard: *As I Knew Them,* p. 157.)

69. *Dictionary of American Biography,* Vol. VII, p. 487.

70. New York *Tribune,* April 3, 1897.

71. *Ibid.*

72. Chicago *Tribune,* April 11, 1912; Detroit *Free Press,* April 12, 1912.

73. New York *Evening Post,* Sept. 30, 1909.

74. The real cause of his death was made public for the first time in May, 1916. It was then that Dr. Robert Abbe, who had signed the death certificate (Detroit *Free Press,* April 13, 1912) ascribing death to a "blood clot," wrote a treatise on "The Legacy of the Intemperate Use of Tobacco" (*Medical Record,* May, 1916), and divulged that Frederick Grant had died of a cancer of the throat superinduced by the excessive use of tobacco. (New York *Times,* May 28, 1916.)

75. New York *World,* April 12, 1912.

76. Detroit *Free Press,* April 13, 1912.

77. St. Louis *Republic,* April 13, 1912.

78. Vicksburg (Miss.) *Herald,* April 13, 1912.

79. New York *World,* April 25, 1912. His brothers did not attend the funeral. (Cincinnati *Enquirer,* April 12, 1912.)

80. "Seventh Report of Class Secretary, Class of 1874," Harvard College, 1899.

81. *Ibid.*

82. San Francisco *Call,* Jan. 11, 1899.

83. *Ibid.,* Jan. 10, 1899.

84. San Francisco *Chronicle,* Jan. 28, 1899.

85. However, there was a decided gain for democratic government: scandalized by these recurrent briberies of state legislators upon whom devolved the selection of United States Senators, the California Legislature adopted a resolution calling upon the Congress of the United States to submit to the states an amendment to the Constitution which would provide for the election of United States Senators by popular vote, and finally the Nation did adopt this procedure.

86. San Francisco *Call,* March 5, 1899.

87. "Fiftieth Anniversary Report of Class of 1874," Harvard University, 1924.

88. Los Angeles *Times,* Sept. 27, 1929.

89. "Report of Class of 1885," Harvard University, 1924.

90. New York *Times,* July 15, 1913.

91. *Ibid.,* July 21, 1913.

92. Los Angeles *Times,* Sept. 27, 1929.

93. New York *Times,* June 9, 1934.

94. New York *Tribune,* May 22, 1897.

95. *Ibid.,* April 27, 1897.

96. *Ibid.,* Nov. 2, 1906.

97. *American Historical Magazine,* Vol. II, 1907, p. 152.

98. New York *Times,* June 21, 1914.

99. *Ibid.,* June 30, 1914.

100. *Ibid.*

101. Los Angeles *Times,* June 10, 1934; New York *Times,* Sept. 8, 1934.

Sons of Rutherford B. Hayes

(Pages 187 to 201)

1. *Diary and Letters of Rutherford B. Hayes,* Ohio Archæological and Historical Society, Vol. I, p. 365.

2. *Ibid.,* Vol. I, p. 366.

3. *Ibid.*

4. New York *Tribune,* Jan. 1, 1878.

5. *Diary and Letters of Rutherford B. Hayes,* Vol. II, p. 289.

6. *Ibid.:* Letter of Aug. 24, 1864.

7. There were millions of Americans then, and scores of historians since, who believed that he had never been elected. Hayes was the Republican candidate in the campaign of 1876; his Democratic opponent was Samuel J. Tilden. The popular vote was 264,000 greater for Tilden than for Hayes. For months after Election Day the American people were not certain who had been chosen President, nor could they foretell who finally would be inaugurated. The campaign managers of each claimed the electoral votes of Florida,

38. *Ohio State Journal*, Feb. 18, 1932; *ibid.*, Feb. 25, 1932.
39. New York *Times*, May 31, 1932.
40. *Ibid.*
41. *Ibid.*, June 5, 1932.
42. *Ibid.*
43. *Ibid.*, June 13, 1932.
44. Text in Baltimore *News*, June 16, 1932.
45. New York *Times*, June 17, 1932.
46. New York *Herald Tribune*, June 17, 1932.
47. Chicago *Tribune*, June 16, 1932.
48. New York *Sun*, June 16, 1932.
49. Wilmington (Del.) *Every Evening*, June 16, 1932; Kansas City *Star*, June 17, 1932; Philadelphia *Enquirer*, June 17, 1932.
50. New York *Times*, June 23, 1932.
51. *Who's Who in Massachusetts*, 1942, published by Larkin, Roosevelt & Larkin, Ltd.; Poor's *Directory of Directors*, 1939; *Who's Who in America*, 1925 to 1943.
52. *Decennial Catalogue and Class Book* of Massachusetts Institute of Technology, August, 1907, p. 53.
53. *The Architect and Engineer*, February, 1931, pp. 124-27.
54. New York *Times*, Nov. 6, 1927.
55. *Ibid.*, May 16, 1928.
56. The journals in the larger cities printed long accounts of the career of Harry Augustus Garfield, and his photograph. Several prominent newspapers commented editorially upon his distinguished work as a teacher and as a college president. The headlines noted that he was a President's son. (New York *Times*, Dec. 12, 1942.)
57. *Who's Who in America*, 1946–47, Vol. 24, pp. 843-44.
58. Martindale-Hubbell: *Law Directory*, 1947.
59. Poor's *Register of Directors*, 1946, p. 1684.
60. New York *Times*, Feb. 14, 1947.
61. Cleveland *Plain Dealer*, Feb. 14, 1947.

Son of Chester A. Arthur

(Pages 220 to 226)

1. W. H. Crook: *Memories of the White House*, p. 160. Contemporary newspapers devoted much space to the renovations of the White House for Arthur's occupancy. "His private apartment was sumptuously decorated," said the Albany *Journal* (Sept. 18, 1883), and the phrase was echoed in other papers. (Philadelphia *Times*, Sept. 16, 1883.)
2. New York *Daily Graphic*, Dec. 2, 1881, and Dec. 5, 1881. After Arthur

became Chief Executive, the assassin Guiteau declared to the press: "I appeal to the President of the United States. I am the man who made him President. Without my inspiration he was a political cypher, without power or importance." (Buffalo *Commercial Advertiser,* Nov. 15, 1881.) In the *Arthur Papers* in the Library of Congress will be found a note from Guiteau to the President asking for aid at his trial.

3. Colman: *White House Gossip,* p. 160.

4. New York *World,* Nov. 19, 1886. Years after Arthur's death, M. C. Hendley (who had been executive clerk at the White House) declared that the President's "nose was not quite right," intimating that the painter of the White House portrait had skillfully hidden the defect. (M. C. Hendley to Charles Moore, April 22, 1925. Library of Congress.) This assertion brought denials from friends of the former President who indignantly asserted that "President Arthur's nose was rather short, but perfectly well shaped." (Arthur H. Masten to Charles Moore, June 16, 1926. Library of Congress.)

5. A typical example was a full-page drawing in the New York *Daily Graphic* labeled the "The arduous labors of the Chief Executive of the Republic." (Oct. 3, 1883.)

6. Wrote Julia Sand to Vice-President Arthur when Garfield was reported near death: "The hours of Garfield's life are numbered—before this meets your eye, you may be President. The people are bowed in grief; but—do you realize it—not so much because he is dying, as because *you* are his successor." (Julia Sand to Chester A. Arthur, Aug. 27, 1881. *Arthur Papers,* Library of Congress.)

7. New York *World,* Nov. 19, 1886.

8. Henry L. Stoddard: *As I Knew Them,* p. 117.

9. *Dictionary of American Biography,* Vol. I, p. 376. This appraisal is amply warranted by contemporary newspapers. An example of the popular sentiment was reflected in the greeting accorded Arthur when he was spied in a New York theater box: "The audience rose to their feet, and in response to their cheers the President bowed." (Albany *Evening Journal,* Sept. 18, 1883.) The press in all sections of the country, when Arthur died, praised his Presidential career: "Called to the Presidency under circumstances that naturally aroused prejudice against him even among members of his own party, Mr. Arthur proved one of the best Presidents this country ever had," was the verdict of the New Orleans *Times Democrat.* (Nov. 19, 1886.) "He left the Presidency with far greater honor than that with which he attained unto it," said the Springfield *Republican;* and the Boston *Post* commented upon his death that "Mr. Arthur's largeness of character was not suspected until a tragedy raised him to the Presidency." (Nov. 20, 1886.) "Above all," commented the New York *Sun,* "Arthur was an American." (Nov. 19, 1886.)

10. Elihu Root to Moore, May 1, 1925, *Arthur Papers,* Library of Congress. Chauncey M. Depew similarly noted that, after Arthur became President, those who had been on familiar terms with him were made aware that there could no longer be informal intimacy between them and their former political leader. (Chauncey M. Depew: *My Memories of Eighty*

Years, p. 116.) However, there is abundant proof that his important friends did call him "Chet." (Shanklin: *American Nicknames*, p. 121.)

11. New York *Tribune*, April 16, 1882. Regarding Arthur's private life while President there is a great divergence of opinion. In contemporary newspapers there were innuendoes that the White House occupant had a liking for wine and women. The austere and abstemious ex-President Rutherford Hayes credited rumors that there had been "nothing like it ever before in the Executive mansion—liquor, snobbery, and worse." (*Diary and Letters of Rutherford B. Hayes*, Vol. IV, p. 417. Ohio State Archeological and Historical Society.) It was Hayes' opinion that "sensual indulgence was the end and aim of [Arthur's] social intercourse. To this he gave his life and by it he lost his life." (*Ibid.*, p. 419.) Another opinion may be cited: Wise, who often visited the White House, recorded in his reminiscences that "Arthur was a high liver. He was not by any means a drunkard, but he was a typical man-about-town and showed it in his fat and ruddiness." (Wise: *Recollections of Twelve Presidents*, p. 163.) It is not within the purview of this treatise to judge the life of Chester A. Arthur, but these contemporary appraisals of the Presidential father *may afford understanding of the President's son.*

12. Crook: *supra*, p. 161.

13. *Ibid.*, p. 162. The attendance of the Presidential son at Princeton brought considerable prestige to that institution. "Princeton College will soon rank with Yale and Harvard, and is every day growing in popularity," declared a leading society magazine, announcing that "General McClellan has just sent his son there to finish his education, as has also Mr. Murat Halstead. Many others of our prominent men who are all able to appreciate the fine educational advantages offered, have also placed their sons there." (*The American Queen*, Oct. 7, 1882.)

14. Princeton University: *Susquidecennial Record of Class of 1885*, January, 1901.

15. Julia Sand to Chester A. Arthur, Sept. 15, 1886. *Arthur Papers*, Library of Congress.

16. Princeton University: *Record of Class of 1885*, 1909.

17. Colorado Springs *Gazette*, July 19, 1937.

18. Arthur Masten to Library of Congress, Jan. 27, 1926; New York *Times*, Dec. 15, 1925.

19. New York *Evening Post*, Nov. 22, 1886: "The first person to leave the home after the coffin was Chester Alan Arthur, the son of the ex-President." Several papers noted that Alan was a graduate of Princeton College, a student in the Columbia Law School, and that "his practical training he received in the law office in which the ex-President was a member up to the time of his election to the vice-presidency on the Garfield ticket." (Springfield *Republican*, Nov. 19, 1886.)

20. New York *Times*, Dec. 7, 1927.

21. Colorado Springs *Gazette*, Nov. 4, 1934.

22. Denver *Rocky Mountain News*, Nov. 4, 1934.

23. New York *Times,* Nov. 4, 1934.

24. *Ibid.,* July 19, 1937. The local newspaper devoted two columns to his career, heading the account, "Chester A. Arthur Dies at His Home. Was President's Son." (Colorado Springs *Gazette,* July 19, 1937.)

Sons of Grover Cleveland

(Pages 227 to 236)

1. Washington *Evening Star,* May 29, 1886.

2. G. Ticknor Curtis: *Life of James Buchanan,* p. 17. James Buchanan rose to fame and power and wealth—Senator, Minister to Great Britain, President of the United States—but he never married. To the end of his days he treasured the love letters penned by the girl he loved, sealed them in a package and willed that, unopened and unread by others, they be destroyed when he himself had joined her in the other world.

3. Allan Nevins: *Grover Cleveland—A Study in Courage,* pp. 164-6.

4. Grover Cleveland was not the only candidate for the Presidency whose private life was made an issue in election campaigns. The political opponents of Andrew Jackson applied to him every term in the dictionary of vituperation (see chapter, "Son of Andrew Jackson"). Much later, in an effort to defeat Woodrow Wilson and also Warren Harding, circulation was given to slanders and rumors regarding their "affairs with women."

5. The two Presidential terms of Grover Cleveland were not successive; they were separated by the term of Benjamin Harrison. Grover Cleveland served, first, from March, 1885 to March, 1889; his second term was from March, 1893 to March, 1897. Chauncey M. Depew summed up the fluctuating popularity of this President: "President Cleveland entered upon his second term with greater popularity in the country than most of his predecessors. When he retired from office, it was practically by unanimous consent." (Chauncey M. Depew: *My Memories of Eighty Years,* p. 127.) The outstanding characteristic of Grover Cleveland was his courage; and his friends exulted that they "loved him for the enemies he had made." Woodrow Wilson, himself a President, considered Cleveland's "practical viewpoint" as his greatest virtue. (David F. Houston: *Eight Years with Wilson's Cabinet,* p. 171.)

6. Scandal mongers in Washington spread the rumor that Cleveland upbraided and slapped his wife because she attended a theater escorted by a publisher; this story, it was said, was repeated by Chauncey Depew at a dinner party. Depew himself asserted that he had heard the story in Chicago, in St. Louis, and in New York. (New York *Times,* Dec. 8, 1888.) From the very beginning of their married life gossipers and newspaper writers spied on the Clevelands; during their honeymoon, in the Maryland mountains, re-

porters "armed with powerful field glasses erected a whispering post opposite the honeymooners' cottage and told the public how a newly married President passed his time." (Robert McElroy: *Grover Cleveland: The Man and the Statesman,* Vol. I, p. 187.) The spying continued when the Clevelands returned to the White House; as a result, the park back of the White House which had always been open to the public was closed by order of the President. (New York *World,* Nov. 29, 1886.) There were also rumors that the President was drinking heavily. All of these reports were proven false. Said the New York *Times,* "Mr. Cleveland has more than his share of these outrages, but Washington and Lincoln had their proper share too." (New York *Times,* April 8, 1895.)

7. Washington *Star,* June 3, 1886.

8. "Oscar Folsom was . . . instantly killed on July 23, 1875. He died without a will. The court appointed Cleveland administrator of the estate." (Allan Nevins: *Grover Cleveland.*) Cleveland's courtship of Frances is described in Nevins: *supra,* pp. 302-6. How the secret was kept from the public is interestingly detailed by another biographer, Robert McElroy. (*Grover Cleveland: The Man and the Statesman,* Vol. I, p. 184.)

9. Crook, in his reminiscences of forty-five years at the White House, wrote, "I have seen many women of various types through all the long years of my service at the White House, but neither there nor elsewhere have I seen anyone possessing the same kind of downright *loveliness* which was as much a part of Mrs. Cleveland as was her voice." (Crook: *Memories of the White House,* p. 184.) The austere Rutherford B. Hayes, who had himself been an occupant of the White House, wrote in his diary: "Mrs. Cleveland has appeared so kindly and full of heartiness that one can't help but think well of her." (*Diary and Letters of Rutherford B. Hayes,* Vol. IV, pp. 339-40.) The newspapers watched her every action; when she kissed the President before he went to the inauguration ceremony, the Brooklyn *Daily Eagle* commented: "The act of Mrs. Cleveland was done so simply and with such womanly grace, that it seemed to be the most natural occurrence in the world and endeared the wife of the President-elect to all those in the apartment." (Brooklyn *Daily Eagle,* March 5, 1893.)

10. Brooklyn *Daily Eagle,* July 8, 1893.

11. New York *Tribune,* June 19, 1898.

12. *Ibid.,* Oct. 29, 1897.

13. *Letters of Grover Cleveland,* edited by Allan Nevins, p. 488.

14. New York *Tribune,* July 19, 1903.

15. *Nassau Herald,* Princeton University, June, 1919, p. 336. During the following year, Richard was in the Army and Princeton had no football teams during his junior and senior years.

16. New York *Tribune,* July 19, 1903.

17. *Ibid.*

18. New York *World,* July 19, 1903.

19. *Letters of Grover Cleveland,* pp. 569-70.

20. Newark *Evening Star,* Feb. 10, 1913.

21. Memphis *Commercial Appeal,* June 21, 1923. An interesting account of this crusade against fraternities at Princeton—"The Quad Struggle"—in which Richard Cleveland was a leading figure among the undergraduates, may be read in Ray Stannard Baker: *Woodrow Wilson, Princeton,* p. 273.

22. *Nassau Herald,* Princeton University, Class of 1919, pp. 75-76.

23. *Ibid.*, pp. 321-22.

24. New York *Times,* June 21, 1923.

25. Memphis *Commercial Appeal,* June 21, 1923.

26. Baltimore *Evening Sun,* May 25, 1943.

27. *American Bar Directory,* 1941.

28. Baltimore *Evening Sun,* May 25, 1943.

29. 1934–35.

30. New York *Times,* May 12, 1932.

31. Baltimore *Sun,* May 13, 1932.

32. Baltimore *News,* May 12, 1932.

33. *Ibid.*, July 1, 1932.

34. Baltimore *News-Post,* Oct. 29, 1936. In subsequent elections, the same newspapers again stressed in headlines that Richard was "Son of Late President Grover Cleveland." (*News-Post,* Oct. 24, 1940; *News-Post,* Oct. 22, 1940.)

35. Baltimore *Sun,* June 7, 1942.

36. *Ibid.*, Feb. 19, 1945.

37. Harvard University Catalog, 1925–26. List of graduates on June 18, 1925.

38. Trenton *State Gazette,* June 20, 1925.

39. *Ibid.*, June 22, 1925.

40. New York *Times,* June 21, 1925.

41. Harvard University: *Decennial Report of Class of 1925,* 1935.

42. Harvard University Catalog, 1928–29, November, 1928, p. 862.

43. 1931. He taught at the Browne and Nichols School.

44. Harvard University: *Decennial Report of Class of 1925.*

45. See chapter, "Sons of John Adams."

46. After 1935, he made no reports to the Harvard class secretary. In the *Sesquidecennial Report,* 1940, his occupation was still noted as "theater."

Son of Benjamin Harrison

(Pages 237 to 246)

1. Philadelphia *Press,* quoted in "Short Reviews of Public and Private Life of Genl. Benj. Harrison."

2. *Ibid.*

3. Sanderson: *Signers of the Declaration of Independence.*

4. *National Cyclopedia of American Biography,* Vol. I, p. 135.

5. There is a wide disparity in contemporary appraisals of Benjamin Harrison's ability and personality. Unquestionably, in the accounts of all associates of Presidents as well as in the autobiographies of their political supporters and adversaries, the personal experiences and relationship of the writer often colored the opinion. Henry Stoddard, the journalist, who knew intimately all the Presidents from Grant to Taft, evaluated Benjamin Harrison very highly. Stoddard named as the outstanding Presidents, Grover Cleveland, Theodore Roosevelt, and Woodrow Wilson; but he added, "I feel as though I were doing an injustice to Benjamin Harrison not to count him into the three; for, intellectually, he outranked them. He was the ablest of all." (Stoddard: *As I Knew Them,* p. 36.) In contrast, another able writer, John S. Wise, who knew thirteen Presidents intimately, expressed the opinion that Benjamin Harrison was the least able, that he lacked tact and understanding. (John S. Wise: *Recollections of Thirteen Presidents,* p. 246.)

6. New York *Daily Tribune,* Feb. 17, 1890.

7. *Lafayette College Journal,* June, 1877, p. 303.

8. *The Men of Lafayette,* 1891. Lafayette College Publication.

9. *The Men of Lafayette,* 1879.

10. New York *Daily Tribune,* April 7, 1889.

11. Brooklyn *Daily Eagle,* March 13, 1892.

12. Crook: *Memories of the White House.*

13. John S. Wise: *Recollections of Thirteen Presidents,* p. 245.

14. New York *Tribune,* Sept. 22, 1891.

15. Brooklyn *Daily Eagle,* March 13, 1892.

16. *Ibid.,* May 9, 1892.

17. John Shiver: *Through the South and West with the President.*

18. Brooklyn *Daily Eagle,* March 5, 1893.

19. New York *Times,* Dec. 29, 1894.

20. New York *Tribune,* Dec. 23, 1898. The flag was presented by the son of Russell Harrison to the Smithsonian Institute in Washington. (William Henry Harrison to the Author, May 14, 1945.)

21. Havana *Herald,* Sept. 12, 1899.

22. New York *Times,* Nov. 18, 1900.

23. New York *Tribune,* March 18, 1901.

24. *Ibid.,* March 20, 1901.

25. "Hearings before the Committee on Pensions," United States Senate. 75th Congress, 1st Session. (June 29, 1937.)

26. Indianapolis *News,* May 28, 1928.

27. Indianapolis *Star,* Aug. 5, 1927.

28. *Ibid.,* Dec. 15, 1936.

29. Indianapolis *News,* Dec. 14, 1936.

30. Helena *Daily Independent,* Dec. 14, 1936.

Sons of the Rough Rider

(Pages 247 to 273)

1. *Editor and Publisher,* Aug. 9, 1902.

2. *Ibid.,* Aug. 16, 1902.

3. Theodore Roosevelt, Jr.: *All in the Family,* p. 7.

4. Corinne Roosevelt Robinson: *My Brother, Theodore Roosevelt.*

5. Bishop: *Theodore Roosevelt and His Time,* Vol. I, p. 4.

6. Theodore Roosevelt: *Autobiography,* p. 30.

7. No President was more democratic than Theodore Roosevelt, yet he never lost respect for the heritage of culture. Long after he had achieved renown, he was pleased that his sons associated with the scions of famous families—even in death. When his youngest son Quentin was shot down in air combat, in the first World War, the ex-President wrote to Henry Cabot Lodge: "I have received very touching letters from France about Quentin. He is in good company, with the young Shaws, and Lowells and Winthrops of the Civil War." (Theodore Roosevelt to Henry Cabot Lodge, April 18, 1918, in *Selections from the Correspondence of Theodore Roosevelt and Henry Cabot Lodge,* Vol. II, p. 535.)

8. *Autobiography:* Chapter 5.

9. Thus far there have served as Assistant Secretary of the Navy: Theodore Roosevelt, Franklin Delano Roosevelt, Theodore Roosevelt, Jr., and Nicholas Roosevelt.

10. *Autobiography,* p. 57.

11. Corinne R. Robinson: *My Brother, Theodore Roosevelt,* p. 23.

12. Foreword to *Autobiography.*

13. Theodore Roosevelt: *Letters to His Children,* edited by Bishop, p. 237.

14. The "Cabots of Boston" in succeeding generations continued to maintain their prestige and their aloofness from the masses, and the undistinguished continued to "hold their distance." A rhyme in the dignified Boston *Transcript* described the cleavage at the funeral of a Judge Cabot in 1932:

> The rich, the learned, *filled the pews*—
> They had an hour to lend;
> And swarthy aliens *thronged the street*—
> They came to mourn a friend.
>
> (Boston *Transcript,* Jan. 11, 1932.)

15. Bishop: *Theodore Roosevelt and His Time,* Vol. I, p. 71.

16. The journalist Henry Stoddard, who witnessed the battle at San Juan, explains that the men were originally called "walkers": "I call them Rough Riders because that was the name the regiment had acquired before sailing for Cuba. History knows them only as Rough Riders. They were not Rough

Riders at all in Cuba, for their horses were never brought over. Down there we called them Wood's Weary Walkers. Leonard Wood was the Colonel in command and Roosevelt was Lieutenant Colonel—hence the alliterative change [from 'Roosevelt's Rough Riders']. They were a wild lot, those Rough Riders. They did not know what discipline meant, though they knew how to fight." (Stoddard: *As I Knew Them,* p. 308.) There is ample corroboration of this; Col. John M. Thompson, who commanded the artillery, has left a description. (New York *Times,* Oct. 1, 1927.) A more dramatic—and less accurate—recollection by one of the participants also exists. (New York *Times,* Oct. 23, 1927.)

17. It has become the habit of biographers to regard Theodore Roosevelt as the sole organizer of the "Rough Riders" and their ranking commander in the Spanish-American War. This is inaccurate. Leonard Wood, who had made soldiering his career and had already reached the rank of colonel at the outbreak of our conflict with Spain, really recruited the cavalry to which the sobriquet was attached. Teddy Roosevelt organized additional riders, and was second in command of a division. Nor was the title "Rough Riders" first applied in that war; a cavalry brigade in the Civil War, led by General Stoneman, was called "Rough Riders"—they pursued Jefferson Davis after the fall of the Confederacy. (New York *Times,* May 9, 1865.)

18. Ike Hoover was right: these Roosevelt sons had more rooms to explore than did their juvenile predecessors. It was during Theodore Roosevelt's occupancy of the White House that the attic was used for the first time, converted into living quarters. (Theodore Bingham's *Collection of White House Functions,* Library of Congress.) It was also this President who officially changed the name of the Presidential residence from "Executive Mansion" to "White House"; the Bingham collection contains the official order for stationery with the new designation. However, the name "White House" was occasionally used by newspapers long before this formal christening; for instance, in an editorial the Boston *Statesman* of April 26, 1828, used as a slogan, "This is the way the second Adams got into the *White House.*"

19. Irwin H. Hoover: *Forty-two Years in the White House,* p. 28.

20. Crook: *Memories of the White House.*

21. Kermit Roosevelt: *The Long Trail,* p. 13.

22. Theodore Roosevelt, Jr.: *All in the Family,* p. 5.

23. *Ibid.,* p. 79.

24. Jacob A. Riis in the New York *Tribune* Illustrated Supplement, Oct. 3, 1902.

25. Hoover: *supra.*

26. New York *Times,* Sept. 18, 1904.

27. St. Louis *Globe Democrat,* Dec. 5. 1898.

28. New York *Tribune* Illustrated Supplement, Oct. 3, 1902. Like his father, young Theodore was always eager for adventure. When the Army, in 1908, experimented with balloons, "young Teddy" climbed into the basket of the first which ascended, remaining in the air from two o'clock in the afternoon until nearly midnight. "Theodore, Jr., An Aeronaut" was a fre-

quent headline. "President's Son Takes First Balloon Trip" was the caption of a long article in a prominent Boston paper which praised his courage. (*Daily Globe,* April 23, 1908.) A detailed account of this escapade may be read in C. deF. Chandler: *How Our Army Grew Wings,* p. 83.

29. New York *Tribune,* Feb. 11, 1902.

30. Theodore Roosevelt to Sir George Trevelyan, Oct. 1, 1911. Bishop: *Theodore Roosevelt and His Time,* Vol. II, pp. 248-49.

31. *Ibid.*

32. Theodore Roosevelt to Henry Cabot Lodge, Aug. 12, 1918. *Selections from the Correspondence of Theodore Roosevelt and Henry Cabot Lodge,* Vol. II, pp. 534-35.

33. New York *Times,* July 13, 1944.

34. New York *Herald Tribune,* July 14, 1944.

35. New York *World,* Nov. 3, 1924.

36. New York *Times,* Sept. 26, 1924.

37. New York *Herald Tribune,* July 14, 1944.

38. New York *World,* Nov. 2, 1924.

39. New York *Times,* Sept. 26, 1924.

40. *Ibid.*

41. New York *Herald Tribune,* Sept. 26, 1924.

42. New York *World,* Sept. 26, 1924.

43. New York *Herald Tribune,* Nov. 2, 1924.

44. New York *Evening Post,* Nov. 7, 1924.

45. San Juan *Progress,* Jan. 4, 1932.

46. *Philippines Herald,* Jan. 11, 1932.

47. New York *Times,* Jan. 10, 1932.

48. Chicago *Daily Tribune,* Jan. 14, 1932.

49. Boston *Transcript,* Jan. 11, 1932.

50. New York *Times,* Jan. 13, 1932.

51. Los Angeles *Times,* Jan. 11, 1932.

52. *Philippines Herald,* Jan. 11, 1932.

53. *Ibid.,* Jan. 19, 1932.

54. New York *Times,* March 27, 1933.

55. *Ibid.,* March 17, 1933.

56. *Philippines Herald,* March 16, 1933.

57. New York *Herald Tribune,* July 14, 1944.

58. Philadelphia *Daily News,* Sept. 21, 1944. After his death a committee of friends began to collect funds for the erection of a library in his memory at Oyster Bay, N. Y. (Washington *News,* June 25, 1947.)

59. Kermit Roosevelt: *The Long Trail,* p. 14.

60. However, Theodore Roosevelt considered Ted the most skillful rider and marksman. Writing to Sir George Trevelyan, he said, "Ted was a better shot and rider than Kermit or myself." (Roosevelt to Trevelyan, Oct. 1, 1911. Bishop: *Theodore Roosevelt and His Time,* Vol. II, pp. 248-49.)

61. Theodore Roosevelt: *Letters to His Children,* ed. by Bishop. Nzoia River, Nov. 13, 1909.

62. William Roscoe Thayer: *Theodore Roosevelt,* p. 320.

63. Theodore Roosevelt: *Through the Brazilian Wilderness,* p. 399. The advertisements for this volume noted, "with illustrations from photographs by Kermit Roosevelt." (Ad of Scribner publications in *National Geographic Magazine,* November, 1914.)

64. Theodore Roosevelt to Henry Cabot Lodge, Aug. 12, 1918. *Selections from the Correspondence of Theodore Roosevelt and Henry Cabot Lodge,* Vol. II, p. 535.

65. New York *Times,* Jan. 6, 1927.

66. *Ibid.,* Jan. 30, 1920.

67. *Ibid.,* April 13, 1923.

68. Theodore Roosevelt, Jr.: *All in the Family,* p. 5.

69. New York *Times,* March 25, 1922.

70. *Ibid.,* March 27, 1922.

71. *Ibid.*

72. *Ibid.,* April 21, 1934.

73. When his will was probated public curiosity was aroused by the bequest of one-fifth of all his property as a life trust for a woman whose identity was shrouded in mystery—the family refusing explanations beyond the statement that she was a "friend of the family." (New York *Times,* July 27, 1943.)

74. New York *Times,* June 10, 1944.

75. Senate Joint Resolution 134, *Congressional Record,* June 21, 1944, p. 6456.

76. While the names of Theodore, Jr., and Kermit appeared in every issue of *"Who's Who in America"* since 1922, no mention was made of Archibald until the volume for 1936–37 was published.

77. Theodore Roosevelt to Sir George Trevelyan, April 9, 1918. Bishop: *supra,* Vol. II, pp. 181-82.

78. *Ibid.,* Vol. II, p. 465. The speech of the ex-President on Oct. 15, 1918, was re-echoed in our second war against the aggressor Germany. Said Theodore Roosevelt: "We must win the peace of overwhelming victory and accept no peace but unconditional surrender. Our whole effort must be to bring Germany to her knees and put a stop once for all to her threats of world dominion." (More of this speech appears in Bishop: *supra,* Vol. II, p. 466.)

79. New York *Times,* Aug. 4, 1919.

80. *Ibid.,* Aug. 5, 1919.

81. In the closing days of 1943, financial journals and the leading New York papers carried the announcement: "Roosevelt & Weigold announces with regret the resignation of Lieut. Col. Archibald B. Roosevelt as President, and the change in name to Chas. E. Weigold & Co., Incorporated." In April, 1946, the financial pages of the New York papers carried dignified two-column announcements that Archibald B. Roosevelt had organized "Roosevelt & Cross, Incorporated" to deal in state, municipal and government bonds. (New York *Herald Tribune,* April 1, 1946.)

82. New York *Times,* Sept. 17, 1943.

83. *Ibid.* Archibald's name seldom appeared in the newspapers after the

close of the war. A rare instance was his photograph in the New York *Times,* when he flew for a vacation to Bermuda. The brief comment noted that he was the "only surviving son of the late President, Theodore Roosevelt." (New York *Times,* July 13, 1947.)

84. Earle Looker: *The White House Gang,* p. 13.

85. Theodore Roosevelt: *Letters to His Children.*

86. Kermit Roosevelt: *Quentin Roosevelt, a Sketch with Letters,* p. 2.

87. *Ibid.*

88. Paris edition, New York *Herald,* Paris, July 17, 1918.

89. *Le Journal,* July 18, 1918.

90. *Le Temps,* July 19, 1918.

91. Bishop: *Theodore Roosevelt and His Time,* Vol. II, p. 454.

92. Theodore Roosevelt: *The Great Adventure.*

Sons of William Howard Taft

(Pages 274 to 291)

1. Several sons of John Tyler enrolled in German colleges; Zachary Taylor's son, Richard, studied in Scotland and France; and a son of Grover Cleveland studied in Switzerland.

2. Mrs. William Howard Taft: *Recollections of Full Years,* p. 275.

3. Although Roosevelt usually refused to discuss the break in his friendship with Taft, on several occasions he did confide in close friends that he considered Taft ungrateful but that the cleavage between them was due mostly to Taft's repudiation of the Roosevelt policies. (Stoddard: *As I Knew Them,* pp. 342-44.) Theodore Roosevelt refused to support Taft for a second term and, as the nominee of the new Progressive Party, he campaigned to defeat Taft. (David F. Houston: *Eight Years with Wilson's Cabinet,* Vol. I, p. 7.)

4. Mrs. Taft inferred that her husband owed his nomination for the Presidency to the efforts of his own family, maintaining that "my husband's brother Charles devoted a full year to it, establishing headquarters in Ohio and Washington, and bore the brunt of the contest." (*Recollections, supra,* p. 322.) Impartial commentators, however, are almost unanimous in the opinion that the dominating factor in Taft's nomination was the support of Theodore Roosevelt.

5. The college class book catalogued other Tafts who had preceded Robert, noting that "Taft's Yale relatives, besides his father, include: Alphonso Taft, 1833, grandfather; C. P. Taft, 1864, H. W. Taft, 1880, and H. D. Taft, 1883, uncles; Hulbert Taft, 1900, Howard Taft, 1906, W. S. Taft, 1907, and W. H. Taft, 2d, 1909, cousins." (Yale University: *History of the Class of 1910,* Vol. I, p. 316.)

6. Yale University: *History of the Class of 1910,* Vol. I, p. 316.

7. *Ibid.*

8. Another President's son—Harry A. Garfield—also held a post in that agency.

9. In addition to the corporations which he listed in his report for the Yale record, Robert Taft held substantial amounts of stock in the Baltimore & Ohio Railroad Company and in the Cleveland & Pittsburgh Railroad. In June, 1935, he asked the Interstate Commerce Commission for authority to serve as director of the Baltimore & Ohio while acting in the same capacity for other railroads. (New York *Times,* June 5, 1935.)

10. Yale University: *History of the Class of 1910,* Vol. IV, p. 186.

11. Cincinnati *Enquirer,* Nov. 3, 1938.

12. Cleveland *Plain Dealer,* Nov. 1, 1938.

13. Cincinnati *Enquirer,* Nov. 1, 1938.

14. New York *Times,* Nov. 13, 1938.

15. New York *Times Magazine,* Nov. 27, 1938.

16. Cleveland *Plain Dealer,* Nov. 9, 1938.

17. Columbus *Dispatch,* Nov. 9, 1938.

18. Columbus *Ohio State Journal,* Nov. 10, 1938.

19. Toledo *Blade,* Nov. 9, 1938.

20. Taft opposed Lend-Lease (*Time,* Feb. 24, 1941); opposed a world pact, arguing for separate pacts with each individual nation (New York *Times,* June 11, 1944); and was a leader in seeking to defeat both the Bretton Woods Agreement and the United Nations Charter formed at San Francisco.

21. New York *Times,* Nov. 15, 1940.

22. *Ibid.,* March 28, 1940.

23. *Ibid.,* March 12, 1940. "ME" was the abbreviation of the Washington telephone exchange "MEtropolitan" on the dial phones.

24. Grove Patterson, editor of the Toledo *Blade,* made the nominating speech. (New York *Times,* June 27, 1940.)

25. Chicago *Daily News,* June 27, 1940.

26. Chicago *Daily Tribune,* June 27, 1940.

27. Chicago *Daily News,* June 27, 1940.

28. With the exception of newspapers which were rabidly antagonistic to the policies of Franklin Roosevelt and repudiated Willkie because he supported some of the policies of the incumbent Administration, the American press generally acclaimed the nomination of Wendell Willkie, considering him superior to Robert Taft in liberalism and a grasp of world affairs. The New York *Times* summed up this widespread opinion: "In the opinion of this newspaper—an independent newspaper—the Republican party has chosen to put forward the best candidate at its command, a candidate who has stood head and shoulders above his rivals for his party's nomination." (New York *Times,* June 28, 1940.)

29. Washington *Post,* Feb. 22, 1945. "Today and Tomorrow."

30. *El Progresso,* quoted by Mrs. Taft in *Recollections, supra,* p. 116.

31. Mrs. William Howard Taft: *Recollections, supra,* p. 122.

32. *Ibid.*

33. Joseph B. Bishop: *Presidential Nominations and Elections.*

34. Yale College: *History of the Class of Nineteen Hundred and Eighteen*, Vol. I, p. 322.

35. *Ibid.*

36. *Ibid.*

37. New York *Times*, Nov. 7, 1927.

38. *Ibid.*, June 1, 1928.

39. *Ibid.*, April 23, 1937.

40. *Ibid.*, June 22, 1937.

41. *Ibid.*, July 21, 1937.

42. Washington *News*, June 12, 1945.

43. Department of State *Bulletin*, March 18, 1944, "Realistic View of Our International Economic Operations," p. 254.

44. *Time*, June 28, 1937.

45. He developed programs for recreation facilities for men in the armed services, and also procedures for control of venereal diseases. (*Time*, March 29, 1943.)

46. New York *Times*, Sept. 23, 1943.

47. Paul Mallon. Philadelphia *Inquirer*, July 13, 1945.

48. New York *Herald Tribune*, Nov. 24, 1945.

49. Washington *Times-Herald*, Nov. 24, 1945.

50. Senate Bill 1580.

51. *Congressional Record*, Nov. 29, 1945, pp. 11339-11340.

52. *Congressional Record*, Nov. 30, 1945, p. 11419.

53. Chicago *Daily Tribune*, Nov. 30, 1945.

54. New York *Times*, Nov. 30, 1945.

55. The vote was 41 to 18.

56. Mason of Illinois.

57. *Congressional Record*, Nov. 5, 1945, p. 10551.

58. Circular of New Jersey Taxpayers' Association, Trenton, December, 1945.

59. Washington *Post*, Dec. 3, 1945.

60. At the dinner of the National Association of Manufacturers, Dec. 6, 1945. New York *Times*, Dec. 7, 1945.

61. Washington *Post*, Jan. 7, 1947.

62. New York *Herald Tribune*, April 3, 1946; *Time*, April 15, 1946; Washington *Post*, April 3, 1946.

63. "A Program for the Republican Party." *Pageant Magazine*, May, 1946.

64. An example of his broadcasts may be read in the *Congressional Record*, June 10, 1946, Appendix, p. 3514.

65. *Time*, June 3, 1946.

66. Thomas Stokes, in Washington *Daily News*, June 5, 1946.

67. *PM*, December 31, 1946. A résumé of Robert Taft's intended program as leader was written by the able commentator Marquis Childs. (Evansville *Press*, Oct. 14, 1946.)

68. *Time,* Jan. 20, 1947.

69. New York *Times,* Jan. 1, 1947.

70. Washington *Daily News,* Jan. 5, 1947.

71. Washington *Post,* Jan. 10, 1947; New York *Herald Tribune,* Jan. 17, 1947.

72. Said one commentator: "At first Bob Taft was riding high. Today his reins are trailing in the dust." (Drew Pearson, in Washington *Post,* March 9, 1947.) Other political observers also noted the abrupt change in Robert's fortunes. "This is an obituary. It is an obituary for a hope that is now definitely and finally dead," were the opening sentences of an article by Marquis Childs discussing Taft's failure to control his own party. (Washington *Post,* March 7, 1947.) Robert Taft resented the argument that his leadership was not acknowledged completely. In a letter to the *Saturday Evening Post* he argued that "it is not easy to get fifty-one Republicans or fifty-one men of any classification to agree on major controversial issues." (Robert Taft to the editor, May 17, 1947.)

73. New York *Herald Tribune,* Feb. 23, 1947.

74. Washington *Post,* Feb. 23, 1947. Robert Taft's own statement regarding his opposition to the appointment was published in the same paper on February 22, 1947. Typical of the condemnation of Taft's arguments was the editorial in the Washington *Daily News,* Feb. 24, 1947.

75. San Francisco *Chronicle,* Oct. 6, 1946.

76. San Francisco *Examiner,* Oct. 6, 1946.

77. *Christian Science Monitor,* Nov. 21, 1946. Said this paper's able Roscoe Drummond: "Every one who knows Senator Taft is aware that he believes profoundly in what he advocates."

78. Arthur Krock, Washington observer for the New York *Times,* summed up Robert's fluctuating popularity: "Mr. Taft has ascended and descended several times in public favor in the last few months." (New York *Times,* April 6, 1947.) While his sponsorship of restrictive labor legislation increased his popularity among the general public which had tired of the excesses of some union leaders, the Congressional act which bore his name aroused the anger of organized labor. Union workers picketed the church in which Robert attended the wedding of his son. (New York *Herald Tribune,* June 29, 1947; New York *Times,* June 29, 1947.) The heads of various unions vied with each other in their scathing denunciation of him, and declared that they would exert every effort to defeat him if he were nominated for the Presidency. (New York *Times,* Aug. 24, 1947.)

79. See the Gallup Poll, Philadelphia Sunday *Bulletin,* May 11, 1947; Philadelphia *Inquirer,* April 26, 1947. Robert Taft's opposition to universal military training brought widespread censure by liberal newspapers; his views stood out in marked contrast to the polls of public opinion and the emphatic pleas of distinguished Americans of all creeds and parties. (Washington *Daily News,* June 30, 1947.) He was severely criticised by eminent men. (Philadelphia *Inquirer,* July 13, 1947.) Nevertheless, by midsummer of 1947, politicians and commentators began anew to discuss Robert's prospects for the

Presidential nomination. (New York *Herald Tribune,* July 13, 1947.) Editorials softened their appraisals of his "reactionary views"; many influential journals praised his sincerity and capabilities. "He has dominated because of his ability, his strong personality, and his never-flagging industry," declared one able commentator who had often criticised Robert's opposition to progressive measures. (Thomas L. Stokes, in the Washington *Daily News,* July 28, 1947.) Most of the important newspapers agreed that Robert Taft deserved praise for his courage in expressing his views when other aspirants for the Presidential nomination were either evasive or silent. (St. Louis *Globe-Democrat,* Aug. 2, 1947; Washington *Post,* Aug. 4, 1947.) A convention of Ohio Republicans endorsed his candidacy for the Republic's highest office; and, in the autumn of 1947, the columns of many newspapers contained either articles discussing Robert's chances for winning the nomination in the 1948 Republican convention, or cartoons depicting his progress toward that goal.

80. Martindale's *Directory of Lawyers* for 1947, the authoritative register of attorneys, lists prominent corporations as Charles' clients.

81. New York *Times,* Feb. 10, 1946.

82. Farrar & Straus. New York *Times* Book Review, May 26, 1946. The announcement made no mention of Charles Taft as a President's son, but described him as "a brother of Senator Robert A. Taft of Ohio."

83. *Time,* Feb. 17, 1947.

84. Washington *Post,* Dec. 6, 1946.

85. New York *Times,* May 22, 1947.

86. Thomas L. Stokes in Washington *Daily News,* June 12, 1945.

Sons of Calvin Coolidge

(Pages 292 to 300)

1. New York *Times,* Aug. 4, 1923.

2. Harding, in apparent good health, had taken a trip to Alaska and returned to San Francisco. There he suffered a heart attack.

3. Article II, section I: "In Case of the Removal of the President from Office, or of his Death, Resignation, or Inability to discharge the Powers and Duties of the said office, the Same shall devolve on the Vice-President."

4. Thus Calvin Coolidge was the sixth Vice-President who became Chief Executive through the death of a President. In similar manner, John Tyler had succeeded William Henry Harrison in 1841; Millard Fillmore succeeded Zachary Taylor in 1850; Andrew Johnson succeeded Abraham Lincoln in 1865; Chester A. Arthur succeeded James A. Garfield in 1881; Theodore Roosevelt succeeded William McKinley in 1901.

5. The *Dictionary of American Biography,* published in 1930, failed to

include the name of Calvin Coolidge; in the 1944 edition—after his death—seven pages were devoted to the account of his career.

6. Stoddard: *As I Knew Them,* pp. 466-69.
7. Chauncey M. Depew: *My Memories of Eighty Years,* p. 342.
8. *Dictionary of American Biography, Supplement* XXI, p. 191.
9. Irwin H. Hoover: *Forty-two years in the White House,* p. 134.
10. Horace Green: *The Life of Calvin Coolidge,* p. 65.
11. New York *World,* Aug. 15, 1923.
12. *Ibid.,* Aug. 4, 1923.
13. Horace Green: *supra,* p. 59.
14. New York *World,* Aug. 4, 1923.
15. New York *Times,* Aug. 6, 1923.
16. *Ibid.,* July 8, 1924.
17. *Ibid.*
18. Washington *Star,* July 8, 1924.
19. New York *Times,* July 8, 1924.
20. Washington *Star,* July 8, 1924.
21. New York *World,* July 9, 1924.
22. The public press, accustomed to describing the imperturbability of the President, generally noted that there was no change in his austere demeanor during his son's illness. This stoicism might have been due to the fact that neither the President nor his wife at first considered that the infection was alarmingly serious. Undoubtedly, the President did feel deeply his son's untimely death; to another bereaved father the President wrote: "To my friend, in recollection of his son and my son who, by the grace of God, have the privilege of beings boys throughout Eternity." (Bartlett's *Familiar Quotations,* p. 819.) Those who knew Calvin Coolidge best asserted that his son's death changed the whole course of the President's conduct, and that he suffered intensely all the time. (James E. Watson: *As I Knew Them,* p. 250.)
23. New York *Times,* July 8, 1924.
24. Another member of the class, Stephen Brown, also of Northampton, Mass., was also called "Butch." Those who opposed the Presidential son in the boxing ring also acquired prestige; one of John's adversaries in an Amherst College tournament was offered $5,000 for three bouts in New York. (New York *Tribune,* Feb. 26, 1926.)
25. New York *Times,* May 1, 1927.
26. Irwin H. Hoover: *Forty-two Years in the White House,* p. 142.
27. New York *Times,* Nov. 16, 1927.
28. As was provided by the Federal statutes, for the protection of all members of the Presidential family.
29. The 1928 *Olio,* published annually by the Junior Class of Amherst, Vol. LXX.
30. New York *Times,* May 20, 1927.
31. Photographs of class members in *Olio,* Vol. LXX.
32. New York *Times,* June 19, 1928.
33. Indianapolis *Star,* May 28, 1928.

34. Hartford *Daily Times,* Sept. 24, 1929.
35. New York *Daily News,* Sept. 24, 1929.
36. New Haven *Journal Courier,* Sept. 24, 1929.
37. Hartford *Daily Times,* Sept. 24, 1929.
38. *Time,* Sept. 5, 1938.
39. Hartford *Courant,* June 27, 1941.
40. New York *Times,* June 27, 1941.
41. *Time,* June 27, 1941.
42. New York *Times,* Sept. 13, 1941.

Sons of Herbert Hoover

(Pages 301 to 309)

1. The copy in the Library of Congress is catalogued: *"De re metallica.* tr. from the first Latin ed. of 1556 with biographical introduction, annotations and appendices upon the development of mining methods, metallurgical processes, geology, mineralogy & mining law, from the earliest times to the 16th century, by Herbert Hoover and Lou Henry Hoover."

2. New York *Times,* June 16, 1928.

3. During his long stay in Europe and in the Orient he acquired the habit of walking on the left side; while Secretary of Commerce, he usually walked in that manner through the corridors of the building. Similarly, an earlier President also was affected by long sojourns in England; Martin Van Buren did not use the American expression, "running for office," but the British equivalent, "to *stand* as a candidate." (*Autobiography,* p. 220.)

4. Like other Presidents, Hoover dropped one of his baptismal names; he discarded "Clark" and called himself Herbert Hoover. See chapters on Grant, Wilson, and Cleveland.

5. His father died when Herbert was six; his mother three years later.

6. He failed in his entrance examination, but his eagerness impressed the college authorities, and he was admitted.

7. Her father was Charles D. Henry, of Waterloo, Iowa. When fame came to her, she was called "a banker's daughter."

8. New York *World,* Nov. 8, 1928.

9. *Register of Graduates of Leland Stanford University, 1892–1901.* Published in 1902.

10. Liverpool *Post and Mercury,* Nov. 7, 1928.

11. London *Times,* Nov. 7, 1928.

12. Liverpool *Post and Mercury,* Nov. 7, 1928.

13. For the first time the "solid South" which, since the Civil War, had invariably given overwhelming pluralities to the Democratic nominee, was now ruptured; three Southern states, traditionally Democratic, gave their

electoral votes to Herbert Hoover. Clashes and bloodshed at the polls were not infrequent; the Los Angeles *Times* tabulated numerous instances in various parts of the country. (Los Angeles *Times,* Nov. 7, 1928.)

14. Los Angeles *Times,* Nov. 7, 1928.
15. New York *Times,* March 4, 1929.
16. New York *World,* March 5, 1929. Other papers saw in the new Administration an era of friendly cooperation with the nations of the world. (Hartford *Courant,* March 5, 1929; Raleigh (N. C.) *News and Observer,* March 5, 1929; Brooklyn *Daily Eagle,* March 4, 1929.) However, to many commentators, Hoover's advent meant continued efforts to retain liquor prohibition. (St. Louis *Globe Democrat,* March 6, 1929; Cleveland *Plain Dealer,* March 5, 1929; Kansas City *Star,* March 5, 1929.)
17. Two centuries earlier, George Washington Adams—son of the sixth President—was born in Berlin, Germany. The namesake of the President succeeding Hoover was also foreign-born; Franklin D. Roosevelt, Jr., came into the world across the border, in Canada, on Campobello Island.
18. New York *Times,* June 20, 1928.
19. *Ibid.,* March 13, 1929.
20. Newark *Star-Eagle,* March 13, 1929.
21. Newark *Evening News,* March 13, 1929.
22. Sponsored by the Aeronautical Chamber of Commerce. Later, the son of another President, Elliott Roosevelt, became an "expert" for this Association.
23. New York *Times,* Aug. 21, 1929.
24. Los Angeles *Times,* Aug. 26, 1929.
25. *Ibid.,* Aug. 27, 1929.
26. He wrote an article in the *Aero Digest,* Jan., 1930.
27. New York *Times,* Feb. 20, Feb. 21, and Feb. 24, 1930.
28. *Ibid.,* Jan. 21, 1930.
29. *Ibid.,* May 13, 1930.
30. Los Angeles *Times,* Sept. 16, 1930.
31. New York *Times,* Oct. 17, 1930.
32. Asheville (N. C.) *Times,* Nov. 26, 1930.
33. *Ibid.,* Jan. 27, 1931.
34. *Ibid.,* May 29, 1931.
35. Asheville (N. C.) *Times,* Aug. 19, 1931.
36. Washington *Star,* March 5, 1929.
37. Irwin Hoover: *Forty-two Years in the White House,* p. 219.
38. New York *Times,* June 19, 1929.
39. Associated Press, July 14, 1929.
40. New York *Times,* July 15, 1929.
41. *Ibid.,* Aug. 1, 1929.
42. Washington *Star,* Aug. 2, 1929.
43. *Ibid.,* Aug. 15, 1929.
44. New York *Times,* Aug. 29, 1929.
45. *Ibid.,* Sept. 15, 1929.

46. *Ibid.*, Sept. 20, 1929.

47. Washington *Star,* Dec. 27, 1929.

48. New York *Times,* Dec. 27, 1929.

49. Washington *Star,* Jan. 2, 1930.

50. *Ibid.*

51. M. B. A.—Master in Business Administration: *Harvard Alumni Directory,* 1940.

52. 1929–31 Western Air Express.

53. 1931–34 Transcontinental & Western Airline, known as TWA. The name is now Trans World Airline.

54. New York *Times,* Feb. 14, 1940.

55. *Time,* Aug. 11, 1941.

56. New York *Times,* March 29, 1942.

57. *Science Service,* quoted in New York *Times,* Dec. 6, 1942.

58. Chairman of the Board, President, and Director of the Consolidated Engineering Corp. of California. Poor's *Register of Directors,* 1945, p. 1922.

59. *Time,* Feb. 3, 1937. In the spring of 1937, in applying for a marriage license, he listed his occupation as "rancher".

60. *Harvard Alumni Directory,* 1940.

61. Under the Agricultural Adjustment Administration Act.

62. New York *Times,* April 20, 1936.

63. *Ibid.,* March 7, 1937.

64. Los Angeles *Times,* March 17, 1937.

65. *Ibid.,* March 18, 1937, p. 9, sec. 2.

66. *Ibid.*

67. New York *Times,* March 18, 1937.

68. *Ibid.,* March 30, 1944. Thereafter, the names of Alan and his brother seldom appeared in the newspapers.

69. There have been divergent views as to whether Hoover should be designated the 30th or 31st President. The consecutive count to 1885 made Grover Cleveland the twenty-second President. He was succeeded in 1889 by Benjamin Harrison, the twenty-third Chief Executive. But Cleveland followed Harrison in 1893, and this second term in office, following Harrison's, is usually numbered twenty-four. Counting Cleveland twice, Hoover was the 31st President.

70. Mrs. Herbert Hoover—the Lou Henry Hoover who helped to translate Agricola—died in January, 1944, leaving most of her property to her two sons. (Washington *Post,* Jan. 30, 1944.) In a letter attached to her will she praised her husband and told Herbert, Jr., and Alan that they were "lucky boys to have such a father." (New York *Times,* Feb. 26, 1944.) The ex-President was attached to his sons, and often visited their homes. (Cincinnati *Enquirer,* Aug. 11, 1947.)

Sons of Franklin D. Roosevelt

(Pages 310 to 346)

1. Notably, the diaries of John Adams, John Quincy Adams, and Rutherford B. Hayes—and the letters which passed between these Presidents and their sons—reveal a comradeship which pervaded and influenced the lives of both fathers and sons; similarly, the activities and correspondence of Theodore Roosevelt and Martin Van Buren reflect a lifelong interdependence between the elders and their offspring. Thus far, in all the prolific writings of Franklin D. Roosevelt, there has been published no correspondence between him and his sons; it is altogether probable that, in after years, there will come to light personal letters which are now hidden from public gaze. However, the events recorded in these pages stand out in sharp contrast to the closeness between other Presidents and their sons.

2. New York *Times,* Feb. 21, 1934. Similarly, as revealed by James A. Farley in an account of the Chicago convention, when Elliott's Presidential father expressed the desire that Henry Wallace be nominated for the Vice-Presidency, Elliott offered to second the nomination of another man. (James A. Farley: "Why I Broke with Roosevelt," in *Collier's,* July 19, 1947.)

3. *Ibid.,* April 30, 1933.
4. Boston *Globe,* Aug. 14, 1938.
5. Boston *Evening Transcript,* Sept. 21, 1933.
6. New York *Times,* Sept. 13, 1933.
7. Said James Roosevelt to his listeners: "As you know, I am probably closest by blood and affection to the man who makes the appointment." (New York *Times,* Sept. 3, 1933.)
8. New York *Times,* Sept. 16, 1933.
9. *Ibid.,* Oct. 10–24, 1933.
10. Paris edition, New York *Herald,* Oct. 15, 1933.
11. New York *Times,* July 13, 1935.
12. *Ibid.,* Nov. 21, 1935.
13. Buffalo *Evening News,* Oct. 1, 1940.
14. New York *Post,* July 1, 1937.
15. *Time,* July 4, 1938.
16. *Christian Science Monitor,* July 2, 1938.
17. Philadelphia *Public Ledger,* July 2, 1938.
18. *Saturday Evening Post,* July 2, 1938.
19. *Time,* July 11, 1938, p. 37.
20. *Collier's Weekly,* Aug. 20, 1938.
21. *Ibid.*
22. A. A. Schecter: *I Live On Air,* p. 391.
23. *Ibid.,* p. 405.

24. James Roosevelt, in National Broadcasting Company interview, Aug. 11, 1938.

25. Philadelphia *Public Ledger,* Aug. 12, 1938.

26. St. Louis *Post-Dispatch,* July 1, 1938.

27. Los Angeles *Times,* Aug. 13, 1938. The "headline writers"—some motivated by their papers' antagonism to the President, but most of them prompted merely by the technique of arousing reader interest—used large blackface type in intriguing fashion; typical captions were: "Jimmy Roosevelt Tells What He Got" (St. Louis *Post-Dispatch,* Aug. 12); "Broker Sues Over Insurance Switched to Son of President" (Los Angeles *Times,* July 2); "Jimmy's Not Doing Badly, Says Income Article Writer" (*Ibid.,* Aug. 12); "Deal Switched to Roosevelt, Suit Charges" (Boston *Herald,* July 2); "Charges Bank Swung Big Fee to Son Jimmy" (Philadelphia *Inquirer,* July 2).

28. Boston *Herald,* Aug. 13, 1938.

29. Detroit *Free Press,* July 4, 1938.

30. Washington *News,* Feb. 24, 1940.

31. Detroit *News,* Jan. 29, 1945.

32. New York *Times,* Oct. 7, 1936.

33. *Ibid.*

34. *Ibid.,* Oct. 11, 1936.

35. *Time,* July 25, 1938. John T. Flynn, in his *Country Squire in the White House,* asserted that "Elliott Roosevelt got $25,000 a year as president and general manager of the Hearst chain of radio stations," and intimated that Hearst, one of Franklin D. Roosevelt's bitterest enemies, engaged Elliott because "Hearst wanted to have four radio-station franchises transferred to him in Texas at a time when he was lambasting the President. He had to get permission of the Communications Commission, appointed by the President. He employed Elliott to get those transfers. Elliott handled the job—and with great success. He was later made manager of the whole Hearst chain at $25,000 a year." (Flynn: *Country Squire in the White House,* p. 117.)

36. Philadelphia *Public Ledger,* Aug. 18, 1938.

37. *Time,* Aug. 29, 1938.

38. In mid-June, 1945, a well-known columnist asserted that, in 1939, Elliott Roosevelt had borrowed $200,000 from the head of a prominent grocery chain and had settled the loan in 1942 for only $4,000. The press associations quoted John Hartford, president of the Atlantic & Pacific Tea Company, who made the loan, as saying that his loss was deducted from his income when he paid his taxes. The sequel to this revelation will be noted chronologically in this review.

39. Buffalo *Evening News,* Sept. 20, 1940.

40. Emporia *Gazette,* Sept. 30, 1940.

41. *Time,* March 15, 1943.

42. *Congressional Record,* 78th Congress, 1st Session, pp. 1610-11.

43. *Time,* Dec. 28, 1942.

44. *Ibid.*

45. Washington *Times-Herald,* July 16, 1943. INS.

46. United Press report, Dec. 28, 1942.

47. Philadelphia *Record,* March 16, 1944. AP.

48. *Newsweek,* July 10, and July 24, 1944.

49. United Press, July 6, 1944.

50. Associated Press, July 8, 1944.

51. Washington *News,* Dec. 4, 1944. UP.

52. New York *Herald Tribune,* Jan. 19, 1945.

53. New York *Times,* Jan. 18, 1945. AP. During World War II, when shipments of war materiel and personnel taxed trains and planes, transportation companies were ordered to allot space to travelers and cargo in a preferential order compatible with the type of permit—called a "priority" issued by the Government—designated "A," "B," and "C." Thus, a holder of an "A-priority" had precedence in obtaining accommodations over a "B"-card holder. This rule also applied on military transports.

54. Washington *Post,* Jan. 22, 1945.

55. New York *Herald Tribune,* Jan. 19, 1945.

56. New York *Times,* Jan. 17, 1945.

57. Philadelphia *Inquirer,* Jan. 21, 1945. AP. The outcry against the use by the President's son of an Army plane to fly his dog across the Atlantic, and the later transportation of the pet across the continent, is not novel in our history. Apparently, a hundred years ago, there were protests against the use of battleships to transport animals which were the private property of officers and men in service. The Navy Department, on November 28, 1838, issued an order that "the bringing home, in public vessels of the United States, various animals such as horses, asses, mules, and *other quadrupeds,* formerly authorized by this Department, having been found by recent experience productive of great inconvenience, and *liable to abuse,* is hereby strictly prohibited in the future." The order was signed by the Secretary of Navy. (Published in the Washington *Globe,* Nov. 28, 1838.) Had Elliott's dog made his trip in time of peace, those who rallied to the defense of the President's son could have cited an earlier example of air transportation for a pet of the Presidential household. In 1927 a collie was sent by airplane from South Dakota to the summer White House in Michigan where President Calvin Coolidge spent his vacation. (San Francisco *Examiner,* July 27, 1927.) In fact, the dogs of the austere Coolidge were accorded such conspicuous attention and prerogatives that editors indulged in jibes and criticism about "Calvin's Canines." (New Orleans *Times-Picayune,* July 28, 1926.)

58. *Congressional Record,* 79th Congress, First Session, p. 1041.

59. *Ibid.,* p. 1042.

60. Senator Bushfield of South Dakota. Readers interested in the ages of commanding generals will find an intriguing discussion in the autobiography of James G. Blaine, *"Twenty Years in Congress."*

61. Senator Thomas of Utah.

62. Franklin D. Roosevelt's personal reply to *Second Report of Harvard Class of 1904;* also subsequent *Decennial Report,* 1914, and *Fifteenth Anniversary Report,* 1919. It has been a custom in some sections of the United

States to give the name of a dead child to a younger brother. (See Theodore C. Smith: *Life and Letters of James Abram Garfield,* Vol. I, p. 5.)

63. New York *Times,* June 17, 1933. Groton was the traditional school of all the Roosevelt clans; Franklin, Jr.'s father had graduated thirty-three years earlier, and another President, Theodore Roosevelt, had also attended Groton. On the program, as prize winners, were several grandsons of the "Rough Rider"—Archibald Roosevelt, Jr., Kermit Roosevelt, Jr., Cornelius Roosevelt, Quentin Roosevelt. Franklin, Jr.'s own younger brother, John, was also a student.

64. New York *Times,* March 25, 1935; April 4, 1935; Nov. 20, 1935; Dec. 23, 1935.

65. Philadelphia *Public Ledger,* July 2, 1938.

66. New York *Times,* April 7, 1934.

67. New York *Herald Tribune,* July 1, 1937.

68. New York *Post,* July 1, 1937.

69. Chicago *Daily Tribune,* July 1, 1937.

70. *Time,* Jan. 6, 1941.

71. New York *Times,* Aug. 18, 1937.

72. *Ibid.,* Aug. 21, 1937.

73. *Ibid.,* Sept. 10, 1937.

74. A century before John Roosevelt's marriage, the town of Nahant was regarded as one of Massachusetts' most charming resorts. In 1829 the Boston *Columbian Centinel* singled out Nahant for its praise, saying editorially: "One of the most elegant luxuries of the summer season, for a tenant of a large and populous city, is a cool and quiet retreat from its dust, heat and clamor. . . . A charming seclusion of this kind is now to be found at Nahant." (Boston *Columbian Centinel,* July 25, 1829.)

75. New York *Times,* June 19, 1938.

76. *Ibid.,* Sept. 1, 1938.

77. M. E. Hennessey, Boston *Sunday Globe,* Aug. 18, 1938.

78. Baltimore *Sun,* Aug. 20, 1944. James took part in the invasions of several Pacific islands.

79. John attended the naval reserve training school at Harvard, became a lieutenant, and toward the close of the conflict was logistics officer for a carrier task force. For this service he received the Bronze Star medal. (Washington *Star,* Aug. 18, 1945.) Franklin, Jr., won a decoration also; the ship which he commanded—the D-E 442—sank a Japanese submarine.

80. Baltimore *Sun,* Feb. 13, 1944.

81. United Press report, June 10, 1944.

82. For instance, although in reports of other invasions only the commanding officer was named, wherever James Roosevelt took part in the engagement he was mentioned as "second in command."

83. Washington *Post,* July 25, 1943.

84. *Ibid.,* Nov. 20, 1944; Washington *Daily News,* July 13, 1945.

85. Beverly Hills *Citizen,* Aug. 1, 1945. Washington *Daily News,* Aug. 2, 1945. The prestige of the Roosevelt name was acknowledged by the advocates

of the national health plan when, in December, 1945, they made an appeal for public support; among the several hundred prominent Americans asked to sign the five-column advertisement approving President Truman's message to Congress "James Roosevelt, Los Angeles" was fifth. (New York *Times,* Dec. 10, 1945.) Significantly, his name was the only one not followed by some phrase indicating the signer's business connection or professional status; James Roosevelt omitted this additional identification—he was a President's son!

86. New York *Herald Tribune,* July 31, 1945.

87. Who revealed to Pegler this secret loan to the President's son? That was never explained. John Hartford asserted that he himself would never have made the transaction public. "Which may well be believed," agreed the *Food Field Reporter,* "for Hartford is little heard or seen. It is said that there are probably not a dozen food manufacturers who would recognize him as one of their best customers if they encountered him on the street." (*Food Field Reporter,* June 25, 1945.)

88. Chicago *Tribune,* June 13, 1945.

89. *Ibid.* In several later editorials, the Chicago *Tribune* continued its condemnation of the loan to Elliott. See editorial of October 3, 1945.

90. Detroit *News,* June 14, 1945.

91. Washington *Post,* June 15, 1945.

92. Washington *News,* Aug. 28, 1945; New York *Times,* Sept. 22, 1945; Washington *Post,* Sept. 22, 1945. Westbrook Pegler devoted a number of his columns to the Elliott loan, mingling his comments with scathing denunciation of other alleged irregularities during the Roosevelt Administration. (Washington *Times-Herald,* Oct. 5, 1945.)

93. Readers interested in Elliott's ownership and management of radio networks will find a comprehensive account in *Advertising Age,* July 16, 1945. Elliott himself declared that he had no moral obligation to pay back either this loan or several others which were revealed later. (Los Angeles *Times,* Oct. 3, 1945.)

94. New York *Times,* June 6, 1945.

95. Washington *Post,* July 8, 1945.

96. New York *Times,* Aug. 28, 1945. Within the Congressional halls the loan to Elliott was discussed with vehemence. A typical example was the speech of Congressman Roy O. Woodruff, Republican, of Michigan. (*Congressional Record,* Nov. 15, 1945, pp. 10907-10909.)

97. New York *Herald Tribune,* Nov. 21, 1945.

98. *Newsweek,* Nov. 12, 1945.

99. Drew Pearson, in Washington *Post,* Nov. 24, 1945.

100. Doris Fleeson, in Washington *Star,* Nov. 23, 1945. The thirty-acre estate on Long Island which became the home of Franklin, Jr., was in a locality traditionally Republican—which, in the words of the New York *Times,* was "the bailiwick of the Oyster Bay-Theodore Roosevelt clan." (New York *Times,* Sept. 22, 1945.)

101. James Roosevelt, too, was held in less awe than during his father's

lifetime. "Col. James Roosevelt Bumped off Plane," was a headline in many papers during August; en route on a plane from California to his Hyde Park home, he was forced to yield his seat to a civilian with a higher priority rating. (AP, Washington *Star,* Aug. 5, 1945.)

102. Washington *Star,* Nov. 30, 1945.

103. *Ibid.*

104. *Newsweek,* Dec. 3, 1945.

105. *Ibid.*

106. Washington *Post,* Nov. 25, 1945.

107. New York *Herald Tribune,* Nov. 24, 1945.

108. When asked why the divorced James Roosevelt had not been barred, Bishop Manning replied, "I didn't know about that." (*Newsweek,* Dec. 5, 1945.)

109. Washington *Post,* Dec. 4, 1945.

110. The *Chronicle,* Dec. 2, 1945; Washington *Post,* Dec. 3, 1945; New York *Herald Tribune,* Dec. 3, 1945.

111. *Newsweek,* Jan. 7, 1946, reviewing Mrs. Roosevelt's own column.

112. New York *Times,* Jan. 2, 1946. This "march of dimes" was in support of Warm Springs, where Franklin Roosevelt died, and for other curative programs for polio sufferers.

113. Some commentators were critical of James' qualifications. (Westbrook Pegler, Washington *Times Herald,* July 5, 1946.)

114. Philadelphia *Inquirer,* March 1, 1946; New York *Times,* March 1, 1946; Washington *Post,* March 7, 1946.

115. Washington *Star,* March 11, 1946; New York *Times,* March 11, 1946.

116. New York *Herald Tribune,* March 15, 1946.

117. Washington *Post,* March 17, 1946; New York *Herald Tribune,* March 17, 1946.

118. New York *Herald Tribune,* March 7, 1946.

119. Speech of Congressman John E. Rankin, *Congressional Record,* Appendix, pp. A1218-19. March 6, 1946.

120. Associated Press, July 21, 1946; United Press, July 22, 1946. Said *Newsweek:* "Jimmy Roosevelt had been named State chairman because of three resounding assets—*his father's name,* his father's charm, and his father's boundless energy." (*Newsweek,* July 14, 1947.)

121. *Time,* July 8, 1946.

122. Phoenix *Gazette,* Sept. 20, 1946.

123. Los Angeles *Times,* Sept. 27, 1946; Los Angeles *Examiner,* Sept. 29, 1946. By midsummer, 1947, Jimmy's difficulties increased—the Democratic party in California was split into two factions. (New York *Times,* July 13, 1947.) Press dispatches still referred to him as "the late President's son," and most of the commentators called him "an amateur in politics—the eldest son of F. D. R." (Washington *Daily News,* July 21, 1947.)

124. *Pageant Magazine,* August, 1946, p. 5.

125. New York *Times* Sunday Magazine, April 7, 1947, p. 10.

126. Danton Walker, New York *Daily News,* June 21, 1946.

127. *Time,* July 8, 1946.

128. *Newsweek,* Sept. 2, 1946. Elliott had the opportunity, more than a decade earlier, to listen to his father's discussion of public affairs with important men. In 1931 he accompanied the elder Roosevelt on a voyage to Europe; on the luxurious *Bremen* was also Charles Dawes, our Ambassador to Britain. The latter recorded in his diary that "Governor Franklin D. Roosevelt of New York sent a note by his son Elliott, inviting me for dinner in his stateroom." (Charles G. Dawes: *Journal as Ambassador to Great Britain,* p. 346.) The conversation lasted four and a half hours. But Elliott wrote no book.

129. Eleanor Roosevelt, "My Day." Washington *Daily News,* Aug. 26, 1946.

130. London *Daily Mirror,* quoted in *Time,* Sept. 2, 1946.

131. *Time,* Oct. 7, 1946.

132. Los Angeles *Times,* Sept. 22, 1946.

133. A sensational charge was made by several commentators in the prominent and conservative Washington *Post* that Elliott's original manuscript of the book was "unpublishable," and that the printed edition was mainly "ghosted" by another writer. (Washington *Post,* Dec. 4, 1946.)

134. Some criticisms were milder. J. and S. Alsop, Washington *Post,* Dec. 2, 1946; Los Angeles *Times,* Sept. 22, 1946; Westbrook Pegler, Washington *Times Herald,* Sept. 3, 1946.

135. *Coronet Magazine,* November, 1946.

136. Washington *Post,* Nov. 10, 1946; New York *Herald Tribune,* Dec. 4, 1946; Washington *Sunday Star,* Dec. 8, 1946; Washington *Daily News,* Dec. 17, 1946.

137. *Newsweek,* Dec. 2, 1946. This reliable and widely circulated magazine was the first to print the startling account of Elliott's reputed remarks.

138. Washington *Post,* Nov. 27, 1946; *Time,* Dec. 9, 1946; Washington *Daily News,* Nov. 27, 1946.

139. Washington *Post,* Dec. 2, 1946.

140. United Press, Dec. 2, 1946.

141. Washington *Post,* Dec. 15, 1946.

142. New York *Times,* Dec. 26, 1946; Washington *Daily News,* Dec. 26, 1946.

143. His mother was more emphatic in a denial that Elliott had made the remarks. In her own column, the Presidential widow said that she *knew* without asking that Elliott did not say it. (Washington *Daily News,* Jan. 16, 1947.)

144. Quoted in Washington *Times Herald,* Dec. 26, 1946.

145. Washington *Post,* Jan. 24, 1947.

146. Elliott's articles were frequently discussed in Congress; both those friendly to him and those critical of his views reprinted in the *Congressional Record* excerpts from his writings, and even entire articles. Thus, what had appeared in the *Nation* was reprinted in the *Congressional Record* of March 28, 1947, Appendix, pp. 1427-28.

147. *Time,* Feb. 17, 1947. While this volume was being set in type Elliott's

name was again blazoned on the front pages of most American newspapers. A Senate committee, investigating war contracts, discovered that Elliott, when a colonel in the air force engaged in selecting planes, had been entertained lavishly at the expense of an airplane manufacturer. His honeymoon expenses had been paid, and costly entertainment at night clubs had been provided for him and his wife. (U. P. Washington *Daily News,* July 26, 1947; *Time,* Aug. 4, 1947; Washington *Post,* Aug. 4, 1947; *Newsweek,* Aug. 4, 1947.) Scathing editorials appeared in prominent journals. "Elliott Roosevelt presents a very shabby picture," commented one paper, heading its editorial "Elliott's Characteristic Indiscretion." (Atlanta *Constitution,* Aug. 4, 1947.) "Outrageous Conduct" was the caption in another influential journal which referred to his "family connections." (Cincinnati *Enquirer,* Aug. 4, 1947.) Those newspapers which had always indulged in bitter censure of the Roosevelt regime now made the most of this flagrant tactlessness on the part of the late President's son; the typical denunciation appeared in the Chicago *Daily Tribune,* which referred to Elliott as a "profligate son" and catalogued all his alleged indiscretions. ("White House Morals," Aug. 6, 1947.) Even those always friendly to the Roosevelt family condemned Elliott's behavior, and one commentator remarked that "whether he (Elliott) would have ever reached his eminence if he had not been the son of the President no one will ever know." (Ernest Lindley, Washington *Post,* Aug. 4, 1947.) But they pointed out, as those acquainted with Washington politics well knew, that there were many others who had accepted favors from war contractors and that Elliott had been singled out because he was the late President's son. "It was not chance that brought Elliott into it," remarked the New York *Times* in discussing the investigation. (Aug. 9, 1947.)

148. One columnist asserted that "except for the props, it's like seeing a ghost when Franklin D. Roosevelt, Jr., comes to Washington." (Douglas Larsen, in the Washington *Daily News,* Dec. 6, 1946.) Other writers also declared that the mannerisms, voice, and pronunciation of Franklin D. Roosevelt, Jr., were reminiscent of the dead President.

149. *PM,* March 7, 1946.

150. New York *Times,* Sept. 1, 1946. The article by S. J. Woolf, is titled "F. D. R., Jr. Speaks for the Veteran."

151. Leonard Lyons, in the Washington *Post,* May 29, 1946.

152. New York *Times,* March 15, 1946.

153. *Time,* June 24, 1947.

154. *Time,* Jan. 27, 1947. Some members of Congress charged that the American Veterans' Committee was still threatened by the Communists' effort to obtain control. (*Congressional Record,* Feb. 24, 1947, pp. 1419-20.)

155. *Federal Register of the United States,* Dec. 7, 1946.

156. Washington *Daily News,* March 17, 1947.

157. New York *Times,* April 19, 1947.

158. New York *Herald Tribune,* April 23, 1947. This decoration was awarded for his "meritorious conduct as commanding officer of a destroyer escort in action against a Japanese submarine."

159. Washington *Post,* May 4, 1947.

160. Americans for Democratic Action.

161. *ADA World,* April 12, 1947. Thus the Baltimore *Sun* captioned a press dispatch, "Housing Situation Held a 'Bust' by F. D. R. Jr." The article referred to him as "the son of the late President." (Baltimore *Sun,* June 22, 1947.) "Police Grab F. D. Jr." was the heading of a news item relating to his arrest for speeding in August, 1947. (New York *News,* Aug. 6, 1947.) When a Chicago newspaper reported his appointment as attorney for a labor union, the column was headed, "F. D. R. Jr. Balks at Comment." (Chicago *Daily Tribune,* Aug. 9, 1947.)

162. New York *Herald Tribune,* Jan. 30, 1946; Washington *Post,* Jan. 29, 1946; *Newsweek,* Feb. 11, 1946.

163. Washington *Daily News,* May 6, 1947.

164. *Life,* May 17, 1947.

"Son" of George Washington

(Pages 349 to 358)

1. Sparks: *Writings of George Washington,* Vol. II, pp. 64 and 327.

2. G. W. P. Custis: *Recollections and Private Memoirs of George Washington.*

3. *Writings of George Washington,* edited by John Fitzpatrick, Vol. 2, pp. 319-25.

4. Sparks: *Writings of George Washington,* Vol. XII, p. 251.

5. Those who approve Napoleon's cynical dictum that "history is a lie agreed to" may find much to support that thesis in tracing the development of the legend that George Washington regarded George Washington Parke Custis as his "adopted son." Even historians accustomed to critical analyses of documentary data have adopted this unsupported claim, either repeating it as a direct assertion or leaving that impression upon the reader by some alluding phrase. Irving says, "He *adopted* the two youngest children of the deceased" (Washington Irving: *Life of George Washington,* Vol. IV, p. 389); Lodge touchingly remarks, "He took to his heart his wife's children as if they were his own" (Henry Cabot Lodge: *Life of Washington*); Rupert Hughes refers to "Washington's own *adopted son,* G. W. P. Custis" as the source of several accounts of events in the life of the first President, then questions Custis' veracity or recollection because "his *adopted father's* letters are always turning up to discredit the reminiscences of his namesake's anecdotage" (Rupert Hughes: *George Washington,* Vol. III, pp. 657-8); Moore even elaborates on the reasons which "caused General Washington to adopt the two younger children at the deathbed of their father" (Charles Moore: *The Family Life of George Washington,* p. 101); Decatur asserts

that, to please Martha, Washington "immediately adopted the two youngest children, Eleanor Parke Custis and George Washington Parke Custis" and proceeds to quote from a letter of a visitor to the Washington home in Philadelphia which refers to Custis not as an "adopted son" but as Martha Washington's grandson! (Stephen Decatur, Jr.: *Private Affairs of George Washington,* p. 174). Thus continues the parade: Lossing quotes George Washington himself, "Your two younger children I adopt as my own" (Benson J. Lossing: *Mount Vernon,* p.113); and others similarly describe in detail the "adoption" scene at the deathbed of the son of Martha Washington, the father of the two "adopted" children. It is significant to note that Jared Sparks, in his exhaustive study of Washington and his writings, refers to Custis not as an adopted son but merely as "Mr. Custis of Arlington" (Sparks: *Writings of Washington,* Vol. II, p. 476). John Marshall, in his *Life of Washington,* makes no mention of any adoption.

6. Washington *National Era,* Oct. 15, 1857.

7. Washington *Evening Star,* Oct. 12, 1857.

8. Introduction to *Recollections and Private Memoirs of George Washington.*

9. Harriet Taylor Upton: *Our Early Presidents,* p. 41.

10. G. W. P. Custis' Preface to *Recollections and Private Memoirs of George Washington.*

11. Alexandria (Va.) *Gazette,* April, 1851. It is true that, while Custis himself never referred to any relationship as the "adopted son" of the first President, some newspapers spread the fiction. Thus, a Philadelphia journal referred to him as "the aged adopted son of Washington." (Philadelphia *Dollar Newspaper,* Nov. 27, 1850.)

12. Benson J. Lossing: *Mount Vernon,* p. 113.

13. Washington to Marquis de Lafayette, Nov. 15, 1781, in *Writings, supra,* Vol. VIII, p. 203.

14. Washington to John McDowell, in *Writings,* Vol. 36, p. 449.

15. Washington to G. W. P. Custis, in *Writings,* Vol. 35, pp. 394-95. It is noteworthy that, in his letters to G. W. P. Custis at this time, George Washington signed himself "affectionate friend" or "sincere friend"; Washington would not have designated himself thus if he considered himself an "adopted father."

16. Washington to David Stuart, Dec. 30, 1798, in *Writings,* Vol. 37, pp. 77-78. On Christmas day, 1798, George Washington wrote to the son of Lafayette about events at Mount Vernon, noting that "Washington Custis preferring a military career to literary pursuits, is appointed Cornet in Lewis's troop." (*Writings,* Vol. 37, p. 63.)

17. Washington to Clement Biddle, or the Quartermaster, June 7, 1799, in *Writings,* Vol. 37, p. 231.

18. Custis' appointment had been in the Troop commanded by George Washington's nephew, Lawrence Lewis (*Writings,* Vol. 37, p. 59). Both in asking for the appointment as Cornet and also for promotion in rank, George Washington protested that he did not wish to use his influence on behalf

of his wife's grandson. At last, however, he admitted that "Friendship have got the better of my Scruples."

19. March 25, 1799, *Writings,* Vol. 37, pp. 162-63.

20. *Autobiography* of Martin Van Buren, Ch. XXXI, p. 418. Van Buren noted that "early in the autumn of 1829 the President and myself rode out to Arlington to pay a visit to Mr. and Mrs. Custis."

21. *Federal Republican,* Sept. 14, 1812. Francis Scott Key had been requested to deliver the address but declined.

22. Sparks: *Life of Washington,* Vol. II, p. 476.

23. Bryan: *History of the National Capital,* Vol. II, pp. 249-50.

24. Among them, Harriet Taylor Upton: *Our Early Presidents.*

25. *National Intelligencer,* Oct. 12, 1857.

26. Eugene E. Prussing: *The Estate of George Washington,* p. 192.

27. *Ibid.*

28. Washington *Evening Star,* Oct. 12, 1857.

29. Washington *Union,* Oct. 13, 1857.

Son of Andrew Jackson

(Pages 359 to 374)

1. Foremost in Jackson's concept of the attributes of a "gentleman" was readiness to meet critics upon the "field of honor" to fight a duel. Thus, when an opposing attorney ridiculed Jackson's legal arguments in a case, Jackson challenged the eminent attorney to a duel. The two men met and fought, but neither was injured. (Bassett: *Correspondence of Andrew Jackson,* Vol. I, p. 5n.) Jackson never left unanswered any comment which he regarded as an aspersion upon his honor. At one time he spent hours searching for a man who had offended him, determined either to cane him or to cut off his ears! Jackson exclaimed that he "had fought through his entire life for his reputation, and would not permit any set of scoundrels to tarnish his character." (Cincinnati *Daily Gazette,* Jan. 4, 1828.)

2. Jackson's role as Peggy's champion is detailed in a preceding chapter, "Sons of the Little Magician." In a letter to Andrew Donelson in February, 1824, Jackson wrote: "My friend Eaton has acted like a friend; he is worthy of and shall receive my warmest gratitude so long as I live." (*Correspondence of Andrew Jackson,* Vol. III, p. 231.) Seventeen years later, Jackson had cause to say, "Never did I so much regret the ingratitude and depravity of man, more than I have the course of Major Eaton." (Andrew Jackson to Amos Kendall, May 15, 1841, in *Correspondence,* Vol. VI, pp. 112-113.)

3. Typical of this trait was Jackson's insistence that the wives of his Cabinet officers should accept his own verdict regarding Peggy O'Neal and associate with her. See chapter, "Sons of the Little Magician."

4. Bassett: *Correspondence of Andrew Jackson,* Vol. II, p. vi.

5. *Ibid.,* Vol. I, p. vii.

6. The story of Jackson's marriage ceremonies is detailed by Mary French Caldwell in *General Jackson's Lady,* pp. 157-158. In 1827, when political opponents were charging that Jackson had lived in adultery with Rachel, his friends in Nashville appointed a committee which made an investigation; its report absolved Jackson from any intentional misconduct.

7. John Quincy Adams: *Memoirs,* Vol. VIII, p. 356.

8. Parton: *Life of Jackson,* Vol. I, p. 339.

9. *Ibid.,* Vol. II, p. 323.

10. *Ibid.,* Vol. I, pp. 337-39.

11. New York *Times,* Sept. 2, 1865.

12. Parton: *supra,* Vol. I, p. 339.

13. Nashville *Dispatch,* April 18, 1865.

14. Andrew Jackson to Rachel Jackson, Jan. 18, 1813, in *Correspondence, supra,* Vol. I, p. 271.

15. *Correspondence,* Vol. I, p. 460.

16. *Ibid.,* p. 477.

17. *Ibid.,* p. 493.

18. *Ibid.,* p. 79.

19. Nashville *Dispatch,* April 18, 1865; New York *Times,* Sept. 27, 1865.

20. Andrew Jackson to Rachel Jackson, March 2, 1824, in *Jackson Papers,* Vol. 64, Library of Congress.

21. *Ibid.,* March 27, 1824.

22. Andrew Jackson to Major Francis Smith, May 19, 1839, in *Correspondence,* Vol. IV, p. 36. While in our own age many women decide for themselves when and whom to marry, in preceding generations there was a strict requirement that the suitor ask the father "for the hand of his daughter." Transplanting to the new world the legal concept of the old, the lawmakers of the Massachusetts colony enacted a "law of courtship"; on October 27, 1647, the General Court ordained "that if any young man *attempt* to address a young woman without the consent of her parents or the county court he shall be fined 5 pounds for the first offense, 10 pounds for the second, and imprisonment for the third." In September, 1649, "Matthew Stanley was tried for drawing the affections of John Tarbox's daughter, without the consent of her parents. He was fined 5 pounds—fees 2s, 6d, and 6s for 3 days attendance by the parents." (Salem *Gazette,* reprinted in the Charleston (S.C.) *Southern Patriot,* Nov. 3, 1838.)

23. Andrew Jackson to Andrew Jackson, Jr., July 20, 1829, in *Correspondence, supra.*

24. Andrew Jackson to Andrew Jackson, Jr., July 22, 1829.

25. *Papers of Andrew Jackson,* Library of Congress, Vol. 73. Andrew Jackson to Andrew Jackson, Jr., July 26, 1829.

26. Andrew Jackson to Andrew Jackson, Jr., Aug. 29, 1829.

27. *Papers of Andrew Jackson,* Library of Congress, Vol. 73. Andrew Jackson to Andrew Jackson, Jr., Sept. 21, 1829.

28. Nashville *Dispatch,* April 18, 1865.
29. Andrew Jackson to Andrew Jackson, Jr., Oct. 27, 1831.
30. *United States Gazette* (Philadelphia), Nov. 26, 1831.
31. *National Gazette,* Nov. 28, 1831.
32. Parton: *Life of Jackson,* Vol. II, p. 660.
33. *Correspondence,* Vol. IV, p. 441.
34. Andrew Jackson to Andrew Jackson, Jr., Feb. 12, 1834.
35. Andrew Jackson to Andrew Jackson, Jr., April 14, 1835.
36. John Quincy Adams: *Memoirs,* Vol. IX, p. 319.
37. Parton: *supra,* Vol. II, p. 663.
38. Andrew Jackson to Hutchings, Dec. 19, 1839.
39. *Correspondence,* Vol. VI, p. 46.
40. *Ibid.,* p. 46.
41. *Ibid.,* pp. 48-49.
42. Parton: *supra,* Vol. III, p. 649.
43. New York *Times,* Sept. 2, 1865.
44. Nashville *Dispatch,* April 18, 1865.
45. *Ibid.*
46. William Ernest Smith: *The Francis Preston Blair Family in Politics,* Vol. I, pp. 195-197.
47. *Correspondence,* Vol. VI, p. 387.
48. *Ibid.*
49. New York *Times,* April 22, 1865.
50. *Ibid.,* Sept. 2, 1865.